# The Photographic Researches of Ferdinand Hurter & Vero C. Driffield

Edited by
## W. B. Ferguson

New Introduction by
## Walter Clark

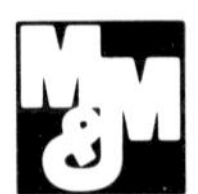

A Facsimile Edition
Published by
Morgan & Morgan, Inc., Dobbs Ferry, New York

Introduction Copyright 1974 by Alfred Clark
International Standard Book Number 0-87100-082-2
Library of Congress Catalog Card Number 74-81184
First Printing of Facsimile Edition, June 1974
Printed in the United States of America

## INTRODUCTION.

In the year 1890, photography was about fifty years old. Although quite young, it had already gone through four major stages: the daguerreotype, the calotype, the "wet plate" collodion process, and the gelatin dry plate. These laid the foundation for photography's phenomenal growth in the succeeding eighty years. They were personal processes. The photographer not only made his pictures, but first prepared his own materials. Then, in the eighteen-eighties, came the dawn of the modern era, when manufacturers made ready-to-use materials for the photographer to buy. The personal aspect for the photographer now involved adapting commercially manufactured materials to his special interests.

The maker as well as the discriminating user of photographic materials was clearly interested in knowing how to relate the photograph to the thing photographed. This was important to permit the manufacturer to know the properties of his products, and to ensure their uniformity and reproducibility. It was equally important to allow the photographer to know his plates, and later his films, at all times: how to use them, and how to adapt their characteristics for his special purposes.

The basic question concerned how the final result was affected by the variables of exposure and development.

In Germany and, especially, in England, some proposals had been made to clarify the relationship between these factors, but it was not until May, 1890, that the results of the first systematic study were made known, in a paper published by Ferdinand Hurter and Vero Charles Driffield. It may seem peculiar today that this paper appeared in the *Journal of the Society of Chemical Industry*. However, the authors were not engaged in the profession of photographic technology, they were industrial chemists and therefore published in the journal of their profession.

Hurter, born a Swiss, took his schooling in Heidelberg, and then made his career for thirty-one years in England with a prominent industrial chemical firm, the United Alkali Company. Driffield, an Englishman, spent his early years with a Swiss master, but studied engineering and eventually became associated professionally with Hurter in the same company. A common interest in music (how many musicians there are in photography!) and a close personal friendship lasted throughout their lives. Driffield had long been interested in photography, and

Hurter in the application of the scientific method. The outcome was their classic research which laid the foundation for what is now known as *sensitometry,* the science of the measurement and description of the relationship between the exposure to light and the final photograph.

It must be realized that at this time photography was much used but little understood. The development of photographic processes was almost entirely in the hands of those who took pictures, amateurs and professionals. There were almost no manufacturers of materials in the modern sense. What we would now call "standardization" could not be applied, and systems of measuring the response of plates to light, so that one photographer could describe to another, or even to the public, the real characteristics of his medium, had not been well thought out.

The paper of 1890, "Photochemical Investigations and a Method of Determination of the Sensitiveness of Photographic Plates," was preceded by others, including patents, relating to measurements important for this subject—in particular, "to devise some means of accurately measuring the actinic power of diffused daylight." Studies of differential thermometers led to the actinometer—"an instrument for measuring light"—called then the *actinograph.* This type of study paved the way for the ultimate investigations. They were followed by a great many papers on the action of light in making negatives and positives, the relation between them, instruments designed for exposing and for measuring density—in fact, the concepts of density and gamma—the principles of enlarging, the factors involved in development and, especially, a system for evaluating sensitivity of photographic emulsions to light: the well-known H&D Speeds.

The broad scope and fundamental significance of the Hurter and Driffield experiments could have filled a monograph of considerable dimensions. Fortunate it was that the Royal Photographic Society, on the death of Driffield in 1915 (Hurter had died in 1898), sought funds to establish a Hurter and Driffield Memorial, which included a biennial memorial lecture; the custody, arrangement and display of the historical apparatus and the numerous manuscripts which Driffield bequeathed to the Society; and the "republication, as a memorial volume, of the more important printed papers of Hurter and Driffield which have been for many years so difficult of access." The response was liberal, and this volume was one of the results.

The editor, W. B. Ferguson, could not have been better chosen. He was a barrister of high esteem—a King's Councillor—a man devoted to the science of photography, a designer of sensitometric equipment (the F.R.B. densitometer, etc.), an ardent supporter of the Royal Photographic Society, and a pioneer in propaganda for the H&D system (it had rough going at the start). His introductory chapter on the early work, 1876-1890, is a masterpiece. It could only have been surpassed if he had carried it through to the end.

Most modern sensitometry is based on the H&D curve. Although the speed system based on the inertia point, proposed by Hurter and Driffield, is not generally used now in its original form, the concepts of the characteristic curve and gamma, and their relationship to the photographic process, are fundamental to all our present derivations of speed, contrast, and other sensitometric values.

This book brings together the most important papers, lists of apparatus and notebooks in the R.P.S. collection; biographical and historical sketches, supplemented with a note by Dr. H. S. Allen, of King's College, London, on the mathematical reasoning of Hurter; and a most extensive and important bibliography—over 700 references—covering the fields dealt with by Hurter and Driffield.

*The Photographic Researches of Ferdinand Hurter and Vero C. Driffield,* originally compiled by the Royal Photographic Society of Great Britain, represents the basis of the modern scientific study of the visible aspects of the photographic process and of most of the methods now used for describing the properties of photographic materials.

Walter Clark

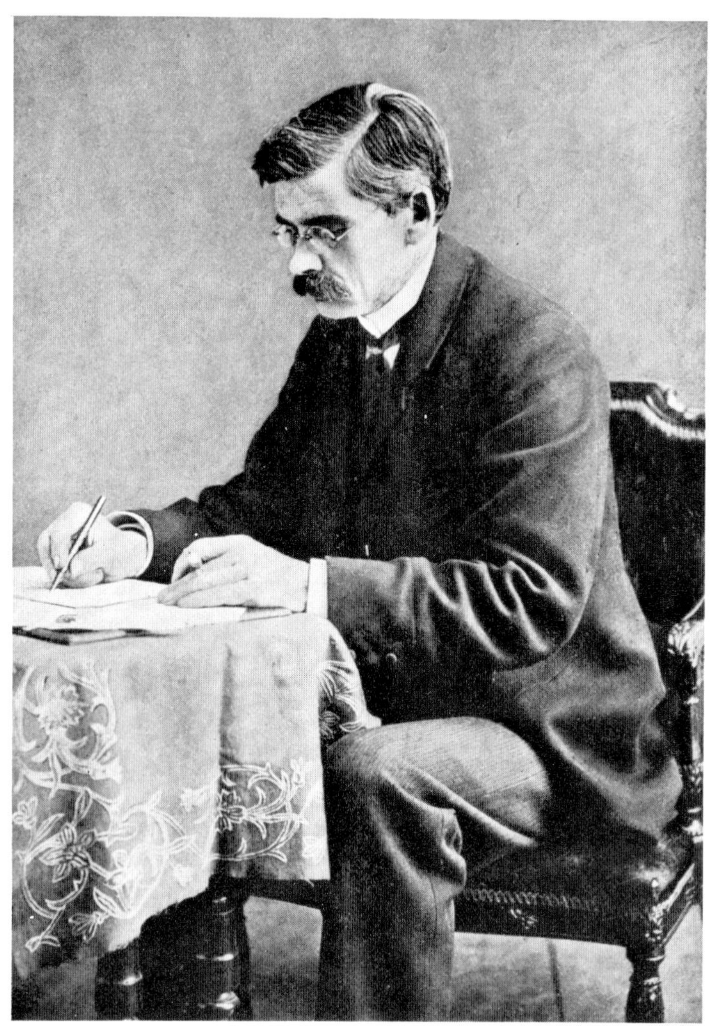

FERDINAND HURTER.

*Born* 15th March, 1844.
*Died* 5th March, 1898.

Royal Photographic Society of Great Britain

*A Memorial Volume*

containing an account of

# The Photographic Researches of Ferdinand Hurter & Vero C. Driffield

Being a Reprint of their Published Papers, together
with a History of their Early Work and a
Bibliography of Later Work on
the same subject

Edited by

## W. B. FERGUSON,

K.C., M.A.Oxon, F.I.C., Hon. F.R.P.S.

Published by
THE ROYAL PHOTOGRAPHIC SOCIETY OF GREAT BRITAIN
35, RUSSELL SQUARE, W.C.

**HARRISON AND SONS**
Printers in Ordinary
to His Majesty
45, St. Martin's Lane, W.C. 2.

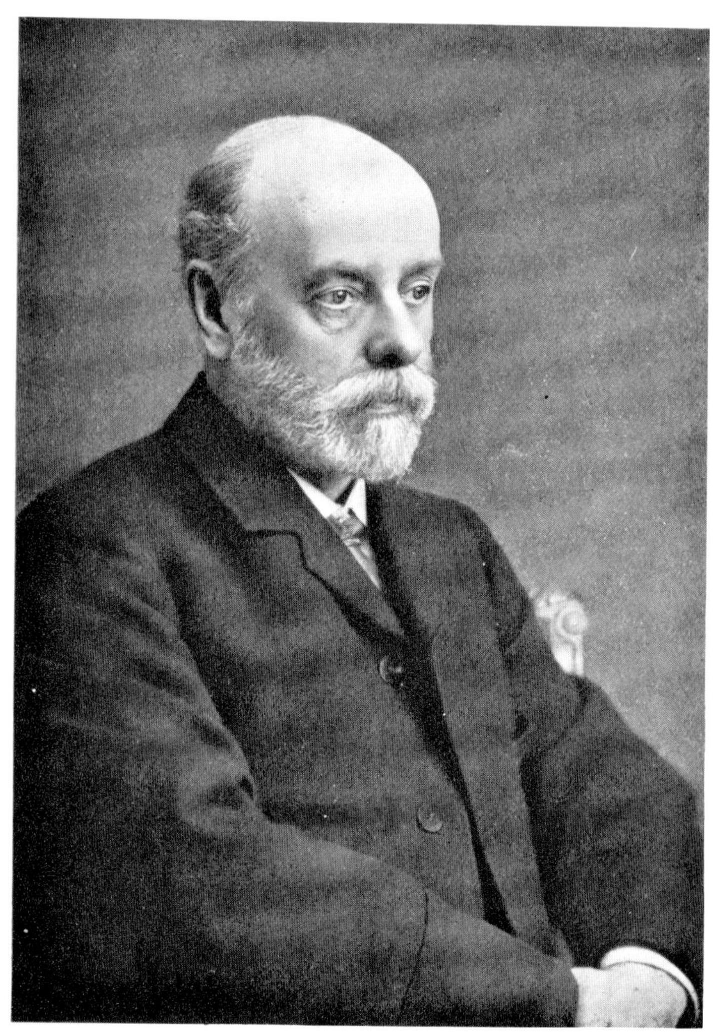

VERO CHARLES DRIFFIELD.

*Born* 7th May, 1848.
*Died* 14th November, 1915.

# PREFACE.

On the death of Vero C. Driffield in 1915 the Royal Photographic Society appealed for funds to establish a memorial to Hurter and Driffield, which it was proposed should take the form of :—

    I. A biennial memorial lecture ;

    II. The custody, arrangement and display of the historic apparatus and manuscripts bequeathed by Driffield to the Society ;  and

    III. The republication, as a memorial volume, of the more important printed papers of Hurter and Driffield which have been for many years so difficult of access.

Photographers and manufacturers of photographic materials throughout the world responded liberally to the appeal.  The first two objects have been already carried out, and I have been requested by the R.P.S. to edit the memorial volume.

A study of the manuscripts led me to conclude that an account of their early work, preceding the publication of the classic paper of 1890, would be a considerable help to the understanding of their views.  I have tried to give such an account as far as possible in their own words as taken from their note books, and to this, as well as to the various reprints, I have appended references to the original manuscripts now in the care of the Royal Photographic Society.

Dr. H. Stanley Allen, M.A., has been kind enough to contribute a review of Dr. Hurter's mathematical work as found in his note books, which should be read in conjunction with the published papers.

The reprints include all the important papers of Hurter and Driffield which their authors deemed to be of special and permanent value as containing a complete exposition of their views.  There are, of course, many other publications of theirs, chiefly in the form of letters to the photographic press, to which reference will be found in the Bibliography, but their interest is chiefly polemical ;  to print them in full would have filled two more volumes, and any conclusions of value which they contain are included in the papers printed herein. The source of the reprints is indicated in every case, and the Society desires to express its thanks to those who have so kindly permitted the reprinting of the various papers, more especially to the Society of Chemical Industry, and to Mr. John Tennant of New York.

The Bibliography has been made a special feature of the book, and for most valuable help in its compilation and arrangement I desire to express my great indebtedness to the late Henry Vaux Hopwood, Librarian of the Patent Office, whose early death last year is so great a loss alike to literature and to science. His unrivalled knowledge of scientific literature and library technique did much to lessen the difficulties of the work, and together with the co-operation of Mr. B. V. Storr, has enabled us to produce such a bibliography of the physics and chemistry of photography as will, it is hoped, prove to be of great value to all engaged in photographic research.

Finally I wish to express my thanks to Mr. F. F. Renwick for all the valuable help he has given, not only in connection with the present volume, but also in the promotion and successful establishment of the Hurter and Driffield Memorial.

W. B. FERGUSON.

*January 6th,* 1920.

# CONTENTS.

# THE HURTER AND DRIFFIELD APPARATUS AND MANUSCRIPTS

Bequeathed by V. C. DRIFFIELD to

THE ROYAL PHOTOGRAPHIC SOCIETY OF GREAT BRITAIN,
and now preserved in their Museum at 35, Russell Square, London, W.C. 1.

## APPARATUS.

### *Exposure Apparatus.*

Case 1 contains :—

1. Dark slide moving past slit with flap shutter.
2. Rotating drum giving radial patches on a quarter plate.
3. First sector wheel in steps (26th April, 1891).
4. Sector wheel for evenly graded exposure.
5. Hand sector wheel for experiments on bromide paper in enlarging.
6. Large enclosed exposing machine with ebonite sector wheel.
7. Special dark slide with cut out steps to hold strips for use in No. 6.

Also part of Amyl acetate lamp, petrol lamp used for larger exposures, rotating apparatus of unknown use, collection of exposure meters, screens and screen holders.

### *Actinometric and Photometric Apparatus.*

Case 2 contains :—

1. Five various forms of Hurter's Actinometer.   One still in working order.
2. Parts of the self-registering Actinometer.
3. Two slide rules used in the calculation of exposures from Actinometer readings.
4. Five different forms of Actinograph.
5. Driffield's Universal Actinograph model.
6. Apparatus used by Dr. Hurter to illustrate his lecture at the Liverpool Physical Society.
7. The early circular photometer.
8. The first bench photometer.
9. The second bench photometer.
10. The third, with splayed sides, illustrated in the *Photo. Miniature.*
11. The final form of Hurter and Driffield bench photometer with Lummer-Brodhun head.
12. Rotating sector as used in Abney's experiments.
13. " Arithmometre " calculating machine used by Dr. Hurter.
14. Hot water developing dish.

And also photometer slips, specimens of densities and Driffield's last note-book.

MANUSCRIPTS.

These are contained in cases in locked Globe-Wernicke Bookcases.   They have been classified under the headings of Note Books, Separate MSS., Charts, Correspondence, Diagrams and Miscellaneous.

They have been marked for purposes of reference as shown below; and a careful Contents List (360 pp.) has been prepared with very numerous cross references both to the manuscripts and the printed matter.

NOTE BOOKS.

| Description. | Mark. | Date. |
|---|---|---|
| NOTE BOOKS OF DR. F. HURTER. | | |
| Quarto, covered red marbled paper .. | H.N.—A. | 1886—1889 |
| ,,  ,,  ,,  ,,  ,, | H.N.—B. | 1889 |
| ,,  ,,  ,,  ,,  ,, | H.N.—C. | 1889 |
| Small quarto, black cover .. | H.N.—D. | 1881—1897 |
| Thin quarto, covered red marbled paper, " Theory of Development " .. | H.N.—E. | |
| Quarto, covered red marbled paper, " Illumination of the Earth," etc. .. | H.N.—F. | 1888 |
| Thin quarto, covered red marbled paper, " Actinograph ".. | H.N.—G. | 1888 |
| Thin quarto, marbled paper, " Actinograph," " Light and Latitude Tables " .. | H.N.—H. | |
| Rough laboratory notes .. | H.N.—I. | 1897 |
| Five small quartos, blue backed, containing " Curves " .. | H.N.—J. to H.N.—N. | |
| NOTE BOOKS OF VERO C. DRIFFIELD. | | |
| Five small octavos, bound together .. | D.N.—A. | 1879—1907 |
| Leather bound octavo rough notes .. | D.N.—B. | 1880—1885 |
| Small black note book .. | D.N.—C. | 1881—1915 |
| Blue marbled paper quarto .. | D.N.—D. | 1887 |
| Vellum bound " Mrs. James Heyes " .. | D.N.—E. | 1888—1890 |
| Blue marbled paper quarto .. | D.N.—F. | 1890 |
| Large red marbled paper quarto .. | D.N.—G. | 1890—1898 |
| Blue marbled paper quarto .. | D.N.—H. | 1894—1898 |
| ,,  ,,  ,,  ,, | D.N.—I. | 1899 |
| ,,  ,,  ,,  ,, | D.N.—J. | |
| ,,  ,,  ,,  ,, | D.N.—K. | |
| ,,  ,,  ,,  ,, | D.N.—L. | |
| Octavo in maroon leather .. | D.N.—M. | |
| Eight blocks or memorandum tablets with notes of density measurements .. | D.N.—Na. to D.N.—Nh. | 1891—1915 |
| Small pocket book, green leather bound .. | D.N.—O. | |
| Small memorandum blocks .. | D.N.—P. | |

## SEPARATE MANUSCRIPTS.

DR. F. HURTER's separate papers are bound up in bundles numbered H. MSS. No. 1 to H. MSS. No. 32.

VERO C. DRIFFIELD's separate papers are numbered D. MSS. No. 1 to D. MSS. No. 18.

## CHARTS.

DR. F. HURTER's charts are in three bundles marked H.C.—1, H.C.—2 and H.C.—3.

V. C. DRIFFIELD's charts are very numerous and have been arranged in order of date as far as possible, collated with the various note-books and cross references marked. They are arranged in four series marked—

D.C.—A.. 1890–1908.

D.C.—B.. Measurements and charts relating to the same, submitted by Driffield to Hurter from 6th December, 1896–1st March, 1898, with letters and comments.

D.C.—C.. Measurements and charts relating to determination of speed from optical qualities, submitted by Driffield to Hurter in December, 1897.

D.C.—D.. Various undated charts.

ALEXANDER COWAN's charts, marked C.C.

## CORRESPONDENCE.

The letters are arranged in 23 bundles in the alphabetical order of the writers and each lot in order of date.

The series is referred to as Cor., with the name of sender, receiver and date. There is also :—

Driffield's Press Copy Letter Book of 86 pages referred to as Cor. D.

## PRESS CUTTINGS BOOK.

This, arranged by V. C. Driffield, contains most of the letters printed in the photographic journals during the controversial time, and is referred to as P.C.

## DIAGRAMS.

Four bundles marked D.1 to D.4, containing diagrams for Actinograph scales and for the various published papers.

## PRINTS.

Various bromide prints to illustrate the application of Hurter and Driffield theories to bromide printing. Marked P.

## ACTINOMETER RECORDS.

A portfolio of the actual records made by the self-recording actinometer of Dr. Hurter.

Year 1885–1886—Marked R.1.

Year 1886—Marked R.2.

---

**There are also some other papers as yet (1919) unclassified.**

# THE EARLY WORK OF HURTER AND DRIFFIELD UP TO THE PUBLICATION OF THEIR PAPER ON 31ST MAY, 1890.

## 1876—1890.

BY

W. B. FERGUSON, M.A., K.C., Hon. F.R.P.S., F.I.C.

---

References to the original documents are indicated thus :—

| | |
|---|---|
| *To* Dr. Hurter's Note Books … … … … | H.N.—A, etc. |
| Dr. Hurter's MSS.… … … … … … | H. MSS.—No. 1, etc. |
| V. C. Driffield's Note Books … … … … | D.N.—A, etc. |
| V. C. Driffield's MSS. … … … … … | D. MSS.—No. 1, etc. |

Correspondence arranged under name of writer. *Journal of Society of Chemical Industry,* " J.S.C.I."

---

## BIOGRAPHICAL.

FERDINAND HURTER was a Swiss, born on March 15th, 1844, at Schaffhausen, in Switzerland. He was the only son of Alderman Tobias Hurter, a famous artistic bookbinder of that place.

In the Gymnasium, or Higher School, of his native town, under Professor Merklein, he began the study of chemistry, for which he at once showed great interest and liking, and was found to have a more than ordinary ability for mathematics.

At the age of sixteen he was apprenticed to a dyer at Winterthur, and three years later he got an appointment with Messrs. Seelig, silk dyers, of Zurich.

While there he was struck by the unscientific methods employed in the business, and he felt the need of a greater knowledge of chemistry than he had then obtained. After consultation with his former teacher at the Schaffhausen Gymnasium, his parents consented to his continuing the study of chemistry at the Zurich Polytechnic under Professor Städeler. In this he showed such ability that at the end of the course Professor Städeler wrote to his step-father suggesting that the young Hurter should be sent to Heidelberg for further scientific study, with a view of taking his degree there.

After some consideration this was arranged, and in the autumn of 1865 Ferdinand Hurter went to Heidelberg, where he studied under those giants of science, Bunsen, Kirchoff and Helmholz, and in 1866 took his degree of Ph.D., with the highest honours—" Summa cum Laude."

At the early age of twenty-two he was offered a Professorship at Aarau, but he refused this, and decided, fortunately for us, that England offered the best opportunity for the employment of his talents. In the spring of 1867, with a few letters of introduction, he came to Manchester, but for some months was unable to obtain employment. However, he heard that Gaskell, Deacon & Co., of Widnes, required an assistant chemist. He had an interview with Mr. Deacon, who engaged him for a month on trial. Here he remained, first as assistant and shortly afterwards as chief chemist, till the works were absorbed in the business of the United Alkali Co., in 1890. He was then appointed chief chemist and technical adviser to that company, a position which he held until his death on March 5th, 1898.

He thus spent the last thirty-one years of his life in England. Apart from his professional work he was much interested in the welfare and progress of education in this country, and took a considerable part in the political movement in favour of Free Education for the people.

Though Swiss by birth, he was at heart and in all his views a most thorough Englishman.

Vero Charles Driffield, the son of a Lancashire coroner, was born on May 7th, 1848, at Prescott, in Lancashire. He received his earlier education at the Liverpool Collegiate Schools and at Sandbach Grammar School, but later on attended the private school at Southport kept by a Swiss, Dr. Knecht, to whom he was indebted for his earliest scientific training, and he considered the time he spent under his Swiss master as the most important part of his early education.

At an early age he had become interested in the practice of photography, and though intended for the profession of an engineer he was allowed to spend half of his seventeenth year in the studio of Henry Sampson, of Southport, a well-known photographer whose name often appears in the earlier numbers of *The Photographic Journal*. Here he learnt all that was known at that day of the principles and practice of photography.

On the completion of his engineering studies and apprenticeship, Vero C. Driffield joined the firm of Gaskell, Deacon & Co., the Widnes Alkali Manufacturers, as engineer in 1871, and there became associated with Ferdinand Hurter, who had occupied the position of chemist in the same firm since 1867.

The two men were both passionately fond of music, and it was this that first brought them together, though no doubt the scientific training which Driffield had got from his Swiss schoolmaster, Knecht, rendered more easy a mutual understanding between them, which before long ripened into a firm and intimate friendship for life.

Driffield, who had for some years been keenly interested in photography, continued to devote much of his leisure time to that subject, as some of his manuscripts[1] show, and to use his own words :—

" In 1876 I induced Dr. Hurter to take up Photography as a recreation, but to a mind accustomed like his to methods of scientific precision, it became intolerable to practise an art which—at that time—was so entirely governed by rule-of-thumb, and of which the fundamental principles were so little understood. Five years' intimate acquaintance with Dr. Hurter and experience of his methods had deeply impressed me with his skill as an investigator, and, when it was agreed that we should jointly undertake an investigation with the object of rendering Photography a quantitative science, it was with a keen appreciation of my privilege that I joined Dr. Hurter as his collaborator."[2]

It should be remembered that at this time the collodion plate was practically the only sensitive medium at the disposal of the photographer, and that such things as the F system of expressing the aperture of lenses, and the construction of exposure tables had not yet been heard of.[3]

The first difficulty was the estimation of the correct exposure. " The photographer," Dr. Hurter says,[4] " has to expose his plate to suit the light. In doing so he cannot take account (only) of those portions of the picture which are illuminated by direct sunlight, he must have details in his shadows, and these are illuminated by the general daylight and diffused light." " The fluctuations of light throughout the year and again throughout the day, are so great that no photographer could adequately allow for them with any certainty of a proper exposure. The best he could do was to make a more or less well-founded guess. It was clear that such a matter as exposure must be governed by a law of nature and with the object in view, therefore, of reducing exposure to a system we made up our minds to work together at the subject."[5]

The first step, therefore, was to devise some means of accurately measuring the actinic power of diffused daylight,[6] and to this problem Hurter and Driffield applied themselves. " After innumerable experiments with a variety of forms of apparatus, a sudden and happy idea suggested itself to Dr. Hurter's mind. He had been examining the spectrum of nitric di-oxide, and it struck him that the light absorbed by that brown gas must do some molecular work, and as this was not chemical decomposition it could only result in a rise of temperature."[7]

---

[1] D. MS.—1.     [2] D. MS.—10.     [3] D.N.—L., p. 4.     [4] H.N.—F., p. 1.
[5] V. C. Driffield, The Actinograph, 1880.     [6] D.MS.—12, p. 2.
[7] *J.S.C.I.*, 30th April, 1890.

" I wonder," said he to Driffield, " whether a yellow gas occupies the same bulk in the light as in the dark? " and a suggestion so likely to lead to a solution of the problem was at once treated experimentally. Two glass bulbs containing this gas were connected by a syphon containing nitric acid ; one bulb was exposed to the light and the other kept in the dark, and " it was with the deepest gratification " (says Driffield) " we found that the column nitric acid indicated by its rise and fall the amount of chemically-active light."

" I saw," says Dr. Hurter,[1] " the application which could be made of this, and I found that if a differential gas thermometer was filled with nitrogen dioxide, one bulb exposed to diffuse light and the other kept in the dark, the gas exposed to the light expanded ; the light absorbed by the nitric oxide was converted into heat, causing an expansion of the gas."

The difficulty of finding a suitable separating fluid, which would not absorb the gas, to act as indicator in the syphon prevented the obtaining of satisfactory results. Convinced, however, that he was on the right track, Dr. Hurter began an extensive series of investigations on the working of differential thermometers of various design, and in his note book[2] of that time there is a mass of notes of work both on the theory of differential thermometers in general and records of the particular results obtained in his experiments.

" The idea that all coloured substances would, in diffuse light, assume a slightly higher temperature than white or colourless substances led to the construction of a differential thermometer the bulbs of which contained a red substance in one, and a white one in the other."[1] Red and white paper, cotton, cloth, and wool were tried in turn in the bulbs, and coloured wool was found to be the most sensitive. The effect was increased by the use of parabolic reflectors so arranged as to concentrate the light rays on the coils of wool in the centre of the tubes.

In 1881, on 23rd April, Dr. Hurter took out a patent (No. 1751 of that year) for the construction of such actinometers. The illustrated specification printed in this volume contains full details of the manufacture, and of the various precautions necessary to the making of a good instrument.

Actinometers so made were, however, found to be unsatisfactory. In the course of time the organic substances in the tubes absorbed the oxygen in the contained air, and at a greater rate in the white[3] tube than in the red, causing not only a displacement of the zero point of the scale, but finally driving the liquid out of the syphon gauge into the white tube and so rendering the instrument useless.[1]

After further experiments, it was found that the best form of instrument

[1] *J.S.C.I.*, 30th April, 1890.      [2] H.N.—D., pp. 1–77.
[3] D.N.—L., p. 6, " the red."

was one in which the one bulb was of thin flashed copper ruby glass, and the other of similar thin white glass containing air and aqueous vapour, the syphon gauge being filled with a solution of potassium carbonate, iodide, and iodine.

" This arrangement," says Driffield,[1] " gave us a reliable instrument, the readings of which we found to be proportional to the amount of chemically-active light measured.   The maximum possible diffuse daylight in this country is represented by a rise in the fluid column of 80 millimetres, which is quite sufficient to allow of the measurement of light of quite feeble intensity."

A complete description of the instrument and of the necessary precautions to be taken in its construction and use is given in the paper of the *J.S.C.I.*, 30th April, 1890, which is reprinted in this volume ; and several of the original instruments are preserved in the Driffield bequest at the house of the Royal Photographic Society.

" Having now secured a means of measuring the light," says Driffield[1] " and so controlling the exposure, we felt that if we could obtain automatically diagrams representing the variations of the light intensity throughout the entire day, and covering the entire year, the information we should obtain could not fail to be of value.   We therefore proceeded to construct actinometers in such a way[2] that we were able to record daily on strips of bromide paper (by photographing continuously the image of the indicating column) diagrams showing from moment to moment the variations in the light as affected by the altitude of the sun and the conditions of the atmosphere."

" This instrument consists of a differential air thermometer, one bulb of which is made of ruby glass, the other being ordinary transparent (white) glass.   The two bulbs are connected by means of a syphon containing a red indicating fluid.

" The following sketch will serve the purpose of explaining how the indications were recorded :—

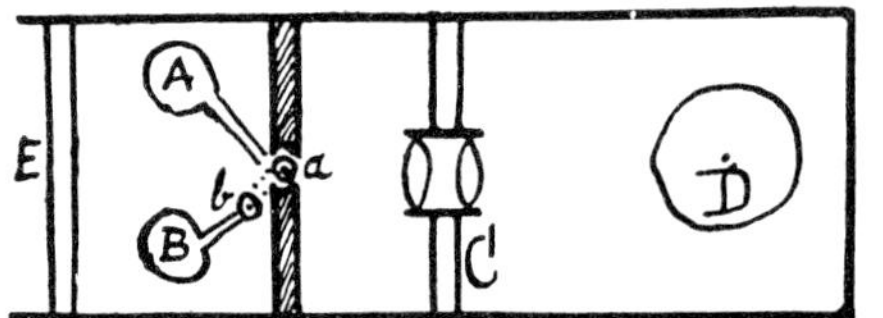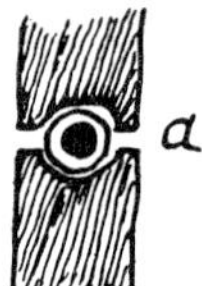

A—transparent (white) bulb.
B—red bulb.
*a* and *b*—the syphon tube containing red fluid, and in communication with A and B.
E—thick plate glass front.

<hr>

[1] D.N.—L., p. 7.                         [2] Details in H.MS. No. 21.

" The light passing through tube *a* falls upon lens C, and is focussed upon a strip of bromide paper wrapped around drum D, which is driven by clock-work.

" A transparent scale, placed behind *a*, gives the degree lines, and the hour lines are secured by means of a wire cage placed over the bromide paper around the drum.  For use, this instrument is exposed to north light, so that no direct rays of the sun can reach it, as any exposure to direct sunlight is fatal to the instrument.

" In order to be independent of barometric variations the instrument must be constructed entirely of glass, no indiarubber or other connections being satisfactory."

Continuous observations were taken every day of the year 1885–1886, and the photographic records[1] of the intensity of diffuse light so obtained were the subject of much study and analysis.

" It became evident," says Driffield, " that the fluctuations of the light from a certain mean value were such that the highest light was never more than double, and the lowest serviceable light was seldom less than half this mean value, and that in consequence, under ordinary circumstances, variations in exposure as 1 to 4 are sufficient to meet alterations in the light due to varying atmospheric conditions."

Dr. Hurter observes[2] that " when there was a steady light throughout the day—which seldom occurred—the curve so clearly indicated that the light was a function of the altitude of the sun, that I had no difficulty in recognizing the sinus curve ; it showed itself really in every diagram."

Dr. Hurter then began an investigation from an astronomical point of view as to what the intensity of diffuse daylight should be at any given place and time.  Lambert, Bunsen, Roscoe and others had done much work on this subject with which—as can be seen from the many memoranda among the MSS[3]—Dr. Hurter made himself familiar.

However, after some time, he began a special note book[4] on " The Illumination of the Earth and Actinograph," in which in some 41 pages he deals with the whole subject from the astronomical-geometrical point of view.  He commences by saying :—

" Diffuse light is the light reflected from particles of nitrogen, oxygen, vapour and dust in the atmosphere ; it bears a certain relation to the amount of sunlight which enters the atmosphere, and may, for a first approximation, be stated to be proportional to the number of rays which enter the visible

---

[1] The original records now at the Royal Photographic Society.
[2] *J.S.C.I.*, 30th April, 1890.　　　[3] H.MS.—No. 21　　　[4] H.N.—F.

portion of the atmosphere. . . . This is equivalent to saying that it is proportional to the sine of the altitude of the sun."

It may be noted that Lambert, Bunsen and Roscoe and others expressed the illumination of the atmosphere as a function of the cosine of the zenith distance of the sun. Hurter expressed it as a function of the sine of the altitude, which amounts to the same thing.

The rest of this note book contains full explanations of the different steps in the theory which led to the methods[1] of calculating the value of the light at all times of the year and day for all latitudes ; and complete light and latitude tables so calculated are contained in other note books H.N.—G., H.N.—H., and D.N.—K.

The intensity of the light was expressed in " actinometer degrees." " The brightest light which ever reaches the earth is at noon on the 21st March and on the 23rd of September, when the sun is vertically over the equator, or has an altitude of 90°. This maximum light we call 100°, and consequently one actinometer degree of light is the one-hundredth part of the brightest light when the sun culminates in the zenith."[2]

As both theory and observation with measurement led to the same conclusion—that the intensity of diffuse daylight was proportional to the sine of the altitude of the sun, the inventors considered that their actinometer was a satisfactory instrument, and, for a number of years, they made their photographic exposures by its aid. The results were such as to leave no doubt as to its capacity for accurately measuring the intensity of diffuse daylight.

---

During the time these researches were being made, the Gelatine Process had been invented by Maddox in 1871, and a gelatine emulsion had been sold by Burgess, of Peckham. Shortly afterwards, ready-prepared silver bromide-in-gelatine dry plates were put on the market by J. W. Swan and Messrs. Wratten & Wainwright.

Driffield had naturally taken much interest in the new process, and his note books[3] show that, from 1879, for some years his leisure time was chiefly occupied in various experiments in emulsion-making, and specially to be noticed are his experiments as to the presence and utility of chlorides in emulsions.

---

[1] H.N.—F., p. 82.

[2] Photo. Soc. Reporter, 30th April, 1889. *J.S.C.I.*, 30th April, 1890.

[3] D.N.—A., " Notes on Gelatine Emulsions." D.N.—B., pp. 2–71. D.N.—C., pp. 3–11.

The great variety of speeds in the new gelatino-bromide plates, so different from the almost uniform rapidity of the wet collodion plate, rendered the problem of correct exposure more difficult than ever, and " indicated strongly to us the importance of discovering some means of ascertaining their relative speeds, and of numerically expressing the same. The first step necessary to meet this need was to carry out a series of investigations in order to ascertain the law which expresses the action of light on the sensitive plate.[1]

The intensity of diffuse daylight could now be measured by their actinometer, the next step in the inquiry was to determine what amount of this light would pass through a lens and fall on a sensitive surface in the camera, and in the first fourteen pages of Dr. Hurter's note book H.N.—A. are full particulars as to the measurements of the lenses used in the succeeding experiments, such as focal length, effective value of diaphragms, losses of light by reflection at the surfaces of the lens, together with other details, such as the distance of the object and consequent alteration in the focal length, which affect the illumination of the image—in short, those qualities on which depend what we now call the " speed " of the lens. In Dr. Hurter's notes, however, the numerical expression of the value of these qualities is expressed as " the slowness," and later, as " the inertia " of the lens.

This is represented by the formula—

$$\frac{1}{k^n}\left(\frac{F}{d}\right)^2$$

where F $=$ focal length of lens.

$d$ $=$ effective aperture of diaphragm.

$k$ $=$ a coefficient indicating what fraction of incident light passes through a single lens.

$n$ $=$ number of lenses in a combination.

The methods of calculation are set out in the more complete MSS.[2] reprinted in this volume, and it will be sufficient here to give as an example the calculation of " the inertia " of a Ross landscape single lens—

$$
\begin{aligned}
F &= 11 \cdot 89 \text{ cm.} \\
d &= 0 \cdot 58 \text{ ,,} \\
k &= 0 \cdot 83
\end{aligned}
\qquad
\frac{1}{0\cdot 83}\left(\frac{11\cdot 89}{0\cdot 58}\right)^2
$$

$$
n = 1 \qquad = \frac{1}{0\cdot 83}(20\cdot 50)^2
$$

$$
\text{Inertia of lens} = \frac{420\cdot 25}{0\cdot 83} = \underline{506\cdot 3}
$$

D.MS.—No. 12, pp. 5 and 6.  D.N.—L., p. 14.

[2] H. MSS.—No. 9.

In the same note book[1] under the somewhat misleading heading, " Actinometry," is set out the first draft of an inquiry into the action of light on a sensitive surface in the camera.   This is an important piece of work which was afterwards expanded by Dr. Hurter into a separate paper found among his MSS. and printed herewith, to which reference should be made.

The note book version begins (on page 15) :—

" Supposing that a source of diffuse white light of intensity one acting directly upon a plate needed a time $t$ to so far alter a bromide of silver gelatine film on that plate that an impenetrable black deposit of silver was caused upon it on development ; then the plate would be the more sensitive the shorter the time $t$ could be made, and a plate would be called slower the greater that time $t$ is ; and if the time $t$ were very great and still did not affect the plate, the plate would be called insensitive or *inert*.

" That time $t$, therefore, measures the *inertia of the plate*, and when ascertained by suitable experiment would yield a coefficient of inertia."

Here, then, is the first mention and definition of that " inertia " in relation to a photographic plate, of which we shall hear so much in Hurter and Driffield's researches.

For the detailed reasoning reference should be made to the H.M.S.—No. 9 printed herewith, but the conclusion arrived at is that if—

    I = the intensity of the light expressed in actinometer degrees.
    $t$ = the time of exposure in seconds,
    S = the slowness of the lens, and
    $i$ = the inertia of the plate :

then, in the case of a properly exposed negative—

$$\frac{I \times t}{S} = i \ (\text{Inertia of plate}),$$

and

$$\frac{S \times i}{I} = t \ (\text{time of exposure}).$$

I, $t$, and S being capable of direct numerical expression, it is clearly possible, first, from a satisfactory negative, to calculate a number which shall express the inertia of a given plate ; and secondly, to calculate the time of exposure necessary with any lens (whose S has been measured) to give a properly exposed negative with a plate whose inertia has already been ascertained.

An example may make the method more clear.

---

[1] H.N.—A., pp. 15–26.

Using a globe lens, with the largest stop, the "slowness," worked out as shown at p. 11, being 487, it was found that when the actinometer registered 17° a good negative was obtained on a Wratten "slow" plate by an exposure of 6 seconds.

Then $\dfrac{17 \times 6}{487} = 0 \cdot 209$ is the inertia of the plate[1].

This means that a sky (density 2) would be obtained by exposing the plate directly to the sky for $0 \cdot 209$ seconds when the actinometer registers $1°$.[2]

If we now require to know what exposure we must give, using this plate, when the light measures 15°— using a lens with a small stop, the S value of which is 2133, we have—

$$\frac{2133 \times 0 \cdot 209}{15} = 29 \cdot 7 \text{ seconds.}$$

Having satisfied themselves that they now possessed a practicable means of numerically indicating the inertia of a plate, and a method of calculating the exposure necessary for the production of a satisfactory negative, Hurter and Driffield turned their attention to *development*, and many experiments were made on the changes in the time of appearance of the image due to variations in the quantities of pyro. bromide and ammonia contained in their developer.

But it soon became evident that it was most important to have some means of estimating the actual reduction of silver due to exposure and development ; in fact, a method of measuring the density of the silver deposit.

The word "density" is first mentioned in the note book H.N.—A., pp. 38–39, and as much confusion afterwards arose in the minds of photographers who were unaware of the special meaning attached by Hurter and Driffield to this word, it is best at once to explain the meaning they attached to this term.

To make their views on these points clear, consider a plate of glass divided into strips. One strip is clear glass, the next is covered with one thickness of developed film, the next with two thicknesses, the next with three, and so on, marked 0, 1, 2, 3, 4, etc. (Fig. 4). You will see that strip 0 allows practically all the light to pass through ; that strip 1 stops some of the light. In this particular case it lets $\frac{1}{3}$ the light come through ; that is, if light of unit intensity falls on one side, $\frac{1}{3}$ is transmitted, and we say its transparency is $\frac{1}{3}$ and its

---

[1] H.N.—A., p. 107.      [2] H.MSS.—No. 9.

opacity we define as the inverse of this, and call it 3. In order to transmit light of unit intensity we must let the incident light be three times as much.

Opacity, then, is the number representing the amount of light which must fall on a plate in order that light of intensity 1 may come through.

Now consider the third band, where there are *two* strips of film. Here $\frac{1}{3}$ of $\frac{1}{3}$ or $(\frac{1}{3})^2$ or $\frac{1}{9}$ will be transmitted, and the opacity will be 9.

In the next strip the light transmitted will be $\frac{1}{3}$ of $\frac{1}{3}$ of $\frac{1}{3}$ or $(\frac{1}{3})^3$ or $\frac{1}{27}$, and the opacity 27.

Now the next diagram will show these figures arranged in their proper order, so that we can consider them and their relation one to another.

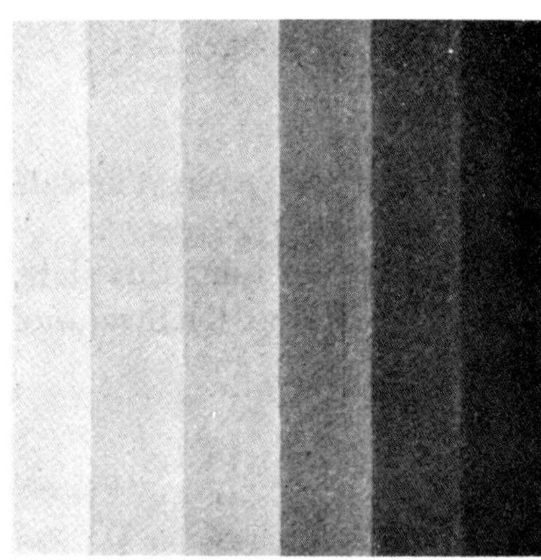



FIG. 4.

Light of Intensity 1.

| No of films .. .. .. | 0. | 1. | 2. | 3. | ... N. |
|---|---|---|---|---|---|
| Transparency .. .. | $\dfrac{1}{1}$ | $\left(\dfrac{1}{3}\right)^1$ | $\left(\dfrac{1}{3}\right)^2$ | $\left(\dfrac{1}{3}\right)^3$ | $\ldots\left(\dfrac{1}{3}\right)^N$ |
| ,, .. .. .. | $\dfrac{1}{1}$ | $\dfrac{1}{3}$ | $\dfrac{1}{9}$ | $\dfrac{1}{27}$ | $\dfrac{1}{(3)^N}$ |
| Opacity .. .. .. | 1 | 3 | 9 | 27 | $(3)^N$ |
| *Density* .. .. .. | 0 | ·477 | ·954 | 1·43 | — |

The first line gives the number of films from 0, 1, 2, 3, to N.

The second line shows the *transparency* expressed as powers of the fraction which is the transparency of one film.

The third line shows these multiplied out, and

The fourth line the inverse of these, or the *opacity*.

Now any number such as 3, 9, 27, etc., may be expressed as some other number raised to a power and the index of the power is called the logarithm of the first number.

Thus the opacity 27 is $(3)^3$ and 3 is said to be the logarithm of 27 to the base 3.

So you will see that in this way the number of films may be considered as the logarithms of the opacities to the base 3, but in ordinary use we have logarithms to the base 10, and I write in the last line the logarithms of the opacities to the base 10, and these are what Hurter and Driffield call the *densities*.

As the amount of silver light stopping stuff in each band is proportional to the number of films, we see that the densities are proportional to the amount of silver in the film or films, and if instead of having 1, 2, 3, or $n$ separate films we had 1 film with bands containing 1, 2, 3, or $n$ times as much silver, the result would be the same.

Density, then, is defined (H.N.—B., p. 1) as the logarithm of the opacity, as the logarithm of the number indicating the intensity of the light which must fall upon the plate in order that light of intensity 1 may be transmitted. To this logarithm the silver on the plate is proportional.

A so-called[1] "Standard Plate for measuring Densities" was made by exposing a plate in steps for 5, 10, 15, 20, 25 and 30 seconds, and a second plate is steps of ten times that amount. The plate was reproduced by contact printing, and the strips of different densities compared with each other singly and superposed in pairs. In what way it was intended to use this plate for the measurement of densities is not clear, but the experiment showed that beyond a certain exposure,—50 seconds—increased exposure did not result in increased density ; that there was a limit to the density due to exposure.

It is probable that about this time Dr. Hurter wrote the interesting paper, H. MSS. No. 7, " Theory of the Action of Light on Sensitive Plates," which deals mathematically with the effects produced by the superposition of two strips from the same step negative, the strips being reversed so that the thickest band on one strip is over the thinnest band on the other. The conclusion arrived at—" The number of molecules of silver salt partially decomposed by light is proportional to the duration of the exposure "—was afterwards found to be erroneous. (See Experiment in H.N—A., p. 45.)

It became evident, however, that some plan must be devised for the comparison of the densities of plates by photometric methods, and on p. 49 of H.N.—A. we come across the subjoined sketch diagram of the first photometer invented by Hurter and Driffield for this purpose.

The apparatus consisted of a circular box, as shown in plan in the sketch, with four openings filled with short tubes at angles of 90° round the circumference of the drum. In the centre of the box was fixed a vertical spindle,

[1] H.N.—A., p. 45.

A series of experiments[1] and measurements led to the conclusion that " in the case of a rightly exposed landscape negative there is a definite ratio of density between the sky and the grass which is about as $1 \cdot 7$ to 1."[2]

At this time the estimation of the inertiæ of the various gelatino-bromide plates appearing commercially, and the calculation of the proper exposures for them, took up a great deal of the leisure time of the two experimenters, and on p. 121 of Hurter's note book, H.N.—A., we find :—" To avoid everlasting calculations we made a slide rule, which answers very well.   Rule : Set degrees of light to lens figures, then opposite the inertia is the exposure." Two of these rules are in the H. and D. collection at the R.P.S.

This rule was the first idea of their " Actinograph—an instrument for the calculation of photographic Exposures,"[3] which was patented in the following year,[4] and as this instrument is fully described and illustrated, with the methods of the construction of its various scales in the patent specification and in its improved form, in *The Actinograph* (Photo. Soc. Reporter, 30th April, 1889), " An instrument for the measurement of diffuse daylight and the actinograph " (*J.S.C.I.*, 30th April, 1890) which are reprinted in this volume, it will be unnecessary to describe it in this place.

It may, however, be noted that the scale in the earlier actinographs, which was marked—as described in the patent—with " inertiæ," was in the next year, and afterwards, marked with " actinograph speeds " of the various plates, the method of arriving at such speed numbers being explained in the paper of 1890.   Specimens of the various forms of the instrument are in the H. and D. collection at the R.P.S.

The actinographs, with simple instructions for their use—both in the calculation of exposures and the determination of plate speeds—at first sold by Hurter and Driffield themselves at Widnes, were later placed on the market by Marion & Co.,[5] of Soho Square, London.   The instrument was favourably reviewed in the photographic press by Captain Abney and others and came into considerable use.

---

" During the ten years from 1876 to 1886 photography underwent a complete revolution owing to the introduction of the gelatino-bromide plate, and as this new phase," says Driffield, " gave us a great deal to think about, and a great deal of new experience to acquire, our work during these ten years was not wholly confined to what has been previously indicated, but had been directed towards discovering some method of testing the speed of plates,

[1] H.N.—A., pp. 107, 112, 118–121.    [2] " The Actinograph " reprint herewith.
[3] H.N.—A., p. 125.    [4] 14th April, 1888, No. 5545.
[5] Correspondence, " Marion & Co."

which was workable in the laboratory and independent altogether of the camera."[1]

In the latter part of 1888 a series of experiments was made with a view of finding the relationship between exposures of various amount and the densities produced by them : to find the law which expresses the action of light upon a plate.

About this time also Dr. Hurter began a special note book (H.N.—B.), which was evidently intended to contain his experiments and conclusions on the rapidly-growing science of photography, and appropriately the book commences with a definition of density previously referred to.

" Density of a plate is the logarithm of the number indicating the intensity of the light which must fall upon the plate in order that intensity one may be transmitted. To this logarithm the silver on the plate is proportional."

Much of the actual experimental results continue to be entered in·the older note book, H.N.—A., while the conclusions arrived at, together with the special facts in support of them, are entered. into the new book, H.N.—B., and it becomes necessary, therefore, to refer to and to compare both note books in order to form a proper idea as to the nature and amount of the work which was being done.

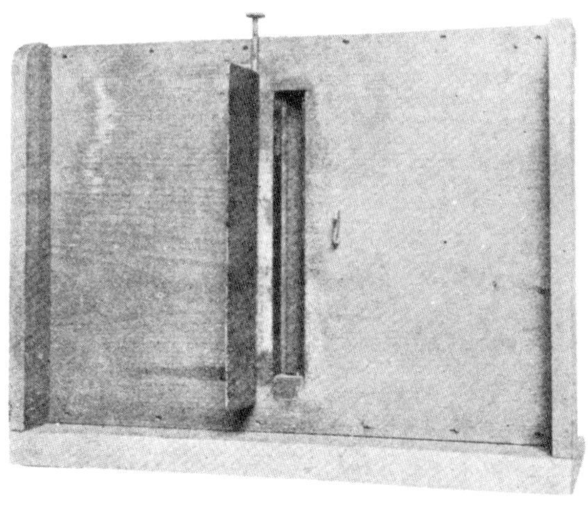

FIG. 8.

As so much depended on impressing the plates with exposures of varied but definite amount, it will not be out of place here to refer to the methods

[1] D.N.—L., pp. 11, 12.

used for this purpose by Hurter and Driffield before they adopted the sector wheel in 1891.

The first piece of apparatus used is that figured below, in which a dark

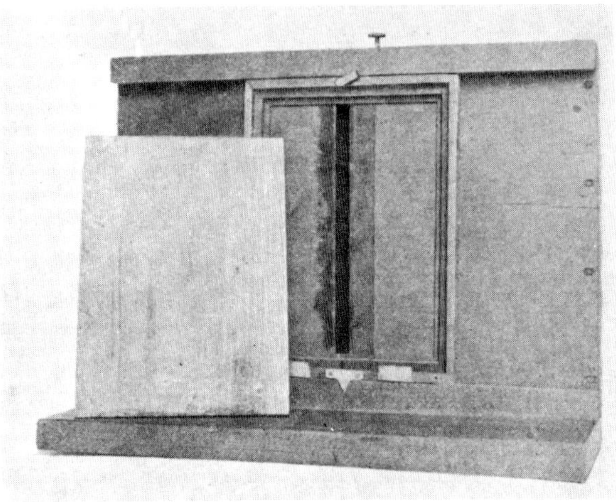

FIG. 9.

slide is so arranged that it can be moved forward by definite amounts behind a narrow slit, which is closed by a flap shutter, and so successive strips of exposure can be impressed upon the plate.

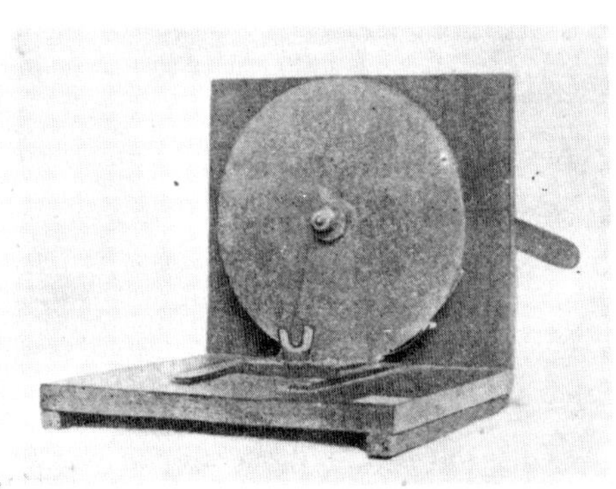

FIG. 10.

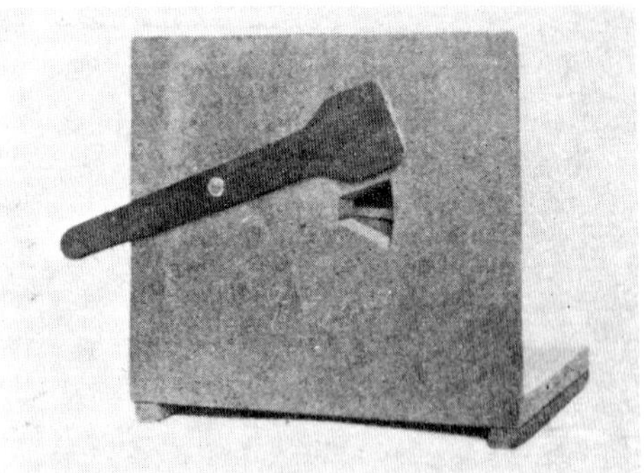

FIG. 11.

The next thing used for this purpose is an arrangement to hold a quarter-plate in a circular drum, which can be rotated behind an aperture covered by a movable shutter, and so eight patches of exposure made on the plate. This is shown in Figs. 10 and 11. Both these were exhibited at the Crystal

Palace exhibition in 1898 and are now in the possession of the Royal Photographic Society.

In addition to these pieces of apparatus a method was adopted of exposing behind rather a crude form of what is now known as a " step wedge."

An artificially-graduated negative was made, one-quarter of which was clear glass and the other three-quarters were respectively covered with one, two and three thicknesses of translucent paper.

The densities of each part were measured in the photometer then in use, and the intensities of incident light transmitted were calculated out. Behind this negative sensitive plates were placed and exposed—in some cases to diffuse daylight and in other cases to candle or lamp light for 2·5, 5, 10, 20 and 40 seconds.

The various densities on the positive so produced were measured, tabulated and compared in every detail, and the following table, part of one which appears in the note book H.N.—A., p. 137, is interesting, as it led to the discovery of the important formula expressing the relation between density and exposure :—

| Exposures. | 3 papers. | 2 papers. | 1 paper. | Clear glass. |
|---|---|---|---|---|
| Secs. | | | | |
| 2·5 | 1·00 | 1·41 | 2·10 | 2·64 |
| 5 | 2·00 | 2·82 | 3·80 | 4·40 |
| 10 | 3·35 | 4·10 | 5·06 | 5·81 |
| 20 | 5·06 | 5·64 | 6·60 | 7·10 |
| 40 | 6·35 | 7·16 | 7·85 | 8·60 |

These figures were obtained by dividing the actual densities measured by the density produced by an exposure to 2·5″ through the part of the negative covered with the three papers.

On examining the column of densities produced under the " three-paper " part of the negative the mean increase of density for each doubling of the exposure is—

$$\frac{6\cdot35 - 1}{4} = 1\cdot34.$$

And if a series of densities are calculated by successive additions of 1·34 to the first density we get :—

|  Calculated. | | | | Observed. |
|---|---|---|---|---|
| 1·00 | .. | .. | .. | 1·00 |
| 2·34 | .. | .. | .. | 2·00 |
| 3·68 | .. | .. | .. | 3·35 |
| 5·02 | .. | .. | .. | 5·06 |
| 6·36 | .. | .. | .. | 6·36 |

The fairly close correspondence of the figures was at once noted, and to get rid, as far as possible, of the effects of experimental irregularities, a table was made by adding together all the densities produced in the previous table by the same time of exposure, and the following series of numbers was obtained :—

| Exposure. | Sum of *Observed Densities.* | *Densities Calculated* by the continued addition of the mean difference to the first density. |
|---|---|---|
| Sec. | | |
| 2·5 | 7·15 | 7·15 |
| 5·0 | 13·02 | 12·85 |
| 10·0 | 18·32 | 18·55 |
| 20·0 | 24·40 | 24·25 |
| 40·0 | 29·95 | 29·95 |

$$\frac{29\cdot95 - 7\cdot15}{4} = 5\cdot70 = \text{mean difference.}$$

The note book[1] then states :—

" This calculates a series as above which shows—

That the Density increases according to a Law—

$$D = a + \gamma \log. t,$$

where $t$ is the time of exposure."

$$D - a = \gamma . \log. t.$$

$$\frac{D - a}{\gamma} = \log. t.$$

$$t = c^{\frac{D - a.}{\gamma}}.$$

The graph which follows expressing the densities in the above table as ordinates, while the logarithms of the time are abscissæ, shows the law in the form of a linear equation, and the close agreement between the observed and calculated results.

There was now no doubt in Dr. Hurter's mind that he had discovered the law of "the influence of light on sensitive plates, and, in his note book H.N.—B., p. 1, he says :—" If an experiment be made in which the time of exposure is prolonged in geometrical progression, the density of the plate is found to be in arithmetic progression." Seven selected experiments in proof of this very important law on Wratten's and Chapman's plates are set out in tables in the note book. For example, it will suffice to set out an experiment by Driffield on a Chapman plate[1]—

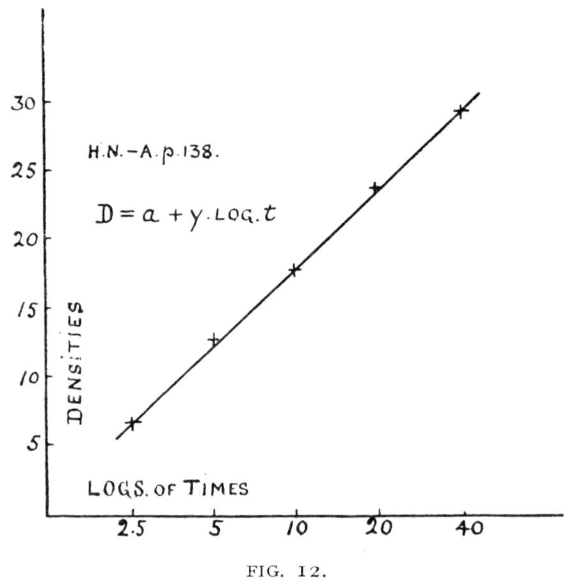



FIG. 12.

| Exposure. | D found | D calculated by addition of mean difference— $\dfrac{1\cdot920 - \cdot750}{5} = 0\cdot234.$ |
|---|---|---|
| Sec. | | |
| 10·0 | 0·750 | 0·750 |
| 14·3 | 0·970 | 0·984 |
| 20·5 | 1·225 | 1·218 |
| 29·3 | 1·470 | 1·452 |
| 41·9 | 1·690 | 1·686 |
| 60·0 | 1·920 | 1·920 |

Here the times of exposure increase by the common factor 1·43, and the resulting densities increase by a common difference of 0·234.

The importance of this relationship between various exposures and the densities resulting therefrom was at once recognised, and Dr. Hurter, in his note book (H.N.—B., p. 4), proceeds :—

" For the direct illumination of a plate, the results obey—

[1] H.N.—B. 3.

*The Law*

$$D_x - D_1 = \gamma \, [\log. T_x - \log. T_1].$$

From this law, and assuming that Driffield's three plates[1] give, in 10 seconds, densities (1) 0·720, (2) 0·750, (3) 0·700, say a mean = 0·720, and taking this and 10 seconds as the standard for Driffield's lamp, we have—

$$D_x - 0 \cdot 720 = \gamma \, (\log. T_n - \log. 10)$$
$$D_x - 0 \cdot 720 = \gamma \, (\log. T_x - 1).$$

For 60 seconds the results are 1·920 and 1·860, or, say, a mean of 1·890. Consequently, we have—

$$1 \cdot 890 - 0 \cdot 720 = \gamma \, (\log. 60 - 1) = \gamma \, \log. 6,$$

or

$$\gamma = \frac{1 \cdot 170}{\log. 6} = \frac{1 \cdot 170}{0 \cdot 778} = 1 \cdot 50.$$

The plates can, therefore, be calculated to any time by the formula :—

$$D = 1 \cdot 5 \, [\log. T - 1] + 0 \cdot 720."$$

This was true of this particular plate and this particular development, but further experiments showed that the factor $\gamma$ was variable and not always 1·5— but that its variation was[2] " independent of light, as it is the same whether the plate is exposed directly or behind thicknesses of paper. It is independent of time of exposure, as it is the same between 10 and 33 seconds as between 16 and 60 seconds. It is evidently variable, not with the plate, for Driffield's plates are specially made, and out of the same batch of emulsion.

As it does not depend either on the light, nor the time of exposure, nor the plate, it can only vary and depend on development, for the factor is not constant."

Further experiments[3] " showed that the density due to light grows with the time of development up to a certain limit . . . and that the factor for the change of exposure into density will grow with each minute (of development) until full density is reached." It will be remembered that the limiting value of density due to exposure had been observed some time before in the measurements of the so-called " standard plate."[4]

Dr. Hurter now began an inquiry into the relationship between the densities of a negative and the densities of a positive produced therefrom by contact printing, and his note book (H.N.—B., p. 9, *et seq.*) contains his first views on this important subject.

---

[1] H.N.—A., pp. 140, 141, 142.  H.N.—B., pp. 2 and 3.
[2] H.N.—B., pp. 5 and 6.    [3] H.N.—B., p. 7.  *J.S.C.I.*, May, 1890, Expt. 1.
[4] H.N.—A., p. 45.

" Relationship between negative and positive.—Assuming the relationship between intensity of light and *time* (query density) until further direct proof, to be—

$$D - 0\cdot720 = \gamma \left( \log.\frac{T\,I}{ti} \right)^1$$

and assuming that light passes through negative of density N, the original intensity will be altered, so that the intensity coming through is $\frac{1}{x}$ of the original, and we have to put—

$$\text{instead of TI,}\quad \frac{TI}{x}$$

But if $\frac{1}{x}$ the light comes through the plate, the density of the plate is log. $x$ according to the definition, or $N = \log. x$.

Consequently, the above formula becomes—

$$D - 0\cdot72 = \gamma\,[\log. T + \log. I - N - (\log. t + \log. I)]$$
$$= \gamma\,[\log. T + \log. I - N - \log. t - \log. I]$$
$$D - 0\cdot72 = \gamma\,[\log. T - N - \log. t]$$

and if $t$ be 10 seconds of open lamp, we have, putting P instead of D—

$$P - 0\cdot72 = \gamma\,[\log. T - N - 1].$$

From this we find, if we transpose—

$$P + \gamma N = \gamma\,[\log. T - 1] + 0\cdot72.$$

If, on the same negative, there are several densities, we have—

$$P_n + \gamma N = \gamma\,[\log. T - 1] + 0\cdot72$$

This, of course, means, as time and development are constant, that for one experiment—

$$P_x + \gamma N_n = \text{a constant} \quad \dots\dots\dots\dots\dots\dots\dots\dots\dots\dots\dots \quad (2)$$

and

$$P_1 + \gamma N_1 = P_2 + \gamma N_2$$

or

$$\frac{P_1 - P_2}{N_2 - N_1} = \gamma \quad \dots\dots\dots\dots\dots\dots\dots\dots\dots\dots\dots\dots \quad (3)$$

(3) This last equation serves to calculate the constant of development ($\gamma$) from the positive, and equation (2) can then be made use of to test the accuracy of the laws."

This theory was then tested as follows :—One of Driffield's negatives[2] was used to make a positive on a similar plate—the exposure given was

---

300 seconds at 8 feet distance from a lamp, and the results tabulated below
were obtained.

| | (1)<br>N found. | (2)<br>P found. | (3)<br>$\gamma$ N + P. | (4)<br>$\gamma$ (log. T − 1) + 0·72 = 3·083. |
|---|---|---|---|---|
| 1 | 0·700 | 1·960 | 3·080 | 3·083 |
| 2 | 0·900 | 1·680 | 3·120 | 3·083 |
| 3 | 1·010 | 1·480 | 3·095 | 3·083 |
| 4 | 1·223 | 1·110 | 3·069 | 3·083 |
| 5 | 1·285 | 1·010 | 3·060 | 3·083 |
| 6 | 1·360 | 0·850 | 3·020 | 3·083 |
| 7 | 1·550 | 0·530 | 3·010 | 3·083 |
| 8 | 1·660 | 0·417 | 3·073 | 3·083 |

The calculation—

$$\frac{P_1 - P_8}{N_8 - N_1} - \frac{1543}{960} = 1\cdot6 = \gamma \text{ (the development constant)}$$

The formula $\gamma$N + P gives series 3.

The formula $\gamma$ (log. T − 1) + 0·72 gives series 4.

$$\text{log. T} = \text{log. } 300 = 2\cdot477$$
$$1\cdot6 \, (2\cdot477 − 1) + 0\cdot72$$
$$= 1\cdot6 \, (1\cdot477 + 0\cdot72$$
$$= 2\cdot3632 + 0\cdot72 = 3\cdot083 \text{ (the constant).}$$

The figures so obtained show the close resemblance of $\gamma$ (log. T − 1) +
0·72 and P + $\gamma$N, the constancy of the value throughout the series and,
consequently, the truth of the law as set out above.

Much work was done at a later date on this subject, *see* H.MSS., No. 14,
D.N.—G., pp. 12–14, 40–44, 50–60, part of which was the foundation for the
paper, " The Relation between Photographic Negatives and Their Positives,"
in the *J.S.C.I.*, read on the 28th February, 1891.


About this time, Hurter and Driffield became more and more dissatisfied
with the results in density measuring given by the photometer then in use.
Two[1] new instruments constructed on the same general plan, but with modified
and, it was hoped, more delicate reading discs, were made and tested with mixtures of Indian ink and water, and the measurements of plates.

[1] H.N.—A., p. 155 *et seq.*   H.N.—B., pp. 17, 36–42.

A thorough and lengthy investigation showed that the instrument could only be trusted for the estimation of such densities as could be measured by a rotation of the disc between 30° and 60°, and that the measurements by direct reading of densities higher than 0·637 could not be relied upon.

The note books of both men about the end of 1889 begin to contain rough sketches of the general design and details of a new measuring instrument—the well-known Hurter and Driffield photometer, described with figures in the paper of May, 1890.

The note book H.N.—A., p. 159, has what seems to be the first sketch of the instrument. Driffield's note books[1] and MSS. contain many sketches of details, while the books H.N.—B., p. 54 and p. 55, and D.N.—E., p 13A (dated "January, 1890"), contain complete diagrams of the photometer, with full instructions as to the method of calculating the scales.

It would appear from the notes[2] that the first photometer measured 18 inches from flame to flame, and others of 17·5 and 15 inches are also referred to, but later on the shorter distance of 12 inches was found to work better, and of the four photometers of this pattern made and used by Hurter and Driffield, and now in the possession of the Royal Photographic Society of Great Britain, three are 12 inches in length and the fourth, of later date, fitted with Lummer-Brodhun prism, is 20 inches from flame to flame. Such full details as to the construction of these photometers and the tests in proof of their accuracy are to be found in the various papers reprinted in this volume that it is needless to describe them here in detail. The instrument proved to be a most valuable aid to research, and, as Driffield says,[3] " is in photographic investigations what the balance is in (quantitative) chemical analysis."

Many of the measurements made in their previous experiments were confirmed by the use of the new photometer, with which it was found possible to measure densities up to 3·5 and to obtain reliable results.

Experiments were continued on a variety of subjects, such as the effect of intensification,[4] the use of a special step wedge negative in

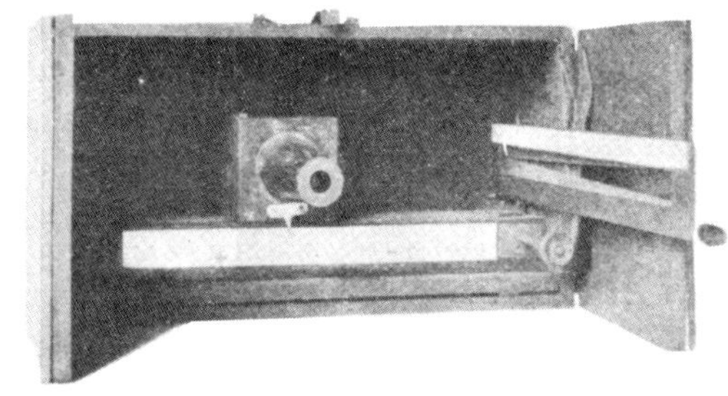

FIG. 13

[1] D.N.—E., pp. 12, 12A.
[3] D.N.—F., p. 7.
[2] H N.—B., pp. 54, 55, 88.
[4] H.N.—A., p. 143. H.N.—B., p. 8.

exposing experimental plates with a view to avoid errors of exposure,[1] the results obtained by exposing one plate behind another,[2] and the laws of reflection and absorption of light by translucent and diffusing media.[3]

Most of these experiments were undertaken under the direction and at the suggestion of Dr. Hurter, a man equipped with a knowledge of the higher mathematics to a degree very uncommon among the chemists of his time, and possessing such a mastery over mathematical method as enabled him to apply it with success to the solution of scientific problems of great difficulty. His note books show that he was now much occupied with a mathematical inquiry into the relationship between the opacity, transparency and density of the deposited silver in the negative, and the laws connecting exposure and its effect on the sensitive gelatino-bromide plate when submitted to development, with a view of discovering some method of determining the inertia (or its inverse —the speed) of plates which would be workable in the laboratory and quite independent of the camera.

Many of the records of experimental work done at this time are missing, but from what remains it appears probable that the work already done on the relationship between a negative and the corresponding positive led them to the following method of arriving at the " inertia " of a plate.

Before describing the method in detail it must be noticed that though in their early work they defined the inertia as the least exposure necessary to produce a sky density of about 2 on their plate when developed, yet when they had discovered the effect of time on the development factor $\gamma$, and the consequent increase of density by length of development, they took as the criterion of a properly-exposed negative that, when developed, the density of the sky should bear to the density of the grass the ratio of $1\cdot7$ to $1$ (see H.N.—A., pp. 107–112, 118–121). Later on, from experiments on the photographing of black paper (H.N.—D., p. 165), they preferred to regard the inertia of the plate as the smallest exposure necessary to produce the slightest deposit on the plate representing the deepest shadow of the original, the reason being that the very slight deposits are little altered by continued development.

At what precise period this change of view took place I am not able to say. However, what was now sought was to find a numerical expression for the smallest exposure which would affect the plate. It was not until some time later that the periods of under, correct and over-exposure were recognised, which effected a further modification of their views on inertia.

---

[1] H.N.—B., p. 71.      [2] H.N.—B., pp. 43, 52, 65.      [3] H.N.—B., pp. 111–117.

The method employed was to give a definite exposure through a step wedge and to measure the densities of the positive thus produced.

A chart was then made in which the densities of the positive were laid off as ordinates, while the corresponding densities of the negative were laid off as abscissæ.

As an example[1] :—

| Negative densities. | | | | Positive densities. |
|---|---|---|---|---|
| 0·900 | .. | .. | .. | 1·84 |
| 1·01 | .. | .. | .. | 1·76 |
| 1·22 | .. | .. | .. | 1·48 |
| 1·36 | .. | .. | .. | 1·23 |
| 1·55 | .. | .. | .. | 0·995 |
| 1·66 | .. | .. | .. | 0·823 |

These, plotted on squared paper as described, are shown in the diagram. It will be noticed that the points lie on a straight line, which produced, cuts the line of negative densities at 2·25.

The meaning of that is that the least light which will affect the plate is the amount which, from the source used, would pass through a density of 2·25. That amount of exposure is the "inertia," and, following the definition of density already given—

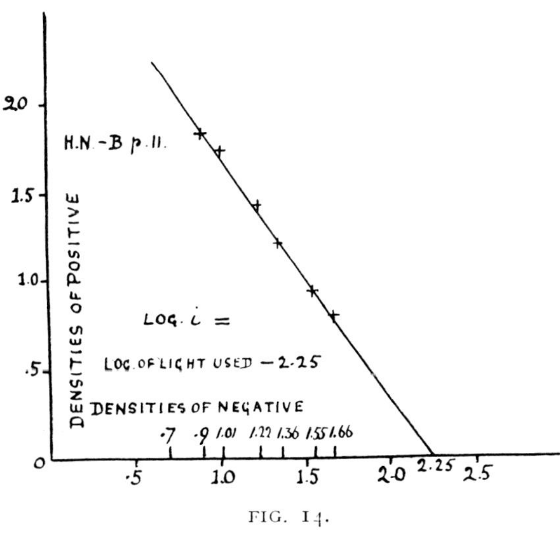


FIG. 14.

$$\text{Log. light used} - 2\cdot25 = \text{log. of } i,$$

from which the numerical value of the inertia is ascertained.

The continued mathematical inquiries of Dr. Hurter (which are to be specially dealt with by Professor H. S. Allen later on) led him to make various suggestions as to other means of determining the inertia.

One ingenious method of calculating the mean inertia of a plate from a number of densities, $D_1 \ldots D_n$, obtained by exposures to a constant source of light for times, $t_1 \ldots t_n$, is specially worthy of notice.[2]

---

[1] H.N.—B., p. 11.     [2] H.N.—B., p. 82.

Add all the densities together.

Divide the sum so obtained by the development factor.

Subtract the quotient from the sum of the logs. of the times, and

The difference so obtained, divided by the number of observed densities, will give the log. of the inertia.

$$\text{Log. } i = \frac{1}{n}\left(\lg t_1 + \ldots \lg t_n - \frac{D_1 + \ldots D_n}{\gamma}\right)$$

As an example of this a worked-out instance from Hurter's note book (H.N.—B., p. 82) may be given here :—

*Wratten's Instantaneous Plate.*

| Exposure. | Log. Exp. | Density. |
|---|---|---|
| Sec. | | |
| (1)  10 | 1·000 | 1·745 |
| (2)  20 | 1·301 | 2·290 |
| (3)  40 | 1·602 | 2·590 |
| (4)  80 | 1·903 | 3·035 |
| | 5·806 | 9·660 |

Density difference between (4) and (1) $= 1\cdot290$—

$$\frac{1\cdot290}{3} = 0\cdot43 = \text{mean difference.}$$

$$0\cdot43 \times 3\cdot3 = 1\cdot43 = \gamma = \textit{development factor.}$$

Sum of densities $= 9\cdot66$.

    ,,    logs. of times $= 5\cdot806$.

Then—

$$\text{Log. } i = \frac{1}{4}\left(5\cdot806 - \frac{9\cdot66}{1\cdot43}\right)$$

$$\text{Log. } i = \frac{5\cdot806 - 6\cdot76.}{4}$$

$$\text{Log. } i = \frac{\bar{1}\cdot044}{4} = \bar{1}\cdot761$$

$$= \lg. \text{ of } 0\cdot577 = i.$$

Which quite agrees with the value obtained by other methods.

The formula finally adopted for the determination of the inertia may be gathered from the various note books referred to below[1], and is the one set out in the classic paper of May, 1890.[2]

Two densities (in the period of correct exposure), $D_1$ and $D_2$, are obtained from exposures $T_1$ and $T_2$. If we plot the densities as ordinates and the logs. of the times as abscissæ, a line drawn through the two density points will hit the log. time line at $i$, which will give the log. of the inertia.

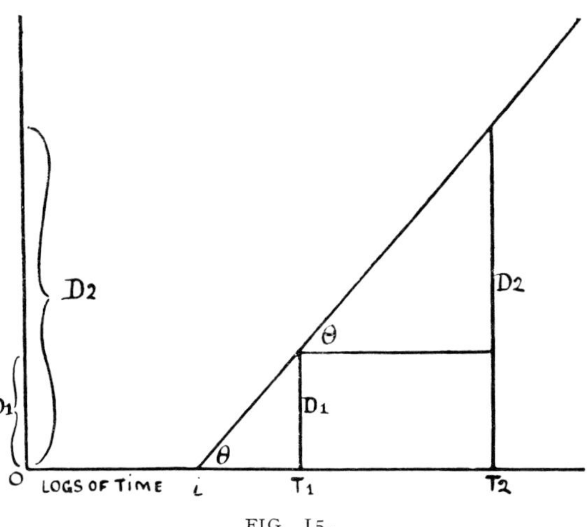


FIG. 15.

$$\frac{D_2 - D_1}{\log. T_2 - \log. T_1} = \tan \theta = \gamma.$$

But—

$$\frac{D_2}{\gamma} = \log. T_2 - \log. i.$$

Transposing—

$$\text{Log. } i - \log. T_2 \quad \frac{D_2.}{\gamma}$$

Or—

$$\text{Log. } i = \log. T_2 - \cfrac{\dfrac{D_2}{D_2 - D_1}}{\log. T_2 - \log. T_1}$$

$$\text{Log. } i = \log. T_2 - \frac{D_2 (\log. T_2 - \log. T_1)}{D_2 - D_1}$$

Getting same denominator.

$$\text{Log. } i = \frac{\log. T_2 (D_2 - D_1)}{D_2 - D_1} - \frac{D_2 (\log. T_2 - \log. T_1)}{D_2 - D_1}$$

Multiplying out—

$$\text{Log. } i = \frac{D_2 \log. T_2 - D_1 \log. T_2 - D_2 \log. T_2 + D_2 \log. T_1.}{D_2 - D_1}$$

---

[1] H.N.—B., pp. 4, 62–63.   D.N.—E., p. 12.   D.N.—O., p. 13,

[2] *J.S.C.I.*, 31st May, 1890, p. 13.

The $+$ and $-\ D_2 \log. T_2$ cross out and we have—

$$\text{Log. } i = \frac{D_2 \log. T_1 - D_1 \log. T_2}{D_2 - D_1}$$

And this is the formula given in the paper of May 31st, 1890.[1]

After devoting their leisure time for more than ten years to researches in the chemistry and physics of photography with a view of rendering the production of a technically perfect negative as far as possible a matter of certainty, Hurter and Driffield had covered the following ground :—

They had in the first place defined transparency, opacity and density and explained the mathematical relationship between the three. They had succeeded in the invention of a reliable method for the measurement of density, and had shown that density in a negative was partly dependent on the exposure and partly on the length of development, and that in both cases it tended to reach a limit.

They had established the fact that if on one and the same plate two different exposures were given, which on complete development would ultimately yield different final densities, then in the case of partial development the two densities would bear the same ratio to each other as the final limiting densities would have—in other words, that the density ratios due to exposure were the same at any stage of development, and they contended that these ratios were unalterable by any variation in development.

Their experiments with long-continued exposures when represented graphically had shown the existence of four different periods of exposure— under-exposure, correct exposure, over-exposure and reversal.

They were able to express mathematically the relations between exposure, development and density, and, finally, had invented methods of determining and expressing numerically the inertia—and consequently the speed of a plate.

The time had now arrived when they decided to bring before the scientific public in the form of a paper the results of their work. Driffield seems to have done most of the experimental work on the lines suggested by Dr. Hurter, but, owing to a habit of recording the results on such scraps of paper as might be handy, most of the enormous mass of experimental data which he accumulated before 1890 has unfortunately disappeared. However, about the end of 1889 he collected into a small green leather-bound pocket book[2] (which was fortunately discovered among the mass of papers) the tabulated results of such of his experiments as seemed to him and to Dr. Hurter to bear on the

---

[1] *J.S.C.I.*, 31st May, 1890.          [2] D.N.—O.

points to be dealt with in the paper, and this little book has been of great help in tracing the history of this part of the subject.

The views of the two experimenters were reduced to a definite and orderly form, and on 17th March, 1890, Dr. Hurter read before the Photographic Society of Liverpool University College a joint paper by Driffield and himself, entitled, "On Recent Photophysical and Photochemical Researches." A manuscript in Driffield's writing (D.N.—F.) was probably the basis of this lecture, but this is not certain. The report in the *Amateur Photographer*, 28th March, 1890, shows clearly that the paper dealt with the same points which were afterwards the subject of Hurter and Driffield's classic paper— "Photochemical Investigations and a New Method of Determination of the Sensitiveness of Photographic Plates," which was read on 31st May, 1890, at Liverpool before the local section of the Society of Chemical Industry, printed in Vol. IX, No. 5, of the *Journal* of that Society, and reprinted in the present volume.

W. B. FERGUSON.

*28th July,* 1917.

# THE MATHEMATICAL WORK

OF

## Dr. FERDINAND HURTER

BY

H. S. Allen, M.A., D.Sc., of King's College, London,

AND

A Letter of 22nd August, 1897, from Dr. Hurter to Mr. Driffield dealing with the Theory of Development, annexed at the request of Dr. Allen.

---

## Dr. HURTER'S MATHEMATICAL WORK.

The note books of Dr. Hurter now in the possession of the Royal Photographic Society contain many pages of mathematical analysis interspersed with records of experimental work. The most important part of the mathematical investigation is concerned with the fundamental formula given in the *J.S.C.I.*, 31st May, 1890. This formula expresses the density after development as a function of the opacity of the unexposed plate, of the time of exposure, and of the "inertia" of the silver bromide.

The physical assumptions on which the formula is based may be, and have been, made the subject of criticism.[1] Some of these assumptions, as that the film obeys the exponential law for the absorption of light, must be regarded merely as approximations. But given the assumptions, there can be no doubt as to the correctness of the mathematical development given by Dr. Hurter. In the following pages, which should be read in conjunction with the published papers, the mathematical reasoning given on various pages of the note books is abstracted. In some cases the notation differs slightly from that finally employed in the joint paper.

[1] *See* Sheppard and Mees, *Investigations on the Theory of the Photographic Process,* pp. 210, 288 (Longmans, 1907).

THE FUNDAMENTAL LAW.

*Dr. Hurter's Note Book,* H.N.—B., pp. 58 and 59.   My law—[1]

$$dx = (1 - a)\frac{I}{i}[e^{-kx} - e^{-ka}]\, dt.$$

$(1 - a) =$ fraction of light not reflected.
$I =$ intensity of light.
$i =$ inertia of silver salt.
$e^{-kx} =$ light not absorbed by changed silver.
$e^{-ka} =$ light not absorbed by total silver.
$e^{-kx} - e^{-ka}$ is light passing by changed less that passing by all.
$dt =$ differential of time.

Result of integration—

$$\log. \frac{e^{ka} - 1}{e^{ka} - e^{kx}} = \frac{k}{e^{ka}} \cdot (1 - a)\frac{It}{i}$$

*Recapitulation of the law* (p. 125).

*Complete derivation of the law of action of light* (p. 154).

$$\int_0^x \frac{dx}{e^{-kx} - e^{-ka}} = \int_0^t (1 - a)\frac{I\,dt}{i}$$

Put   $e^{-kx} = y$ and $e^{-ka} = A$   then
$$dy = - e^{-kx}\, dx \cdot k \text{ or}$$

$$dx = -\frac{dy}{y}\,\frac{1}{k}\quad \text{or}$$

$$\int_0^x \frac{dx}{e^{-kx} - e^{-ka}} = -\frac{1}{k}\int_1^{e^{-kx}} \frac{dy}{y\,(y - A)}$$

(3)
$$\int_1^{e^{-kx}} \frac{dy}{y(y - A)} = - k\,(1 - a)\frac{I}{i}t$$

$$\int \frac{dy}{y\,(y - A)} = \frac{1}{A}\int \frac{dy}{y - a} - \frac{dy}{y}$$

$$\frac{1}{y\,(y - A).} = \frac{c}{y} + \frac{B}{y - a}$$
$$1 = C\,(y - A) + B\,y$$
$$1 = - CA$$
$$C = -\frac{1}{A}$$
$$B + C = 0 \quad B = - C = \frac{1}{A}$$

(4)
$$\int_1^{e^{-kx}} \left(\frac{1}{y - A} - \frac{1}{y}\right) dy = - A\,k\,(1 - a)\frac{I}{i}\,t\quad \text{or}$$

[1] *See* p. 11 of Reprint from *J.S.C.I.*, 31st May, 1890.

$$\log. \frac{e^{-kx} - e^{-ka}}{e^{-kx}(1 - e^{-ka})} = -A\,k\,(1-a)\frac{1}{i}t$$

$$\log. \frac{e^{-kx}(1 - e^{-ka})}{e^{-kx} - e^{-ka}} = e^{-ka}\,k\,(1-a)\frac{1}{i}t$$

Multiply by $e^{ka}$ gives—

$$\log.\frac{1 - e^{-ka}}{1 - e^{-ka}\,e^{kx}} \quad \text{and by } e^{ka}$$

$$\log. \frac{e^{ka} - 1}{e^{ka} - e^{-kx}} = \frac{k}{e^{ka}}(1-a)\frac{1}{i}t$$

Substituting O for $e^{ka}$ and D for $kx$, we have—

$$\frac{O - 1}{O - \epsilon^{D}} = \epsilon^{\frac{k}{O}(1-a)\frac{1}{i}t}$$

collecting symbols $k\,(1 - a)$ and $i$ into $i_{o}$—[1]

$$\frac{O - 1}{O - \epsilon^{D}} = \epsilon^{\frac{1}{O}\frac{I}{i}t} \quad \text{or}$$

$$O - \epsilon^{D} = (O - 1)\,\epsilon^{-\frac{1}{O}\frac{I}{i}t}$$

$$\epsilon^{D} = O - (O - 1)\,\epsilon^{-\frac{1}{O}\frac{I}{i}t}$$

$$D = \log.\left[O - (O - 1)\,\epsilon^{-\frac{1}{O}\frac{I}{i}t}\right].$$

## THE POINT OF INFLEXION ON THE CURVE.[2]

*Dr. Hurter's Note Book*, H.N.—C., pp. 69-75.

$$D = \log.\left[O - (O - 1)\,\epsilon^{-\frac{It}{io}}\right].$$

Put $\dfrac{It}{io} = a$, then—

$$D = \log.\,[O\,(1 - \epsilon^{-a}) + \epsilon^{-a}].$$

Differentiate according to log. $a$ as follows :—

If $u = O\,(1 - \epsilon^{-a}) + \epsilon^{-a}$

then $D = \log._{\epsilon} u$ and

$$\frac{dD}{du} = \frac{1}{u} = \frac{1}{O\,(1 - \epsilon^{-a}) + \epsilon^{-a}},$$

[1] The MS. reads $i_{o}$, but the sense seems to require $io$.
[2] Compare Sheppard and Mees, *loc. cit.*

$$\frac{du}{da} = O\epsilon^{-a} - \epsilon^{-a} \text{ hence } \frac{dD}{da} = \frac{O\epsilon^{-a} - \epsilon^{-a}}{O\,(1 - \epsilon^{-a}) + \epsilon^{-a}} \; ,$$

$$\frac{dD}{da} = \frac{O\epsilon^{-a} - \epsilon^{-a}}{O - (O\epsilon^{-a} - \epsilon^{-a})}.$$

If $m = \log._\epsilon a$, then $a = \epsilon^m$; hence—

$$\frac{da}{dm} = \epsilon^m = a \,; \text{ hence}$$

$$\frac{dD}{dm} = \frac{O\epsilon^{-a} - \epsilon^{-a}}{O - (O\epsilon^{-a} - \epsilon^{-a})} \cdot a$$

this is the tangent of the curve when log. $a$ is made abscissa and D ordinate.

This tangent is important.

For if $a$ is o, the tangent is o, and when $a = \infty$ the tangent is o again, for the fraction may be written—

$$tg = \frac{\epsilon^{-a}\,(O - 1)}{O - \epsilon^{-a}\,(O - 1)}\, a \text{ or}$$

$$tg = \frac{O - 1}{O\,\epsilon^a - (O - 1)}\, a.$$

Since $a$ can only have positive values, and $O\,\epsilon^a$ is always greater than $O - 1$, the values are always positive, and vary from $O$ to a maximum, decreasing again to O. This maximum will be obtained when $\dfrac{a}{O\,\epsilon^a - (O - 1)}$

is itself a maximum, or when $\dfrac{d}{da}\,\dfrac{a}{O\,\epsilon^a - (O - 1)} = 0$, but this is the case when

$$(1 - a)\,\epsilon^a = \frac{O - 1}{O}\,.$$

This is the point of double curvature.

The density at the point of double flexure is—

$$D = \log. \left[1 - \left(\frac{O - 1}{O}\right)\epsilon^{-a}\right] + \log. O,$$

but $\dfrac{O - 1}{O} = \epsilon^a\,(1 - a)$, consequently—

$$D = \log. \left[1 - (1 - a)\right] + \log. O$$
$$D = \log. a + \log. O.$$

The tangent of the angle at that point is—

$$tg = \gamma = \frac{\epsilon^{-a}}{\left(\dfrac{O}{O - 1}\right) - \epsilon^{-a}} \cdot a.$$

Substituting for $\dfrac{O}{O-1}$ its equal value $\epsilon^a (1-a)$ we get—

$$\gamma = \frac{\epsilon^{-a}\,\epsilon^a\,(1-a)}{1-\epsilon^{-a}\,\epsilon^a\,(1-a)}\,a$$

$$= \frac{1-a}{1-(1-a)}\,a = 1-a.$$

These two values are important, viz. :—

$$\left.\begin{aligned} D &= \log.\,(aO) \\ tg &= \gamma = 1-a \end{aligned}\right\} \text{ for point of double flexure.}$$

(Copy.)

West Shandon House,<br>
Shandon, N.B.<br>
22nd August, 1897.

My Dear Driffield,—

Here we have been in a lovely spot for now five days, and there has not been a day that heaven did not weep over " the time wasted." It pours every day, if not all day, yet at times so hard that being out is unpleasant. Still, we have made some nice excursions, and if ever you want to do a week's camera work on some worthy landscapes this is the place for you to come to. There are plenty of cameras at work, but most of them without any brains or knowledge to work them. I have kept my word and thought of nothing. But to-day being Sunday, and having been to church and listened to a grand long sermon on " being nigh to the Kingdom of God," I could not help my thoughts wandering, and here is what half an hour's quiet produced on paper. As I have no experimental evidence here I cannot go on, but I will just impart to you the thought for your criticism and consideration. The chaos of experimental evidence which you have accumulated wants an analytical expression to sift what is due to development of latent image from that due to fog, and to bring clearly out what is simply due to alteration of developer. You know already that the *starvation* theory did not satisfactorily explain matters, and that diffusion seems to work so fast, that there is no need for assuming a limit to the development for want of developer. Equally (in the opposite direction) there is not clear evidence that the *bromide* generated in the film by decomposition of bromide of silver materially affects results, since it escapes by diffusion just as fast as the pyro can enter.

Still, to some extent, all these phenomena will affect the results, and these results will naturally deviate in consequence from any simple rule, which cannot possibly be so formulated as to take account of everything—constitution of film, quality of gelatine, velocity of diffusion to and fro, temperature, etc.

All that mathematical analysis can do is to trace the *main* features of the course of development.

The following thoughts have thus taken shape.

Let the total quantity of silver on any part of the plate be A. After illumination this consists of two portions, unaffected bromide $=$ B and an affected part $a$, and always will, B $+ a =$ A. *The difference between the two portions is not one of kind, but simply one of degree in rapidity of* development,[1] and this thought applied to the density of the resulting image makes that (in imagination) also consist of two parts, *i.e.*, of developed *fog* and developed *image.* Call the one $x$ (image) and $y$ the fog, then the density will be $x + y =$ D.

The small amount of latent image developed at any moment will be, say— $dx$ and that amount is developed in the moment $dt$, hence the velocity of development is expressed as $\dfrac{dx}{dt} \dfrac{\text{(image)}}{\text{(time)}}$.

This velocity will be proportional to a factor $k_1$, which depends upon the constitution of the developer, and to the amount of undeveloped latent image present at that moment which we are considering. Let the latent image already developed be $x$, then $(a - x)$ is the amount of undeveloped latent image and the velocity of development (growth of density in unit time) is—

$$\frac{dx}{dt} = k_1 (a - x).$$

But while the latent image is thus developing, the ordinary bromide of silver B is attacked as well, and at the moment we are considering the density of fog is already $y$, so that B $- y$ is the amount of unaltered bromide not yet developed. The rapidity of development will depend upon a factor $k_2$, depending upon the developer, and also, like the former, proportional to the bromide still present.

We have thus for fog-velocity—

$$\frac{dy}{dt} = k_2 (B - y). \qquad \text{(Similar in kind, different in degree from the other!)}$$

By integration, this gives for the latent image density in time $t$—

$$x = a \left(1 - \epsilon^{-k_1 t}\right)$$

and for fog—

$$y = B \left(1 - \epsilon^{-k_2 t}\right)$$

and the total developed density at time $t$ is the sum of these two.

This sum expressed in its simplest form comes out—

$$D = A \left(1 - \epsilon^{-k_2 t}\right) + a \left(\epsilon^{-k_2 t} - \epsilon^{-k_1 t}\right)$$

or

$$D = A \left(1 - \epsilon^{-k_2 t}\right) + a \left(\frac{\epsilon^{k_1} - \epsilon^{k_2}}{\epsilon^{k_1 + k_2}}\right) t$$

[1] *See pp.* 88, 227, 231.

This shows how, with a given developer, the whole density grows. The first term is the fog, and is a constant and an excuse for deducting it as we have done, but the second term is also affected by that fog, hence this deduction is not permissible when the fog is at all appreciable. If a developer be *so* constituted that within the time of development there is no fog, that means that $k_2$ is $= 0$, and the above expression changes to—

$$D = a (1 - \epsilon^{-k_1 t})$$

and if $\epsilon^{-k_1}$ is put as in our original paper $= \alpha$, then we have $D = a (1 - \alpha^t,)$ which is the formula *exactly* of our original paper (*a*) being the highest possible density reachable for the particular exposure with the particular developer (a non-fogging one !).

There now remains only to replace $k_1$ and $k_2$ by functions which depend upon the composition of developers. This I do not think is difficult when I get home. I cannot do it here. You may see that now I shall be able to put order into the whole thing. I expect that—

$$k_1 = \frac{\text{Pyro} \times \text{Alkali}}{\text{Bromide}} \times \text{constant}$$

$$k_2 = \text{the same} \times \text{other constant,}$$

and that the two constants are given by the speed of plate, thus—

$$\frac{\text{Constant No. 1}}{\text{Constant No. 2}} = \text{speed of plate,}$$

or it may be that Constant No. 1 alone will be affected by the speed and Constant No. 2 remain. That I can only tell from the experiments.

But I think I shall now be able to put matters straight. Please keep this letter ; it is the only record in ink of this thought, and I may lose my pencil copy.

Trusting all is going on well, and that you are not working unnecessarily at this subject.

I remain,

Yours sincerely,

F. HURTER.

Give Mrs. Hurter's, Annie's, and James's love to May. They all wish to be kindly remembered by you.—F. H.

*One very important* experiment is to be made.

*Unexposed* strips of Cadett 21 and Cadett 103 or 111 are to be developed for 2, 4, 8 minutes **in** a fogging developer but together ! Can you do that ?

(To find fog related to speed—if it is.)—F.H.

NOTE.—This manuscript, H. MSS. No. 9, is in Dr. Hurter's handwriting, and is the earliest record of an inquiry as to the relationship of light, plate speed, inertia exposure, etc., which was the foundation of his later researches. *See also* H.N.—A., p. 15 *et seq.*

## ACTINOMETER.

---

# ACTION OF LIGHT ON PHOTOGRAPHIC PLATES.

SUPPOSING a source of light of intensity $1^0$ to act directly upon a photographic plate, without use of lens, and to produce in the time $t$ such a density that the deposit of silver almost completely intercepts any light. Then a plate would be said to be rapid if the time $t$ is small, or slow if that time $t$ is large, and the plate would be said to be *inert* if, however large the time $t$ be made, no black deposit is produced. Consequently, the time which it takes to blacken intensely a plate with $1^0$ of light is a measure of the *inertia* of the plate.

In order to produce the same effect upon the plate if the source of light be of any other intensity, that light would have to act for a longer or shorter time, so that, if the intensity of the light is $I_0$ and the coefficient of inertia of the plate be E, there would be necessary a time $t$ so that $I_0 t = E$.

For, if in that equation $I_0$ become $= 1$, then $t = E$, as above defined, the time with $1^0$ of light is the measure of the inertia.

If the source of light is not permitted to act directly upon the plate but through the medium of a lens, then the intensity of light of the image would be different from the intensity of the source of light $I_0$, and would be for

infinite distance (sky) in (1), $I_1 = k\dfrac{d^2}{f^2}I_0$, where $I_1$ is the intensity of the image,

$d$ the diameter of the aperture, $f$ the focal length of the lens, and $k^1$ a coefficient depending upon the amount of light lost owing to absorption by and reflection from the glass.

In order, therefore, to produce a given density with a plate of inertia E it will be necessary to use a time $t$ so that the intensity of the image $\times$ by the time is equal to the inertia of the plate.

---

[1] $k$ is that fraction of the light impinging upon the front surface of lens, which really comes from the back surface, and is for one single lens 87 per cent. of the light (7 per cent reflected from front and 7 per cent. from back of lens).

We must have—

$$(2)\ \ I_1\, t = E, \text{ or } I_1 = \frac{E}{t}.$$

Putting for $I_1$ its value, we get from (1) and (2)—

$$I_1 = \frac{E}{t} = k\frac{d^2}{f^2}\cdot I_0.$$

Hence the inertia of a plate can be found by means of any lens, and is—

$$E = k\frac{d^2}{f^2}\cdot I_0\, t.$$

If a lens be employed consisting of several separate pieces of glass, the reflection on each piece must be considered. The absorption is so small as to be immeasurable. If two pieces of glass are employed the coefficient $k$ must occur twice, which is $k^2$. If three pieces, $k^3$. If diaphragms are used in front of the lens, their diameter is taken as the aperture of the lens, but if the diaphragms are in between the lenses or behind, then the aperture of the diaphragm must be projected upon the next lens immediately in front of it, from the equivalent focus of all the lenses in front of the diaphragm as centre of projection. Thus, if $f$ is the equivalent focus of a combination of two lenses in front, $d_1$ must be found by projecting $d$ upon the next lens in front of the diaphragm from $f$ and that value must be taken as the aperture of the lens.

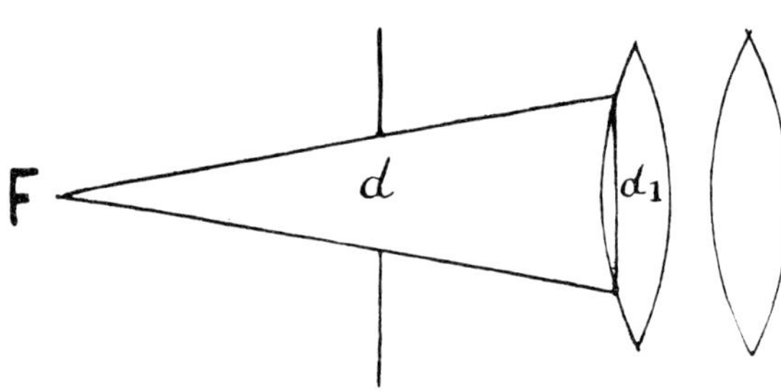


Having thus ascertained the inertia of a plate, for a given kind of plate, it is easy to calculate for any other lens the time of exposure—it is simply the slowness of the plate multiplied by the slowness of the lens.

$$I\, t = E \times \frac{F^2}{d^2} \times \frac{1}{k^n}.$$

And similarly if for any given lens $I\, t$ has been ascertained, E can be found—

$$E = \frac{I\, t \times k^n}{\left(\dfrac{F}{d}\right)^2}.$$

It is best to have the fraction $\left(\dfrac{F}{d}\right)^2$ calculated and to use the inverse value of $k$ so as to multiply $\left(\dfrac{F}{d}\right)^2$ with it. $k$ is $0\cdot87$ for two surfaces of one lens, the inverse is $1\cdot15 = a$.

For two lenses $k^2$ is $0 \cdot 759$ and the inverse is $1 \cdot 317 = a^2$.
For three lenses $k^3 = 0 \cdot 661$ and the inverse is $1 \cdot 512 = a^3$.
Hence, for finding inertia of plate time—

$$E = \frac{I\,t}{\left(\dfrac{F}{d}\right)^2 \times a^n}$$

*Example.*—Wratten's slow plates take with a lens for which $\left(\dfrac{F}{d}\right)^2 = 1600$ an exposure of 550 second degrees, the lens consists of two separate lenses only, hence $\left(\dfrac{F}{d}\right)^2$ is multiplied by $a^2 = 1 \cdot 317$, $1600 \times 1 \cdot 317 = 2107$, dividing 550 by this figure $2,107$ we get $\dfrac{550}{2107} = 0 \cdot 261$, and this is the coefficient of inertia of the plate, which means, that a sky density $2 \cdot 000$ is obtained by exposing the plate *directly* to the sky for $0 \cdot 261$ seconds when the actinometer registers $1°$.

The exposure for any other lens for Wratten's slow plates is found by multiplying the product $\left(\dfrac{F}{d}\right)^2 . a^n$ by the inertia. The result is second degrees.

For instance, a portrait lens for which $\left(\dfrac{F}{d}\right)^2 = 18$ and $a^3 = 1 \cdot 51$, we have $\left(\dfrac{F}{d}\right)^2 \times a^3 = 18 \times 1 \cdot 51 = 27$, and multiplying by inertia $0 \cdot 26$ gives $7 \cdot 02$ second degrees required, because $27 \times 0 \cdot 26 = 7 \cdot 02$.

# ACTINOMETERS OR INSTRUMENTS FOR MEASURING LIGHT.

LETTERS PATENT to Ferdinand Hurter, Ph.D., of Widnes, in the County of Lancaster, Alkali Manufacturer, for an Invention of " IMPROVEMENTS IN ACTINOMETERS OR PHOTOMETERS, OR INSTRUMENTS FOR MEASURING LIGHT."

PROVISIONAL SPECIFICATION left by the said Ferdinand Hurter at the Office of the Commissioners of Patents on 23rd April, 1881.

FERDINAND HURTER, Ph.D., of Widnes, in the County of Lancaster, Alkali Manufacturer. " IMPROVEMENTS IN ACTINOMETERS OR PHOTOMETERS, OR INSTRUMENTS FOR MEASURING LIGHT."

My Invention relates to improvements in instruments for measuring the intensity of light from any source, but more particularly diffused daylight and direct sunlight.

According to one mode of carrying out my Invention I cause rays of different refrangibility of the light to be absorbed by the two bulbs of a differential air thermometer, which are so arranged as to absorb or reflect wholly or partially the respective rays. A difference of temperature is thus produced, which is measured in the ordinary manner upon a syphon gauge or other pressure gauge, and which is a measure also of the intensity of the light, the absorption of which causes a rise of temperature.

In order to cause the bulbs to absorb rays of different refrangibility I either coat them outside with substances of different colours, but which should be equal absorbents of radiant heat, that is to say, rays of lower refrangibility than luminous rays.

Or in lieu of coating the bulbs with different coloured substances I place such substances inside the bulbs, as (for example) I may employ strips of coloured papers, placed one colour in one bulb, another in the other. Or I coat both the bulbs inside or outside with lamp black, and cause rays of light to fall upon them, after having passed through coloured glass or coloured liquids, or other coloured transparent media. The one bulb receiving the light which passed through the glass of one colour, whilst the other bulb is illuminated by the light which has passed through glass of another colour. Or in lieu of filling the bulbs with air I fill them with a coloured vapour, such, for example, as nitrogen dioxide or bromine, and cause the light to fall upon the bulbs, after having passed through different coloured transparent substances, such, for example, as different coloured glasses.

The choice of the colours depend upon the purpose for which the instrument is used, and the kind of rays which are to be measured. For photographic and photo printing purposes I use red and white substances, or red and colourless substances and liquids ; for general photometric purposes I prefer lamp black and a white substance, such, for example, as white lead.

Extreme care should be taken to guard against differences in the heat-absorbing power of the two bulbs and the coloured glasses and substances used. I place the bulbs in a box made of wood or other imperfect conductor of heat, and coat it outside with polished metal or other imperfect radiator. The side of the box through which the light enters is covered with thick plate glass or with a vessel of glass filled with water or a solution of various salts capable of almost completely absorbing heat rays.

In lieu of using differential air thermometers I may employ thermometers filled with other gases and vapours ; or I may use ordinary thermometers of extreme sensitiveness ; or I may use a thermopile and galvanometer as an indicator of the difference of temperature, and consequent upon the absorption of rays of different refrangibility by the two sensitive sides of the pile.

I also use reflectors and condensers in order to concentrate as much light as possible upon the sensitive parts of the apparatus. Such condensers and reflectors may, again, be of different colours and materials, but they also should be chosen so that radiant heat shall pass equally through them, or be reflected equally by them, otherwise the indications of the instruments will not be due to light rays only, and become absolutely useless.

For the purpose of illuminating the bulbs or sensitive surfaces of piles with rays of different refrangibility I may also use the dispersive power of prisms, placing, for instance, one bulb in one part of the spectrum while the other is placed in another part.

SPECIFICATION in pursuance of the conditions of the Letters Patent filed by the said Ferdinand Hurter in the Great Seal Patent Office on 19th October, 1881.

FERDINAND HURTER, Ph.D., of Widnes, in the County of Lancaster, Alkali Manufacturer. "IMPROVEMENTS IN ACTINOMETERS OR PHOTOMETERS, OR INSTRUMENTS FOR MEASURING LIGHT."

My said Invention relates to improvements in instruments for measuring the intensity of light from any source, but more particularly diffused daylight and direct sunlight.

According to one mode of carrying out my said Invention I cause rays of different refrangibility of the light to be absorbed by the two bulbs of a differential air thermometer, which are so arranged as to absorb or reflect wholly or partially the respective rays. A difference of temperature is thus produced, which is measured in the ordinary manner upon a syphon gauge or other pressure gauge, and which is a measure also of the intensity of the light, the absorption of which causes a rise of temperature. The differential thermometer used may be of the type of that known as Leslie's, or a differential thermometer of any other suitable description.

In order to cause the bulbs to absorb rays of different refrangibility I either coat them outside with substances of different colours, but which should be equal absorbents of radiant heat, that is to say, rays of lower refrangibility than luminous rays ; or in lieu of coating the bulbs with different coloured substances I place such substances inside the bulbs, as for example, I may employ strips of coloured papers placed one colour in one bulb, another in the other ; or I coat both the bulbs inside or outside with lamp black, and cause rays of light to fall upon them after having passed through coloured glass or coloured liquids, or other coloured transparent media, one bulb receiving the light which passed through the glass of one colour, whilst the other bulb is illuminated by the light which has passed through glass of another colour. Or in lieu of filling the bulbs with air I fill them with a coloured vapour, such, for example, as nitrogen dioxide or bromine, and cause the light to fall upon the bulbs after having passed through different coloured transparent substances, such, for example, as different coloured glasses.

The choice of the colours depends upon the purpose for which the instrument is used, and the kind of rays which are to be measured. For photographic and photo-printing purposes I use red and white substances, or red and colourless substances and liquids ; for general photometric purposes I prefer lamp black and a white substance, such, for example, as white lead.

Extreme care should be taken to guard against differences in the heat-absorbing power of the two bulbs and the coloured glasses and substances used. I place the bulbs in a box made of wood or other imperfect conductor of heat, and coat it outside with polished metal or other imperfect radiator. The side of the box through which the light enters is covered with thick plate glass or with a vessel of glass filled with water, or a solution of various salts capable of almost completely absorbing heat rays.

In lieu of using differential air thermometers I may employ thermometers filled with other gases and vapours. Or I may use ordinary thermometers of extreme sensitiveness. Or I may use an electric differential thermometer, that is to say, a thermopile and galvanometer as indicator of the difference of temperature and consequent upon the absorption of rays of different refrangibility by the two sensitive sides of the pile.

I also use reflectors and condensers in order to concentrate as much light as possible upon the sensitive parts of the apparatus. Such condensers and reflectors may, again, be of different colours and materials, but they also should be chosen so that radiant heat shall pass equally through them or be reflected equally by them, otherwise the indications of the instruments will not be due to light rays only, and become absolutely useless.

For the purpose of illuminating the bulbs or sensitive surfaces of piles with rays of different refrangibility I may also use the dispersive power of prisms, placing, for instance, one bulb in one part of the spectrum while the other is placed in another part.

The method of carrying my said Invention into effect which I have found most satisfactory is the following :—

I construct entirely of glass, without any cemented or indiarubber joints, a differential thermometer represented on the annexed drawing in front elevation, and elevation, and plan in Figs. 1, 2 and 3 respectively. A, A$^1$ are two glass cylinders ending in small tubes, made altogether of as thin glass as possible. To these two cylinders, which form the sensitive parts of the thermometer, is fused on a capillary syphon gauge B$^1$, B$^2$, B$^3$, B$^4$, bent exactly as shown in the figure. At the bend between B$^2$ and B$^3$ a small nozzle H is drawn out, which serves to introduce into the syphon the coloured liquid C.

While the small tubes in which the cylinders A, A$^1$ terminate are still open I insert into them coils of Berlin wool D wrapped loosely upon fine capillary glass tubes, serving as supports. The wool for tube A is red coloured, that for A$^1$ is pure white. Both these coils of wool should be perfectly dry, and in order to ensure the more perfect absence of all moisture I draw through the apparatus a current of air absolutely dry, and I place in each of the tubes a few small lumps of fused chloride of calcium, as shown at *a*. When the coils have been placed in the tubes A and A$^1$ I introduce the liquid into the syphon through the nozzle H by placing this liquid first into a wide test tube, and then lowering the syphon into the liquid. When the syphon has thus been filled to about half its length in both $B^2$ and $B^3$ I rapidly withdraw the syphon and incline it so as to cause the liquid to flow into the bends $B^1$, $B^2$, taking care that none of the liquid flows into the cylinder A.

The nozzle H is then fused up, and when cool the liquid is again caused to flow into the bend $B^2$, $B^3$. The whole apparatus is then immersed in cold water to such an extent only that no water flows into the cylinders. When the whole has cooled to a uniform temperature the ends of the cylinders A and $A^1$, which are still open, are fused up also.

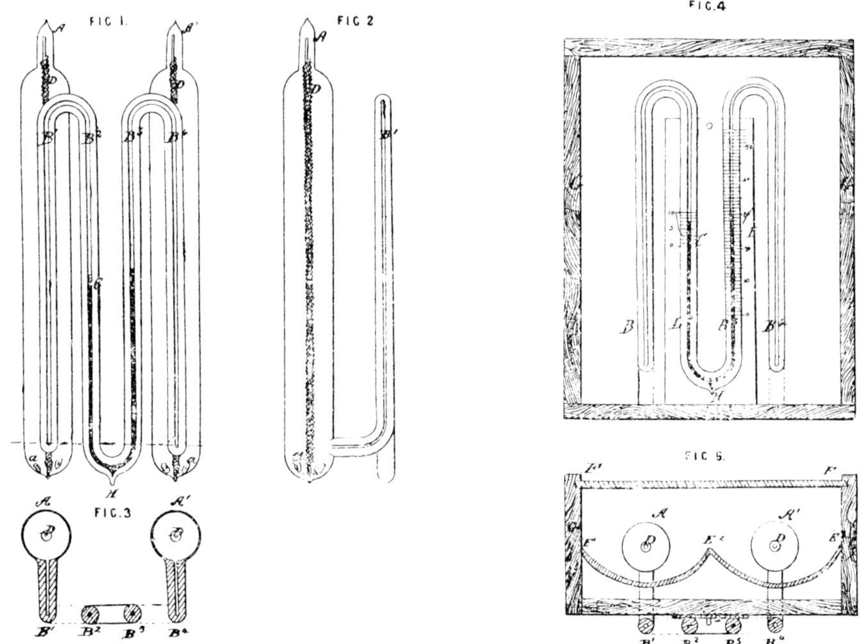


The differential thermometer so prepared is then placed in a wooden box lined with polished metal inside and outside. This box is shown in plan and elevation, Figs. 4 and 5. G, G, is the box. The front of the box is made of a glass plate F, F. The large cylinders A, $A^1$ are in the centre of the box ; the syphon $B^1$, $B^2$, $B^3$, $B^4$ is outside at the back of the box. Suitable openings or slits are provided to allow the connecting tubes to pass through the wood.

Behind the cylinders are placed two parabolical reflectors $E^1$, $E^2$, and $E^2$, $E^3$, made of sheet lead silvered on one side, in order that they may reflect the light coming through the glass plate F, F, and concentrate it upon the coils D of wool in the centre of the tubes A, $A^1$. It is necessary that the centres of these tubes be exactly in the focus of the parabolic reflectors.

Behind the syphon, between it and the wood, I place a sliding scale I in order to admit of conveniently reading the change of level in the liquid which takes place when the apparatus is exposed to diffuse daylight. The scale is divided into arbitrary degrees. The intensity of the light is proportional to the number of degrees registered. This, however, is only the case when the apparatus is very carefully constructed, and when a liquid is used for filling the syphon, which has a very small vapour tension. The most satisfactory liquid I have yet found is oil of turpentine coloured with alkanet root.

In order to be good the apparatus should stand the following tests :— (1) When placed in water of different temperatures in the dark the level of the liquid should not change as the temperature of the water is altered. This is only the case when all moisture is completely removed ; (2) when placed opposite a dark source of heat, such as a stove, the level of the liquid should not alter.

Should it alter it is a proof that the cylinders are not affected equally by radiant heat. I then cover that side of the glass F, F, which is opposite the cylinder most easily heated, with transparent colourless varnish, such, for example, as negative varnish, or I screen both cylinders A and A¹ with a larger glass cylinder, and by adjusting the length of these screening tubes I can make the apparatus almost insensitive to heat.

These extreme precautions, however, are only necessary for instruments which are intended to measure low degrees of light, for the ordinary work of the photographer the apparatus does not need the extremely fine adjustment for radiant heat, and the changes of level caused by alteration of temperature are so small as to interfere very little with the measurement of light, and can be taken into account if necessary.

Having now described and particularly ascertained the nature of my said Invention and the manner in which the same is or may be used or carried into effect, I would observe in conclusion that what I consider to be novel and original, and therefore claim as the Invention secured to me by the hereinbefore in part recited Letters Patent, is :—

Measuring the intensity of light by causing rays of different refrangibility to be received by or pass through different colours, and to be absorbed by the two sensitive parts of a differential thermometer, and measuring the difference of temperature thus produced, whence the intensity of the light may be ascertained, substantially as hereinbefore described.

In witness whereof, I, the said Ferdinand Hurter, have to this my Specification set my hand and seal, this Fourteenth day of October, One thousand eight hundred and eighty-one.

FERDINAND HURTER. (L.S.)

*Date of Application, 14th April,* 1888.
*Specification Accepted, 18th May,* 1888.

## SPECIFICATION OF FERDINAND HURTER AND VERO CHARLES DRIFFIELD.

### A.D. 1888, 14th April.   No. 5545.

## IMPROVEMENTS IN INSTRUMENTS FOR CALCULATING PHOTOGRAPHIC EXPOSURES.

---

### COMPLETE SPECIFICATION.

We, FERDINAND HURTER, of Wilmere House, Bold, Widnes, in the county of Lancaster, Analytical Chemist, and VERO CHARLES DRIFFIELD, of Mount Pleasant, Appleton, Widnes, in the county of Lancaster, Engineer, do hereby declare the nature of this invention, and in what manner the same is to be performed, to be particularly described and ascertained in and by the following statement :—

Our improvements consist in so arranging logarithmic scales as to enable a photographer to ascertain at a glance, and with a considerable degree of certainty, the length of time during which the sensitive plate must be exposed in the camera in order to procure a satisfactory negative.

Four factors enter into any such calculation : 1st, the time of exposure ; 2ndly, the intensity of the light ; 3rdly, the focal length, aperture, and construction of the lens ; and 4thly, the sensitiveness to light of the photographic plate.

We therefore employ four logarithmic scales corresponding respectively to the four factors mentioned above—time, light, lens, and plate.

Two of those scales are attached to a movable slide working between the other two scales, which are fixed.

Upon one of the fixed pair of scales we mark the intensity of the light expressed in arbitrary degrees, and upon the other we mark what we call and hereinafter define as the " inertia," or slowness of the plate.

Upon one of the movable pair of scales we mark the various speeds of lenses in a manner which will hereafter be explained, and upon the other, the time of exposure in seconds.

Either of these pairs of scales may be fixed, and the other pair movable, but, owing to the peculiar construction of the light scale, we prefer to have the light and the " inertia " scales fixed, and the lens and exposure scales movable.

In order to avoid the use of an instrument for directly measuring the light at the moment of exposing the sensitive plate we employ, as a light scale, a diagram showing the average relative intensity of the light for every hour throughout the year for any particular latitude. This diagram consists of a number of curves, each of which indicates the variation of the light for any given hour of the day throughout the year. It is necessary to construct separate diagrams for various latitudes.

In order to construct these diagrams we proceed as follows :—

We have ascertained by daily observations extending over several years that the mean intensity of light at any given hour in the day is about one half of the highest intensity possible at that hour. We have further ascertained that at or immediately after sunset or before sunrise the photographic value of the twilight on clear days is uniform throughout the year, and we have ascertained the numerical value of the twilight expressed in arbitary degrees.

We therefore calculate first the highest intensity of the light for every hour of the day for a certain number of days, say two in each month of the year, for a given latitude, on the basis that the difference between the intensity of light at 12 noon and at sunset is 100 units in places where the sun culminates in the zenith. We perform this calculation by multiplying the sine of the altitude of the sun at the particular hour by 100. The values thus found for the intensity of light would lead to absolute darkness at the time of sunrise and sunset. We therefore add to each of these numbers the value of the twilight which we have ascertained to be equal to about 5 units on this arbitrary scale, the sum we divide by two, and the number so obtained we term the mean light for that hour.

Having calculated in this way the value of the mean light for a particular hour, say 10 a.m., for two days in each month, we proceed to construct the logarithmic curve for that hour. We find in a table of logarithms, the logarithm of the numbers, we use the logarithmic values as abscissæ, and the dates as ordinates, and draw through the points thus found a curve connecting them. This curve represents the variation of the mean intensity of light at 10 a.m. throughout the year.

In order to still better illustrate the mode of constructing these curves we have annexed a sheet of drawings.  Fig. 1 shows the curve for 10 a.m. for the latitude 53° 7′.

We mark on the vertical line A B the 182 days from 21st December to 21st June.  We find by calculation, as indicated above, that 100 times the sine of the altitude of the sun at 10 a.m. on 21st December is 15·8, to which

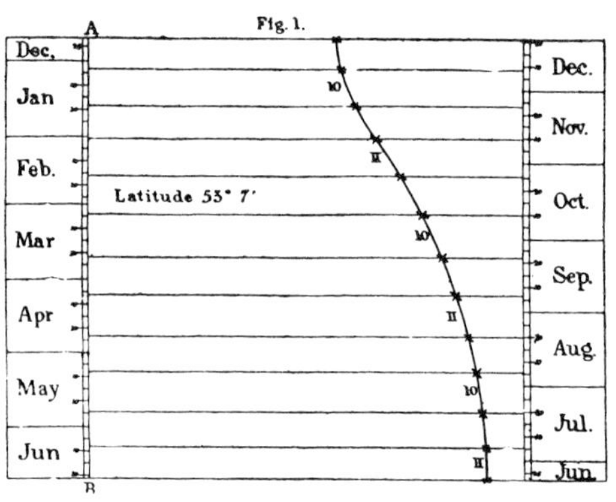


we add 5 = 20·8.  Half of this number, viz., 10·4, is what we call the mean light for 10 a.m. on 21st December.  The common logarithm of 10·4 is 1·017.  Representing graphically the logarithm of 10 by a length of 100 millimetres we mark off on a horizontal line drawn through the point corresponding to the 21st December 101·7 millimetres, and mark that point as 10 a.m.  Proceeding in like manner for two days in each month, the other points of the curve are obtained, and the curve is drawn through them.

In like manner we proceed to obtain the curves for every other hour of the day that the light is photographically active.  We calculate the hour at which light ceases to be active as corresponding to the time when the sun is 6° below the horizon.  We draw all the curves belonging to one latitude upon one diagram, as shown in Fig. 2, and mark them with the hours to which they correspond.  On the margins we indicate the corresponding dates.  Fig. 2 represents the diagram for places situated on the equator.

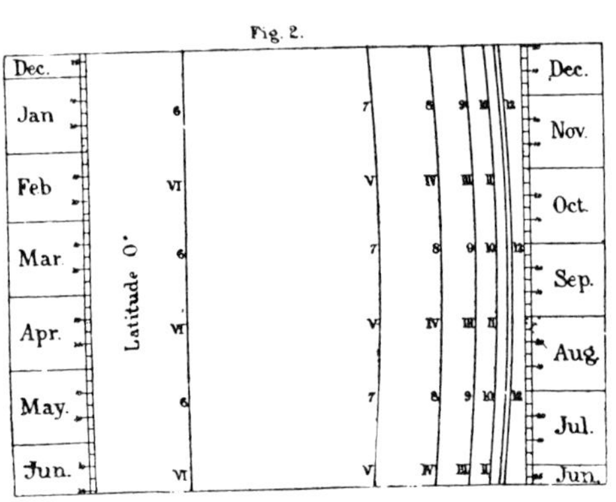


Owing to the fact that the intensity of the light of the afternoon hours corresponds exactly to the intensity of the light of the morning hours of the same day, each curve is marked with two figures, the ordinary figure showing the morning hour, the Roman figure the corresponding afternoon hour.

And owing to the fact that to each day between the 21st December and the 21st June there is a corresponding day between the 21st June and 21st December on which the intensities of the light are the same, it is not necessary to mark the curves for the whole of the year ; it suffices to calculate and mark them for half the year ; and to place on the opposite side another scale of dates returning from 22nd June to the 21st December in contrary direction, as shown in Figs. 1 and 2.

As already stated, we provide a number of such diagrams for the different latitudes.

On the second fixed scale we mark what we have previously spoken of as the " inertia " or slowness of the sensitive plate.  By this term we express the time, measured in seconds, which the sensitive plate must be exposed to a direct diffuse daylight, of the intensity 1° on our arbitrary scale, in order that on development sufficient of the silver salt on the plate may be reduced to silver, so as to become as dense as the sky of a well exposed landscape negative ought to be.  It will be perceived that the slower the plate the greater will be the time necessary for obtaining this result.

As the " inertia " of the plates of different manufactures vary, we provide a whole scale of " inertias " ranging from 0·01 of a second to 1 second, but we may state at once that most of the gelatino-bromide plates in the market have, according to our experiments, " inertias " ranging from about 0·08 to 0·35 of a second, but those generally known as " ordinary," " rapid," and " extra rapid " have " inertias " of about 0·2, 0·14 and 0·08 respectively.

We have ascertained these " inertias " of the plates by means of accurate measurements of the light at the moment of exposure, but we shall hereafter show how, by means of our present invention, every operator can ascertain the " inertia " of any plates he may desire.

In constructing this " inertia " scale, we simply take the logarithms of the numbers as abscissæ and mark the points with the natural numbers as is well understood in the construction of ordinary slide rules.  Care must be taken that the same unit be chosen for the logarithmic value of 10 in this scale as in the light scales.  Fig. 3 shows the arrangement and special marking of the " inertia " scale.

In consequence of the various " inertias " of different plates, we prefer to apply a complete " inertia " scale as described, but it is obvious that in the case of plates of known " inertia," a single line would suffice, or a movable index might be substituted for it.

The first of the movable pair of scales is what we call the lens scale.  It is shown in Fig. 4.  It consists simply of a number of lines in groups of three, marked respectively 1, 2 and 3, and below each group with the usual mode of expressing the value of the aperture of the lens as a fraction of its focal length, which in our example is the system adopted by the Photographic Society of Great Britain, but any other system can be easily adapted.  Thus the group of lines marked $\frac{F}{16}$ belongs to lenses the apertures of which have been stopped down so that the optical value of the diameter of the aperture is $\frac{1}{16}$ of the focal length.

As is well known, the intensity of the light in the image produced by such a lens, if the lens were perfectly transparent and reflected no light from its surfaces, would be $(\frac{1}{16})^2 = \frac{1}{256}$ of the intensity of the light sent out by the object, and it would consequently require, with this lens $(16)^2 = 256$ times the exposure which would be necessary if light of the same intensity as the object sends out had acted upon the plate without the interposition of a lens. We find, however, by experiment that this is not correct. Owing chiefly to reflection from the surface of the lens more time is requisite, and more time in proportion to the number of reflecting surfaces which the lens has. We find that the time is about 15 *per cent.* more in the case of single lenses, 32 *per cent.* more in the case of double combinations, and 53 *per cent.* more in case of triple combinations. For this reason we have three lines for each ratio of aperture to focal length.

The lines marked 1 refer to single lenses, the lines 2 to double combinations and the lines marked 3 to triple combinations.

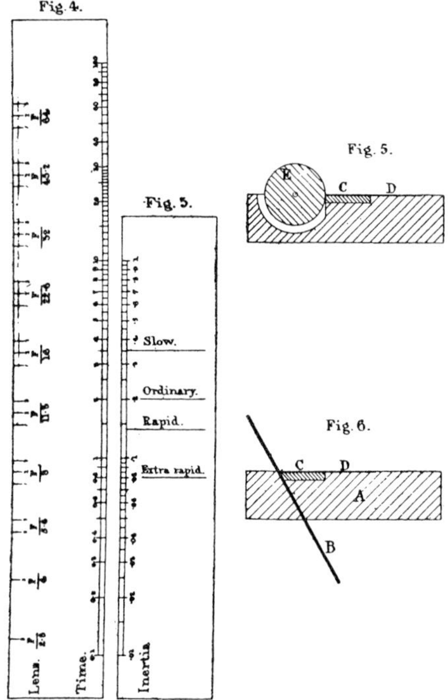


The exact place where each line has to be marked upon the scale is found as follows :—

We square the denominator of the fraction indicating the ratio of aperture to focal length. We multiply this by 1·15 for single lenses, by 1·32 for double combinations, and by 1·53 for triple combination lenses ; of the products thus obtained we take the logarithms : considering the logarithm of 10 expressed by 100 millimetres, we mark off the corresponding logarithms, and at the respective lines we write the figures 1, 2 and 3, and under them the ratio o, aperture to focal length. As there are no lenses which yield figures smaller than 10, our scale begins with 10 and proceeds to 10,000 ; the spaces between 10 and 100, 100 and 1,000, 1,000 and 10,000 being all 100 millimetres each.

For example, it is required to find the place at which to mark $\frac{F}{32}$ for a double combination.

The square of 32 is 1,024, this figure multiplied by 1·32, for reasons above stated, gives 1,351. The logarithm of 1,351 is 3·1306. If our Lens scale started with 1, we should have to mark at 313 millimetres the place for $\frac{F}{32}$ (2). But as the scale starts with 10, for reasons already stated, the place will have to be marked at 100 millimetres less, *i.e.*, at 213 millimetres. In exactly the same way we proceed to mark the ordinary ratios in use as shown on Fig. 4.

The last scale, the time scale, is simply an ordinary logarithmic scale of the natural numbers as used in ordinary slide rules. It expresses the time of exposure in seconds, beginning with 0·1 of a second and proceeding to 100 seconds. The scale is shown in Fig. 4. It, together with the Lens scale, forms the movable slide.

It will be readily understood that any other unit instead of millimetres may be adopted for the construction of these logarithmic scales, but the same unit must be adopted for all of them.

The four scales which we have now described in detail may be combined into one instrument in various ways, two of which are shown in Figs. 5 and 6.

Fig. 6 represents a sectional elevation of the form we prefer to adopt when using several light diagrams for different latitudes.

A is a block of wood perforated with an oblique slot through which the diagram B, mounted on card or other stiff material, slides up and down. In close proximity to this diagram is the sliding strip C bearing the lens and time scales, and fixed on the block in juxtaposition to the sliding scale is the " inertia " scale D, the initial point of which must be exactly opposite the initial point of the light scale on the diagram.

Fig. 5 shows a form of instrument which we prefer when restricting ourselves to one latitude only. In this case we wrap the paper diagram round a roller E, in such manner that the dates become successively visible on turning the roller. The other scales are fixed as shown in the other form, the lens scale being as close as possible to the cylindrical light scale.

To ascertain by means of this instrument the " inertia " of any given plate, we assume the plate in the first instance to be of medium sensitiveness, to which corresponds the " inertia " 0·14.

Supposing the experiment to be made on the 25th May at 9 a.m. or 3 p.m., we take an ordinary landscape, say, with a doublet lens stopped to $\frac{F}{32}$. We set the diagram till this date corresponds with the edge of the lens scale, and move the lens scale until $\frac{F}{32}$ (2) is exactly opposite the curve marked 9 and III.

Opposite the assumed " inertia " 0·14 on the " inertia " scale we find an exposure indicated on the time scale of 5 seconds. If we believe the light to be a mean light we expose for 5 seconds.   If upon development this exposure yields a satisfactory negative, the assumed " inertia " is correct.   On the other hand, if the negative is under or over exposed, the " inertia " was respectively too small or too large, and a second experiment, with another " inertia " is desirable, and will generally decide the question.

Having ascertained the " inertia " by such experiments, it is afterwards easy to find the exposure necessary at any other time and with any other lens. Suppose, for instance, a landscape had to be taken on the 10th of January at 12 noon with a single lens $\frac{F}{32}$ and with a plate of which the " inertia " is 0·2, we set the light diagram to the date as before and move the point $\frac{F}{32}(1)$ on the lens scale opposite the curve 12 on the diagram, and find opposite the " inertia " 0·2 an exposure of 15 seconds indicated.

The method of using the cylindrical diagram will be obvious after these explanations.

The exposures thus indicated by our instrument are strictly correct only for mean light and ordinary landscape work.

Of course, when taking pictures differing materially in their illumination from ordinary landscapes, suitable allowances must be made.

Instead of employing one of our light diagrams, the photographer may use an instrument for directly measuring the light at the time of exposure. In this case the light diagram must be replaced by an ordinary logarithmic scale of natural numbers similar to our " inertia " scale, but marked from 1 to 100, and instead of setting the lens scale to the particular day and hour, as in the case of our light diagrams, it is set to the figure indicated by the instrument for measuring the light, the " inertia " of the plate being found as previously explained.

Having now particularly described and ascertained the nature of our said invention and in what manner the same is to be performed, we declare that what we claim is :—

1. An instrument for calculating photographic exposures consisting of a combination of specially-marked logarithmic scales substantially as hereinbefore described.

2. The application of several light scales for different latitudes to one instrument, substantially as hereinbefore described.

Dated this Thirteenth day of April, 1888.

FERDINAND  HURTER.
VERO  C.  DRIFFIELD.

[*Reprinted from The Photographic Societies' Reporter, 30th April, 1889.*]

# THE ACTINOGRAPH.[1]

*A Paper read before the* LIVERPOOL AMATEUR PHOTOGRAPHIC SOCIETY,
*25th April,* 1889,

BY

## VERO  C.  DRIFFIELD.

ONE of the greatest difficulties the photographer, and especially the amateur, has to encounter, lies in correctly estimating his exposure. Of course, by one who is in the habit of making almost daily exposures, experience is gained, which is a more or less certain guide, but by the photographer, who only occasionally exposes a plate, some better guide is required if certainty of result is to be expected. The fluctuations of the light throughout the year, and again throughout the day, are so great that we believe nobody, be he professional or amateur, can adequately allow for them unless he has some reliable data to go upon. Then, again, with the era of gelatino-bromide dry plates, a new difficulty arose in consequence of the great variety in their speeds. This is a very serious complication, and has never hitherto been scientifically dealt with, a satisfactory unit of speed never having been found.

To-night we have the pleasure of bringing before your notice our actinograph, which is the outcome of an effort to reduce exposure to system, and to put the speeds of plates on to a satisfactory basis.

I propose, in the first place, to show you, in a few words, how the invention of the actinograph came about. For fifteen years I photographed with no better guide to exposure than notes I had myself carefully made of exposures which had proved satisfactory ; and though the experience I had gained and tabulated was of considerable assistance, I felt that it would be a great boon if the matter could be reduced to a system, if only to avoid inspection of notes and mental calculations at the moment of exposure. About

---

[1] *See* H.N.—F., p. 82.

twelve years ago I was fortunate enough to enlist the interest of my friend, Dr. Hurter, and we made a number of attempts to measure the light directly. These attempts were, at first, unsatisfactory, but were soon followed by the application of a simple, but original, idea of the  doctor's, which his knowledge and skill enabled him to carry out ;  and the outcome of which was the production of an actinometer, which I believe to be the only means of accurately and rapidly measuring diffused daylight, at present in existence. For a number of years Dr. Hurter and I made our exposures solely by the aid of this instrument, and the results were such as to leave no doubt as to its capacity for accurately measuring the light.  Unfortunately this actinometer is a most difficult instrument to make ;  it is exceedingly fragile, and there are such difficulties in the transportation of it, that it was never made a marketable commodity.

One form of the instrument is self-recording, and for upwards of a year we took, by means of it, daily diagrams of the light.  We will now throw upon the screen facsimiles of three typical diagrams, taken by means of this instrument.   The top diagram shows the duration and intensity of chemically active light in December, the centre one in March, and the bottom one in June.  They may be considered therefore to represent the amount of light on the longest and shortest days, and at the time of the equinoxes.  The vertical lines divide the day into hours from 3 a.m. to 9 p.m.  In December the actinic light only commences at about 7.30 in the morning, and has gone again at 3.30 in the afternoon.  In June the duration of the light extends from 3.30 in the morning to 8.30 in the evening, and in March from 5.30 a.m. to 6.30 p.m.  The vertical height of the wavy lines shows how the light increases in intensity as the year advances, and also shows the fluctuations that take place in the light from passing clouds and other causes.

Now I need hardly say that when we had secured daily diagrams of the light for an entire year, we learnt a great many lessons from them, and the most important lesson we learnt was that our actinometer could be advantageously dispensed with in favour of another instrument, the arrangement of which we then only obscurely pictured to ourselves, but which has since been matured into what we have termed the " actinograph."

In order to facilitate the calculation of exposures from the readings given by the actinometer, we had for some time made use of a special logarithmic slide rule, and the actinograph, in its essentials, consists simply of this slide rule, with this difference :  that the light value, instead of being ascertained from the actinometer, is ascertained from a specially constructed light diagram.

We also learnt from the diagrams taken by means of the actinometer that, though the light fluctuates considerably, these fluctuations are limited deviations from a certain mean value, which itself varies with the altitude of the sun ; and we found that when this mean value was known, the fluctuations of the light could be judged by the eye with sufficient accuracy to permit the calculation of an exposure such as, with suitable development, would certainly yield a satisfactory negative.

Having shown you how the actinograph came about, I will now proceed to explain this instrument, and will throw a photograph of it upon the screen. It is contained in a small box about $4\frac{1}{2}$ inches long, $2\frac{3}{4}$ inches wide and $1\frac{1}{4}$ inch deep, so that it is no encumbrance, and can easily be carried in the pocket. The instrument consists of four logarithmic scales, two of which are fixed and two are movable, and which relate respectively to the light, the speed of the plate, the lens and the exposure. The light scale is wrapped round a revolving roller, and in contact with this roller is a slide bearing the lens and exposure scales, and fixed in a particular position at the bottom is the speed scale. Sliding between the movable exposure scale and the fixed speed scale is an index bearing six marks : the five upper marks point simultaneously to five different exposures, and the single lower mark is set to the speed of the plate in use.

In order to explain these different scales, I will now show them to you just as they are printed, and before they are put together to form the actinograph. I will explain them in their order, and will commence with :—

I. *The Light Scale.*—The light varies from a definite mean value according to the state of the atmosphere, and the light scale of the actinograph represents these mean values in a series of curves. Each curve shows the mean value of the light for a certain morning and corresponding afternoon hour throughout the year. We find that the fluctuations in the light due to atmospheric conditions are such that the highest light is never more than double, and the lowest serviceable light is seldom less than half the mean value indicated by the actinograph for any given time. Having the value of the mean light

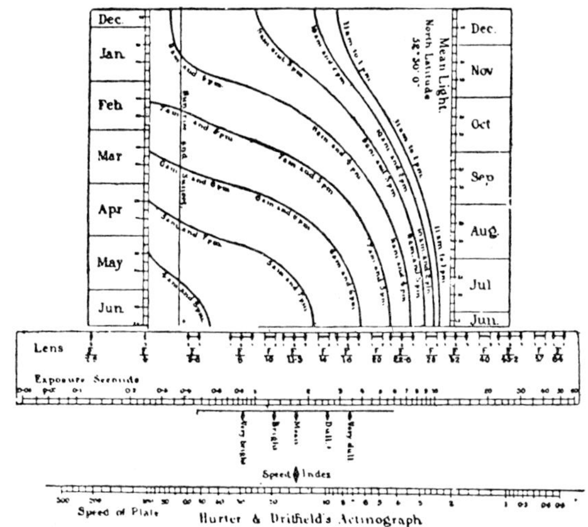

given, and knowing the possible maximum and minimum, it is no difficult matter to decide whether to choose an exposure corresponding to the maximum, the mean, or the minimum, or to select an exposure lying in between the mean and either extreme. As the light has, on any one day of the year (apart from atmospheric influence), its exact counterpart on another day, the dates for the first half of the year are placed on one side, and those for the other half of the year on the opposite side, of the diagram. Every fifth day is distinctly marked, and the intermediate days can be easily interpolated. On the left-hand side of the diagram you see a line marked " sunrise and sunset." This line divides the curves into two unequal portions—the longer portions, on the right-hand side of the line, representing the light from sunrise to sunset ; and the smaller portions, on the left-hand side of the line, the value of twilight. The former are arrived at by direct calculation, but we are again indebted to the actinometer for helping us to the value of the latter. Of course we do not attach much importance to the twilight portion of the curves, as it is seldom this part will come into requisition, but it is just possible that circumstances might arise when it became an object to secure a negative, even at such a time ; and the twilight values certainly render the actinograph more complete. Before concluding my remarks about the light, I will define what our unit of light is, as I shall have to refer to it again when I describe our speed scale. The brightest light which ever reaches the earth is at noon on the 21st March and the 23rd September, in places situated exactly on the equator. This maximum light we call 100, and consequently one degree of light is the 1/100th part of the brightest light when the sun culminates in the zenith.

II. *The Lens Scale.*—There are three different kinds of lenses in general use—the single landscape, the doublet (such as the rapid rectilinear), and the triplet (such as the portrait lens). Now if we simultaneously took three negatives, one with each of the above kinds of lenses, so arranged as to have precisely the same ratio of aperture to focal length, we should find that the three negatives would not apparently be equally exposed, though they actually did receive the same exposure. The single lens would prove the quickest, the rectilinear the next, and the portrait would be the slowest. This is due to the absorption and reflection of light, which is greater the larger the number of separate lenses in the combination. Now we ascertained by experiment what allowance to make for this absorption and reflection, and, with a view to making the actinograph as perfect as possible, we took the matter into consideration. You will see that we have indicated the ratios of aperture to focal length in accordance with the two systems in general use— that of the Photographic Society of Great Britain, and the Decimal System.

You will notice that over each of the ratios of the former system there are three distinct marks, numbered respectively 1, 2 and 3, and these marks are accordingly used as the lens is a single one, a doublet, or a triplet. In the case of the decimal system only two marks are given—for single lenses and doublets ; the third mark is omitted in order to prevent confusion, but its position can be easily judged by the eye should it be required. From these remarks it will be evident that the ratio existing between the diaphragms and the focal length of the lens must be accurately adjusted to one of these systems, otherwise the value of the actinograph will be greatly impaired.

III. *The Exposure Scale.*—With respect to this, I need only say that it indicates directly exposures ranging from 0·05, or 1/20th of a second, up to 1 minute.

IV. *The Speed Scale.*—It has been customary hitherto to compare plates of different rapidities with the collodion wet plate as a standard, and modern dry plates are spoken of as being so many times as sensitive as wet plates. Apart from the fact that the majority of photographers of the present day have no experience whatever of wet plates, that these alleged speeds are otherwise most arbitrary and unreliable, and that wet plates themselves vary in speed, the system of referring one plate to another as standard is bad. We feel strongly that one of the most pressing photographic requirements of the day is the adoption of a scientific unit of speed, which will admit of an accurate comparison of the rapidity of different plates. We must all feel what a boon it would be if plate-makers were in a position to state definitely on each packet the speed of the plates it contained. We know this is attempted, in a manner, by referring in some cases to Warnerke's sensitometer numbers ; but this is a most crude and unsatisfactory method of judging the speed of the plates. You may purchase to-day a plate by a certain maker and with a certain label, and you may find it to be a certain speed, but this is no criterion that if you purchase another sample of what professes to be the same plate, in a few months' time, you will find it of the same speed. I could name a certain commercial plate which some months ago had an actinograph speed of 7, while the last packets I procured of the same plate had a speed of 18, or were nearly three times as rapid. In another case I worked with some plates the speed of which was 35 ; all at once, without the slightest notification of alteration, the speed dropped to 20, or, in other words, the plates were about half their original speed. Till plate-makers therefore are provided with, and adopt some method of estimating the speed of their plates, the best plan for photographers who wish to save annoyance and expense, is to purchase a large stock of plates at the same time, with a guarantee from the maker that they are all made from the same batch of emulsion.

Now we have attempted to remedy this defect in the nomenclature and comparison of plates, by choosing as measure for the speed of the plates the length of time it takes to produce a definite result upon the plate. Let us consider, for a moment, a landscape negative, in which there is a considerable expanse of sky, and say of green pasture in the foreground. We all know that in the case of over-exposure the density of the grass will come more or less nearly up to that of the sky, and a flat uninteresting negative will result. On the other hand, in the case of under-exposure, in the effort to force detail in the grass, the sky will become extremely dense while the grass may be represented by almost bare glass. Now we cannot fix upon a definite density for the sky alone, because almost any density is compatible with either under- or over-exposure, but in the case of a rightly exposed negative, be it either generally thin or dense, there is a definite ratio of density between the sky and the grass, which we find to be about as 1·7 is to 1.[1] We have, therefore, decided to take the exposure required to produce this definite ratio of density, under special conditions of light and lens, as a measure of the speed of the plate. Hence we call the speed of that plate 1, which produces this necessary ratio of density between sky and foreground in 1 second with 1° of light, the intensity of the light reaching the plate being equal to that sent out by the object ; and we call that plate speed 100, which produces the same result under the same circumstances, in the 1/100th part of a second. It will be obvious that it is impossible, in practice, to comply with the above-named conditions, and the speed has therefore to be calculated from results obtained under practical conditions. An example will best show how this calculation is made. We will assume that a negative with the requisite ratio of density was obtained on the 8th June, at 11 a.m., in the brightest possible light. The light at this time, in our latitude, would be 85 actinograph degrees. The lens used was a rapid rectilinear working at intensity $f/32$, and the exposure given was $2\frac{1}{2}$ seconds. With such a lens and stop, the light reaching the plate is $32^2$, or 1,024 times less in intensity than that emitted by the object. As I said before, however, the lens absorbs and reflects a certain proportion of this light, and the amount, in this instance, which actually reaches the plate consequently becomes 1,351 times less than the light reflected by the object. This figure 1,351 we divide by 85, the degrees of light ; and by $2\frac{1}{2}$, the time of exposure in seconds ; and the result, viz., 6·3, is the speed of the plate.

All this may sound rather alarming to some of our fellow-amateurs, but it is not in the least necessary that they should know anything about it in order to work the actinograph successfully. The calculation we have just made is

---

[1] H.N.—A., pp. 107–112, 118–121.

precisely the inverse of what the actinograph makes itself every time it is consulted. We have given the definition and the example merely to show that our speed scale is no arbitrary arrangement, but that it is based upon scientific principles.

The speeds indicated on our scale range from 0·5 up to 300 ; 0·5 is about the speed of a wet plate, and 50 is about the speed of the quickest dry plate we have yet come across, so that though the tendency is to make plates faster and faster, we have left a considerable margin which is hardly likely to be reached just yet. It will also be found in practice that the speeds above 50 are frequently of value when working with factors.

Roughly we subdivide the speeds of commercial gelatino-bromide plates as follows :—Slow, 2 to 6 ; ordinary, 6 to 15 ; rapid, 15 to 25 ; and extra rapid, 25 to 50. As, however, we have come across plates which professed to be extra rapid, and the speed of which was actually only 10, it is never safe to rely upon the maker's estimate of speed. It is absolutely necessary for the photographer to ascertain the speed of his plates for himself, and I shall presently show you how simply this may be done by means of the actinograph.

Below the speed scale you will notice another very short scale. This bears on its upper edges five points, marked respectively " Very bright," " Bright," " Mean," " Dull " and " Very dull." These points, as I said before, indicate simultaneously five different exposures, and the selection of the right one to use, which, with a little experience, presents no difficulty, is almost the only thing left to the judgment of the photographer who uses the actinograph. Of course, an exposure lying between any two of these points may be chosen in case a doubt arises which to select. On the bottom edge of this little scale is a single mark termed the " speed index." This is set to the figure on the speed scale which indicates the speed of the plate about to be used.

I should here like to say a few words on the subject of development. It is popularly supposed that a great deal can be done in development to modify the effect produced on the plate by the light ; that in case of over-exposure detail can be checked while density is allowed to proceed ; and that, in case of under-exposure, detail can be forced while density is restrained. We hold most strongly that this control during development is, to say the least of it, greatly exaggerated. A technically perfect negative can only be produced by an accurate exposure. It is quite true that there is considerable latitude of exposure, but only such as will affect the general character of the resulting picture. On the one hand we call the picture " soft," and on the other hand " brilliant." Exceed these limits and you produce decided under- or over-exposure. The effect of abnormal quantities of alkali in the developer is simply to hasten development, and eventually to fog the plate ; and the effect of abnormal additions of a bromide is simply to retard development, and eventually to prevent it altogether. It is perfectly clear that development cannot produce detail when the light has not had time to affect the plate, and it is equally clear that if the light action has been allowed to continue till the deepest shadows have themselves affected the plate, development cannot prevent the relatively small difference between the high lights and the shadows asserting itself in the finished negative. Our views on this subject will probably be considered heterodox, but they are the result of careful experiments carried out purposely to decide the question. Opinions to the contrary are usually formed upon the behaviour of isolated negatives taken in the ordinary way without reliable data to go upon, and, what is of paramount importance, without any certain method of estimating the strength of the light. We cannot lay too much stress upon the importance of a correct exposure, and if this be given you need have no anxiety as to the resulting negative, whatever the developer, so long as it is well balanced.

Before we proceed to the practical working of the actinograph, there is one other matter to which I must call your attention. It must be borne in mind that the light diagram before you strictly applies only to places situated on north latitude 52° 30′, which passes through the centre of England. This diagram is no doubt sufficiently accurate for the whole of England and Ireland, but the light in other latitudes varies from ours so much that, in order to secure certain results all the year round, it would be requisite to have another light diagram, even for places as near as the north of Scotland.

I will therefore show you some light diagrams for other latitudes, in order to give you an idea of the variation of the light in different parts of the world The diagram you have just seen for our own latitude is drawn to a logarithmic scale, but those I am about to show you are drawn to a natural scale, the difference in the light being thus rendered more apparent. I will first show you the light diagrams for the Equator and for the North Pole, not that I expect we shall any of us be called upon to photograph in the latter spot, but because it enables me to show you the extreme variation in the light. Now you must understand that the more nearly the curves, or light lines, approach the right-hand side of the diagram the more intense is the light, the scale at the bottom of each diagram expressing the intensity of the light in actinograph degrees. On the lower or Equator diagram there are six lines of light, from which we see that the light extends every day, throughout the entire year, from 6 a.m. to 6 p.m. We also see that the highest lights occur there in March and September. One curious point is that the light line for 6 a.m. and 6 p.m. is perfectly straight, so that, assuming the atmosphere to be constant, the exposure at 6 o'clock is absolutely the same every day in the year.

We will now refer to the upper diagram, the one for the North Pole. The chief characteristic of this is that it has only one light curve, and that this curve is not marked with any hour, as time of day, photographically speaking, does not exist at the Poles. To put it another way, whenever the curve is found opposite a date, as it is from March to September, the exposure on that day is exactly the same throughout the whole twenty-four hours, and when there is no part of the curve opposite a date, as is the case from September to March, there is no light either day or night, so that for six months of the year you may photograph there day and night, but for the other six months, if you want to photograph at all, you will have to resort to the flashlight. While at the Equator the highest possible light is 100° (actinograph), at the Poles it does not exceed 39·8°.

Now it is obvious, if these two diagrams represent the two extreme conditions of light on the earth, that for places situated anywhere between the Equator and the Poles the light more or less nearly approaches one or other of these extremes, and it is most interesting to see how the light at the Equator represented by the six light lines gradually merges, as we go north or south, into the solitary curve at the Poles. At first sight it would seem, as we leave the Equator, that the tendency is for the number of light lines to become less and less, but if you remember that at the Equator it is only possible, at any time of the year, to photograph during twelve hours of the day, while in our own latitude, during the summer, we may photograph for sixteen hours out of the twenty-four, you will see that this cannot be the case.

In order to show you how this merging of the six Equator lines into the single North Pole line really takes place, I will show you the light diagrams for north latitudes 20° and 70°, which correspond with Bombay, and the north of Norway, and are equidistant from the Equator and the North Pole. In the lower diagram you will see that the curves are more nearly akin to those of the Equator, though they have already lost the symmetry of the latter, and begin to incline downwards from left to right. There are also the same number of curves as on the Equator diagram, but the highest light now occurs in April and August, and you see that the 6 o'clock curve only comes into use for half the year.

In the upper diagram you will see that the curves have considerably increased in number, and yet we are only 20° away from the solitary curve of the North Pole. But, at the same time, you see how the curves tend to compress themselves together to the left-hand side of the diagram, and, as you go still farther north, they become more and more compressed till they eventually coalesce into the single North Pole curve. In north latitude 70° you may photograph from May to August all day and all night, while from November to January you have no light at all. In latitude 20° the maximum light is 100° (actinograph), and in latitude 70° it is only 68·7°.

Though these diagrams show conclusively the impossibility of timing exposures in one part of the world from the light-values of another, you may think we have taken rather extreme cases, so I now propose to show you two more diagrams more closely connected. The upper one is for north latitude 52° 30′, our own latitude ; and the lower is for north latitude 37° 30′, which corresponds with the south of Spain. In the former case the light lasts, in summer, for sixteen hours of the day, and in the latter for fourteen hours. The curves themselves show how much more intense the light is generally in the south of Spain compared with what we have it here.

An inspection of these diagrams shows that the variation in the light in different north latitudes tells most seriously in the winter months, and in south latitudes, of course, in the summer months, and, in either case, in the earlier and later hours of the day.

In order to adapt the actinograph for any part of the world, we have decided to supply instruments with special light scales for any latitude north or south of the Equator, at intervals of $2\frac{1}{2}$°. If the photographer desires to be able to work at any practicable time of the day, and all the year round, we do not think that each diagram can be used, with accuracy, for a greater zone than 5° ; if, however, he confine himself to several months when the light is at its best, and to the middle hours of the day, a single diagram will probably serve for a zone extending over 10°.

We have now, I think, fully explained the principles upon which the actinograph is based, and it only remains for me to show you, as far as I can, the method of using the instrument. In order to do this, by means of the lantern, I have constructed a transparent actinograph.[1] It is obvious, however, that in the lantern I cannot deal with our revolving light scale in its entirety. We shall therefore have to be content to restrict ourselves to one date, and all our examples will consequently refer to the date I have taken, viz., the 21st June. I think I cannot do better than follow the course we have taken in our pamphlet of instructions. After describing the instrument we give an example of the methods of finding the exposure for an ordinary landscape. And here let me say, that by an " ordinary " landscape we embrace a wider range of subjects than this term is generally supposed to imply. It is sometimes amusing to notice the fine distinctions under which land-

---

[1] Now in the H  and D. collection at the R.P.S.

scapes are classified, and the fine shade of exposure these distinctions are supposed to render necessary, when, after all, the final selection of the exposure is very possibly decided upon data more of the nature of a guess than anything else. By an " ordinary " landscape we mean general landscape and architectural work, and we do not consider any modification in the exposure to be necessary, unless, on the one hand, we approach the object with the camera at a distance of from twenty to fifty focal lengths, or, on the other hand, unless we wish to secure pictures of extremely distant objects. Of course, it is obvious that we do not include abnormally lighted views, such as forest scenery, in which the light is obscured by heavy foliage.

In the examples I have chosen to give you to-night, I have selected data in such a way as to give simple figures to deal with. To proceed with our first example : Let us suppose we are about to take an ordinary landscape at 4 p.m., with a single lens, working at $f/16$, that the light is " very bright," and that the speed of our plate is 5. We first of all set the " speed index " to 5 on the speed scale, we then move the long slide till $f/16$ (1) is opposite the curve marked 8 a.m. and 4 p.m., and now, opposite the point marked " very bright," we find the correct exposure, viz., one second. From this example you see what a very simple operation the finding of an exposure involves. Had the time been 4.30 instead of 4 o'clock, we should have placed the point marked $f/16$ (1) midway between the four and five o'clock curves.

I fancy I hear some of you saying, " But how are we to ascertain the speed of our plate ? " There are two ways of doing this, which I will now proceed to describe. Probably most of you have a favourite plate with which, at any rate, you have secured one satisfactorily exposed landscape negative. Now, supposing you have a record of the conditions under which this landscape negative was produced, it is a very simple matter, by means of the actinograph itself, to ascertain the speed of that plate. We will assume that it was taken on the 21st of June at 3 p.m., with a rectilinear lens working at $f/22 \cdot 6$, that the light was the brightest possible, and that the exposure you gave was one second. To find the speed of that plate, set $f/22 \cdot 6$ (2) opposite the curve marked 9 a.m. and 3 p.m., then set the point " very bright " to one second on the exposure scale, and, opposite the " speed index," you will find the speed of your plate, viz., $9 \cdot 5$.

In case, however, you have no reliable record of a satisfactory landscape exposure, it will, of course, be necessary to proceed in another way. Choose a day, if possible, for the experiment when the light corresponds with " very bright," as, under these conditions, the result is always most reliable. Proceed to take an ordinary landscape, and, if you have literally no clue to the rapidity of the plate, assume a medium speed, say 15. Ascertain the exposure by

means of the actinograph with this assumed speed, and expose the plate.
If, upon development, the negative is satisfactory, the assumed speed is the
actual speed of that plate.   Should the negative prove to be under-exposed,
the speed of the plate is less than 15.   If, on the other hand, it proves to be
over-exposed, the speed of the plate is more than 15 ; and a little experience,
and, if necessary, a second experiment, will enable you to decide what the
speed really is

The exposure scale of the actinograph commences with 0·05, or one-
twentieth, of a second.   Circumstances frequently arise when a smaller
exposure than this is necessary, as in the case of using a large lens aperture
with an exceedingly rapid plate, and in a " very bright " light.   We will
now work an example to show how to use the actinograph in such a case.
Let us assume that the picture is to be taken at noon on the 21st of June, with
a rectilinear lens working at $f/8$, that the light is " very bright," and the speed
of the plate is 50.   We will set the actinograph to these data, and you see that
we are unable to read off any exposure opposite the point " very bright."
As, however, our speed scale is exactly the inverse of the exposure scale, we
can help ourselves out of the difficulty in this way : Assume the speed of the
plate to be one-tenth of what it really is, and accordingly set the " speed
index " to 5 instead of to 50.   You will now find opposite the point " very
bright," an exposure indicated of 0·2, or one-fifth, of a second, but this is ten
times too great because we took the speed ten times too small, and therefore
the required exposure is 0·02, or one-fiftieth, of a second.

So far we have merely considered the taking of what we have called an
ordinary landscape.   I shall now proceed to show you how to use the actinograph for other purposes.   We take the ordinary landscape as our unit, and
we obtain the exposure for any other class of subject simply by multiplying
the ordinary landscape exposure by a certain factor.   I shall confine myself
to two examples as, of course, the only distinction in dealing with different
subjects lies in the factor employed.   We will assume that we are about to
take a cloud negative.   The factor for this subject is one-tenth, that is to
say, we must take one-tenth of the exposure indicated for an ordinary landscape.   We will take the conditions as follows :—Time, 6 p.m. ; lens, single,
$f/32$ ; light " mean " and speed of plate 5.   We will set the actinograph
accordingly, and opposite point " mean," we find the exposure 15 seconds ;
but as we have to multiply this exposure by one-tenth, the exposure we require
will be one-tenth of 15, or 1·5 second.   Now, I want to impress upon you that
multiplying an exposure by a certain number is precisely the same thing as
dividing the speed by that number, and *vice versâ*.   In this case, for example,
instead of dividing the indicated exposure by 10, we might have multiplied

the speed by 10, and assumed for this particular purpose that the speed was 50 instead of 5, when the correct exposure, viz., $1\cdot5$, or a second and a half, would be directly indicated.

As a last example, we will assume that we are about to take a portrait in diffused light out of doors. Time, noon ; lens, rectilinear, $f/8$ ; light " bright," and speed of plate 15. For this subject we will take the factor as 5, that is to say, the indicated exposure will require to be multiplied by 5. Having set the actinograph in accordance with these data, we find an exposure opposite " bright," of $0\cdot1$ or one-tenth of a second, and as 5 times one-tenth is half, half a second is the exposure we require. Here again we might have divided the speed by 5, in the first place, instead of afterwards multiplying the exposure by 5. If accordingly we set the " speed index " to 3 instead of to 15, our exposure of half a second will be directly indicated opposite point " bright."

And now I think I may bring my subject to a close, for I feel that it has probably already exceeded the limits of your patience. Having explained, to the best of my ability, the working of the actinograph and the principles upon which it is based, I suppose I might, in conclusion, expatiate upon its virtues and advantages. This, however, I have no intention of doing ; we are perfectly satisfied to leave the verdict in the hands of the photographic public, and if the actinograph can eventually claim to have done anything to render the technical work of photographers more certain, and to place upon a more scientific basis matters which at present are involved in ambiguity, our chief ambition will have been attained. At best we have but found another tool, and placed, as it were, another pigment in the painter's hand ; its use may help him in the prosecution of his art, but neither it, nor any other scientific aid, can possibly usurp the function which belongs to art alone.

[*Reprinted from The Journal of the Society of Chemical Industry*, 30th April, 1890. *No. 4, Vol. IX.*]

# AN INSTRUMENT FOR THE MEASUREMENT OF DIFFUSE DAYLIGHT AND THE ACTINOGRAPH.

BY

## F. HURTER, Ph.D.

THE actinometer which I have devised for measuring diffuse daylight depends upon entirely different principles than the instrument Mr. Ballard has just brought to our notice. In most instruments designed for measuring light the eye has to decide when two things are equal, in Mr. Ballard's instrument, when the luminosity of the paint is equal to the light coming through the blue glass, in the ordinary silver paper actinometers the eye decides when two tints are equal.

Once when examining the spectrum of nitric dioxide the thought struck me that the light absorbed by that gas must do some molecular work, and as this was not chemical decomposition, it could only result in a rise of temperature. I saw the application which could be made of this, and I found that if a differential gas thermometer was filled with nitrogen dioxide, one bulb exposed to diffuse light, the other kept in the dark, the gas exposed to the light expanded. But owing to the difficulty of finding a suitable separating fluid, one which should not absorb the gas, I could not obtain satisfactory results. Equally unsatisfactory I found an instrument filled with bromine vapours. The idea that all coloured substances would in diffuse light assume a slightly higher temperature than white or colourless transparent substances led to the construction of differential thermometers, the bulbs of which contained a red substance in one, and a white one in the other. Very sensitive instruments were obtained with red and white wool, next in sensitiveness was cotton and paper. The red substances absorb most of the rays of the spectrum, except the red ones, whereas the white substances absorb very little of any of the rays, and the absorption of the light causes a slight rise in the temperature of the red substance, which expands the air of the bulb containing this substance. The consequent increase in pressure is read off on the scale behind the syphon gauge, and as experiments in this direction proved this rise of pressure was proportional to the chemical action of the light on silver salts.

But instruments so made were very unsatisfactory. Besides the temporary alterations in pressure in the bulb containing the red substance there was also a permanent change, which increased with every exposure to the light, and though little perceptible in one day, in the course of a few months became so large as to completely destroy the instrument by driving the liquid out of the syphon gauge into the bulb containing the white substance.

An investigation of what this was due to revealed the fact that the oxygen of the enclosed air gradually vanished, and it disappeared faster in the white one than in the red one. What becomes of the oxygen I am unable to say. It was clear I had to abandon organic substances.

But even when I began to use coloured glass the same difficulty still arose. I used either alcoholic solutions or benzine solutions of alkanet as indicator in the syphon gauge, and even after I had abandoned them also I still found the zero points of the instrument unsteady. It varied very little, but in the course of a year the change was quite perceptible.

A good instrument can, however, be made as follows :—Two test tubes holding from 10 to 15 c.c. are chosen; one of them must be made of very thin glass flashed inside with copper ruby glass, the other one must be of similar thin clear white glass. They should both be of the same weight and the same capacity, a slightly larger capacity for the white tube is favourable. These tubes must be well cleaned with nitric acid and caustic potash, carefully rinsed with boiled distilled water, dried and fused on to capillary glass tubes. When this has been done they must be repeatedly exhausted under the air pump to remove all products of combustion which enter during the operation of fusing to the capillary. They are finally made red hot and when cool a single drop of pure distilled water is allowed to enter into each tube, and is shaken into the bulb. The syphon gauge is filled either with a solution of potassium bichromate, or better, with a solution of potassium carbonate, to which is added sufficient potassium iodide and iodine to give it a deep colour. The bulbs are then sealed on to the syphon gauge, two very fine hair tubes being drawn out first, through which the air can escape and enter, on either side of the liquid in the syphon gauge.

When the instrument is so far completed it is again exhausted repeatedly to remove products of combustion, and the hair tubes are sealed up, the bulbs being at the time immersed in cold water to keep their temperature alike. The instrument has then to be tested to see that it is absolutely air-tight, and that both bulbs behave alike when the temperature is raised.

The position of the liquid in the gauge must not move under the receiver of the air pump, nor when the bulbs are immersed in hot water. A temporary change during the latter operation always occurs, but it must be only temporary.

If the instrument be found good it is mounted in a wooden box with a glass front, and to render it more sensitive the bulbs are placed in front of two concave reflectors, which are best made of silvered sheet copper and very thin.

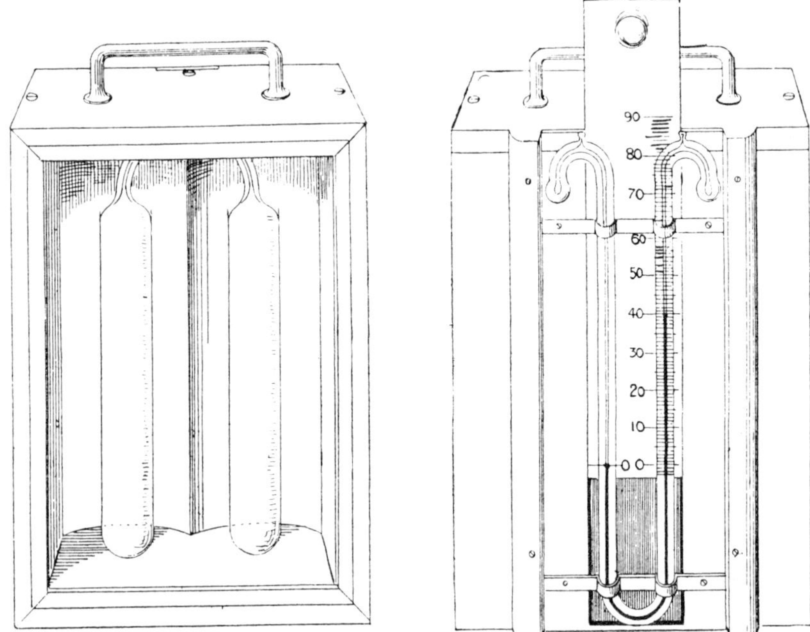

The side of the box opposite the reflectors is closed by a sheet of thick patent plate glass, coated on the outside with transparent gelatin and varnish, which helps to prevent the entrance of heat rays into the box.

A millimetre scale behind the syphon gauge, which is outside the box at the back, completes the instrument. (*See* illustrations.)

Yellowish-brown glass is almost as good as ruby glass and easier to procure.

An instrument of this description will indicate the brightest diffuse daylight obtainable in this country, as reflected by the northern sky by a variation in the level of the liquid of about 80 millimetres. It is therefore possible to measure the diffuse light to one per cent. of its greatest intensity with ease, and this is more than sufficiently accurate for all photographic processes.

By means of this instrument it is quite possible in steady light to time very accurately the exposure of a photographic plate. But my friend Mr. Driffield soon discovered that a very accurate measurement of the light was not necessary and the reason for this we decided to ascertain, and he has been my fellow-worker in all subsequent investigations.

We made self-recording actinometers by registering the position of the liquid in the syphon gauge photographically upon gelatino-bromide paper, which was fastened on a revolving drum driven by a clock. We continued to take observations for every day of the year 1885-86, and some of these photographs of the intensity of diffuse daylight are represented by the diagrams.

When there was a steady light throughout the day, which seldom occurred, the curve so clearly indicated that the light was a function of the altitude of the sun that I had no difficulty in recognising the sinus curve. This curve showed

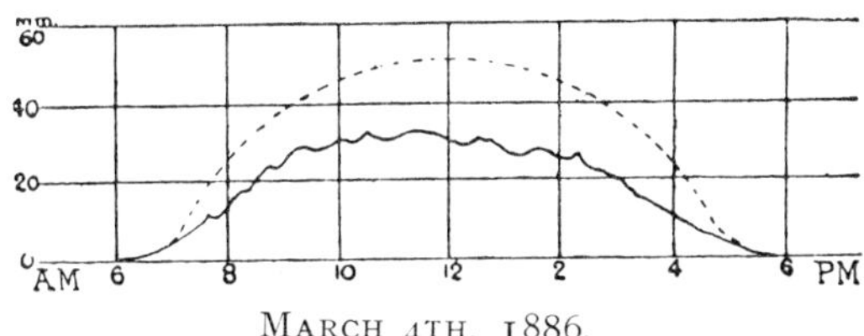

MARCH 4TH, 1886.

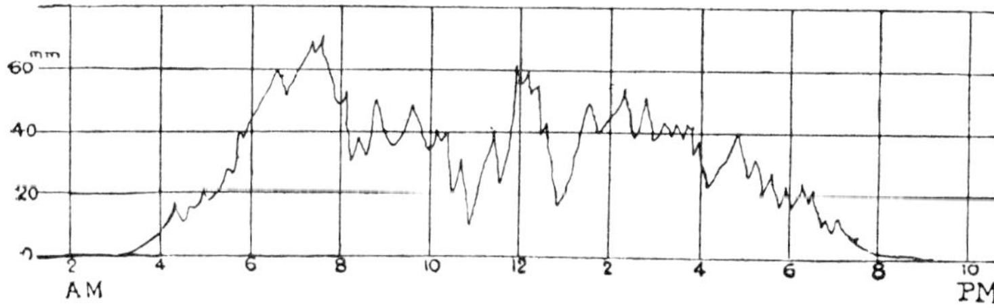

JUNE 12TH, 1886.

itself really in almost every diagram. It is broken up by passing clouds. The dotted curve in the diagram of 4th March shows the sinus of the altitude of the sun on that day for latitude 53° 8′. By measuring at the same time the diffuse light with the actinometer, and the sinus of the altitude of the sun by well-known means, we obtained the connexion between the altitude of the sun and the degrees of our actinometer.

We thus found that the diffuse light at any given hour of any given day is seldom less than 25 per cent. of the maximum light possible at that hour, except when it is foggy or raining, but under those circumstances no one thinks of taking pictures outside.

It is therefore clear that exposures of photographic plates at any particular moment under ordinary conditions vary only in the ratio 1 : 4. But as other investigations which Mr. Driffield and myself made showed that the latitude of exposure within which a good picture is possible is in many cases comprised in exposures varying from 1 : 2, it will be seen that accurate measure of the light is quite unnecessary.

We therefore together devised the little instrument called the actinograph, which Mr. Ballard recommended as a calculating machine.  The fact is, it is not only a calculating machine, it is in reality a machine for telling at any hour of the year the maximum light possible, and for converting that indication directly into times of exposures of plates of varying speed, with various lenses.

The manipulation of the instrument is exceedingly simple, and it has this great advantage over actinometers, it tells beforehand what the exposure on any day at any hour has to be, according to the condition of the atmosphere, and the eye soon judges that.   With this instrument photographic exposures can be ascertained with so great a degree of probability as to be almost equal to certainty.

The instrument has four scales : a light scale on a revolving cylinder, a slide carries the lens scale and the time scale, and on a fixed scale is marked the speed of the plate.   The speed of the plate must be ascertained by the operator by a simple experiment.

The lens scale is set to the hour and date at which an exposure is to be made, the speed index is set to indicate the speed of the plate ; when that is done, five different exposures in seconds can be read off at once, corresponding to five different conditions of the light : Very bright, bright, mean, dull, and very dull.

The sketch shows the instrument.

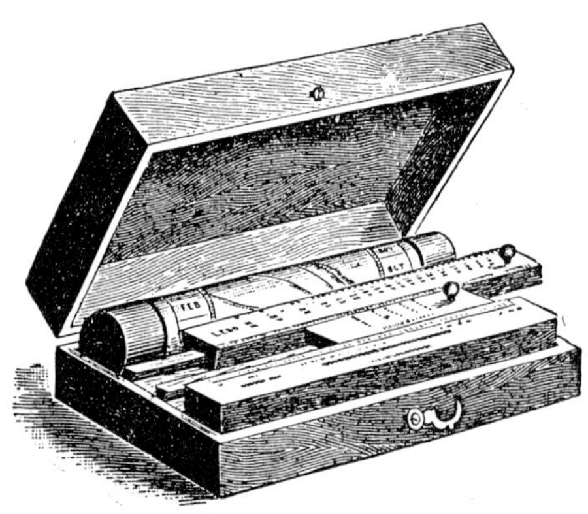

To give an idea of speed, I will add that Wratten's slow plates are about 10 on our scale, and Ilford Ordinary about 15 to 20.

The degree of light and the unit of speed are chosen for the instrument as follows :—The highest possible diffuse light corresponding to the altitude of the sun = 90°, is divided into 100 equal parts, one of which we call an actinograph degree.   The unit of speed is the speed of a plate which with one such degree of light will take an ordinary landscape in as many seconds as the square ratio of the focal length and aperture indicates.   Thus a plate would be of the speed 1, which with one actinograph degree of light, and a lens of F ÷ 4 it would take 16 seconds to produce a good landscape negative.

This system of degrees of light and speed of plates I venture to say is the only scientific one which has yet been proposed, and the actinometer I have described I believe to be the only satisfactory instrument for measuring diffuse light yet devised. The photographed records show that it is somewhat slow in following the light. Indeed the variations of light are frequently so sudden that the use of actinometers for photographic purposes will always remain unsatisfactory, because some time must necessarily elapse between the observation of the light and the exposure owing to a calculation having to be made.

The actinograph, on the other hand, avoids all calculation, takes into account variations in light, in lenses, and in plates, and will be a truly scientific substitute for actinometers, so long as the earth does not deviate from her time-honoured journey round the sun.

*(Reprinted from The Journal of the Society of Chemical Industry,* 31st *May,* 1890.
*No.* 5, *Vol. IX.*)

# PHOTO - CHEMICAL INVESTIGATIONS AND A NEW METHOD OF DETERMINATION OF THE SENSITIVENESS OF PHOTOGRAPHIC PLATES

BY

FERDINAND HURTER, PH.D., AND V. C. DRIFFIELD.

---

### I. WHAT IS A PERFECT NEGATIVE ? DENSITY, OPACITY, TRANSPARENCY.

THE production of a perfect picture by means of photography is an art ; the production of a technically perfect negative is a science.

A perfect negative demands, in the first place, a perfect plate, and as the manufacture of dry sensitive plates is a large and rapidly-growing chemical industry, we need offer no apology for bringing this subject before this Society.

Our researches, which have covered a period of over ten years, were made with a view to rendering the production of perfect negatives as far as possible a matter of certainty.

What is a perfect negative ? A negative is theoretically perfect when the amount of light transmitted through its various gradations is in inverse ratio to that which the corresponding parts of the original subject sent out.

The negative is mathematically the true inverse of the original when the opacities of its gradations are proportional to the light reflected by those parts of the original which they represent.

Before we can clearly understand this definition, it will be necessary to state shortly the laws of absorption of light by opaque black substances, and to define clearly the meaning we attach to the terms opacity, transparency and density of a negative. It is the more necessary to do this, as the whole of our investigations depend upon these laws.

For substances which do not reflect much light, such as black opaque bodies or transparent coloured bodies, the relation between the light absorbed and the quantity of the substance present is very simple.  If between the eye and a source of light we place a thin layer of dilute Indian ink, that layer absorbs light, and thereby reduces the intensity of the light transmitted.  Assume that such a layer absorbs one-half of the light, then one-half of the light will be transmitted.  Whatever may be the intensity of the original light, the intensity after passing this layer of ink will be one-half of what it was.  The interposition of two such layers will reduce the light to one-quarter the original intensity ; three such layers will reduce it to one-eighth, and so on, each layer reducing the intensity to one-half of what it receives.

Had the first layer allowed one-third of the light to pass through, then two such layers would reduce the intensity to one-ninth, three layers to one-twenty-seventh, &c.  In general any number of layers would reduce the intensity of the light to a fraction, which is equal to the fraction the first layer allows to pass, but raised to a power, the index of which is the number of layers employed.  If $n$ equal layers were employed, and the first one reduced the intensity of the light to a fraction $\dfrac{1}{m}$, the $n$ layers would reduce it to $\left(\dfrac{1}{m}\right)^{n}$.

If instead of using so many successive layers, the first layer were made to contain as much Indian ink as the $n$ successive layers contain altogether, we should find that the one layer now reduces the intensity of light by exactly the same amount as the $n$ layers did.  The reduction of the intensity is, of course, due to the black particles, and depends simply upon the number of them which are interposed per unit of area.  We can thus replace the number of layers by the number of particles, and the law takes this form :—The intensity $I_x$ of light after passing A molecules of a substance is a fraction of the original intensity I, such that—

$$\frac{I_x}{I} = \left(\frac{1}{C}\right)^{A}$$

For purely mathematical reasons the fraction $\dfrac{1}{C}$ is usually expressed as a negative power of the base of the hyperbolic logarithms $\epsilon$, say $\dfrac{1}{C} = \epsilon^{-k}$ and we can write—

$$\frac{I_x}{I} = \epsilon^{-kA}.$$

where $k$ is called the coefficient of absorption.  This form of the law we shall frequently use again.  The fraction $\dfrac{I_x}{I}$ represents and measures the *trans-parency* of the substance.  The inverse of that fraction, or $\dfrac{I}{I_x} = \epsilon^{kA}$

measures the *opacity* of the substance. It indicates what intensity of light must fall on one side of the substance in order that unit intensity may be transmitted.

In our investigations we use the letter T to denote transparency, and O to denote opacity, and the two symbols are related thus :—O $\times$ T = 1.

We must further define what we mean by density as distinct from opacity. By density we mean the number of particles of a substance spread over unit area, multiplied by the coefficient of absorption ; $k.A$ is what we term density, and mark by the letter D.

For our purposes, *i.e.*, in its application to negatives, the density is directly proportional to the amount of silver deposited per unit area, and may be used as a measure of that amount.

The relations between the three terms, transparency, opacity and density, are the following :—

$$T = \epsilon^{-D}$$
$$O = \epsilon^{D}$$
$$D = \log. \epsilon\, O = -\log. \epsilon\, T.$$

The density is the logarithm of the opacity, or the negative logarithm of the transparency.

These relations hold good for some substances with regard to ordinary white light, for others only with regard to monochromatic light, and for others they do not hold good at all. We have satisfied ourselves that they do hold good for the silver deposited as a black substance in negatives so long as the silver does not assume a metallic lustre, and reflects but a very small amount of light.

By means of these definitions we are now in a position to trace the connection between the densities of a theoretically perfect negative and the light intensities which produced them.

Since the density is the logarithm of the opacity, and since, in a theoretically perfect negative, the opacities are directly proportional to the intensities of the light which produced them, it follows that each density must be proportional to the logarithm of the light intensity which produced it. (More correctly, the density is a linear function of the logarithm of the intensity of light and time of exposure.)

The result is this :—In a theoretically perfect negative, the amounts of silver deposited in the various parts are proportional to the logarithms of the intensities of light proceeding from the corresponding parts of the object.

The question arises, can such a negative be produced in practice ?

In order to answer this question, we had first to find a simple method of measuring the density of the silver deposited in negatives. We had then to study the influence of the developers upon the density of the deposits, and we were then in a position to investigate the action of the light itself.

## II. Instrument for Measuring Densities.

We proceed to describe the instrument for measuring the density of the deposit. It is based on the relation existing between density and opacity. We measure the opacity of the plate, and in order to avoid calculations and references to tables of logarithms, the scale of the instrument is so arranged as to read the logarithm of the opacity, which is the density. The reason why we prefer to have the results expressed as density is because the density is a measure of the amount of silver deposited, or of the chemical work done by the light.

*Fig. 1*

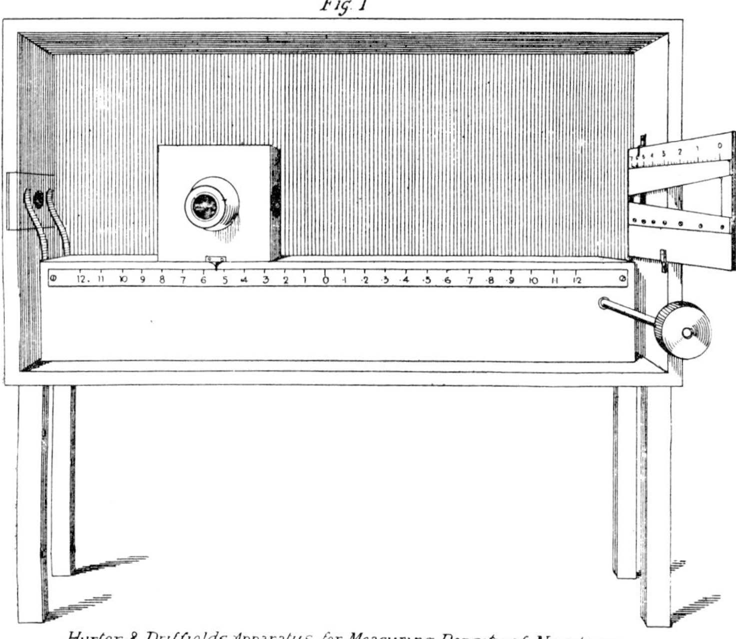

*Hurter & Driffields Apparatus for Measuring Density of Negatives*

The instrument pictured in Figs. 1 and 2 consists essentially of a small Bunsen photometer similar to those used for testing the illuminating power of gas, &c. The paper disc with its grease spot is placed in a small cubical chamber. The chamber carries an eye-piece, through which an image of each side of the disc can be viewed in two small mirrors, and so compared. The chamber can be made to slide in a straight line on a support by turning a key connected to one of two pulleys, over which passes an endless cord attached to the chamber. This arrangement is placed within a larger box, the ends of which have apertures through which light is admitted from two powerful petroleum lamps. Corresponding exactly with these apertures, similar apertures are bored into the sides of the small chamber, which admit the light to either side of the Bunsen disc. The dimensions we have adopted are, for the larger box, 12 in. long, 6 in. high and 4 in. deep. The small chamber is a cube measuring 2 in. inside. We find it necessary to blacken everything within the box except the scales, and it is also important to exclude all extraneous light by means of a screen. The heat of the lamps also very soon injures the woodwork unless it is covered with asbestos cardboard and sheet metal.

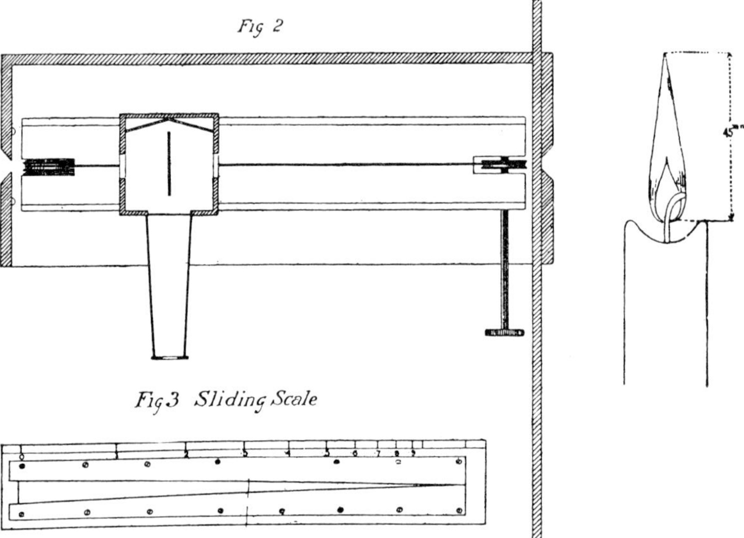


The aperture in the left-hand end of the large box we reduce to about $\frac{1}{4}$ in. diameter by a diaphragm. At this end is placed the plate to be measured, held in position by springs. The hole at the right-hand end of the box is reduced by a rectangular diaphragm, $\frac{1}{4}$ in. wide and $\frac{1}{2}$ in. long, the length being vertical. This diaphragm can be reduced in length by moving a taper diaphragm past it.

The instrument is provided with two scales, one fixed, the other movable, the use and construction of which we will now explain. The fixed scale indicates the position of the disc chamber, and is constructed as follows :—

Suppose that the lamp on the left-hand side gives light of the intensity $I_1$, and that on the right-hand side light of intensity $I_2$, and that both lamps are equidistant from the centre of the instrument, and that this distance is $l$. Then, when the disc chamber has been moved to a distance $x$ from the centre of the instrument, so that—

$$(1) \qquad \frac{I_1}{(l-x)^2} = \frac{I_2}{(l+x)^2} \quad \text{or} \quad \frac{I_1}{I_2} = \left(\frac{l-x}{l+x}\right)^2$$

the two images of the disc will be alike. If a plate is now inserted, which reduces the light from the intensity $I_1$ to intensity $i$, then the disc chamber will have to be moved to another place nearer to the plate before the two images of the disc are alike again. Supposing the distance of the disc from the centre of the instrument is now $y$, then—

$$(2) \qquad \frac{i}{(l-y)^2} = \frac{I_2}{(l+y)^2} \quad \text{or} \quad \frac{I_2}{i} = \frac{(l+y)^2}{(l-y)^2}$$

By multiplying the two equations we find the fraction, which measures the opacity—

$$\frac{I_1}{i} = \left(\frac{l-x}{l+x}\right)^2 \left(\frac{l+y}{l-y}\right)^2$$

Taking logarithms on both sides, we have, since log. $\frac{I_1}{i}$ is the density D of the plate—

$$D = \log. \left(\frac{l+y}{l-y}\right)^2 - \log. \left(\frac{l+x}{l-x}\right)^2$$

If, therefore, at the distances $x$ and $y$ we write on the scale the values of log. $\left(\frac{l+x}{l-x}\right)^2$ and log. $\left(\frac{l+y}{l-y}\right)^2$ we can simply read off these logarithms, subtract one from the other, and the result is the density of the plate. For general convenience we use vulgar and not hyperbolic logarithms. In order to avoid all errors arising from the distance of the lamps, we make the apertures in the box small compared with the luminous portion of the flame of the lamps ; it can be shown that in that case the distance $l$ must be measured between the centre of the instrument and the diaphragm.

The following table gives the relative distances of the various points of the scale from the centre of the instrument, at which the logarithms of $\left(\frac{l+x}{l-x}\right)^2$ have the values $0 \cdot 1$, $0 \cdot 2$, $0 \cdot 3$, &c., $l$ being half the distance between the diaphragms.

TABLE I.—*Fixed Scale of Instrument.*[1]

| Log. $\left(\dfrac{l + x}{l - x}\right)^2$ | Distance from centre of instrument. | Log. $\left(\dfrac{l + x}{l - x}\right)^2$ | Distance from centre of instrument. |
|---|---|---|---|
| 0·000 | $l \times 0·000$ | 0·900 | $l \times 0·476$ |
| 0·100 | $l \times 0·057$ | 1·000 | $l \times 0·519$ |
| 0·200 | $l \times 0·114$ | 1·100 | $l \times 0·560$ |
| 0·300 | $l \times 0·171$ | 1·200 | $l \times 0·599$ |
| 0·400 | $l \times 0·226$ | 1·300 | $l \times 0·634$ |
| 0·500 | $l \times 0·280$ | 1·400 | $l \times 0·667$ |
| 0·600 | $l \times 0·332$ | 1·500 | $l \times 0·698$ |
| 0·700 | $l \times 0·382$ | 1·600 | $l \times 0·726$ |
| 0·800 | $l \times 0·430$ | 1·700 | $l \times 0·752$ |

Suppose, as in our case, the box were 12 in. long between the diaphragms, then $l$ is 6 in. The centre of the instrument is marked with zero, and we find from the table that 0·500 must be placed at $6 \times 0·280$ in. from the centre on both sides of the centre. Similarly, other points of the scale are found by means of the table. The scale on both sides of zero is symmetrical. The distances between the points so found are subdivided into equal parts. This is not absolutely necessary, but it is convenient.

The movable scale (see Fig. 3) is attached to the upper edge of the taper diaphragm, which is used for reducing the amount of light admitted through the rectangular opening. This taper diaphragm is made of sheet metal about 12 in. long and 2 in. wide, out of which is cut a triangular opening about $10\frac{1}{2}$ in. in length from base to apex, the width of the base being $\frac{1}{2}$ in. It is essential that the sides of this triangle be absolutely straight lines. The scale attached to this taper diaphragm is constructed as follows :—From the apex we measure 10 in. exactly towards the base ; this gives the zero point of the scale. The other points of the scale are marked so as to read directly the densities. At any distance $x$ from the apex the area of the opening and, with it, the intensity of the light, will be reduced as $10 : x$, and the vulgar logarithm of the fraction $\dfrac{10}{x}$ is the corresponding density with which the scale is marked. For convenience we append table showing the distances from the apex, at which the figures 0·1, 0·2, 0·3, &c., are to be placed :—

[1] H.N.—B., p 55.  D.N.—E., p. 13A.

Table II.—*Movable Scale.*

| Value of log. $\frac{10}{x}$. | Distance from apex. | Value of log. $\frac{10}{x}$. | Distance from apex. |
|---|---|---|---|
| | Inches. | | Inches. |
| ·00 | 10 | 0·50 | 3·16 |
| ·05 | 8·91 | 0·60 | 2·51 |
| ·10 | 7·94 | 0·70 | 2·00 |
| ·20 | 6·31 | 0·80 | 1·58 |
| ·30 | 5·01 | 0·90 | 1·28 |
| ·40 | 4·00 | 1·00 | 1·00 |

Intermediate points are obtained by subdivision into equal parts.

An index is fixed to the inside of the box over the centre of the rectangular diaphragm pointing to the number to be read. The Figs. 1 and 2 will help to make this description clearer.

Two examples will show how the instrument is used.

1. When measuring a small density we move the sliding scale to zero, and the disc chamber to such a position that the images of the Bunsen disc are alike. We then insert the plate to be measured, and without altering the position of the disc chamber slide the movable scale until equality is restored. The density will then be indicated by the fixed index on the diaphragm scale.

2. In the case of a high density we place the sliding scale to 0, and by placing a piece of opal glass outside the box, between it and the lamp, we reduce the light on the right-hand side until the disc chamber requires to be moved almost up to the right-hand end of the box in order to secure equality of the images. If necessary, we move the lamp further away. When equality is thus secured, we read the number below the index of the disc chamber on the fixed scale. We then insert the plate to be measured, and move the disc chamber to the left until equality is again restored. If that cannot be done by the movement of the disc chamber alone, it can be obtained by using the movable scale in addition.

Suppose the index stood at 1·100 on the right, and afterwards at 1·55 on the left of zero, then the density would be 1·100 + 1·55 = 2·65.

If the index stood at 1·10 to the right and afterwards at 1·7 to the left, and equality could then only be restored by using the movable scale as well, and its index pointed to ·75, then the density would be 1·10 + 1·7 + 0·75 = 3·55. Higher numbers than 3·55 do not occur in ordinary negatives. A plate, the density of which is 3·55, only transmits $\frac{1}{3548}$th part of the light it receives.

The general rule for finding the density is :—Consider the numbers to the right of zero as negative numbers, those to the left as positive. Subtract the first reading from the second ; the result is the density. If the movable scale be used as well, the amount it indicates must be added.

It will hardly be necessary to say that a plate of density 1 permits one-tenth of the light to pass, and that a plate of density 2 permits one-hundredth of the light to pass, since 1 is the log. of 10, and 2 that of 100.

With this instrument we have obtained fairly accurate results. Analyses of mixtures of Indian ink and water, indigo solution and water, and of many other substances have been made by it. The following analyses are given to show the capabilities of the instrument :—

1. *Experiment with Indian ink.*—An Indian ink solution was mixed with water in known proportions, and the density of one solution being known, that of the others was calculated. The following table shows the observed and calculated densities. The calculated density is simply proportional to the amount of Indian ink employed :—

TABLE III.—Experiment with Indian Ink.[1]

| Indian ink employed to 100 c.c. of water. | Density calculated. | Density found. | C.c. of Indian ink found. |
|---|---|---|---|
| c.c. | | | |
| 5 | ·240 | ·240 | 5·00 |
| 10 | ·480 | ·500 | 10·42 |
| 15 | ·720 | ·750 | 15·62 |
| 20 | ·960 | ·950 | 19·80 |
| 25 | 1·200 | 1·245 | 25·90 |
| 30 | 1·440 | 1·440 | 30·0 |
| 35 | 1·680 | 1·665 | 34·7 |
| 40 | 1·920 | 1·885 | 39·3 |

The greatest error made does not reach 4 per cent. of the total amount, and even better results can be obtained if more than one reading be taken. But this accuracy is quite sufficient for photographic purposes, where, from other causes, still greater errors are liable to arise, as will presently be shown.

Sometimes, when using the instrument for analysing solutions of coloured salts, a peculiar difficulty arises from the different colours of the two images of the Bunsen disc. This is easily overcome by viewing the disc through appropriately coloured glass—red, green and blue glasses being the most

[1] H.N.—B., pp. 94, 95,

useful. The following experiment with indigo solution is representative of one of the most difficult, since dark blue glass was used to view the disc.

TABLE IV.—Indigo Solution.[1]

| Indigo solution employed. | Indigo found. | Density calculated. | Density found. |
| --- | --- | --- | --- |
| c.c. | c.c. | | |
| 100 | 96·0 | 1·554 | 1·487 |
| 50 | 50·6 | ·777 | ·787 |
| 25 | 24·1 | ·388 | ·375 |
| 10 | 10·0 | ·155 | ·155 |

It will be seen, again, that the results are only accurate within 5 per cent. of their value.

With regard to the lamps, they should be powerful petroleum lamps with duplex burners. The flames should be in planes, at right angles to the axis of the instrument. Very erroneous results are obtained if Argand burners are used. The lamps should be placed close to the diaphragms, and it is advisable to provide a small stage outside the diaphragm to hold coloured glasses, when a substance requires investigation in light of a particular colour.

Captain Abney has also devised an instrument for measuring transparencies. His instrument consists of a Rumford shadow photometer as indicator, and of a revolving sector, which can be closed or opened whilst revolving, as a measure of the transparency. Apart from the fact that a Bunsen disc is more sensitive than the shadows, there is a fallacy in the assumption that the amount of light which passes through a revolving sector is proportional to the angle to which the sector is opened. Experiments made for the purpose show that the amount of light passing through a revolving sector is more correctly represented by a formula—

$$I_x = I \frac{\phi}{360} + C.$$

Where $I_x$ is the light transmitted by the sector, I the intensity falling upon the sector, $\phi$ the angle of opening, and C a constant, which depends upon the relative position of the lamp, the sector and the screen, and is, in fact, due to the semi-shadow on both edges of the sector openings. The error caused by this constant is small with plates of low density, but it rises to over 100 per cent. with plates of high densities, which renders the results utterly untrustworthy.

[1] H.N.—B., pp. 94, 95.

We have thought it necessary to give this lengthy description of our instrument since we consider it a very important one ; it is for photographic experiments as indispensable as the balance is in analysis. The instrument is capable of other applications ; its indications can always be translated into weights by simply multiplying them with a factor. It is, therefore, capable of applications in analysis.

III.—DEVELOPMENT.

There is a generally-accepted belief among photographers that a great amount of control can be exercised in development over the density and the general gradations of a negative, and in this respect alkaline pyrogallol enjoys a special reputation. On this account we have chosen this developer for the following series of experiments, except where otherwise stated. These experiments conclusively show that the only control the photographer has over development lies in securing a greater or less density of image (the former often only at the expense of fog), and that he has no control whatever over the gradations of the negative.[1]

The plan we have adopted in carrying out these experiments is to subject *pieces of one and the same plate* to the varying conditions, the influence of which, on the density or the gradation, is the subject of our investigation. A precaution we have always taken, except in our earliest experiments, is never to develop a piece of a plate which has been exposed to the light without simultaneously submitting to the same developer a piece of the same plate which has *not* been exposed, and which we term the " fog strip." The object of this precaution is to ascertain exactly how much of the resulting density is due to the action of the light and how much is due to incidental fog, including therein fog inherent in the plate or caused by injudicious development, and also the density due to glass and gelatine.

In the following series of experiments, made to ascertain the influence of time, of development, and composition of the developer on the density, we covered up one-half of a plate and exposed the other half to a standard light, as will be presently more fully explained. After exposure we cut up the plate in such a way that each piece included a portion of the unexposed and a portion of the exposed plate. Each strip was then developed, such modification in time of development or composition of developer being made as formed the subject of the investigation. The resulting densities were then measured after fixing, washing and drying.

---

[1] " Gradations " here means " the relative amounts of silver deposited in various portions of the negative " ; there is considerable control " over the relative transparencies." *See* letter Hurter—Bothamley, 5th July, 1890, in D.N.—F., pp. 6, 8.

*Time of Development.*

[1] *Experiment 1.*—Plate : " Wratten Ord."  Exposure (?).

Developer, 100 c.c. contain $\begin{cases} 0 \cdot 085 \text{ g. } NH_3. \\ 0 \cdot 400 \text{ pyrogallol.} \\ 0 \cdot 250 \ NH_4Br. \end{cases}$

*Results.*

| Time of development | Minutes | 2·5 | 5·0 | 7·5 | 10·0 | 12·5 | 15·0 |
|---|---|---|---|---|---|---|---|
| Densities produced | .. .. | ·183 | ·543 | ·793 | 1·160 | 1·10 | 1·17 |
| Percentage | .. .. .. | 15·6 | 46·0 | 67·8 | 99·1 | 94·0 | 100·0 |

[2] *Experiment 2.*—Plate : " Wratten Ord."  Exposure = 60 C.M.S.

Developer, 100 c.c. contain $\begin{cases} 0 \cdot 162 \ NH_3. \\ 0 \cdot 342 \text{ Pyro.*} \\ 0 \cdot 228 \ NH_4Br. \end{cases}$

| Time of development | | Minutes | 1·25 | 2·5 | 5 | 10 | 15 |
|---|---|---|---|---|---|---|---|
| Density exposed plate | .. .. .. | | ·775 | 1·175 | 1·725 | 2·275 | 2·475 |
| Density unexposed plate | .. .. .. | | ·155 | ·270 | ·510 | ·590 | ·790 |
| Density due to light | .. .. .. | | ·620 | ·905 | 1·215 | 1·685 | 1·685 |
| Percentage developed | .. .. .. | | 36·8 | 53·7 | 72·1 | 100 | 100 |

* Sulpho-pyrogallol equivalent to pyro.

[2] *Experiment 3.*—Plate : " Wratten Ord."  Exposure = 20 C.M.S.

See Diagram No. 1.  Developer, 100 c.c. contain :—

0·162 $NH_3$.

0·342 Pyro.

0·228 $NH_4Br$.

| Time of development | Minutes | 2·5 | 5 | 7·5 | 10 | 15 | 20 |
|---|---|---|---|---|---|---|---|
| Density exposed plate | .. | ·670 | ·965 | 1·245 | 1·420 | 1·755 | 1·945 |
| Density unexposed plate | .. | ·200 | ·345 | ·415 | ·505 | ·575 | ·710 |
| Density due to light | .. .. | ·470 | ·620 | ·830 | ·915 | 1·180 | 1·235 |
| Percentage developed | .. | 38·0 | 50·2 | 67·2 | 74·1 | 95·5 | 100 |

[1] H.N.—A., pp. 37, 39, 98.  H.N.—B., p. 7.  [2] D.N.—O., pp. 28, 29 ; 26.

These experiments show that the total density grows with the time of development, but that the density due to light reaches a limit in about 15

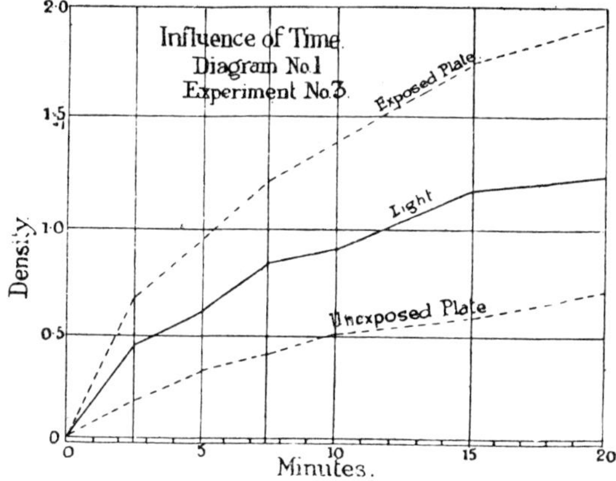



minutes.   The continued growth of the total density is due to the action of the developer upon the bromide of silver which had not been affected by the light.

*Variation of Pyrogallol.*

[1]*Experiment* 4.—Plate : " Wratten Ord."   Exposure (?).

Developed each strip four minutes in a developer containing in 100 c.c. =
$$\begin{cases} 0 \cdot 1156 \ NH_3. \\ 0 \cdot 2000 \ NH_4Br. \end{cases}$$

| Pyrogallol . . . . . . . . grms. | 0·08 | 0·16 | 0·32 | 0·64 |
|---|---|---|---|---|
| Relative amount . . . . . . . . . . | 1 | 2 | 4 | 8 |
| Density . . . . . . . . . . | 1·036 | 1·506 | 1·526 | 1·500 |

*Experiment* 5.—Plate : " Wratten Ord."   Exposure = 60 C.M.S.   See diagram No. 2.

Developed four minutes in a developer, 100 c.c. =
$$0 \cdot 162 \ NH_3.$$
$$0 \cdot 228 \ NH_4Br.$$

| | | | | | | |
|---|---|---|---|---|---|---|
| Pyrogallol used grms. | ·057 | 0·114 | 0·228 | 0·457 | 0·914 | 1·828 |
| Relative amount . . . . | 1 | 2 | 4 | 8 | 16 | 32 |
| Density exposed plate . . | ·595 | ·840 | 1·060 | 1·215 | 1·150 | 1·040 |
| Density unexposed plate . . | ·180 | ·195 | ·190 | ·130 | ·135 | ·105 |
| Density due to light . . . . | ·415 | ·645 | ·870 | 1·085 | 1·015 | ·935 |

[1] H.N.—A., p. 98.   H.N.—J., p. 4.

From these results we gather that an excess of pyrogallol beyond a certain limit tends to retard development and the production of density. This limit appears to be the equivalent of pyrogallol necessary to convert the ammonia into tribasic pyrogallate, $C_6H_3(ONH_4)_3$.

A similar experiment is here given, made with "sulpho-pyrogallol" compounded with sodium sulphite and citric acid. It will be evident that the presence of the acid, by neutralising the ammonia, is responsible for the much more marked falling off in density.

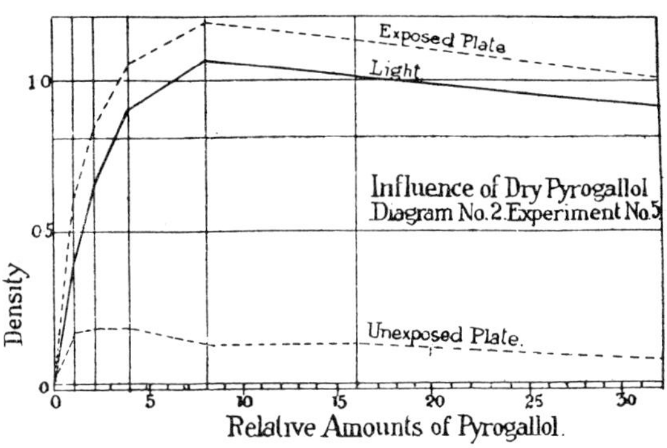


[1] *Experiment* 6.—Plate : " Manchester Slow."  Exposure $=$ 40 C.M.S.

Developed 4 minutes, 100 c.c. $= \begin{cases} 0 \cdot 162\ NH_3 \\ 0 \cdot 228\ NH_4Br, \end{cases}$ and " sulpho-pyrogallol " corresponding to $x$ grms. pyrogallol.

| Pyro        grms. $x =$ | 0·114 | 0·228 | 0·457 | 0·914 | 1·371 | 1·828 |
|---|---|---|---|---|---|---|
| Relative amount | 1 | 2 | 4 | 8 | 12 | 16 |
| Density exposed plate | ·940 | 1·710 | 1·610 | 1·350 | ·700 | ·105 |
| Density unexposed plate | ·360 | ·660 | ·495 | ·240 | ·110 | ·080 |
| Density due to light | ·580 | 1·050 | 1·115 | 1·110 | ·590 | ·025 |

*Variation of Ammonia.*

[2] *Experiment* 7.—Plate : " Wratten Ord."  Exposure (?).

Developed 4 minutes in developer, 100 c.c. $=$

$x$ grms. $NH_3$.

0·40 Pyro.

0·20 $NH_4Br$.

| Ammonia        grms. | 0·0231 | ·0462 | ·0925 | ·185 | ·277 | ·370 |
|---|---|---|---|---|---|---|
| Density .. | 0·00 | ·613 | 1·276 | 1·816 | 2·136 | 2·266 |

<hr>

[1] D.N.—O., pp. 25, 33, 24.            [2] H.N.—A., p. 99.

[1] *Experiment 8.*—Plate : " Wratten Ord."   Exposure 20 C.M.S.   See diagram No. 3.

Developed 4 minutes in 100 c.c. $= \begin{cases} x\ NH_3. \\ 0\cdot34\ \text{Pyro.} \\ 0\cdot23\ NH_4Br. \end{cases}$

| | | | | | | |
|---|---|---|---|---|---|---|
| Ammonia    grms. $x =$ | ·103 | ·207 | ·414 | ·828 | 1·656 | 3·312 |
| Relative amount       | 1 | 2 | 4 | 8 | 16 | 32 |
| Density exposed plate    | ·340 | ·530 | ·960 | 1·675 | 1·710 | 1·470 |
| Density unexposed plate    | ·090 | ·120 | ·265 | ·700 | 1·310 | 1·300 |
| Density due to light       | ·250 | ·410 | ·695 | ·975 | ·400 | ·170 |

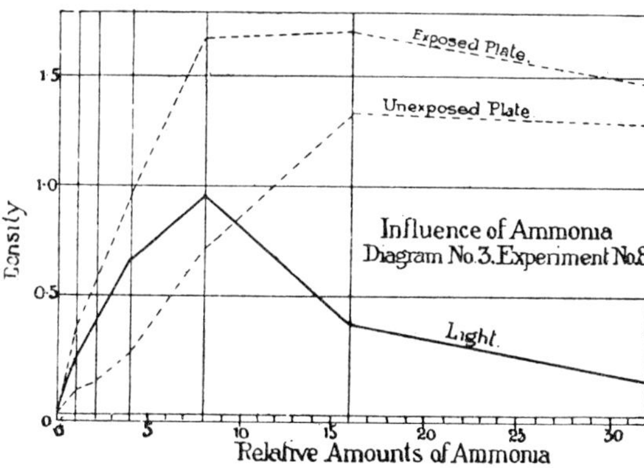


[1] *Experiment* 9.—Plate :  " Manchester Slow."   Exposure 40 C.M.S.  See diagram No. 4.

Developed 4 minutes in 100 c.c. $= \begin{cases} x\ NH_3. \\ 0\cdot34\ \text{Pyro.} \\ 0\cdot23\ NH_4Br. \end{cases}$

| | | | | | | |
|---|---|---|---|---|---|---|
| $x$ grms. $NH_3$       | ·207 | ·414 | ·828 | 1·242 | 1·656 | 3·726 |
| Relative amount       | 1 | 2 | 4 | 6 | 8 | 18 |
| Density exposed plate    | ·250 | 1·530 | 2·290 | 2·470 | 2·470 | 1·865 |
| Density unexposed plate    | ·090 | ·550 | 1·400 | 1·880 | 2·015 | 1·445 |
| Density due to light    | ·160 | ·980 | ·890 | ·590 | ·455 | ·420 |

The general result of these experiments is that the addition of ammonia, up to a certain extent, increases the density in a given time, but that the amount of ammonia which can be added without giving rise to fog, and without simul-

[1] D.N.—O., pp. 25, 33, 24.

taneously adding bromide, is very limited.   The so-called accelerating action of ammonia being due almost entirely to its solvent action on bromide of silver, which, if the ammonia is increased sufficiently, results in greatly diminishing the density.

The following table shows the solubility of silver bromide[1] in very dilute ammonia, such as is used for development of plates :—

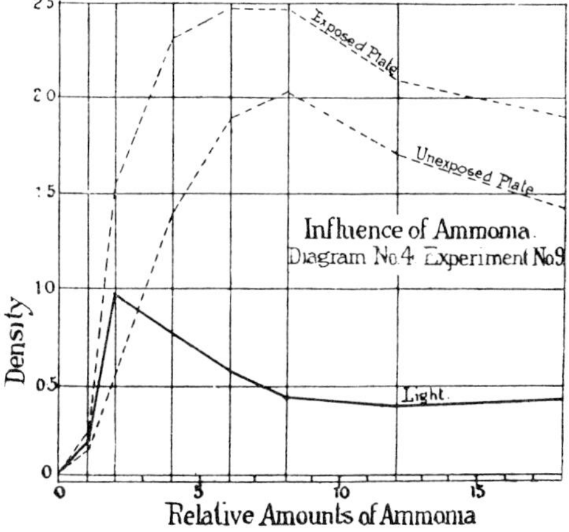


100 c.c. of dilute ammonia containing—

| | | | | |
|---|---|---|---|---|
| 1·105 grms. | NH$_3$ dissolve | 0·0376 | AgBr. | |
| ·555 | ,, | ,, | 0·0206 | ,, |
| ·162 | ,, | ,, | 0·0100 | ,, |
| ·0897 | ,, | ,, | 0·0052 | ,, |

The last two solutions represent the extreme concentrations usually employed by photographers for development.

If to any of these solutions of silver bromide in ammonia, bromide of ammonium be added, an immediate precipitate of bromide of silver is the result.   The so-called accelerating action of ammonia, and the retarding action of ammonium bromide, are probably due entirely to this solvent action of the one and the anti-solvent action of the other of these two reagents.   The rapid production of fog when ammonia is increased is due to the fact that when pyrogallol solution is added to an ammoniacal solution of bromide of silver, the silver in solution is precipitated immediately in the metallic state.

The following experiments show the influence of—

*Variation of Ammonium Bromide.*

[2] *Experiment* 10.—Plate : " Wratten Ord."   Exposure (?).

Developed for 4 minutes, 100 c.c. $= \begin{cases} 0 \cdot 123 \text{ NH}_3. \\ 0 \cdot 375 \text{ Pyro.} \end{cases}$

| Ammonium bromide, grms. in 100 c.c. | 0·00 | 0·10 | 0·20 | 0·40 | 0·80 | 1·28 |
|---|---|---|---|---|---|---|
| Relative amount | 0 | 1 | 2 | 4 | 8 | 12·8 |
| Density | 1·81 | 1·73 | 1·61 | 1·43 | 0·34 | 0·00 |

[1] D.N.—A., p. 124.     [2] H.N.—A., p. 98.   H.N.—J., p. 3.

[1] *Experiment* II.—Plate : " Wratten Ord."   Exposure $= 40$ C.M.S.

Developed 4 minutes in 100 c.c. $= \begin{cases} 0 \cdot 162 \ NH_3 \\ 0 \cdot 342 \ Pyro. \end{cases}$ and various amounts of bromide.   See Diagram No. 5.

| | | | | | | |
|---|---|---|---|---|---|---|
| Ammonium bromide  ..  .. | ·057 | ·114 | ·228 | ·457 | ·918 | 1·828 |
| Relative amount  ..  .. | 1 | 2 | 4 | 8 | 16 | 32 |
| Density exposed plate  .. | 1·450 | 1·335 | 1·235 | 1·025 | ·685 | ·120 |
| Density unexposed plate  .. | ·560 | ·455 | ·315 | ·255 | ·130 | ·090 |
| Density due to light  ..  .. | ·890 | ·880 | ·920 | ·770 | ·555 | ·030 |

It is clear that development in both experiments was entirely prevented in these four minutes when the amount of bromide was about ten times that of ammonia present.

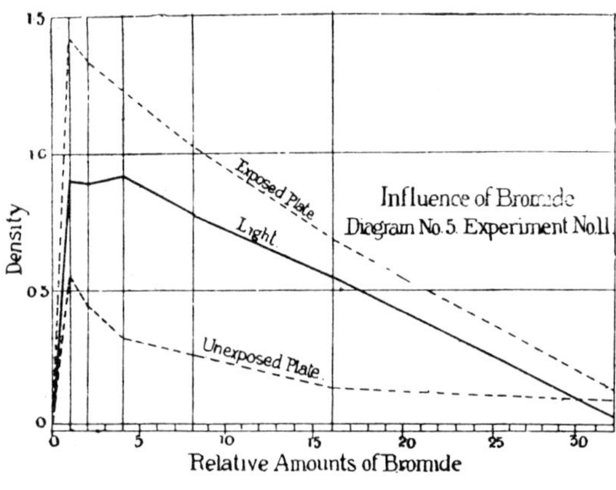


It also appears from our experiments that a rational developer would consist of a decinormal solution of ammonia, containing so much pyrogallol and ammonium bromide as would correspond with the formula—

$$C_6H_3(NH_4O)_3 + NH_4Br.$$

We have represented many of these results in the form of diagrams.  It will be interesting just to point to Diagrams Nos. I, 3 and 4, to show the great amount of action which the alkaline developer may have on the bromide of silver, although it has never been exposed.

This disagreeable property is common to all alkaline developers, and it renders them unsuitable for scientific investigations.  In all our important work we use exclusively the ferrous oxalate developer, for the reason that it attacks unexposed bromide of silver so slowly, that within one hour and even more no appreciable density can be developed upon a really good plate.  Nor does its action vary much with its composition.  The addition or omission of bromide from the constitution of this developer does not seem to have any great influence, and a greater or less concentration of the reagents within considerable limits does not affect its action ;  indeed, we have not found any variation to arise from alterations in its composition, excepting the length of time needed for completion of development.

[1] D.N.—O., p. 30.

The following table shows how the density of an exposed plate grows as the time of development is prolonged from five minutes to one hour :—

[1] *Experiment* 12.—Ferrous Oxalate.

| Time. | Density exclusive of fog. | | | | |
| --- | --- | --- | --- | --- | --- |
| | I. | II. | III. | IV. | V. |
| Minutes. | | | | | |
| 5 | ·365 | ·350 | — | — | ·215 |
| 10 | ·525 | ·460 | — | — | ·305 |
| 15 | ·615 | ·550 | ·795 | ·570 | ·410 |
| 20 | ·615 | ·575 | — | — | ·420 |
| 25 | ·700 | ·650 | — | — | — |
| 30 | ·700 | ·660 | ·860 | ·670 | ·450 |
| 45 | — | — | 1·000 | ·715 | ·515 |
| 60 | — | — | — | ·740 | — |

Columns I and II are the results obtained upon the same plate, one (I) portion of the strips developed in a developer consisting of four parts of a saturated solution of potassium oxalate, mixed with one part of a saturated solution of ferrous sulphate, the other (II) portion of the strips developed in the same developer diluted with an equal volume of water. Columns III and IV represent other experiments, the plates being developed with the saturated solution. Whilst I to IV were developed with a small amount of bromide of potassium added to the developer, No. V was developed without bromide. In not one instance did the density of the unexposed portions of the plate amount to more than 0·098, which is the density due to clear glass and gelatin. That ferrous oxalate does not, however used, attack silver bromide which has not been exposed to light is a most valuable and characteristic property of this developer.

An important result of this series of experiments is that the density reached is dependent upon the time of development as well as upon the exposure of the plate. The time it takes to reach a given density varies much with the gelatin employed in making the emulsion and the age of the plate. But with each plate it obeys a certain law, which is more or less clearly visible in every one of the five experiments. The density grows rapidly at first, its growth becoming slower as time advances, and finally tends to a limit. Each experiment is, taken by itself, liable to many errors ; but by reducing every experiment to the densities obtained in No. IV, in simple proportion, the following tabulated series of numbers is obtained :—The columns marked I,

[1] D.N.—F., p. 21.

II, &c., are the reduced densities of the corresponding columns of Experiment 12. The column marked " Mean " shows the arithmetical mean for any period of development obtained from the five series. The column " Calculated " is obtained by means of a formula based upon the idea that the number of particles of bromide of silver affected by the light is greatest in the front layer of the film and decreases in geometrical progression as each succeeding layer of the film is reached, an idea which will be better appreciated when we have explained the action of the light upon the film. This idea expressed algebraically leads to the formula—

$$D_t = D (1 - a^t),$$

where $D_t$ is the density after $t$ minutes development, D the limit of density reached by very prolonged development, and $t$ the time of development, $a$ is a fraction depending upon the nature of the film, concentration of developer, temperature, &c. The constants for the series of figures below are D = 0·720, $a = 0·9015$.[1]

| Time. | Recalculated —Densities. | | | | | | |
|---|---|---|---|---|---|---|---|
| | I. | II. | III. | IV. | V. | Mean. | Calculated. |
| Min. | | | | | | | |
| 5 | ·349 | ·350 | — | — | ·298 | ·332 | ·290 |
| 10 | ·502 | ·460 | — | — | ·423 | ·462 | ·464 |
| 15 | ·588 | ·550 | ·569 | ·570 | ·569 | ·569 | ·568 |
| 20 | ·588 | ·575 | — | — | ·583 | ·582 | ·628 |
| 25 | ·670 | ·650 | — | — | — | ·660 | ·665 |
| 30 | ·670 | ·660 | ·615 | ·670 | ·625 | ·645 | ·687 |
| 45 | — | — | ·715 | ·715 | ·715 | ·715 | ·713 |
| 60 | — | — | — | ·740 | — | ·740 | ·719 |

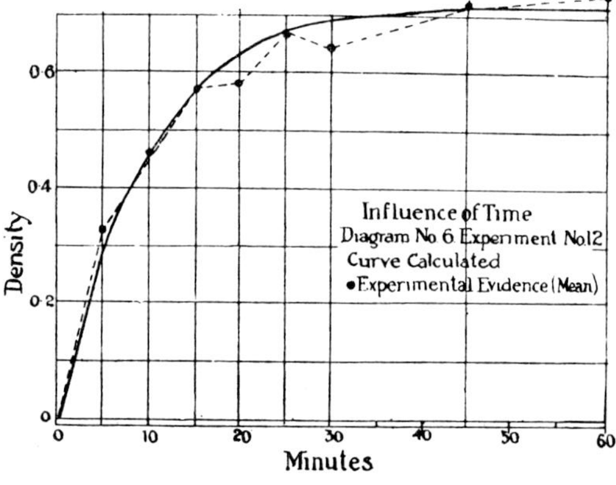


The relation of the calculated figures to the experimental data is best seen in Diagram No. 6.

A very important conclusion can be shown to proceed from the formula representing the course of development.

If on any one plate two exposures are given, one of which would ultimately yield density $D_1$ and the other $D_2$, and if this plate

[1] H. MSS., No. 17.

were developed for a time $t$, then two densities, $d_1$ and $d_2$, would result such that :—

$$d_1 = D_1 (1 - a^t)$$
$$d_2 = D_2 (1 - a^t)$$

and it will be seen that, on dividing these equations—

$$\frac{d_1}{d_2} = \frac{D_1}{D_2}$$

the resulting ratio is independent of the time of development, and is equal to the ratio of the ultimate densities which would be reached, so that the gradation[1] of negatives appears to be independent of the time of development.


## IV.—GRADATION.

The above experiments have shown that with a well-balanced developer there is a limit to density, which depends upon the action of the light, and that, so far, the only control the photographer has lies in deciding whether he will reach that limit or not.

It also became evident that if two different densities be developed upon the same plate to their extreme limits, the ratio existing between these limits must depend solely upon the action of the light. The question we have now to consider is whether it is possible by any modification of development to influence this ratio, and whether this same ratio exists at all stages of development.

In making these experiments the source of light we have adopted is a standard candle placed at 1 metre distance from the plate. We then produce a number of gradations upon the plate by exposing different portions of it to the light for different periods of time, always leaving one portion of the plate unexposed.

In order to show that the length of time of development does not affect the ratio of densities among themselves, but increases every density by proportional amounts, we give the following experiments, made with various plates, ferrous oxalate being the developer used. The table show the densities obtained, their ratio among themselves, and the ratios of the two corresponding densities obtained by long and short development.

All densities are given exclusive of fog (the density of unexposed plate bring subtracted from density of exposed plate).

---

[1] " Gradation " here means the ratio of the densities.

*Experiment* 13.—Gradations.  Ferrous Oxalate.

| Plate used. | Exposure, C.M.S. | Short development, 4 minutes. | | Long development, 12 minutes. | | Ratio $\dfrac{D_2}{D_1}$ | Remarks. |
|---|---|---|---|---|---|---|---|
| | | Density $D_1$. | Ratio. | Density $D_2$. | Ratio. | | |
| Ilford Red Label. (1.) | 10 | ·775 | 1·0 | 1·260 | 1·0 | 1·63 | Greatest error, ± 2·4 per cent. |
| | 20 | 1·000 | 1·29 | 1·660 | 1·31 | 1·66 | |
| | 40 | 1·180 | 1·52 | 1·96 | 1·55 | 1·66 | |
| | 80 | 1·250 | 1·61 | 2·08 | 1·65 | 1·60 | |
| | | | | Mean .. .. | | 1·64 | |
| Wratten's Drop Shutter. (2.) | 10 | 1·17 | 1·0 | 1·74 | 1·0 | 1·50 | Greatest error, ± 3·4 per cent. |
| | 20 | 1·67 | 1·42 | 2·37 | 1·36 | 1·42 | |
| | 40 | 2·06 | 1·76 | 2·91 | 1·67 | 1·41 | |
| | 80 | 2·26 | 1·93 | 3·33 | 1·91 | 1·47 | |
| | | | | Mean .. .. | | 1·45 | |
| " United Kingdom." (3.) | 10 | ·160 | 1·0 | ·275 | 1·0 | 1·70 | Greatest error, ± 5 per cent. |
| | 20 | ·313 | 1·95 | ·485 | 1·76 | 1·55 | |
| | 40 | ·518 | 3·23 | ·830 | 3·01 | 1·60 | |
| | 80 | ·703 | 4·39 | 1·145 | 4·14 | 1·63 | |
| | | | | Mean .. .. | | 1·62 | |

The greatest errors are comprised within those limits within which our method of measuring densities is only reliable.

The results clearly show that the ratio of densities is given by the light alone, and is not affected by the time of development, a fact quite in accordance with the conclusions previously arrived at.

This ratio, we find, is altogether unalterable.  No modifications we have made in developers or in development has ever seriously disturbed this ratio of the densities.  We quote the following few experiments in support of this statement.

[2] *Experiment* 14.—The plate, a " Manchester Slow," having received three different exposures, was cut into four portions ; two were developed with

[1] D.N.—O., p. 2.  H.N.—I., p. 1.    [2] D.N.—O., p. 21.  H.N.—I., pp. 1 and 2.

hydroquinone and two with eikonogen for different lengths of time. The densities are given exclusive of fog, which, with both developers, was very considerable :—

| Developer. | Exposure, C.M.S. | Short develop. | | Long develop. | | Ratio $\dfrac{D_2}{D_1}$. | Remarks. |
|---|---|---|---|---|---|---|---|
| | | Density $D_1$. | Ratio. | Density $D_2$. | Ratio. | | |
| Hydro-quinone. | 10 | ·485 | 1·0 | ·785 | 1·0 | 1·61 | Short time = 2·5 m. Long time = 7·5 m. Mean ratio, 1·55. Greatest error, 4 per cent. |
| | 20 | ·875 | 1·80 | 1·385 | 1·76 | 1·58 | |
| | 40 | 1·450 | 3·0 | 2·120 | 2·70 | 1·47 | |
| Eikonogen. | 10 | ·310 | 1·0 | ·580 | 1·0 | 1·87 | Short time = 4 m. Long time = 12 m. Mean ratio, 1·79. Greatest error, 4·4 per cent. |
| | 20 | ·560 | 1·81 | ·980 | 1·7 | 1·75 | |
| | 40 | ·905 | 2·92 | 1·600 | 2·76 | 1·76 | |

[1] *Experiment* 15 shows that the same result is obtained with pyrogallol development. Plate used : " Manchester Slow." Densities exclusive of fog :—

| Exposure, C.M.S. | Developed, 3 minutes. Ammonia added at once. | | Developed, 18 minutes. Ammonia added in six doses every 3 minutes. | | Ratio $\dfrac{D_2}{D_1}$ | Remarks. |
|---|---|---|---|---|---|---|
| | Density $D_1$. | Ratio. | Density $D_2$. | Ratio. | | |
| 10 | ·385 | 1·0 | ·420 | 1·0 | 1·09 | Mean ratio, 1·15. |
| 20 | ·770 | 2·0 | ·850 | 2·0 | 1·10 | Greatest error, 5 per cent. |
| 40 | 1·095 | 2·84 | 1·315 | 3·1 | 1·19 | |
| 80 | 1·455 | 3·7 | 1·765 | 4·0 | 1·21 | |

[2] *Experiment* 16 is important because it contradicts emphatically the belief that gradations of an over-exposed negative can be altered by using greater amounts of bromide. Plate : " Manchester Slow."

[1] D.N.—O., p. 20.  H N.—I., p. 2.  [2] D.N.—O., p. 23.

| Exposure, C.M.S. | Developed, 4 minutes. 100 c.c. = 0·22 NH$_4$Br. | | Developed, 12 minutes. 100 c.c. = 0·66 g. NH$_4$Br. | | Ratio $\dfrac{D_2}{D_1}$ | Remarks. |
|---|---|---|---|---|---|---|
| | Density D$_1$. | Ratio. | Density D$_2$. | Ratio. | | |
| 10 | ·440 | 1·0 | ·485 | 1·0 | 1·10 | Mean ratio, 1·15. |
| 20 | ·840 | 1·91 | ·965 | 1·98 | 1·15 | Greatest error, 4·3 per cent. |
| 40 | 1·200 | 2·73 | 1·440 | 2·97 | 1·20 | |
| 80 | 1·625 | 3·70 | 1·900 | 3·90 | 1·16 | |

*Experiment* 17.—For this experiment a " Wratten Ordinary " plate received four different exposures. It was then cut into four portions, and each portion was developed with a different developer. The result is extremely interesting and important, since it shows that the ratio between the various densities is identically the same whatever developer is employed, except in the case of eikonogen, in which the ratios are a little different. We shall recur to this difference in another place.

TIME OF DEVELOPMENT DIFFERENT FOR EACH DEVELOPER.[1]

| Ex-posure. | Ferrous oxalate. | | Pyrogallol. | | Hydroquinone. | | Eikonogen. | |
|---|---|---|---|---|---|---|---|---|
| | Density. | Ratio. | Density. | Ratio. | Density. | Ratio. | Density. | Ratio. |
| C.M.S. | | | | | | | | |
| 10 | ·310 | 1·0 | ·320 | 1·0 | ·410 | 1·0 | ·300 | 1·0 |
| 20 | ·535 | 1·7 | ·550 | 1·7 | ·695 | 1·7 | ·470 | 1·6 |
| 40 | ·810 | 2·6 | ·805 | 2·5 | 1·000 | 2·4 | ·645 | 2·2 |
| 80 | 1·080 | 3·5 | 1·005 | 3·1 | 1·400 | 3·4 | ·820 | 2·7 |

These experiments all confirm the statement that the gradations of a negative, as expressed by the ratios of the densities, are independent of time of development, cannot be affected by alterations in the composition of the developers, and are almost identically the same whatever developer is employed. We are thus driven to the conclusion that the photographer has no control over the gradations of the negative, the ratios of the amount of silver deposited on the film being solely dependent upon the exposure. The photo-

[1] D.N.—O., p. 14 ; H.N.—K., p. 25.

grapher has the power to increase the total density by prolonged development, but by no means at his disposal can he alter the ratios existing between the amounts of silver reduced in the various parts of the negative. They are regulated entirely by the exposure.

These ratios are not even altered by intensification after development, as is shown by the following results :—

### INTENSIFICATION.

[1]*Experiment* 18.—Plate " Wratten Ordinary," exposed and developed with ferrous oxalate, measured and afterwards intensified and measured again :—

| Exposure. | Before intensification. | | After intensification. | | $\dfrac{D_2}{D_1}.$ |
|---|---|---|---|---|---|
| | Density $D_1$. | Ratio. | Density $D_2$. | Ratio. | |
| 10 | ·31 | 1·0 | ·60 | 1·0 | 1·93 |
| 14 | ·50 | 1·61 | ·91 | 1·5 | 1·82 |
| 20·5 | ·67 | 2·16 | 1·30 | 2·16 | 1·94 |
| 29·3 | ·86 | 2·77 | 1·71 | 2·85 | 1·98 |
| 41·9 | 1·03 | 3·32 | 2·15 | 3·5 | 2·08 |
| 60 | 1·30 | 4·19 | 2·56 | 4·2 | 1·96 |
| | | | | Mean ... | 1·95 |

It will be seen that the process of intensification has almost exactly doubled the amount of silver[2] on the plate. Almost the same result was found in the following experiment :—

[3] *Experiment* 19.—Similar to last experiment.

| Exposure. | Before intensification. | | After intensification. | | Ratio $\dfrac{D_2}{D_1}.$ |
|---|---|---|---|---|---|
| | Density $D_1$. | Ratio. | Density $D_2$. | Ratio. | |
| 10 | ·260 | 1·0 | ·475 | 1·0 | 1·82 |
| 20 | ·460 | 1·8 | ·850 | 1·8 | 1·85 |
| 40 | ·700 | 2·7 | 1·270 | 2·6 | 1·81 |
| 80 | ·950 | 3·6 | 1·700 | 3·6 | 1·79 |
| | | | | Mean .. | 1·82 |

[1] H.N.—A., p. 143.  H.N.—B., p. 8.

[2] This should be " density," not "silver."  *See* Corr. Hurter—Chapman Jones, October, 1890.  [3] D.N.—O., p. 22.

In this case intensification did not quite, but very nearly, double the amount of *silver*[1] in each density, but the ratio existing between the several gradations is, again, not affected at all.

We see, therefore, that whatever may have been the mode of development employed, and whether intensified or not, the ratios of densities are characteristic of the action of the light, and can be alone relied on in investigations respecting the action of the light on the sensitive film.

### REDUCTION.

There is only one process known to us, so far, which will totally alter the ratios existing between the deposits of silver on a negative, viz., the process of reduction, that process consisting in immersing the developed plate into a solution of potassium ferricyanide and sodium thiosulphate (hyposulphite). This process so alters the ratios that photographers ought to use it very cautiously.

[2] *Experiment* 20.—Plate exposed, measured, and reduced by immersion in potassium ferricyanide and sodium thiosulphate :—

| Exposure. | Before reduction. | | After reduction. | | Ratio $\dfrac{D_1}{D_2}$. |
|---|---|---|---|---|---|
| | Density $D_1$. | Ratio. | Density $D_2$. | Ratio. | |
| 10 | ·410 | 1·0 | ·020 | 1·0 | 20·5 |
| 20 | ·655 | 1·6 | ·130 | 6·5 | 5·0 |
| 40 | 1·010 | 2·46 | ·365 | 18·2 | 2·7 |
| 80 | 1·450 | 3·5 | ·680 | 34·0 | 2·1 |

### V.—ACTION OF LIGHT ON SENSITIVE FILM.

Our investigations have not only revealed the fact that one single density taken by itself is not characteristic of the exposure which the sensitive film received, since the density may be partially due to "fog," or may not be developed to its extreme limit, but the experiments have also clearly shown that the ratio of two densities, exclusive of fog, is a function of the action of the light on the plate. It will be noticed that in all these experiments the exposures given varied between 10 seconds and 80 seconds, and the source of light was always a standard candle placed exactly one metre off the plate. If we tabulate the ratios found between the 10 seconds and 80 seconds

---

[1] Should be "density."  Corr. Hurter—Chapman Jones, Oct., 1890.  [2] D.N.—G., p. 22.

exposures in these experiments, we see at once that the ratio, though constant for one particular plate, is very different for different plates.

| Name of plate. | Ratios of densities for | | Experiment No. |
| | Exposures $\frac{40''}{10''} = 4.$ | Exposures $\frac{80''}{10''} = 8.$ | |
|---|---|---|---|
| Ilford " Red Label "  .. | 1·53 | 1·63 | 13 |
| Wratten " Dropshutter "  .. | 1·71 | 1·92 | 13 |
| " United Kingdom "   .. | 3·12 | 4·27 | 13 |
| " Manchester Slow "  .. | 2·97 | 3·82 | 15 |
| Do.  ..  .. | 2·85 | 3·80 | 16 |
| Do.  ..  .. | 2·84 | — | 14 |
| Own make ...  ...  ... | Batch A  ..  ..Exposures $\frac{160''}{20''}$ .. | 8·00 | |
| | „ A  ..  ..  „ $\frac{240''}{30''}$ .. | 5·30 | |
| | „ A  ..  ..  „ $\frac{1440''}{180''}$ .. | 3·00 | |

The ratio is for the same exposures, smaller for rapid plates than for slow plates, but even with the same plate the ratio between two densities varies for exposures which bear the same ratio to each other, but are different in absolute value, as is seen from the experiments given in the above table, and made with plates prepared by ourselves.

It is certain, therefore, that the ratio between two densities depends not only on the ratio of the exposures, but also on the sensitiveness of the plate and the absolute values of the exposures. The following investigations were made to discover the connection existing between exposure, sensitiveness and density produced :—

*Unit of Exposure.*—For these investigations it was necessary to adopt a standard unit of exposure. As unit of light we have chosen the intensity of a standard candle at one metre distance, and as unit of time the second, so that our unit of exposure is the product of the intensity of the standard candle at one metre distance and the second, and we call this unit of exposure one " candlemetre-second." We find for experimental purposes, with plates of average speed, it is an excellent unit, easily procured, and of sufficient constancy to permit of satisfactory repetitions of experiments. There are a few precautions necessary to ensure uniform results. The flame of the candle cannot be relied on until it has settled to a height of nearly 45 mm., measured from the top of the spermaceti to the top of the flame, as shown in Fig. 4. The candle must be protected against draughts, and this is best done by placing it within a black box having one side open.　This also prevents the illumination of bright objects on the working table and consequent reflections.　The candle should be extinguished by an extinguisher and kept covered up while not in use.

As regards measuring time of exposures, we use a chronograph watch, or a metronome for short exposures, but we find that errors of exposure become too great if less than 10 seconds are measured.　If we wish to give shorter exposures than 10 candlemetre-seconds (C.M.S.) we place the standard candle two metres off, thus reducing its intensity to one-quarter.

It is scarcely necessary to say that we have carefully ascertained that within such limits of exposures as our experiments embrace it is immaterial whether an exposure be made with a light of one-quarter candlemetre for 40 seconds or a light of one candlemetre for 10 seconds.　We have also proved by experiment that, as far as the ratios of densities are concerned, they remain constant, whether the exposure be made with a candle, with a petroleum lamp, or with daylight, so long as the product of intensity of light and time of exposure be the same.　The intensities of such different sources of light cannot, however, for this purpose be compared by the ordinary Bunsen photometer, but must be compared by photographic experiments.　But with careful work even single densities can be reproduced with tolerable accuracy.　For instance, on three separate days we obtained on three separate plates of the same batch by carefully measuring the time, both of exposure and of development, densities 0·750, 0·730 and 0·720 respectively.　Four different standard candles gave upon one plate in 10 seconds the following densities :—0·490, 0·490, 0·500, 0·480.

With the standard candle we investigated, in the first place, the general effect of prolonged exposure on the density, *i.e.*, we ascertained how much silver was reduced by different exposures.

[1]*Experiment* 21.—A " Manchester Slow " plate exposed, developed with ferrous oxalate, and measured, gave :—

| Exposure, C.M.S. | Density. | Difference. | Exposure, C.M.S. | Density. | Difference. |
|---|---|---|---|---|---|
| 0·625 | ·045 | — | 80 | 1·010 | ·255 |
| 1·25 | ·055 | 0·010 | 160 | 1·270 | ·260 |
| 2·50 | ·085 | 0·030 | 320 | 1·555 | ·285 |
| 5·00 | ·175 | ·090 | 640 | 1·885 | ·330 |
| 10·0 | ·250 | ·075 | 1,280 | 2·088 | ·203 |
| 20 | ·460 | ·210 | 2,560 | 2·262 | ·174 |
| 40 | ·755 | ·295 | 5,120 | 2·352 | ·090 |

[1] D.N.—O., pp. 7, 8.　Corr. Driffield—Chapman Jones, 17th July, 1890.

It will be seen that, every time the exposure is doubled, the density increases, at first slowly, then considerably, and (disregarding errors of experiment) from 40 C.M.S. up to 1,280 C.M.S. every time the exposure is doubled, nearly an equal addition to density is the result, the addition to the density being on an average 0·266, but after an exposure of 1,280 C.M.S. further doubling produces less and less increase in density. The first few densities are too small to admit of accurate measuring.

This series of results is represented graphically on diagram No. 7, the exposures being chosen as abscissæ, the densities as ordinates ; from this diagram it will be seen at once how rapidly densities grow at first as exposure is increased, and how slowly at last the densities tend towards a limit.

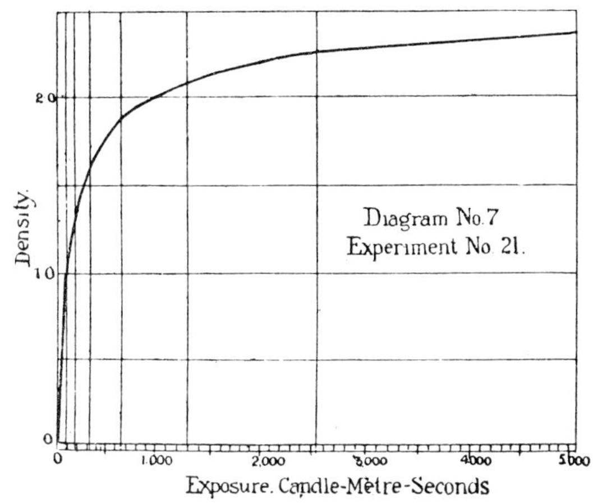


The following series of exposures is carried still further in order to ascertain the character of the curve representing the action of the light on the silver bromide, and to learn, if possible, something of the limit towards which the curve tends.

[1] *Experiment* 22 :—

| Exposures, C.M.S. | Densities. | Difference. | Exposures, C.M.S. | Densities. | Difference. |
|---|---|---|---|---|---|
| 1 | ·060 | — | 1,024 | 2·985 | + 450 |
| 2 | ·160 | + 100 | 2,048 | 3·115 | + 130 |
| 4 | ·340 | + 180 | 4,096 | 3·280 | + 165 |
| 8 | ·500 | + 160 | 8,192 | 3·405 | + 125 |
| 16 | ·715 | + 215 | 16,384 | 3·508 | + 103 |
| 32 | ·940 | + 225 | 32,768 | 3·474 | — 0·034 |
| 64 | 1·345 | + 405 | 65,536 | 3·280 | — 0·194 |
| 128 | 1·875 | + 530 | 131,072 | 3·128 | — 0·162 |
| 256 | 2·290 | + 415 | 262,144 | 2·920 | — 0·208 |
| 512 | 2·535 | + 245 | 524,288 | 2·464 | — 0·456 |

This series of results could not be graphically represented to advantage by choosing exposures as abscissæ since they vary from one candlemetre-

[1] H.N.—B., p. 136.

second to over half a million. But it is evident that prolonged exposure gradually reduces the density attainable after development.

The graphic representation of Experiment 22 on the same scale as Experiment 21 would require a diagram about 500 times as long as Diagram No. 7, and nothing of any value would be learnt from such a diagram.

What we really wish to ascertain is whether it is possible to produce a theoretically perfect negative, such as was defined, and what the connection is between the densities and the exposures.

If in any part of the curve of densities, as represented in Diagram No. 7, the densities were proportional to the logarithm of the exposures, we should discover that portion of the curve if, instead of choosing the exposures as abscissæ, we used the logarithms of the exposures as abscissæ. This is easily done when the exposures progress, as they always do in our experiments, in a geometric series. We have only to mark every new exposure equi-distant from the previous one as abscissæ. In this manner the results of Experiment 22 are plotted in Diagram No. 8.

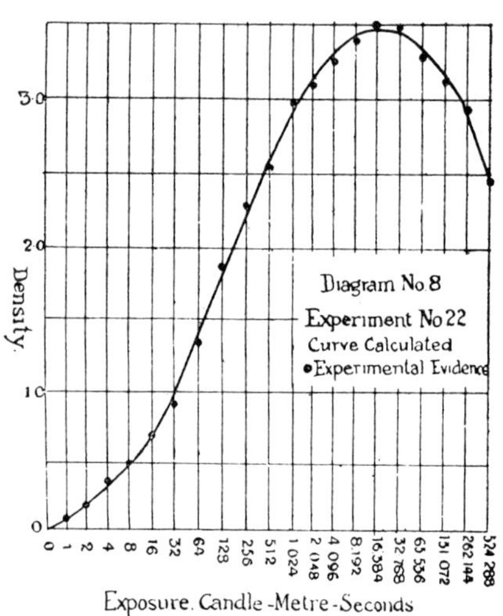


It will be perceived that the curve now consists of four distinct branches. It proceeds from exposure 1 in almost horizontal direction, ascends slowly to exposure 16, from thence it proceeds almost in a straight line to exposure 2,048, when the growth of densities becomes slow. The densities reach their maximum at exposure 16,384, and from thence the curve returns, the densities diminishing slowly with increased exposures.

We accordingly distinguish four different periods of exposures. The first period we term the period of " under-exposure " ; it is comprised in the first curved portion. The second period, that during which the curve is almost a straight line, we call the " period of correct representation." The third period is that during which the curve is again strongly bent as far as its maximum. This is the period of " over-exposure," and the last portion of the curve we term the period of " reversal."

I. *Period of Under-exposure.*—During this period the ratios between two densities are at first accurately equal to the ratio of the corresponding exposures. It is very difficult to study this portion of the curve accurately, owing to the short exposures which it demands, but still more owing to the small densities which this period yields, and which are difficult to measure. By making very slow emulsions we have, however, succeeded in showing clearly that at first the amount of silver reduced is proportional simply to the exposure. Thus, a plate made by ourselves, with pure bromide of silver, gave the following results :—

Exposure, 20 C.M.S.  Density, ·125 or 1.

,,  160  ,,  ,,  1·055 or 8·4.

The ratio between the densities being very nearly 8, the ratio of exposures.

Again, a " United Kingdom " plate gave the following results :—

Exposure, 2·5 C.M.S.  0·160.  Ratio, 1.

,,  5·0  ,,  0·313.  ,,  1·95.

A very slow " Manchester " plate gave the following results :—

1 C.M.S.  0·260.  Ratio, 1.

2  ,,  0·550.  ,,  2·1.

But of course there is no definite point which marks the end of this period and the beginning of the next. But it is from this period that we learn that, for short exposures, *the amount of silver reduced is directly proportional to the exposure.*

*Period of Correct Representation.*—The second period of exposures we have thus named because during this period a plate is capable of giving a negative differing as little as possible from that which, at the beginning, we defined as theoretically perfect. That definition demanded that the densities of the negative should be proportional to the logarithms of the exposures which produced them. It is characteristic of this period that *the densities are proportional to the logarithms of the exposures.* This is shown on Diagram No. 8, where the densities are the ordinates, the logarithms of exposures are abscissæ, and the period of correct representation a straight line. We have measured densities of dozens of plates falling within this period, and we find them all to conform to this very simple linear equation—

$$D = \gamma\, [\log.\ I.t \pm C],$$

D being the density, $\gamma$ a constant depending on time of development, I.t the product of intensity of light and time, *i.e.*, the " exposure," and C a constant depending upon the speed of the plate. As we shall give further detailed proof of this, we will here merely insert one example of a plate the constant

C of which is zero.  It is Plate 2 of Experiment No. 13.  That plate gives the following results with equation :—

$$D = 1{\cdot}75 \times \log. \text{ exposure.}$$

| Exposure. | Density found by experiment. | Density calculated. |
|:---:|:---:|:---:|
| 10 | 1·74 | 1·75 |
| 20 | 2·37 | 2·27 |
| 40 | 2·91 | 2·75 |
| 80 | 3·33 | 3·30 |

Many similar examples will be quoted presently.

We have thus arrived at the answer to the question, Can negatives be produced such as we defined to be theoretically perfect ?  And this answer is, They *can* be produced, but only by so carefully adjusting the time to the intensity of the light that the exposures may fall within that period of correct representation.  No variations whatever in development will correct an under or over-exposure.

*Period of Over-exposure.*—Little need be said about this period.  As the curve tends to become parallel to the axis of abscissæ it is clear that when exposures fall within this period, shadows and high lights will all be represented by densities which are almost equal.  There will be no contrasts.  In the first period of under-exposure the contrasts are too great.  Here they are too small.

*Period of Reversal.*—This period we have named the period of reversal because within this period happens that peculiar phenomenon, the transformation of the negative into the positive, the " solarisation," " reversal," &c.  It is easy to understand how the negative becomes a positive.  Whilst the deep shadows still act upon the plate, increasing the density, the high lights have passed their maximum and their densities grow less and less.  The more the exposure is prolonged the less dense the high lights become, the shadows exceeding them in density.  It is quite easy to observe this phenomenon of reversal with a powerful petroleum lamp or gas burner, or to produce by direct contact printing a secondary negative, instead of a positive, from the original negative, by about 15 to 20 minutes' exposure at 6 in. distance from the light.  When, in the camera, exposure is prolonged, it is well known that a positive is obtained instead of a negative.  It has been stated by Jansen that a secondary negative and a secondary positive can be obtained by prolonging the exposure still further.  We have not, however, been able to verify this statement, and we believe it to be erroneous.  Our investigations show that the density tends to a limit, and a picture produced by prolonged exposure in the camera is gradually lost in a uniform veil of fog, though it is still visible even after three days' exposure.

A " United Kingdom " plate received various prolonged exposures, with the following results :—

| | | | | Difference. |
|---|---|---|---|---|
| 75,000 C.M.S. gave density .. .. | 1·415 | | | |
| | | | | ·304 |
| 150,000 ,, ,, .. .. | 1·111 | | | |
| | | | | ·141 |
| 300,000 ,, ,, .. .. | ·970 | | | |
| | | | | ·045 |
| 600,000 ,, ,, .. .. | ·925 | | | |

A piece of the same plate exposed to direct daylight for 90 minutes (about six million C.M.S.) gave a density 1·200. From this it appears to us that there is an equilibrium established between the action of the refrangible and less refrangible rays.

The period of reversal is, theoretically, exceedingly interesting, and deserves further careful study, but the reversing action is so slow, and requires such enormous exposures, that it does not need to be considered from a practical point of view, and we shall disregard it entirely for the present. The three first periods, that of under-exposure, that of correct representation, and that of over-exposure, are the only practically interesting portions of the curve. We have already stated that, during the first period, the ratio of densities is equal to the ratio of exposures, *i.e.*, the amount of bromide of silver reduced is proportional to the exposure, whilst, during the second period, the density only grows in proportion to the logarithm of the exposure. It almost ceases to grow during the third. Of course, these assertions are only two approximate statements of one single law connecting the densities with the exposures.

All photo-chemical investigations which have hitherto been made have proved that the amount of chemical action is proportional to the " exposure " (*i.e.*, the product of intensity of light and time). The sensitive film of the photographic plate forms no exception to this general law, and we take it as a fundamental truth that the amount of action upon the plate is, at any moment of the exposure, proportional to the energy which the plate receives at that moment. During the first period, when the surface, or chiefly the surface of the film, is acted upon, the results of the investigations have shown this to be true accurately. But when the action of the light upon particles of bromide of silver below the surface has to be considered, the question arises, How much of the light which impinges on the surface really reaches those particles ?

Of the rays of light which impinge upon the surface of the sensitive plate, some are reflected and some pass right through the plate.[1]  If one sensitive plate be exposed to light behind another, it will be found that it also is affected.

The energy of the reflected and transmitted light cannot, obviously, play any part in the molecular work to be done in the film.  It is useless photographically.

The light absorbed in the film is the only light which contributes towards the formation of the " latent image," but not even the whole of the light which is absorbed does useful work.  It can be proved experimentally that a plate which has received such an exposure as to yield maximum density on development absorbs exactly as much light as a plate which has not been exposed at all, yet the light absorbed by a plate already so exposed obviously contributes nothing towards increase of density.

From this it is clear that the light absorbed by a particle of silver bromide, which has already received sufficient energy to bring it into that condition in which it is capable of development, is useless.

It will therefore be evident that, of the light impinging upon the plate, there is only one portion useful, viz., that which is absorbed by unaltered silver bromide, the light reflected, the light transmitted, and the light absorbed by particles of silver bromide already changed, being altogether useless.

The amount of work done at any moment of the exposure is therefore proportional to the amount of energy received by the unaltered silver bromide only.[2]

It is very easy to state this proposition mathematically, and thus find the law which connects the densities with the exposures.

If the intensity of the light (with respect to chemically active rays) is I, and the fraction of the light reflected from the surface of the film is $a$, then the amount $(1 - a)$ I enters the film.  If the film contains, at the moment we are considering, $x$ particles of silver bromide per unit area, which are already changed, then the transparency of the plate with respect to the changed particles is $e^{-kx}$, i.e., this is the amount of light which passes the particles already changed.  If from this amount we deduct the amount of light which passes *all* the particles of silver, changed or unchanged, the difference represents the amount of light absorbed by the silver bromide not yet affected. Now the light which passes all the particles of silver, if there are $a$ of them per unit area, will be measured by the transparency of the plate, viz., $e^{-ka}$. Deducting this from $e^{-kx}$ and multiplying the difference with the total amount of light entering the film will give the mathematical expression for

[1] H.N.—B., pp. 43, 53, 59.

[2] H.N.—D., p. 83, and Dr. Allen's paper in this vol., p. 34.

the amount of light which, at the moment we are considering, can do useful work. This amount is : $(1 - a) I (\epsilon^{-kx} - \epsilon^{-ka})$. If this expression is multiplied by the short time of exposure $dt$, it will represent the amount of useful energy conveyed to the plate during that time.

Suppose it requires an amount of energy $e$ to change one particle of silver bromide into the condition capable of development, then the number of particles $dx$ so changed during the time $dt$ will be—

$$(1.)\ dx = \frac{1}{e}\ (1 - a)\ [\epsilon^{-kx} - \epsilon^{-ka}]\ dt.$$

This is the complete mathematical expression of the idea that it is only that portion of the light which is absorbed by unchanged silver bromide which contributes to the growth of density.[1]

By integration of equation (1), and by substitution of the symbol O for $e^{+ka}$, we find that the density of the "latent image" (before development) is—

$$D = \log_{\cdot \epsilon} [O - (O - 1)\ \beta^{k(1-a)\frac{It}{e}}]$$

where $\beta$ is a fraction, the hyperbolic logarithm of which is $-\frac{1}{o}$, O is simply the opacity of the plate to the chemically active rays before exposure.

In this derivation of the connection between the density D and the exposure $It$, two assumptions have been silently made which need explanation. The coefficient of absorption $k$ has been assumed to have the same value both for the altered and the unaltered silver bromide. We have, however, experimentally ascertained that this is a fact. It can be easily proved photographically. If, behind a plate, one portion of which has been already exposed so as to yield maximum density, the other portion having received no exposure at all, a very sensitive plate is placed, and if now a suitable exposure be given, it will, on development, be found that the shielded plate has uniform density all over. This proves that $k$ is the same as regards blue light both for the altered and for the unaltered silver bromide.

The second assumption is that the sensitive film obeys the laws of absorption, as explained at the beginning of this paper. It would prolong this paper very much if we had to furnish here the proof that, as far as the chemically active rays are concerned, and as far as the light *not reflected* is concerned, the law of absorption does hold good. Suffice it to state that, to the more refrangible portion of the spectrum, the sensitive film is as black as Indian ink is to white light.

[1] H.N.—D., p. 83.

To recur to our formula, it requires still more alteration to complete it. The density as given by the formula is the maximum density, and expressed as regards the behaviour of white altered silver bromide towards the blue rays of the spectrum.  As we know already, we can develop of that maximum density as much as we please, and the change from white to black during development makes the density more or less equal for all rays of the spectrum. We therefore simply multiply the equation by a constant to express this change, and we call this the development constant.  The formula then stands—

$$D = \gamma \log._\epsilon [O - (O - 1) \beta^{k\,(1-a)\frac{It}{e}} ] .$$

$k$, $a$ and $e$ represent physical and chemical properties of the bromide or silver, which together constitute its sensitiveness to light.  We combine them into one single symbol, and write $i = \dfrac{e}{k(1-a)}$ , so that we have finally—

$$(2.)\ D = \gamma \log._\epsilon [O - (O - 1) \beta^{\frac{It}{i}} ].$$

This formula[1] represents the density after development as a function of the opacity of the unexposed plate, of the exposure, and of the symbol $i$, which is a measure of the slowness of the silver bromide, and which symbol we shall call the " inertia " of the silver bromide.

To show the approximation of densities calculated by this formula to those obtained in Experiments 21 and 22, we append here the calculated and the observed densities.  For this purpose the plates used for Experiments Nos. 21 and 22 were investigated for their opacity to the rays of the spectrum from F to H, and this opacity was found to be 332.

Experiment 21 compared with theory.

| Exposure, C.M.S. | Density found. | Density calculated. | Exposure, C.M.S. | Density found. | Density calculated. |
|---|---|---|---|---|---|
| 0·625 | ·045 | ·035 | 80 | 1·010 | ·992 |
| 1·25 | ·055 | ·065 | 160 | 1·270 | 1·272 |
| 2·5 | ·085 | ·121 | 320 | 1·555 | 1·531 |
| 5 | ·175 | ·214 | 640 | 1·885 | 1·780 |
| 10 | ·250 | ·339 | 1,280 | 2·088 | 2·022 |
| 20 | ·460 | ·520 | 2,560 | 2·262 | 2·218 |
| 40 | ·755 | ·743 | 5,120 | 2·352 | 2·352 |

[1] H.N.—B., pp. 155, 159.

*Experiment* 22 compared with theory.

| Exposure. C.M.S. | Density found. | Density calculated. | Exposure. C.M.S. | Density found. | Density calculated. |
|---|---|---|---|---|---|
| I | ·060 | ·092 | 128 | 1·875 | 1·800 |
| 2 | ·160 | ·172 | 256 | 2·290 | 2·165 |
| 4 | ·340 | ·302 | 512 | 2·535 | 2·518 |
| 8 | ·500 | ·482 | 1,024 | 2·985 | 2·860 |
| 16 | ·715 | ·735 | 2,048 | 3·115 | 3·138 |
| 32 | ·940 | 1·050 | 4,096 | 3·280 | 3·328 |
| 64 | 1·345 | 1·405 | 8,192 | 3·405 | 3·405 |

On examining the " calculated " series of results it will be found that they have exactly the same characteristic properties as those we pointed out as appertaining to the three periods. For the short exposures the calculated densities are nearly proportional to the exposures, whilst from 16 C.M.S. to 1,200 C.M.S. the densities increase by nearly equal amounts for every successive double exposure, and differ very little from densities calculated by the simple formula—

$$D = \gamma \, [\log. \, It - C].$$

In order that this may be very clearly seen we append another table comparing in column 1 the densities obtained by the correct formula (2), with densities in column 2 calculated by the approximate formula—

$$D = 1 \cdot 176 \, [\log. \, It - 0 \cdot 579].$$

| Exposure, C.M.S. | (1) Density by correct formula. | (2) Density by approximation. | Exposure, C.M.S. | (1) Density by correct formula. | (2) Density by approximation. |
|---|---|---|---|---|---|
| 16 | ·735 | ·735 | 256 | 2·165 | 2·151 |
| 32 | 1·050 | 1·089 | 512 | 2·518 | 2·505 |
| 64 | 1·405 | 1·443 | 1,024 | 2·860 | 2·859 |
| 128 | 1·800 | 1·797 | 2,048 | 3·138 | 3·213 |

We think it necessary to draw attention to this agreement, because the approximate formula is extremely easily applied, whilst the correct formula requires very tedious calculations, and we shall make a very important practical application of such calculations.

Although there is a close general agreement between the experimental results and the numbers calculated by means of the equations, yet in individual cases there are discrepancies. Diagram No. 9 shows the theoretical curves in full lines, the actual observations being indicated by dots. This diagram leaves little doubt that the action of the light on the sensitive film is fairly represented by our equation, and consequently it may be assumed as proved that the action of the light at any moment is proportional to the amount of light absorbed by unaltered silver bromide.

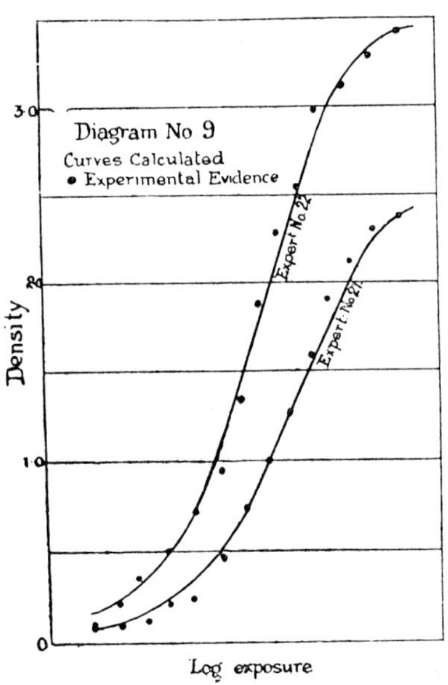


Nevertheless, we felt that more experimental proof was wanted to support our equation, which represents the resulting density as a function of the opacity of the unexposed plate to blue light. When it is remembered that the density of the unexposed plate is proportional to the silver bromide spread over its area, it will be perceived that this statement means, in fact, that the density of the image depends upon the amount of silver on the plate in some way, and this is almost a self-evident proposition.

We prepared sensitive plates of different opacities by spreading on equal areas different amounts of silver bromide. These plates were measured to ascertain their opacity to blue light, and the following results obtained :—

| Plates No. 1. | Amount of silver bromide per 100 sq. cm. | Opacity to blue light. |
| --- | --- | --- |
|  | Grms. |  |
| 1 | 0·016 | 1·738 |
| 2 | 0·031 | 3·00 |
| 3 | 0·062 | 10·0 |
| 4 | 0·124 | 83·0 |

By means of these opacities four curves were calculated, which are represented in Diagram No. 10. To ascertain whether the relative distances between those curves were true, points in each curve belonging to the same exposure (or abscissæ) had to be determined in at least two different portions. For this purpose four plates, one of each opacity, were simultaneously exposed, and two different exposures were given of 30 and 240 C.M.S. respectively. The plates were then developed and the ratios of the densities were taken alone for comparison.

The following results were thus obtained :—

| Exposure. | Plate I. | Plate II. | Plate III. | Plate IV. |
|---|---|---|---|---|
|  | Density. | Density. | Density. | Density. |
| 30 C.M.S. .. .. | ·065 | ·095 | ·260 | ·272 |
| 240 C.M.S. .. .. | ·120 | ·275 | ·700 | ·852 |
| Ratio .. .. .. | 1·84 | 2·89 | 2·69 | 3·31 |

The ratios which are obtained for the theoretical densities, calculated by the equation (2), are the following ones :—

| —— | Plate I. | Plate II. | Plate III. | Plate IV. |
|---|---|---|---|---|
| Ratio .. .. .. | 1·70 | 2·50 | 2·83 | 3·22 |

It will be seen that the theoretical ratios agree as well with the observed ratios as could possibly be expected from so difficult an experiment. In Diagram No. 10 the relative distances of the curves, as calculated from the ratios obtained by the experiment, are marked by dots.

Diagram No. 10 is worthy of some remarks. It will be at once perceived that the more thinly the plates are coated the shorter is that portion of the curve which is a straight line. This means that the period of correct representation is very short, and great contrasts cannot be truly rendered by a thinly-coated plate. It will also be found on closer inspection that the centre of the straight portion is in each curve in a different place, and that the thinner the plate the shorter is the exposure necessary to reach the centre portion. This means that a thinly-coated plate is somewhat faster than a thickly- coated one, though they are made of the same emulsion. A thinly-covered plate, however, appears very much faster than it is in reality. It is incapable of rendering wide contrasts, and

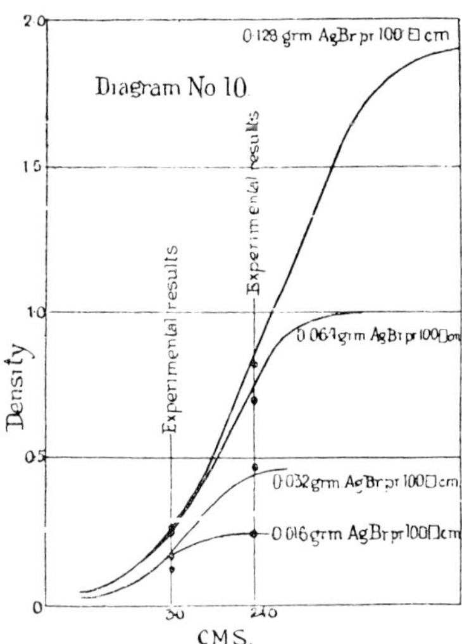

hence the negative always looks flat, and thereby gives to the eye the impression of over-exposure.

We have now learnt the great influence which the opacity of the unexposed plate has on the density of the resultant image, and we must now point out a most important source of error in photographic experiments such as we have described.

If a plate be not perfectly evenly coated, the densities, after development, arising from equal exposures will be different on different parts of that plate. We give here an example of a plate, not a bad one either, on which, in different parts, different exposures were given.   The table shows the densities which the same exposure produced on the one half and on the other half of the plate :—

| Exposure. | I. | II. | Ratio. |
|---|---|---|---|
| | Density. | Density. | |
| 10 | ·275 | ·240 | 1·14 |
| 20 | ·535 | ·480 | 1·12 |
| 40 | ·825 | ·775 | 1·06 |
| 80 | 1·185 | 1·080 | 1·10 |

The errors on this plate amount to from 6 to 14 per cent., owing to unequal thickness of the film.   It is needless to say that in the dark room, in ruby light, such differences in the thickness of the film cannot be observed.   The only remedy for this is to use only very thickly coated plates.   We may here say that for our most important experimental work we used slow plates specially prepared for us by Mr. Chapman, of Manchester, every care being taken to secure a thick and even film.

Thickly-coated plates give also very much greater latitude in exposure. The plates used in experiments 21 and 22 would have given good pictures of subjects with contrasts varying from 1 : 80, though the exposures had varied from 1 : 2, so that an exposure of 10 seconds, or one of 20, would have resulted in but little difference in the negatives, excepting that the one would have been much slower in printing, because generally denser.   Thinly-coated plates, on the other hand, need very accurately-timed exposures.

## VI.—Speed of Sensitive Plates.

We gave two formulæ as the result·of our investigations ; one of them, the approximate one, is the direct result of our experimental work, the other is the mathematical expression of the idea that a certain definite amount of energy is needed to bring a particle of silver bromide into the condition in which it can afterwards be developed, and that it is only to the light absorbed by unaltered silver bromide that increase of density consequent on increased exposure is due.

Whilst the approximate formula is never strictly true, and can be used only for exposures which fall within the period of correct representation, it is extremely simple, and we are about to describe an important application of it, viz., the determination of the speed of the sensitive plate.

The more correct formula cannot be used for practical applications, owing to its complication, but it serves to indicate the limits within which the approximate formula may safely be used.

In the formula[1]—

$$D = \gamma \cdot \log \cdot \left( O - (O - 1)\, \beta^{\frac{It}{i}} \right)$$

we may replace $(O - 1)$ by the symbol O when that represents a large number, that is, when the plate is richly coated with silver bromide. If, in addition, we remember that $\log_\epsilon \beta$ is $-\dfrac{1}{o}$, the equation can be transformed into another viz. :—

$$D = \gamma \cdot \log \cdot \left( \frac{It}{i} \right)$$

which equation holds good only when the numerical value of $\dfrac{It}{i}$ is greater than 1 and less than the opacity O.[2] It is between these two limits only that this equation gives tolerably correct results. Comparing this last equation with the approximation we gave before, it will be seen that the constant C of that approximate formula is the logarithm of $i$, the symbol measuring those properties of the film which together constitute its sensitiveness, and which we termed the inertia of the plate.

Supposing we had two richly-coated plates, with different inertias, $i$ and $i_1$, and we wished to impress the same density upon them by a given intensity of light I. They would require different exposures, and the exposures would have to be such that—

$$\frac{It}{i} = \frac{It}{i_1}$$

or the times would have to be chosen so that—

$$\frac{t_1}{i_1} = \frac{t_0}{i_0}$$

[1] H.N.—B., p. 156.     [2] H.N.—B., pp. 63, 156.

This means that if the values of $i$ are known for different plates, the exposures required to obtain the same results are also known for those plates, if the exposure is known for any one of them.

The determination of the numerical value of the symbol $i$ is therefore an important problem.

Since the density of the image is an abstract number, it follows that the ratio $\dfrac{It}{i}$ is an abstract number also, and that $i$ is therefore an exposure. We termed this symbol the inertia, and it really measures that exposure which will suffice to change a particle of silver bromide into the developable condition. But for its practical application it has another meaning. It measures the least exposure which will just mark the beginning of the period of correct representation.

The speed of the plate is the inverse value ; the longer the exposure needed to bring the plate just to the beginning of the period of correct representation the slower is the plate. Therefore we measure the speed of the plate by the value $\dfrac{1}{i}$.

The method we adopt for measuring the value of $i$ is briefly as follows :— We give to the plate at least two exposures falling within the period of correct representation, and develop.[1] We then measure the densities exclusive of fog. We thus obtain two equations connecting the two densities $D_1$ and $D_2$ with the two known exposures $E_1$ and $E_2$, viz. :—

$$D_1 = \gamma.\log. \frac{E_1}{i} \text{ and } D_2 = \gamma.\log. \frac{E_2}{i}$$

from which we obtain by elimination—

$$\log. i = \frac{D_2 \log. E_1 - D_1 \log. E_2}{D_2 - D_1}$$

and—

$$\gamma = \frac{D_2 - D_1}{\log. E_2 - \log. E_1}$$

The value of $i$ is expressed in candlemetre-seconds, and can be found by reference to ordinary tables of logarithms.

We will now describe our practice. For the determination of the inertia only the central portion of the plate should be used ; the margin should be avoided, as it is liable to be irregular in thickness of film. In order to insure at least two exposures falling within the period of correct representation we give to the plate eight different exposures of 2·5, 5, 10, 20, 40, 80, 160,

---

[1] D.N.—O., p. 13.   H.N.—B., pp. 63, 71.

and 320 C.M.S., leaving a portion of the plate unexposed. We develop this plate with ferrous oxalate, and, after properly washing, fix in a perfectly clean bath of thiosulphate. We then wash and dry spontaneously or by means of alcohol. The length of time for development is judged by the density of the image. We avoid too great density, but develop sufficiently long to obtain a decided deposit for the lower exposures. When all the densities have been measured we subtract from every one of them the density of the fog strip in order to obtain densities " exclusive of fog."

From this series of densities we may calculate the value of $i$. For that purpose we find the differences between the consecutive densities, and we choose from the series those points which give differences most nearly alike. As an example we quote the series of results obtained with the Manchester slow plate of experiment No. 21 :—

| Exposures | | | 2·5″ | 5″ | 10″ | 20″ | 40″ | 80″ | 160″ |
|---|---|---|---|---|---|---|---|---|---|
| Densities | | | ·085 | ·175 | ·250 | ·460 | ·755 | 1·010 | 1·270 |
| Differences | | | | ·09 | ·075 | ·210 | ·295 | ·255 | ·260 |

We should take the results of exposures from 20 C.M.S. to 160 C.M.S., as those falling within the period of correct exposure. Choosing the exposures 20 and 160 for the calculations, we should obtain, in accordance with the formula given—

$$\log. i = \frac{1 \cdot 270 \times \log. 20 - 0 \cdot 460 \times \log. 160}{1 \cdot 270 - 0 \cdot 460}$$

or $\log. i = 0 \cdot 787$, and from an ordinary logarithm table we should find $i = 6 \cdot 12$ candlemetre-seconds.

In another experiment with a plate of the same make the following results were obtained :—

| Exposures | | | 10″ | 20″ | 40″ | 80″ |
|---|---|---|---|---|---|---|
| Densities | | | ·300 | ·590 | ·910 | 1·260 |
| Differences | | | | ·290 | ·320 | ·350 |

Choosing only the 20″ and 80″ points, we have—

$$\log. i = \frac{1 \cdot 260 \times \log. 20 - 0 \cdot 590 \times \log. 80}{1 \cdot 260 \times 0 \cdot 590} = 0 \cdot 771$$

or $i = 5 \cdot 90$ candlemetre-seconds.[1]

It will be seen that these values for the inertia of the " Manchester Slow " plate are almost alike. With faster plates it is not so easy to obtain quite such

[1] Correspondence :—Driffield—Cowan, 25th July, 1892.

concordant values, but they are always sufficiently accurate for practical purposes, for whether an exposure in practice be four or five seconds it will not appreciably alter the resulting negative, so that in the determination of the inertia an error of 10 per cent. is fortunately not of very great consequence, and in most cases two determinations carefully made will not differ more than 10 per cent.

We prefer, however, to obtain the result by a graphic method, by means of which we avoid all calculations and all references to tables of logarithms. We scratch on an ordinary slate a horizontal scale of inertias similar to the scale of an ordinary slide rule, but we repeat the scale four times instead of twice, as in the case of the slide rule. Diagram No. 11 shows this arrangement. We scratch at points 2·5, 5, 10, 20, 40, 80, 160, and 320 of this scale vertical lines (exposure lines), and divide them each into 20 equal parts, marking the highest as density 2·0, the lowest as 0. Having measured the densities we mark them on the scales of the corresponding exposure lines, and draw a straight line through those points which appear to fall most accurately within such a line. It is better to stretch a white thread across these points, as the portion of the line can thus be more easily determined. Where the thread or the straight line intersects the inertia scale we can at once read off the inertia of the plate.

The solutions of the problem of ascertaining the inertia or its inverse the speed of the plate have hitherto been unsatisfactory, and always depends finally upon the judgment of the comparative visibility of letters or numbers printed upon a sensitive plate.

Our method, by referring the speed to a standard candle as unit will enable different operators to obtain almost identical and definite numerical results. Should at any time a better practical unit of light be found, the method is at once applicable with it also. The fact is, we have based our method on the measured effects produced by a given unit of light, excluding the influence of alterations in development, whilst the present method, by means of Warnerke's sensitometer, depends entirely upon development. We could so alter the composition of the developer as to make a rapid plate give most misleading results.

Such a proceeding is impossible with our method.

There is a theoretical possibility that a plate may be rapid to one developer and slow to another, so as to require different exposures according to the developer used. If silver bromide be reduced to metallic silver, 22,700 units of heat must be supplied to replace the heat of combination. Of this amount of heat the developer in the act of development supplies a portion. Ferrous oxalate, for instance, would probably supply 12,900 units, so that the light need only supply the difference, viz., 9,800 units. But if another developer could supply more than 12,900 units, then the light, clearly, need not supply quite so much, and in that case the plate would be faster to one developer than to another.

We have not paid such close attention to this question yet as to enable us to decide it finally, but as far as our experiments have gone we have found very little difference, if any, between the various developers, and we do not feel justified in assigning to the small differences we have observed any great importance.

If a developer could be found which would render a plate materially faster, that developer would strike a serious blow at the hypothesis that the latent image consists of sub-bromide of silver.

We append a number of interesting diagrams representing our graphic method of determining the inertia of a plate.

Diagram No. 11 shows the general arrangement we adopt for finding graphically the value of the inertia. An ordinary " slide rule " furnishes the mode of subdividing the scale (the distances of the numbers being proportional to their logarithms). The two curves are the curves of Wratten and Wainwright " ordinary " and " instantaneous " plates. It will be noticed that the " instantaneous " plate shows, within the given exposures, a portion of the period of over-exposure, whilst the " ordinary " shows a portion of the period of " under-exposure." The inertia of the one is $1\cdot4$, that of the other $5\cdot5$, and in round numbers the one plate is four times as fast as the other.

Diagram No. 12 shows the results of experiment 15 graphically, for the purpose of showing that variations in the mode of development do not influence the determination of the inertia ; the densities of the two modes of development being different, yet the straight lines practically converge to the same point.

Diagram No. 13.—This diagram represents another variation in pyro development, viz., in the amount of bromide (experiment 16). It will be again seen that the values of the inertia are almost identical, in spite of a considerable difference in the composition of the developer and the time of development.

Diagram No. 14 shows four determinations of the inertia of one plate (see experiment 14), two determinations being made with eikonogen and two with hydroquinone. The duration of development being different for each determination, yet the results of all four determinations are practically identical.

Diagram No. 15 shows that the inertia of a plate can be determined after intensification, *but not after reduction.* It is, therefore, better to develop

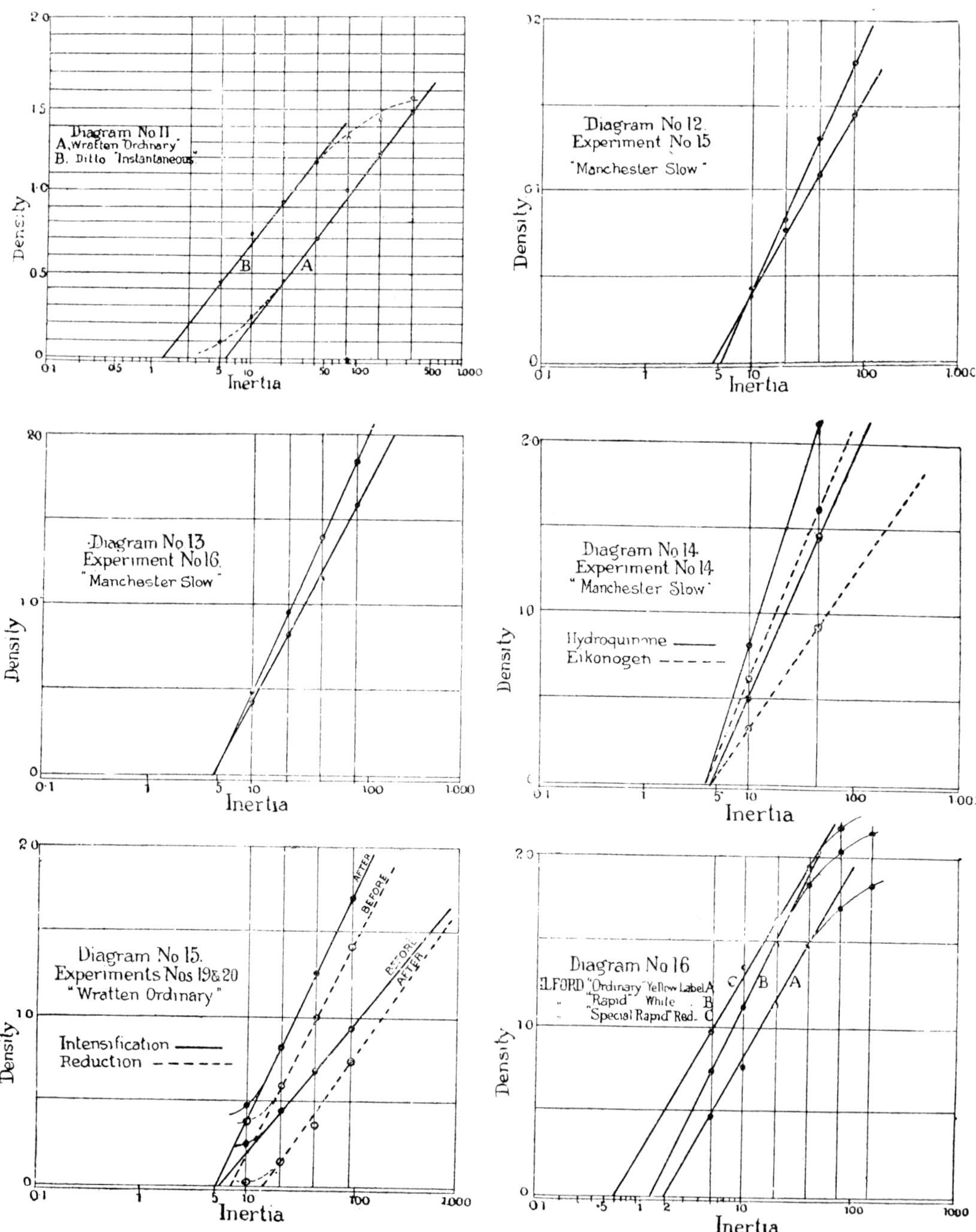
Diagram No II
A. Wratten Ordinary
B. Ditto Instantaneous
Density
B
A
Inertia

Diagram No 12
Experiment No 15
Manchester Slow
Density
Inertia

Diagram No 13
Experiment No 16
Manchester Slow
Density
Inertia

Diagram No 14
Experiment No 14
Manchester Slow
Hydroquinone
Eikonogen
Density
Inertia

Diagram No 15
Experiments Nos 19 & 20
Wratten Ordinary
Intensification
Reduction
AFTER
BEFORE
BEFORE
AFTER
Density
Inertia

Diagram No 16
ILFORD Ordinary Yellow Label A
Rapid White B
Special Rapid Red C
C B A
Density
Inertia

too little rather than too much. We clearly must not resort to reduction, but we may intensify if the trial plates have been under-developed. (Experiments 19 and 20.)

Diagram No. 16 shows the determination of inertia of the Ilford plates, "ordinary," "rapid," and "special rapid" (red label). Their inertias are respectively 2·0, 1·4, and 0·56, and their speeds are relatively as 1 :: 1·41 : 3·5. The "red label" plates are the most rapid plates we have so far investigated, but we found it very difficult to ascertain their true speed in the camera, on account of the difficulty in securing adequate density.

When the inertia of the plate is known, it is possible to time the exposures in the camera so that the densities of the gradations are almost exactly proportional to the logarithms of the light intensities which produced them. By this means negatives can be produced which satisfy very nearly the definition we gave of a theoretically perfect negative. It must be borne in mind, however, that such a negative is not necessarily true to nature. The optical density after development differs from the density of the latent image. If the negative is to be true to nature, a plate must be used which is richly coated, the exposure must be carefully timed, and the development must be carried only so far that the value of the development constant $\gamma$ is numerically equal to 1. Experiments which we have made indicate that for the production of artistic effects on ordinary silver chloride paper, it is necessary to exaggerate the densities, *i.e.*, to prolong the development until $\gamma$ is greater than 1, and nearly reaches the value 2. This requires further investigation; suffice it to have pointed out that what Captain Abney terms "photographic untruth" is not necessarily inherent in photography, since the photographer has it in his power to decide the degree of exaggeration.

The exposure to be given in the camera can be found by means of the actinograph,[1] when the inertia of the plate is known.

The "actinograph speed" of the plate is found by means of the formula $S = 34/i$, where S is the speed and $i$ the inertia in candlemetre-seconds. We find, for instance, the speed of the Ilford plates from their inertia (as shown on Diagram 16) :—

|  | | Speed. |
|---|---|---|
| Ilford "ordinary"  .. .. .. .. | $= \dfrac{34}{2}$ | $= 17$ |
| Ilford "rapid" .. .. .. .. .. | $= \dfrac{34}{1\cdot4}$ | $= 24$ |
| Ilford "special rapid" .. .. .. .. | $= \dfrac{34}{0\cdot56}$ | $= 60$ |

[1] See *J.S.C.I.*, 1890, 370, or the Photographic Societies' Reporter for 30th April, 1889.

This method of referring the  sensitiveness of the plate to the candlemetre-second as unit will, we believe, greatly promote progress both in the preparation of the plates and in their application.   We flatter ourselves that we have supplied one of the greatest needs of plate makers and photographers in general, by enabling them, for the first time, to ascertain accurately the sensitiveness of different plates, and by means of the actinograph to apply this information in practice.

The above is the main practical result which has accrued from our investigations, but, incidentally, we have shown the fallacy of many popular views on the subject of development, and the paramount importance of correct exposure.

From a purely scientific point of view, perhaps, the most interesting result of our labour is the elucidation of the numerical relation between the exposure and its effect on the sensitive film, and the simple explanation of these relations, based upon the optical properties of the unexposed sensitive film.   It would not have been difficult to extend these considerations so as to include in them the reversing action of the less refrangible rays.   This would not, however, have served any practical end at present, and it would have complicated the formulæ very considerably.   We reserve for a future communication this extension of the law which we have discovered.

*Reprinted from the Journal of the Society of Chemical Industry, 31st July, 1890, Vol. IX., page 722.*

# COMMUNICATION ON THE ACCURACY OF THE GREASE-SPOT PHOTOMETER FOR MEASURING THE DENSITY OF PHOTOGRAPHIC PLATES AND A NOTE ON THE SECTOR PHOTOMETER

BY

Captain W. de W. ABNEY, C.B., R.E., D.C.L., F.R.S.

---

The publication of a paper by Messrs. Hurter and Driffield in the *J.S.C.I.*, on " Photo-chemical Investigations and a New Method of Determination of the Sensitiveness of Photographic Plates," has induced me to offer a few criticisms on the subject.

I have two reasons for doing this. One is that I have written a good deal regarding part of it, and the other that some doubt is thrown in the paper on the accuracy of the results I have obtained, owing, it is asserted, to the photometer I use being faulty.

I should have been unwilling to enter into a criticism of the paper now the season is over were it not that it will no doubt be largely quoted at home and abroad as giving an authoritative exposition of the law of density, and that no opportunity of having a say in the matter would occur before November.

We may take the paper as practically divided into four parts :—Definition of terms employed ; instrument for measuring and method of measuring the density of deposit in photographic plates ; methods of producing density ; and a mathematical investigation of the subject.

Under the first heading I may have one or two criticisms to make subsequently—such as on the law of absorption applied to a film in which opaque particles are embedded—but for the present I wish to confine myself to the second division, viz., the instrument and the mode of measuring densities, for, if these are in fault, the measured densities and the application of theory to them will require revision.

To begin with the instrument itself as used by the authors. There is a statement made regarding the method of photometry employed to which I must take exception, and that is that the Bunsen disc is more sensitive than the (Rumford) method of shadows. The leading authorities on photometry in London, viz., the Gàs Referees, have adopted the shadow test, and certainly the measurements made by Mr. Vernon Harcourt are not wanting in delicacy. The well-known drawback to the grease-spot method is the necessity of excluding all reflected light from the grease spot, and when it is recollected that the blackest lampblack reflects more than 2 per cent. of white light, the exclusion of all reflected light becomes a problem very hard to solve, more especially in an instrument 12 by 4 by 6 inches, such as used by Messrs. Hurter and Driffield. I am not saying that they have not overcome this difficulty, but I bring forward a possible objection to this instrument. This may be passed over, however; but, unless I am very much mistaken, a much more serious, if not fatal, objection must be taken to it when measuring the density of photographic deposits, and is one I have long been practically acquainted with, and which I have again investigated recently. Let anyone, after focussing a view, replace the ground glass of a camera by a photographic negative, and place his head under the focussing cloth. He will see two objects, the lens through the plate and the view, more or less dim, on the negative itself. In other words, the film acts like ground glass and is partially translucent. Now, if the negative be replaced by a glass of apparently the same darkness, in which the colouring matter is part of the glass itself, the view is no longer visible, or, if visible at all, very faintly so, but the lens will be clearly seen. Now, ground glass, if illuminated, becomes practically a source of light, the light being scattered in every direction, but it naturally illuminates more strongly in the direction from which the original light falls on it, if the glass be perpendicular to that direction. Thus, when a piece of ground glass is placed at the end of a narrow tube, which is inserted in the walls of a dark and black-painted room (the ground surface being inside the room), it will be found that if a beam of light be sent through the tube, not only is the room illuminated exactly opposite the tube, as it would be were the ground glass removed, but also at every angle with the axis of the tube. The illumination of a white surface gave the following results in one case, the surface being always at the same distance from the aperture.

TABLE I.

| Angle from axis.<br>Deg. | | | | | | | Relative<br>illumination. |
|---|---|---|---|---|---|---|---|
| 0 | .. | .. | .. | .. | .. | .. | 100 |
| 10 | .. | .. | .. | .. | .. | .. | 64 |
| 20 | .. | .. | .. | .. | .. | .. | 21 |
| 30 | .. | .. | .. | .. | .. | .. | 14 |
| 40 | .. | .. | .. | .. | .. | .. | 8·2 |
| 50 | .. | .. | .. | .. | .. | .. | 7·2 |
| 60 | .. | .. | .. | .. | .. | .. | 6·0 |

Evidently the amount of scattered light would have to be taken into account, as, if not, it would be immaterial if the ground glass were in front of the tube or not, except for the small amount of light which would be reflected back towards the source of light ; and, further, the brightness of the light which illuminated the grease spot would not vary exactly inversely as the square of the distance, since the light is not symmetrically scattered, if we may use such a phrase.

If the ground glass in the above experiment be replaced by a piece of a negative the same scattering of light will be readily seen by holding a piece of white card about 1 foot from the orifice.

Now, let us see how the results obtained by the instrument under consideration would be affected by the " ground glass " effect of the negative. Suppose we have two lights properly enclosed in a darkened room, one being stationary, with an aperture in front of it, the flame being of such dimensions that it more than fills the aperture (in fact, just as the authors arrange both their lights) and the other movable. Let a movable Bunsen disc be placed at some fixed distance from the aperture, and the other light be moved till equality of illumination of the grease spot is secured, and let the distances of the aperture and of the movable light from the grease spot be noted. Next, let the Bunsen disc be moved to a different distance from the aperture and the movable light be again moved till equality of illumination is secured, and let the two distances be again measured. The distances of the aperture and of the movable light from the grease spot, in the first case, should be proportional to the two distances in the second case. Suppose, in the first instance, the distance of the aperture from the grease spot was 6 inches, and that of the movable light 3 feet, then, if the grease spot be moved to 12 inches from the aperture, the distance of the movable light should be 6 feet, and so on. Now, if the measurement of density of a plate by the grease-spot method be correct when a film is placed in contact with the aperture, the same should hold good, but if the scattering of light by the film affects the result it should not.  To test this, I have made a good many very careful experiments, and I cite one here which is a sample of the results obtained in all cases.  The plan adopted was to make measures of a lighted aperture as stated, and then, without any alteration of the general arrangement, to place a portion of a plate with a photographic deposit on it against the aperture, and measure the light coming through it by placing the grease spot at different distances from the aperture, and then to get equality of grease-spot illumination by moving the second light.  Table II gives the measures of the unmarked aperture, which was about $\frac{1}{4}$ inch in diameter as taken.

TABLE II.

| Distances of Aperture from Grease Spot. | Distance of Movable Light from Grease Spot. | | |
|---|---|---|---|
| | Readings. | Mean. | Adopted. |
| C.M. | | | |
| 3·5 | 4, 3·75, 4·2 | 4 | 4 |
| 7 | 8, 8, 8 | 8 | 8 |
| 14 | 16, 16 | 16 | 16 |
| 28 | 31·5, 31·5, 32 | 31·7 | 32 |
| 42 | 47·5, 48·5, 48·5 | 48·2 | 48 |
| 56 | 63, 64, 63 | 63·3 | 64 |
| 70 | 80, 78, 79, 79 | 79 | 80 |

The readings are sufficiently close to show that for naked lights the results are concordant.  Table III gives the measures of the light passing through a negative, and at different distances reaching the grease spot.

TABLE III.

| Distance of Aperture from Grease Spot Negative in Front. | Distance of Movable Light from Grease Spot. | | | Ratio of Distance of Aperture and Movable Light from Grease Spot. |
|---|---|---|---|---|
| | Readings. | Mean. | Adopted. | |
| C.M. | | | | |
| 3 | 42·5, 42, 42·5 | 42·7 | 42·7 | 14·2 |
| 4 | 48, 49, 49 | 48·7 | 48·7 | 12·2 |
| 5 | 57, 58, 56·5 | 57·2 | 57·2 | 11·4 |
| 6 | 63, 62, 64 | 63 | 63 | 10·5 |
| 8 | 84, 85, 84 | 84·3 | 84·3 | 10·5 |
| 9 | 93, 95, 95 | 93·7 | 93·7 | 10·4 |
| 10 | 102, 99, 100 | 100·3 | 100·3 | 10·03 |

If we critically examine this table we shall at once notice that large discrepancies appear.  For instance, at 6 in the first column the distance of the
movable lamp should be double that at 3, or it should be 85·4, but it is only
63 ; so at 8, if it were double that at 4, it should be 97·4, whereas it is 84·2 ;
at 10 it should be double that at 5, or 114·4, whereas it is 100·3.  The last
column gives the ratios of the distances.

The squares of the ratios of the first and last measures, viz., at 3 and 10,
the distances of the aperture from the source are as 201·6 to 100·6, or nearly
2 to 1.  The nearer distance of the screen to the aperture therefore gives a
lower value of the transmitted light than the further one.  The question is
which, if either, is correct, and, looking at it from a theoretical point of view,
it appears that neither is.  According to the two measures, the light transmitted through the negative was about one hundred and fifty-fourth and
one seventy-seventh, whereas by a correct means of measurement the amount
transmitted was found close upon one-fortieth.

The trial of their instrument by the authors with Indian ink and indigo
solution is totally different to its trial with films.  In a minor degree Indian
ink scatters, but the indigo solution is transparent.  Now, from the published
description of the instrument as used by Messrs. Hurter and Driffield, it is
probably impossible for the grease spot to be nearer to the aperture than
$1\frac{1}{4}$ inches, or about 3 cm., seeing that the inner box is 2-inch cube and that
we have to add for the thickness of the glass of the negative and the thickness
of the box itself.  We may take it that the distance of the grease spot in the
measures made varies between 6 inches and $1\frac{1}{4}$ (15 and 3 cm.) inches, and in
this range there can be a remarkable variation of densities to be obtained
from the different readings.  It may be said that the measures obtained are
concordant one with another.  This may be so, since it will be seen from
Table III that after a certain range is passed, the ratios of the two distances
become almost the same, but they will not be true measures of the light transmitted.  Taking all things into account, it seems not unreasonable to conclude
that the measures of light given as transmitted through deposits are too small ;
and, as has been shown, when the densities are great and the grease spot
has to be moved close to the aperture, the variation may be as great at 100
per cent. less than would have been obtained if a longer box had been employed
and the disc were further away from the aperture.

In this part of the paper to which I am confining myself the authors
allude to the photometer which I use, and which works on the principle of
cutting off light by rotating sectors of varying apertures, but a remark is
made which more than suggests a want of accuracy in its measure.  The
authors say that with it the density measured " rises to over 100 per cent.

(of error) with plates of high densities, which renders it utterly untrustworthy." From the formula of light transmitted through my photometer given by the authors the 100 per cent. evidently means making the density too great.   In taking exception to the results obtained by their grease-spot method, I have indicated experiments which anyone interested can try, and I shall now give some made with my own photometer.   I might stop here and use an " *argumentum ad hominem*," which would be thus :—The grease-spot photometer having been proved capable of giving results *inter se* 100 per cent. in error and mine having in the same hands  given results 100 per cent. in error when compared with them, may it not be assumed that my photometer gives correct results, or, at all events, more nearly correct results than  the grease-spot method gives ?   Setting this kind of argument on one side, I will for a brief space examine the statements that have been made regarding my photometer.

They say the light transmitted is more correctly represented by—

$$I_x = I\,\frac{\phi}{360°} + C$$

(when $I_x$ is the light transmitted, I the light falling on the sector, $\phi$ the aperture of the sector, and C a constant), than by—

$$I_x = I\,\frac{\phi}{360°}$$

which I have always taken as the true transmission.   Their formula, of course, if pushed to extremes, results in an absurdity, for, if the aperture be 0°, that is, if the sectors be closed, still C light will be transmitted.   The reason assigned for adopting this formula is said to " be due to the semi-shadow on  both edges of the sector openings."   Evidently, then, if we increase the number of  these openings, keeping the total aperture the same, the magnitude of  C will increase. If with two sectors it is C, then with four sectors it will be 2 C and with eight sectors 4 C, and so on, till we arrive at a point when $n$ C $= 1$, which is the total intensity, leaving no light to pass through the  apertures.   Had the formula been—

$$I_x = \left(I\,\frac{\phi}{360} - C\right)$$

there might have been something to say in its favour, for, if the light be close to the sectors, the thickness of the metal of which the sectors are made might possibly cut off a fraction of a degree, but, as I never use the photometer in such a manner, any error caused  by this is quite negligible, more especially as the photometer, for other reasons, is rarely read below 7° or 8°, the light being adjusted to make higher readings when low readings with one position of the light would be obtained.

I may as well here give some experimental results of the correctness of the photometer. Two incandescent lights, approximately similar in dimensions, were used and kept glowing with a constant current. One lamp was fixed at a distance of about 18 inches from the screen, the other placed on a block sliding on a bar, and the illuminated shadows cast by a rod fell on a white patch, and were equalised in brightness. The rotating sectors were introduced between the first light and the screen and were fixed at different apertures. Equality of illumination was obtained by sliding one light along the bar. The following are the results :—

TABLE IV.

| Sector Set at. | Mean Reading of the Distance of the Movable Lamp. | Calculated Value. |
|:---:|:---:|:---:|
| ° | | ° |
| 180 | 16·25 | 180 |
| 90 | 23 | 90 |
| 46 | 32 | 46·5 |
| 20·5 | 48·5 | 20·2 |
| 10 | 69 | 10 |
| 4·8 | 101 | 4·7 |

In the next two tables we have a large luminous source, viz., an Argand burner $\frac{3}{4}$ inch in diameter.

The first shows the worst measures made and the second one usually obtained :—

TABLE V.

| Sector Set at. | Mean Readings of Lamp from Source. | Calculated Intensity. |
|:---:|:---:|:---:|
| ° | | |
| 180 | 37·75 | 176·8 |
| 88 | 19·5 | 88 |
| 60 | 23·5 | 60·5 |
| 45 | 27·25 | 44·5 |
| 30 | 33 | 30·8 |
| 10 | 59 | 9·6 |
| 5 | 83 | 4·8 |

TABLE VI.

| Sector Set at. | Mean Reading of Lamp from Source. | Calculated Intensity. |
|:---:|:---:|:---:|
| $^{\circ}$ | | |
| 180 | 13·25 | 180 |
| 90 | 18·75 | 90·3 |
| 44·5 | 24·75 | 44·6 |
| 10 | 57·25 | 9·6 |
| 5·2 | 79·0 | 5·1 |
| 3 | 196·5 | 2·8 |

Equally good results were obtained when the sectors were placed in the beam of light, which was focussed on the screen by means of a lens.

In the foregoing remarks I have given my criticisms on the accuracy of the grease-spot photometer for measuring densities, and it has seemed to me that the whole paper more or less hangs on this. I have also endeavoured to vindicate the sector photometer from the slur which has been placed upon it. All the experiments I have given on both subjects are easy to repeat, and I trust that some independent physicist will take the matter up and judge between myself and the authors.

It would be premature to go into the proofs which can be adduced that the method employed by myself for measuring densities is correct. If necessary, such proof can be given. Doubt has only been thrown on the instrument I use, and not on the manner of using it in its latest development. My admiration of the paper is not diminished by any fault I have found in the methods employed by Messrs. Hurter and Driffield, but I thought it right in the interests of photographic science to point out what I believe to be a weak spot in the proofs of their theory.

[*Extract from the Journal of the Society of Chemical Industry, July* 31*st,* 1890.]

# REPLY TO THE COMMUNICATION OF CAPTAIN ABNEY "ON THE ACCURACY OF THE GREASE - SPOT PHOTO-METER, &c."

BY

## FERDINAND HURTER, Ph.D., and V. C. DRIFFIELD.

---

CAPTAIN ABNEY has conferred a great honour upon us by his kind criticism of part of our paper.

The objections which Captain Abney brings against our photometer are two. In the first place, he objects to the light reflected from the walls of the blackened large chamber as likely to interfere with the readings of our instrument. But we placed the photometer disc within a second chamber for this very reason, and the light reflected from the walls of the second chamber are equal on both sides when the disc is at point of equality.

The second objection is of greater importance. The phenomenon of "scattering" represents one of the great difficulties to contend with. It is more readily observed with white opaque substances, such as ground glass or emulsions, but it also undoubtedly exists, though to a small extent, in negatives. Fortunately, it interferes only in plates of very high densities.

The experimental results given by Captain Abney agree fairly with our own, though they are rather worse. We have, however, guarded against serious errors by showing in Table I the extreme limits to which we use the instrument. It will there be seen that the last figure we use is $1\cdot7$, corresponding to $l \times 0\cdot75$, which in our instrument means a distance of $1\cdot5$ inches between the Bunsen disc and the plate to be measured. If we accept Captain Abney's results, given in Table III, as correct, the relative densities shown for this distance of 4 cm. and one of 10 cm. would be proportional to the logarithms of the numbers $12\cdot2$ and $10\cdot03$ respectively, *i.e.*, to $1\cdot086$ and $1\cdot00$, and the error made in this extreme case would be 8 per cent. only, and not 100 per cent., as stated by Captain Abney. But it is very seldom indeed that the disc has to be moved so close to the plate as is assumed in this example, and we have clearly and carefully stated that we do not claim any greater accuracy than 5 per cent.

With regard to the angle subtended by the spot of the Bunsen disc and the diameter of the diaphragm, it is even in this extreme case less than 10°.

Respecting the objection we made to the revolving sector, we asserted that the light transmitted by the sector was not exactly the half or the quarter of that which the lamp gives directly, when the sector is open to 180° and to 90° respectively, and the experiments quoted by Captain Abney are no answer to this objection. We also stated that the error was small with plates of low density. The formula we gave was the result of experiment and not of any theoretical considerations.

Like other empirical formulæ, it has the property of leading to absurdities when pushed to extremes. We may have occasion to quote an important formula published by Captain Abney which has the same disagreeable property, but it is interesting, perhaps, to state that we assured ourselves of the existence of the error by the very experiment Captain Abney mentions, viz., by multiplying the sector openings.

We have to apologise to Captain Abney for the omission in our paper of an important statement which was made when the paper was read, viz., that this error does not in any way affect the results of his researches on the sensitiveness of the silver compounds to the various parts of the spectrum. We thank Captain Abney for his expression of admiration of our paper, and we can assure him that we do not undervalue or wish to detract from the importance of his classical researches.

# MEASURING THE DENSITY OF NEGATIVES.

BY

F. HURTER, Ph.D., and V. C. DRIFFIELD.

*[Reprinted from " Photography," August 28th, 1890.]*

---

A RAPID method of measuring the density of negatives is a desideratum not only for the scientific investigator but also for the practical photographer. In a paper published in the *Journal of the Society of Chemical Industry* we have shown that the speed of photographic plates can be ascertained by a very simple method, provided an instrument be at hand which rapidly, and with a sufficient degree of accuracy, measures the relative amounts of silver deposited on a plate by a series of different exposures. We described in the same paper the instrument we ourselves use for this purpose, and we asserted that the results obtained by means of it were correct within 5 per cent. Whilst Mr. Chapman Jones and Mr. Pringle have directed their criticisms to our conclusions on the subject of development, and to our denial of the possibility of correcting errors in exposure by means of development, the foremost of our scientific photographers, Captain Abney, has devoted his attention to our instrument for measuring densities. Having ourselves criticised Captain Abney's photometer adversely, we cannot complain if his criticisms of our instrument are possibly more severe than they otherwise would have been.

We should have passed no remarks on Captain Abney's instrument were it not that we know that a repetition of many of our experiments, if made with his photometer, would lead to entirely different and, as we believe, erroneous results. We purposely avoided in our paper any criticism of the results obtained by Captain Abney himself by means of his instrument, and we candidly pointed out in Liverpool, and since then in the *Journal of Chemical Industry*, that even the errors, which we believe to be inseparable from his photometer, do not affect in any way his classical researches on the sensitiveness of the silver salts. We are still reluctant to do more than take a passing notice of the " laws " which he deduces from his photometric results.

If plates on which different amounts of silver have been developed are measured by means of Captain Abney's instrument his own investigations show that the logarithm of the amount of silver on the plate is proportional to the square root of the logarithm of the opacity, the inverse of the transparency. This very complicated relation between the amount of silver and the transparency, as measured by Captain Abney's photometer, supposing it to be correct, renders his instrument unsuitable for the purpose of determining rapidly the relative amounts of silver on a plate.

Professor Rücker, as Captain Abney tells us, has drawn his attention to the fact that this complicated relationship is not in accordance with accepted views, nor with the theoretical investigations of Lord Rayleigh and of Maxwell. The "law" of Captain Abney certainly differs very much from the laws which Bunsen and also Vierordt found to apply to transparent media.

Our instrument differs essentially from Captain Abney's in that its indications are perfectly in accord with the laws which have for a long time past been held to apply in such cases, and it is certainly in complete accord with Lord Rayleigh's and Maxwell's theoretical conclusions. These conclusions are that the amount of matter and the opacity are so related that the logarithm of the opacity is directly proportional to the amount of matter. Our instrument is so arranged that, without any calculations, the relative amount of silver can be directly read off. We asserted that the results were carried within 5 per cent. The proofs of this assertion are so simple that we did not think it necessary to indicate them. There are many ways in which the instrument can be tested.

(1) If a negative of uniform density be cut into pieces, and the density of one piece be ascertained, it will be found that the density of three or four pieces superimposed will be exactly three or four times that of the single piece. If pieces of different densities be measured separately and afterwards together, it will be found that the density of the pieces together is the sum of the densities of the several pieces.

(2) If plates of sufficient size be exposed and developed so as to yield different but uniform densities, and be then measured in our instrument, the films being afterwards removed from the plate, the metallic silver converted into chloride of silver and weighed (a delicate operation, which can only be carried out by chemists), it will be found that the several weights of silver chloride will correspond with the respective densities.

(3) If, with an emulsion of metallic silver in gelatine, various mixtures be made with known but varying amounts of water, and the densities of these various emulsions be measured in a small glass cell (similar to the life box of

microscopists), it will be found that the densities will be directly proportional to the amount of metallic silver in the various emulsions.[1]

We give below the results of a few experiments made as we have just indicated.

We never, however, claimed perfect accuracy for our photometer ; it is liable to errors, as is every other which depends finally upon the eye as judge of equality.   Its liability to error is 5 per cent. of the value of the density to be measured, and may, with better eyes than we possess, be even more accurate, while an unpractised eye may make even greater errors.  We find that most observers are capable of handling the instrument after a few minutes' practice.

The whole of our experimental research depends upon this property of our instrument to give numbers proportional to the amount of silver on the plate, and if Captain Abney can prove that our instrument does not do so, as we now again assert it does, then our results are valueless, and we shall withdraw them unhesitatingly.   We are confident that, if our directions are adhered to, Captain Abney, as any other investigator, will confirm our results.

This valuable property of our instrument, to give numbers directly proportional to the amount of silver on the plate, or, what is the same thing, to the work which the light has done on the plate, rendered it comparatively easy for us to prove that the work done by the light is *not* proportional to the intensity of the light and the time of exposure simply, but that it varies in a somewhat complex manner, the action of the light being also influenced by the gradually decreasing amount of unaltered silver salt on the sensitive plate.

This, it will be readily admitted, is an extremely probable result ; much more probable, indeed, than that deduced by Captain Abney's instrument, which is that the amount of silver deposited after development is simply proportional to the intensity of the light (strictly speaking, to some power of the intensity of the light, the index of which power cannot be learnt with certainty from Captain Abney's researches).

We were in possession of our own results before Captain Abney published his " Law of Error," and we are as fully convinced now as we were at the time of its publication that the " Law of Error," as applied to photography, is an error itself.   We could point to measurements of Captain Abney's which show that the " Law of Error " does not apply to some of his own plates.

With regard to the reproach we cast upon his photometer, we distinctly said that for low densities the error was small.  As far as we can ascertain,

[1] H.N.—B., pp. 114, 115.

Captain Abney has never measured any plates of very high densities, and, indeed, we do not think it is possible to do so with his instrument.

The extreme simplicity, absence of all complicated mechanism, of electro-meter and battery, of lantern arrangements and reflectors, &c., &c., and of tedious calculations, must surely speak in favour of our instrument from a purely practical point of view.

But it will be said that Captain Abney has proved by experiment that Hurter and Driffield's photometer is wrong. *Our answer is, he never tried it.* When he has done so, we are confident he will alter his opinion.

The scattering of light, which Captain Abney says interferes with measurements made by our instrument, exists in the case of white opaque substances and, to a minute extent, in the case of black. It can be proved by means of a sensitive plate that, compared with the light of the flame, transmitted directly, the light scattered is very small. The scattering of the light does not interfere with measurements made in our instrument, because the " scattering " plate and the source of light are practically at the same point. Captain Abney's assertion that, on account of this scattering of light, the law of inverse square of distance does no longer apply, is true only for the experiment with a tube and ground glass, but it is incorrect for the apparatus we designed. The silver deposit in a negative scatters very little light indeed. If in a camera the flame of a lamp, such as we use, be focussed, and a sensitive plate exposed, a dense negative of uniform tint being interposed immediately behind the lens, the image when developed would be blurred and veiled if the interposed negative became itself a considerable source of light. This does not occur. The image of the flame is as sharp and clear when a negative of density $2\cdot5$ is interposed as if that negative had not been there. This experiment proves that the amount of light transmitted by the negative directly is large compared with the light it scatters.

This cannot, therefore, be the cause of the discrepancies which Captain Abney found in his experiment, which was not made with our instrument. We have critically examined his results, and we are led to the conclusion that he either used a grease spot of too large a diameter or read the vanishing instead of the equality point of the grease spot. Either will account for the discrepancies. A plate has naturally different opacities for rays which traverse it at different angles, and it is therefore necessary to utilise only those rays which fall as nearly perpendicularly as possible, both on the plate to be measured and on the grease spot. This cannot be completely attained in practice, but we have so arranged our instrument that no rays of greater angle than $10°$ fall on the grease spot (the diameter of which is only about 1 mm.), and the error from this source is at most 2 per cent. in the density.

We subjoin the experimental proofs that our instrument gives numbers proportional to the amount of silver on the plate accurately to 5 per cent. :—

(1) Several negatives were measured separately, then superimposed.[1] The densities were found to be :—

| | |
|---|---|
| No. 1 .. .. .. .. .. .. .. | 0·775 |
| ,, 2 .. .. .. .. .. .. .. | 1·075 |
| ,, 3 .. .. .. .. .. .. .. | 1·325 |
| ,, 4 .. .. .. .. .. .. .. | 1·575 |

Nos. 1 and 2 ought to give 1·850, found 1·885, error 1·4 per cent.

  ,, 1, 2, 3   ,,   ,,    3·175,   ,,    3·075,   ,,    3·1      ,,

  ,, 3 and 4   ,,   ,,    2·900,   ,,    2·850,   ,,    1·7      ,,

  ,, 1, 3 and 4   ,,   ,,    3·675,   ,,    3·600,   ,,    2·4      ,,

(2) Four half-plates were exposed and developed to different densities. They were then measured in different places and the densities averaged. After that the films were taken off, treated with nitric acid, the silver precipitated with hydrochloric acid, filtered and weighed on a fine balance. The following table gives the results :—[1]

| Plate No. | Density Found. | Grms. AgCl Found. | Density Calculated from AgCl. |
|---|---|---|---|
| 1 | 0·525 | 0·0163 | 0·525 |
| 2 | 0·960 | 0·0299 | 0·963 |
| 3 | 1·470 | 0·0450 | 1·449 |
| 4 | 1·970 | 0·0611 | 1·968 |

(3) A silver emulsion was made by taking the films off two negatives and dissolving them in warm water.[2] No gelatine was added. The emulsion was filtered through muslin and diluted with water until it became measurable. Its density, including the glass cell, was found to be 3·225. Various mixtures of this emulsion and water were then made and measured in the same cell. The densities were found to be, inclusive of the cell :—

| | |
|---|---|
| 10 c.c. emulsion + 5 c.c. water .. .. .. | 2·200 |
| 5   ,,    + 5   ,, .. .. .. | 1·650 |
| 5   ,,    + 16   ,, .. .. .. | ·815 |
| 5   ,,    + 45   ,, .. .. .. | ·400 |
| 5   ,,    + 95   ,, .. .. .. | ·225 |

[1] H.N.—B., p. 170            [2] H.N.—B., p. 169

Deducting from each density the value of the cell filled with pure water, which was 0·070, the densities of the emulsions are :—

| Density Found. | Per cent. of Strong Emulsion. | Density for one per cent. Calculated. |
|---|---|---|
| 3·155 | 100 | 0·0315 |
| 2·130 | 66·6 | 0·0315 |
| 1·580 | 50 | 0·0316 |
| 0·745 | 23·8 | 0·0313 |
| 0·330 | 10·0 | 0·0330 |
| 0·155 | 5 | 0·0310 |

It will thus be seen that our instrument gives numbers which are directly proportional to the amounts of silver contained either in an emulsion or in the film of a negative.

It clearly follows that our instrument, which measures with considerable accuracy the amount of matter (silver in the case of negatives), also measures equally correctly the transparency, which is simply a function of the amount of matter.

[*Reprinted from the Journal of the Society of Chemical Industry*, 31*st January*, 1891.  *No.* 1, *Vol. X.*]

# THE SECTOR AND GREASE-SPOT PHOTOMETERS AND THEIR RESULTS.

BY

## F. HURTER, Ph.D., AND V. C. DRIFFIELD.

---

IT will be within the recollection of the Section that, in a paper read at the end of last session, we very briefly criticised an instrument which Captain Abney devised for measuring the transparencies of negatives. In consequence, Captain Abney practically accuses us of having, to use his own words, " blown upon " his instrument without sufficient investigation.  Such a proceeding on our part would have been most unjust, and we hope that our present paper will prove to the satisfaction of this Society that the charge is perfectly groundless.

In our former paper we based our criticisms entirely on experimental grounds ; our conclusions were, however, even more strongly based upon an investigation of the results Captain Abney obtained by means of his photometer. Of these results we purposely said nothing ; but the course Captain Abney has since seen fit to take leaves us no alternative but, in self-defence, to bring them forward.  We shall therefore proceed to show that, by our experiments and by a careful analysis of Captain Abney's own researches, we were driven to the conclusion that we must warn our readers against the use of his instrument. We wish, at the same time, to answer disparaging criticisms of our own photometer and of our results.  We shall do this as shortly as is consistent with the importance which has been attached, by many journals, to our paper.

The instrument which Captain Abney uses as a standard measure for light consists of a revolving disc with angular apertures which can be opened and closed whilst the disc is revolving, and which he shortly terms a " rotating sector."  When this disc is caused to revolve in front of a lamp, a screen, illuminated by this lamp, appears darker and darker, as the sector is gradually closed.  The screen really receives the full intensity of the light but, owing to the rapid revolution of the sector, periods of illumination and periods of darkness intervene so rapidly that, to the eye, they coalesce and produce the impression of continuous illumination of lesser intensity ; and the real question at issue is : can the eye judge the exact arithmetical average of the various intensities of light which act upon the nerves in rapid succession ?   If the eye can do this, the rotating sector is a perfect photometer and our criticism was unjust ; but, if the eye cannot do this, our criticism was just, and the angular aperture of a rotating sector is not an accurate measure of light intensity.

Now, if the aperture of the sector be large enough and the sector be at rest, a lamp placed behind it will illuminate a portion of a screen with the same intensity as if the sector were not present.   On revolving the sectors slowly, the eye still perceives that intensity as long as it can follow the image of the sector opening on the screen ; as the revolutions are increased and the eye can no longer follow the image of the sector opening, a complete circle of light of considerably reduced intensity is the visible result.   If the opening of the sector extend over half the circumference (180°) and the revolutions be made very rapidly indeed, a point is reached when the intensity of this circle of light approaches more and more nearly the exact half of the intensity of direct

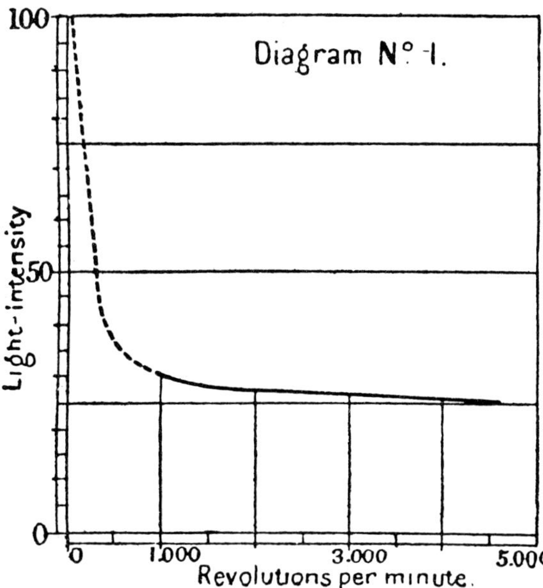



illumination of the lamp. It requires, however, from 4,000 to 5,000 revolutions per minute to attain this result. Diagram No. 1 shows how, with increasing revolutions, a sector of 90° opening (two openings of 45° each) gradually gave light of less and less intensity. This was measured by the grease-spot photometer, the first measurement being made at 900 revolutions per minute. The curve between this point and complete rest is imaginary only and simply indicates the alteration in intensity which must take place as the sector passes from complete rest to 900 revolutions per minute. A sector opening of 90° should, of course, give 25 per cent. of the original light intensity, but it will be seen from this diagram that this fraction of the original intensity was only reached when upwards of 4,000 revolutions of the sector were attained.

We consider it a most serious objection to the rotating sector that its indications depend upon the number of its revolutions.

With large openings of the sector the task which the eye has to perform is comparatively simple. It receives a number of impressions of the full intensity of the light interrupted by periods of darkness, and it has to average these, But the task becomes more difficult as the openings become smaller. Diagram No. 2 represents the light intensities measured by the grease-spot photometer as the opening of the sector revolves slowly past a line joining the grease spot and the centre of the flame. The abscissæ represent the various positions of the sector in angular measure, o being the position when the sector opening was bisected by the line joining grease spot and flame. The diagram shows the variations of illumination which the grease spot received when

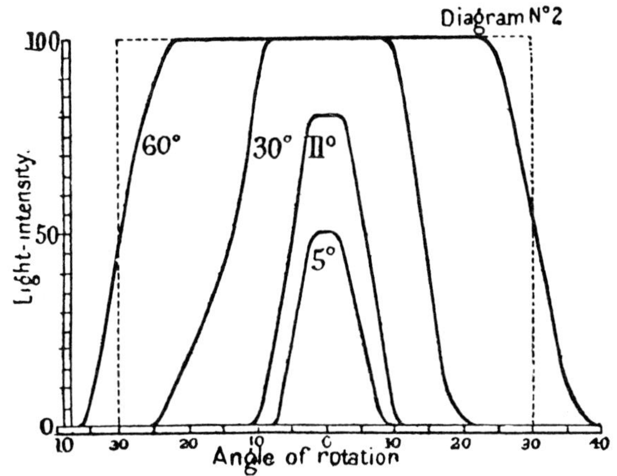


sectors of different angular openings, viz., 60°, 30°, 11°, and 5°, were interposed. It will be seen that, with the largest opening of 60°, there was measurable light, not for 60°, but for 76° of its revolution. The full intensity of the light of the lamp (taken as 100) is maintained during 45° to 46° of the revolution.

The light gradually grows from darkness at one end, and gradually diminishes to darkness again at the other. These periods of growth to and from the full intensity we called in our paper the " semi-shadow at both edges of the sector opening." As the sector opening is reduced, a point is reached when the full intensity of the light is no longer obtained ; an opening of 11° giving only 81 per cent. of the full intensity, and one of 5° only 51 per cent., the semi-shadow being all that is left. The total amount of light which reaches the grease spot during the complete passage of the sector opening is proportional to the sector opening ; it is so theoretically, and it is so practically. The areas of these diagrams were measured by means of Amsler's planimeter, and the following results were obtained :—A rectangle, shown in dotted lines on the diagram, one side being equal to 60° and the other side to the full intensity of the light, measured 2,938 = 60°. The diagram for 60° measured 2,942 = 60·1° ;

for 30°, 1,445 = 29·5° ; for 11°, 469 = 9·5° ; for 5°, 239 = 4·9°.  These measurements leave no doubt that the amount of light transmitted by a revolving sector is proportional to the opening of the sector.  This may also be proved by means of photographic plates.  If the light passing through a revolving sector fall upon a sensitive plate, the number of revolutions will have no effect so long as every point of the plate receives each intensity equally often.

When, however, we tried to average these rapidly varying intensities by means of the eye, we found that it was not equal to the task.  We still hoped that the eye might prove capable of averaging alternate periods of illumination and darkness with tolerable accuracy if the intensity of the light itself were constant, as it would be if the source of light were a luminous point or a bundle of parallel rays ; but we found that, even in this case, the eye is unable to average correctly, as we shall now proceed to show you practically.

For this purpose we shall employ an ordinary optical lantern, which is our source of light.  We place in it a black disc having two openings of equal angular dimensions.  Upon causing this disc to revolve, we produce two concentric circles of equal light intensities.  This proves that our apparatus does not introduce errors, in that the two equal openings in the disc produce upon the eye equal effects.

In order to show you the difference between the two intensities due to openings of 60° and 70°, we place into the lantern another disc having such openings.  The difference is, of course, small, but you will probably have no difficulty in deciding which intensity is due to the 60° and which to the 70° opening.  We show you this in order that in our next slide you may be prepared not to look for any very striking difference.

We now place the third slide into the lantern and leave it to you to decide which circle of light, if either, is the brighter.[1]

We ourselves think the inner circle decidedly the brighter ; but assuming them to be equal in intensity, they clearly demonstrate the errors of the sector for this reason :—The inner circle has a single opening of 60° ; the outer circle has six openings of 12° each, or a total of 72° ; yet it was this inner circle which was, if anything, the brighter.  This clearly proves that, to the eye, 6 × 12° is not equal to 72°, but is more nearly equal to 60°.  So much for the effect upon the eye.  Upon a sensitive plate, however, the effect is different, the action of the light being strictly proportional to these openings.  We produce a plate exposed to the action of light passing through this same disc, and the resulting

---

[1] Opinion was divided ; some members thinking the inner circle the brighter, others the outer circle, and others, again, that they were equal in intensity.  All agreed, however, that the difference between the two circles was decidedly less than in the case of the second slide.

densities measure, for the inner circle of 60°, 0·820, and for the outer circle of 72°, 0·920.

These experiences point to but one conclusion, viz., that the impressions made on the eye by rapidly changing intensities of light are not sufficiently accurate to serve as basis for photometric experiments. Captain Abney claims great accuracy for his apparatus, and we ourselves stated that its errors only became seriously appreciable in the case of high densities ; but an analysis of his results obtained by means of it, and of which we proceed to give a short epitome, entirely corroborates the experimental proof we have given that the rotating sector is not a reliable instrument of research.

Captain Abney, like ourselves, investigated the action of light on sensitive plates, and, from measurements made with the sectors, he arrived at a law which expresses the relation of transparency to the number of a hole in the particular sensitometer which he uses. After making the necessary algebraical transformations in order to substitute the relative intensity of the light for the purely arbitrary number of the hole, the formula stands thus :—

$$T = \epsilon^{-u\,(\log. I)^2}$$

Taking logarithms on both sides we find—

$$-\log. T = u\,(\log. I)^2,$$

$u$ being a constant and I the intensity of light which produced the transparency T, the unit of light being that due to the sensitometer hole which just failed, on development of the plate, to produce any deposit. This law Captain Abney terms the "law of error," and upon examination it leads to very extraordinary conclusions. It tells us, in the first place, that as the intensity of the light increased indefinitely, the transparency diminishes indefinitely also ; that is, the amount of silver on the plate increases indefinitely and without limit with increased exposure. The camera would, if this were true, become a kind of alchemistic laboratory wherein silver may be produced from nothing. Captain Abney knows perfectly well that the density of a negative is limited by the amount of silver placed on the plate by the manufacturer, and we trust he will now see reason to doubt the truth of a law which leads to so absurd a conclusion. If this were the only fault to be found with his law, it would be of comparatively little consequence, as many other laws, generally accepted, lead to similar absurdities when pushed to extremes.

A much more serious objection to the formula, as a law, is that symbols enter into it, the meaning of which is ill-defined. It starts from a perfectly arbitrary number of a hole in a particular sensitometer, and it contains a constant of which we do not know the meaning. The real truth of the formula is this : The law, when deprived of its transcendental character, represents a parabola ; and, given a short piece of any curve having no singular point, it is always easy to find a parabola which resembles it as closely as desired ; for it is always possible to lay a parabola through four points of any given curve, and that is all Captain Abney can claim for his formula.[1]

Captain Abney further showed that if the quantity of silver on a plate be gradually increased, the transparency follows the same law—

$$T = \quad - m \, (\log. \, Q)^2,$$

which is again our algebraic transformation of his.   From this law an equally absurd conclusion follows as from the last, and that without pushing the formula to extremes.   According to Captain Abney's results, if we were to super-impose on a plate which permitted 26 per cent. of light to pass another plate of equal density (*i.e.*, double the amount of silver), the combination would allow 12·3 per cent. of the original light to pass.   (*Photographic News* 33, 634, gives the necessary data for this calculation.)   Thus the second plate becomes greatly more transparent than it would be if used as a first, since it allows $\dfrac{12 \cdot 3}{26 \cdot 0} = 47 \cdot 3$ per cent. of the light which it receives to pass.   This result is amazing indeed ; the more silver we deposit on the plate the more transparent becomes each single unit of silver !   We need not say that this is in direct contradiction to all researches hitherto made in this direction.   With ordinary transparent media Bunsen and Roscoe, and Vierordt also, proved those laws which we gave in our former paper, and we shall presently see that a negative behaves almost exactly like a deeply-coloured transparent solution.

By a combination of the results of these two investigations Captain Abney arrives at the deduction that the amount of silver reduced by the light and subsequent development is simply proportional to the intensity of the light which acted on the plate.   This conclusion cannot be deduced mathematically from his formula ; nor is it true, except for very short illuminations, or very feeble intensities of light.

Then Captain Abney showed that a plate, after intensification, still obeyed the "law of error."   After the necessary algebraic transformations of his formula, the relation between the transparencies of the intensified plate and of the original plate is simply expressed—

$$\frac{- \log. \, Ti}{- \log. \, To} = \frac{0 \cdot 01015}{0 \cdot 00603} - 1 \cdot 68.$$

It will perhaps be remembered that we called the negative logarithm of the transparency T the density, and that, for an intensified plate, we also made the

---

[1] Our results, however, clearly show that this curve *cannot* be a parabola.

assertion that the ratio of densities was constant. When, however, we examine Captain Abney's numerical results, we find that they deviate very considerably from this constant ratio, the deviations ranging from $1 \cdot 0$ to $2 \cdot 27$, the true mean being $1 \cdot 64$. From these large deviations we judge that the rotating sector is not so accurate a tool, even in Captain Abney's hands, as the grease-spot photometer is in our own. And when our critics find fault with deviations in ratios of 5 per cent., we think we may fairly point to these results which deviate from 30 per cent. to 40 per cent. from the mean.

A further very curious result is brought to light if the " law of error," as applied to quantity of silver, be combined with the " law of error," as applied to intensification. It is not difficult to combine them, and we will only say that the result of so doing is that a given atom of silver will precipitate, from a solution of mercuric chloride, various amounts of mercury which depend upon the number of the sensitometer hole behind which that atom of silver was reduced. This, of course, is utterly untrue ; it is entirely opposed to all chemical experience, and, in the face of Mr. Chapman Jones' researches on intensification, it is simply absurd.

We trust we have now said sufficient to prove to the Society that we have not warned our readers against the use of the rotating sector without cause. We are certain that Captain Abney is as able an experimental investigator as anyone living, and we ascribe these erroneous results solely to the faulty measuring instrument which it has been his misfortune to adopt.

We have ourselves, on the other hand, made use of the grease-spot photometer throughout our research. We asserted that its indications were proportional to the weight of silver on the plate, and we never made any claim that it was absolutely accurate, or that it measured the whole of the light transmitted in all directions by the negative. The main practical result of our investigations, which we communicated to the Society, was a method of determining the speed of a sensitive plate. As the results of our investigations have been called into question, owing to some alleged inaccuracy in the measurements of the plates, we have made a determination of the speed of a plate both by gravimetric analysis and by photometric measurements. For this purpose we used four half-plates, exposed respectively for 10, 20, 40, and 80 seconds to a standard candle at a distance of one metre. The four plates were developed together, and, after carefully fixing, washing and drying, they were measured photometrically. The films were then removed from the plates, and the silver determined. The results obtained were as follows[1] :—

---

[1] H.N.—B., p. 167.

| Exposure, C.M.S. | Measured density. | Calculated density. | Weight of silver chloride. |
| --- | --- | --- | --- |
|  |  |  | Grm. |
| 10 | 0·525 | 0·525 | 0·0163 |
| 20 | 0·960 | 0·963 | 0·0299 |
| 40 | 1·470 | 1·449 | 0·0450 |
| 80 | 1·970 | 1·968 | 0·0611 |

On the assumption that density, as indicated by photometric measurement of plates developed with ferrous oxalate, is proportional to the weight of silver, the densities calculated from the weights are as given in the above table. Diagram No. 3 shows the graphic method of finding the inertia of the plate, and the absolute coincidence of the gravimetric and photometric results proves the extent to which the grease-spot photometer may be relied upon ; and it also proves that there is, as we asserted there was, a range of exposures during which the weight of silver reduced by the light is proportional to the logarithm of the exposure. This is proved by the almost entire coincidence of the points and the straight line drawn through them. The abscissæ are the logarithms of the exposures, and the ordinates the milligrammes of silver chloride weighed. This experiment, we consider, disposes, once for all, of the adverse criticism which has been passed upon our photometer.

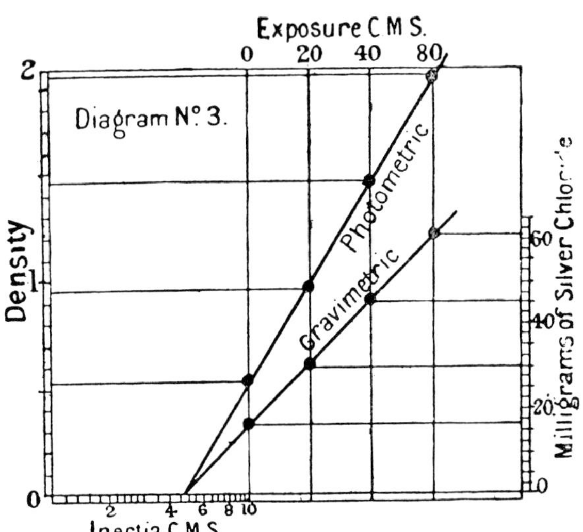


Captain Abney has discovered that negatives "scatter" so much light that our instrument cannot possibly measure all the light which a negative transmits ; and owing to our instrument measuring the correct amount of light transmitted directly plus an excess of "scattered" light, as he told the Camera Club, we ought to find the transparency too great. But, in his criticism in the *Journal* of this Society, he found that a negative, measured by our method, gave a transparency of $\frac{1}{100}$ which, when measured by his "new and correct" plan (still using the sector), transmitted one-fortieth of the light.   These criticisms, which are in direct antagonism, demand no reply.

In connection with this " scattering " of light we wish to show you one or two experiments made by Captain Abney to prove what he thinks an insurmountable difficulty in our method of measuring plates.

We project upon the screen, by means of a lantern, a well-defined disc of light.   Holding in front of the lens a piece of ground glass, this disc absolutely disappears and the light is now spread over the whole screen.   This phenomenon is what Captain Abney terms the " scattering " of light.   The fact is that the ground glass has itself become a source of light, and in calculating intensities of light as from this source, the distance of the illuminated screen would have to be measured from this ground glass.

If two pieces of the ground glass be placed in front of the lens, you will see that the general illumination is but slightly diminished.

If, instead of the ground glass, we place in front of the lens a solution of ammonio-cupric sulphate, the phenomenon is essentially different.   The disc of light remains as it was (except that it is blue), and there is a very faint general illumination of the screen.   Simply breathing upon the cell containing the solution will produce the " scattering " effect.

We now exchange this solution for a fairly dense negative which measures about 1·8, and again the phenomenon is slightly different.   A well-defined disc of light is the most conspicuous effect, and around this disc you will perceive a halo of diffused light.   There can be no doubt, however, that this phenomenon resembles much more closely that produced by the transparent solution than by the ground glass.

If a second negative of the same density be now placed in front of the first, both the disc and the halo are very considerably reduced in intensity—in fact vanish—which was not the case with the ground glass.   This proves that both the directly transmitted light and the scattered light diminish, as the amount of silver on the negative is increased.   And if, as in our photometer, the distance of the illuminated screen from the source of light and from the " scattering " negative be identically the same, then the total intensity of the light both " scattered " and directly transmitted by the negative, diminishes as the silver is increased, in accordance with the laws which we published in our former paper.

Many other criticisms have been passed on our paper which are too frivolous to call for notice, though we may just instance one respecting our use of logarithms and the effect which the employment of other systems of logarithms would have had upon our results.   We would, in reply to this, simply refer our critic to Chapter XVII. of Knight and Hall's Algebra.

We admit that, to many of the readers of our paper, the use we made of the word density proved a stumbling block.  We can now see that if we had converted all the results into milligrammes of silver, we should have been better understood.  Our " density " is in reality, however, synonymous with weight of silver.

It was by referring our results to weight of silver that we discovered that important and interesting curve, the characteristic curve of the sensitive plate. No other way of stating the results ; no other method of plotting this curve would ever have revealed such a simple and important explanation of photographic phenomena.  On this ground alone we claim a distinct score for our grease-spot photometer.  The " law of error " is, on the other hand, utterly opposed to the photographer's everyday experience of the existence of distinct periods of under-, correct-, and over-exposure.

Another very important fact brought to light by means of the grease-spot photometer is that the photographer has no power to alter the ratio of the weights of silver reduced in various parts of the negative by alterations in development.  These ratios are due to the action of the light alone.

To this statement many have taken exception, notably Mr. Chapman Jones,[1] who, while he agrees with us that under-exposure cannot be corrected by development, still believes that, in some measure, over-exposure can be remedied.  To prove this he made an experiment, and sent us the plates for measurement.  The experiment consisted in illuminating two plates equally by means of a sensitometer, so as to obtain a similar series of gradations on each plate.  The time of exposure was, in the case of both plates, 30 times that needed to give a perceptible deposit with the smallest hole of the sensitometer. The light intensities ranged from 1 to 775.  One plate (No. 7) was developed for two minutes in a strong developer of soda and pyrogallol.  The other plate (No. 8) was first immersed in a solution of potassium bromide, and the entire development occupied no less than 38 minutes, the alkali being added in minute quantities from time to time.  Of this experiment Mr. Chapman Jones wrote :—" Thus in Plate 8 I did the best I could to  remedy the evil of over-exposure."  Diagram No. 4 shows you how far he succeeded.  The curve No. 7 is a mean path on which the points which indicate the densities, as measured on Plate No. 7, ought to have been situated.  The higher curve, No. 8, is exactly the same curve as No. 7, each ordinate being multiplied by the mean density ratio 1·54.  This simply means that, had the development of Plate No. 7 been prolonged for one minute, the densities of Plate No. 7 would have been situated on the same curve as are those of Plate No. 8.  In other

---

[1] D.N.—G., 26–28.  Correspondence :—Chapman Jones—Driffield, 15th August, 1890.  Driffield—Chapman Jones, 16th August, 1890.

words, Mr. Chapman Jones, in doing his best to remedy the evil of over-exposure, only succeeded in making one plate generally denser than the other, but the ratios of the silver deposited are, on the whole, the same in Plate No. 8 as in

Plate No. 7. The density ratio between the extremes of Plate No. 7 is 3·22, that between the extremes of Plate No. 8 is 3·25, so that the density ratio was increased by less than 1 per cent. We do not therefore think that Mr. Chapman Jones can claim to have remedied the evil of over-exposure, considering that a correct representation of his

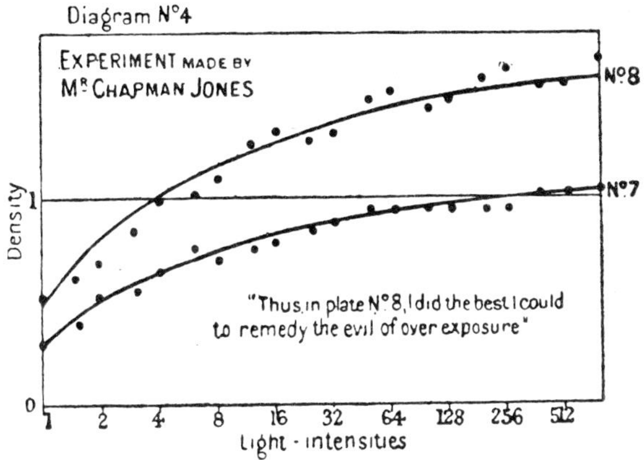


light intensity would have demanded a density ratio between the extremes of at least 1 : 30.

This experiment clearly shows the inability, even of an expert, to correct over-exposure in development. Mr. Chapman Jones does not agree with us, however, because he regards the errors in these results as evidence that he *has* done something to remedy over-exposure. But when we arrange the true density ratios of the corresponding squares of Plates Nos. 7 and 8 in their original sequence on the plate, as we have done in Diagram No. 5, the errors group themselves in such a way as to leave no doubt that they are due, almost entirely, to inequalities in the coating of the plates, particularly on the left-hand margin, where it will be seen the highest density ratios all lie. In our former paper we pointed out that inequalities in the coating of the plate constitute the most serious source of error of all. Mr. Chapman Jones bases his claim to have remedied over-exposure chiefly upon the averages of *four* groups, each consisting of *five* consecutive density ratios. The diagram will show the fallacy of such a proceeding, as two of the groups each include two of the high marginal density ratios, one group includes only one, and the fourth group does not include any at all. The averages of *five* groups, each consisting of *four* consecutive density ratios, as indicated on the diagram, fail altogether to support Mr. Chapman Jones' claim.

Diagram N°5.

| 1 | 2 | 3 | 4 | MEAN. |
|---|---|---|---|---|
| 1·60 | 1·48 | 1·29 | 1·50 | 1·47 |
| 8 | 7 | 6 | 5 | |
| 1·67 | 1·54 | 1·32 | 1·52 | 1·51 |
| 9 | 10 | 11 | 12 | |
| 1·69 | 1·52 | 1·50 | 1·57 | 1·57 |
| 16 | 15 | 14 | 13 | |
| 1·66 | 1·55 | 1·51 | 1·61 | 1·58 |
| 17 | 18 | 19 | 20 | |
| 1·70 | 1·52 | 1·52 | 1·61 | 1·59 |

We ourselves consider that this experiment upon which Mr. Chapman Jones exerted his utmost skill a most striking proof of our assertions, and, as experiments of this kind are most welcome to us, we here record our thanks to him for the trouble he has taken to put our conclusions to a practical test.

We will conclude this paper with a quotation from an address by Captain Abney to the British Association at Newcastle. He said : " Photography deserves to have followers of the highest scientific calibre, and if only some more real physicists and chemists could be induced to unbend their minds and study the theory of an applied science which they often use for record or for pleasure, we might hope for some greater advance than has hitherto been possible."

We do not flatter ourselves that we are physicists or chemists of the highest scientific calibre, nor do we claim to have had Captain Abney's opportunities and experience in photographic matters ; but we do claim, for our investigations, superiority over his, in that they are based upon a scientific and satisfactory nomenclature and system of units, and that they were carried out in such a way as to be capable of repetition by anybody else.

We claim also to have given formulæ which, unlike Captain Abney's, lead to truth, explain photographic phenomena, and admit of practical application. We have had the misfortune to discover the errors of his results, and have thereby incurred his serious displeasure.

*[Reprinted from " Photography," 19th and 29th February, 1891.]*

# THE ACTION OF LIGHT ON THE SENSITIVE FILM.

*Inaugural Address Delivered to the Photographic Section of the Liverpool Physical Society
January 19th, 1891.*

BY

## F. HURTER, Ph.D.

THE function of photography is the production of permanent images of natural objects as true to nature as possible.   The various applications of photography require truthful rendering of the object from different points of view.   The astronomer and the surveyor require truth with regard to the relative distances of the various points in the picture, and, in order to attain this end, they look for a degree of perfection in the construction of lenses and cameras of which the ordinary photographer has no conception.

The construction and adjustment of a photo-theodolite (as the surveyor's camera is called) and the determination of its errors are in themselves a study. The use of photography as an aid to surveying is rapidly extending, particularly for the survey of mountainous districts, and there is a great probability that before very long the photo-theodolite will be called into the service of meteorologists, who, it is expected, will by means of it, be able to determine and measure with considerable accuracy the formation, height, and movement of clouds, and the form and path of electric discharges, such as flashes of lightning.   The truthful rendering of dimensions, however, depends upon the perfection of the apparatus only, and has nothing whatever to do with the rest of photographic operations, except in so far as they tend to distort the film of gelatine ; but it is satisfactory to know that, with proper care, these distortions are so small as to cause errors of only $\frac{1}{100}$ per cent. of the dimension.

Whilst the artist also looks for truthful drawing, he, in addition, seeks truth to nature from another point of view ; he requires light and shade to be rendered as it is seen by the eye : he looks for truth in tone.   But while great perfection has been reached in correctness of drawing, the truthful rendering of tone is still more or less a matter of chance ; and indeed, so long as our plates are less sensitive to light of great wave length than to light of short wave length, absolute truth of tone will not readily be obtained.   There is a large field of research still open in the matter of orthochromatic plates.  A compound sensitive to light of various wave lengths, in proportion to the effect which they produce upon the human eye, would solve the problem of truth of tone. Perfection in this direction would be reached if the substance rendered truthfully the natural colours ; and though the solution of this problem is still far in the distance, I should not like to say positively that it will never be found.

Truth to nature, as far as light and shade are concerned, is therefore only possible with respect to those rays of the spectrum to which the film is sensitive. These rays are, unfortunately, usually such as do not contribute much to the luminosity of the object.

When my friend, Mr. Driffield, first induced me to take up photography as a pastime, the phenomena of under and over-exposure came more frequently under my observation than the phenomenon of correct exposure.   Still, I was familiar with the fact that many prints very fairly represented the light and shade of objects as seen in nature.   Very early I asked myself the question— What are the laws of the action of light in obedience to which a picture is at one time true to nature, and at another (under or over-exposure) it is false ? I had, however, to work for many years before I could, with any degree of satisfaction, answer the question.   From the outset I recognised that truth to nature in a photograph—for example, a positive transparency—was an impossibility if the action of the light on a film were such that the amount of metallic silver produced on the plate were proportional to the intensity of the light.   Yet these transparencies were often the finest, and, to all appearances, the most truthful representations of natural objects.

It is easy to prove that direct proportionality between the intensity of the light and the amount of silver would lead to pictures in which the gradation of tone would be similar to that resulting from under-exposure.

I have here a small apparatus,[1] by means of which I hope to make this clear.  It consists of two black cylinders, which can be made to revolve rapidly.   Upon the circumference of the upper cylinder are fastened two pieces of white paper, cut to the shape of right-angled trapezoids, as shown in Fig. 1.

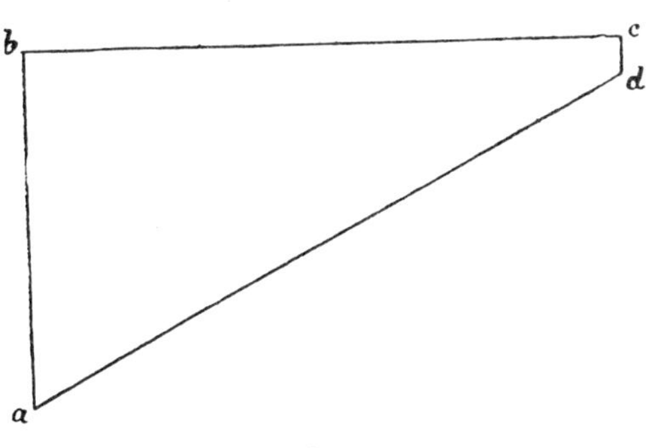


FIG. 1.

---

[1] Now in the collection of the Royal Photographic Society.

The length (BC) is the length of the cylinder, the side (AB) is half the circumference of the cylinder, and CD is the one-tenth part of the side AB. On the lower cylinder are also fastened two pieces of white paper, but a logarithmic curve is substituted for the straight line AD, as shown in Fig. 2.

When these cylinders are caused to revolve rapidly they both show a complete gradation of tone, merging from the same white on one side to the same grey on the other. But the gradation of the upper cylinder appears almost imperceptible to the centre, and then, somewhat abruptly changes into the grey tint ; whilst on the lower cylinder we perceive a beautifully uniform gradation from white to grey, without any abrupt transition. From the upper cylinder the eye receives reflected light, which decreases in arithmetical progression, and from the lower cylinder the eye receives light which decreases in geometrical progression. Whenever we see a beautifully uniform transition from light to dark we may be sure that the light decreases more nearly in geometric than in arithmetic progression.

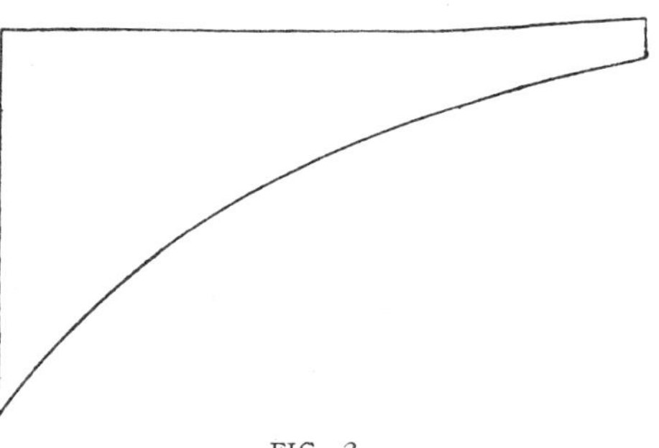

FIG. 2.

Suppose, now, that the upper revolving cylinder (arithmetical progression) were to be photographed, and suppose that the lower cylinder (geometrical progression) represented the photographic positive which resulted, the photographer would then say that this was an under-exposed picture, because there would not be nearly as much white in the picture as there was in the object. If, therefore, a photographer were to produce a geometrical progression of tints from an object reflecting light in arithmetical progression, he would come to the conclusion that he had under-exposed.

I now show you a wedge-shaped glass vessel, tapering in a length of 15 c.m. from a point to a width of 1·5 c.m., *i.e.*, 1 in 10. This glass vessel is filled with a jelly of gelatine, which is intimately mixed with finely-divided metallic silver obtained from a negative. This vessel represents a negative in which the metallic silver increases gradually from one end to the other in arithmetical progression ; but if we examine it by transmitted light we at once perceive that the character of its gradations coincides with the regular and gradual transition of tone of the lower cylinder. The light transmitted by the wedge diminishes, therefore, from one end to the other in geometrical progression, whilst the silver it contains decreases in arithmetical progression.

Now, assume light intensities, as on the upper cylinder, decreasing in arithmetical progression. If the silver on the negative were proportional to the intensity of the light, then an arithmetical progression of silver would result and the negative would be exactly like this wedge. But the light transmitted by this negative would be a geometrical progression, and would, of course, by the same law produce a geometrical progression of silver on a positive, which, in its turn, would, by transmitted light, look a terribly false representation of the original ; that is, it would appear like an under-exposure.

Thus, if the law of proportionality between the light and the amount of silver on a negative held good, we should have the following :—

       Light reflected by object                     Arithmetical progression,
       Silver deposited on negative             Arithmetical progression,
       Light transmitted by negative           Geometrical progression,

and hence the negative would give a range of gradations of light, which could be false in progression.

It is now easy to perceive what the law must be if photographs are to be absolutely truthful in tone. If a geometrical progression of light intensities produce a deposit of metallic silver in arithmetical progression, it will readily be seen that the transmitted light of the negative would be of the same progression as the original light intensities, thus :—

       Light reflected by object                     Geometrical progression,
       Silver deposited on negative              Arithmetical progression,
       Light transmitted by negative           Geometrical progression,

and that the photograph would consequently be true in tone.

To some the arithmetical and geometrical progressions may be clearer expressed in numbers, thus :—

       Light intensities in geometrical progression  2, 4, 8, 16, 32, 64.
       Silver deposited in arithmetical progression  1, 2, 3, 4, 5, 6.
       Light transmitted in geometrical progression 32, 16, 8, 4, 2, 1.

In this case alone would the negative transmit light in the same progression as that reflected by the original object.

The mathematician calls each term of an arithmetic series which corresponds to any given term of a geometric series, the logarithm of that term ; and the law which alone would produce absolutely true tones in photography would be expressed by saying that the quantity of silver reduced on the negative is proportional to the logarithm of the light intensity. The question now arises, is this really the law ?

Bunsen and Roscoe found that when light acts upon a mixture of chlorine and hydrogen, the amount of hydrochloric acid produced in a given time is proportional to the intensity of the light. By analogy, this law has been held to apply to other reactions induced by the light also. But Bunsen likewise studied the action of light upon a solution of chlorine gas in water. When light acts upon chlorine dissolved in water, hydrochloric acid is also formed and oxygen is given off.   Bunsen, however, found that this reaction does not obey the simple laws which he found to apply in the other case, and he did not succeed in tracing the law.   Another investigator, Wittwer, took the matter in hand, and he soon discovered the difference between the laws expressing the two reactions.   When light acts upon a mixture of hydrogen and chlorine in Bunsen's apparatus, the hydrochloric acid is removed as fast as it is produced, and the light acts uniformly upon an almost constant mixture of the two gases.   When, however, light acts upon chlorine water, this chlorine being converted into hydrochloric acid constantly decreases in quantity, and Wittwer found that this gradual disappearance of the chlorine was the reason why the simple law of proportionality did not apply in this reaction.   He found that the amount of chlorine changed during any short interval of time was proportional both to the intensity of the light and to the amount of chlorine still left  in the solution. Now, it is well known to mathematicians that, when the rate of growth or of decrease is proportional to the magnitude of the thing that grows or diminishes, the connection between the magnitude and the time of  growth is the same as exists between a geometric and an arithmetic series.   The growth of the one is proportional to the logarithm of the other.   But the connection between the time and the chlorine which disappeared is just the reverse of that which must apply to photographic plates if they are to be capable of yielding truthful representations.   Similar conditions do, however, exist in the case of photographic plates.   The light changes the silver-salt, and, as the unchanged silver-salt gradually decreases in amount, there is less and less still to be changed in each successive moment.   There are other factors, too, which further tend to complicate the matter : the amount of light which reaches each successive layer of the film also becomes less and less ; as those particles of silver-salt already acted upon and changed screen other particles which are not yet changed.   The result of all these influences is that the connection between the amount of silver changed and the intensity of the light is not accurately logarithmic, but is somewhat complicated.   I found, together with my friend Mr. Driffield, however, that for every plate there is a range of exposures during which the connection between the amount of silver and the exposure is so nearly logarithmic that no human eye could possibly detect the difference between the truth and the approximation.   The more richly coated the plate, the wider is this range, and the more extended is the scale of gradations which the plate is capable of rendering truly.

But when the light acts upon the plate for a very short time, or when the light intensity is very feeble, the amount of silver is almost proportional to the intensity of the light.   When this is the case, the resulting picture is, as I pointed out before, necessarily false in tone. Its gradations are terrible exaggerations. There is too abrupt a transition from white to black, and the photographer would judge it to have been under-exposed. When, on the other hand, exposure is unduly prolonged, the growth of the reduced silver gradually ceases, the gradations are lost in one uniform tint, light and shade are indistinguishable, and the picture is again untrue, but in the opposite direction.

I have throughout spoken of silver as " reduced." This is, of course, a figure of speech, the complete reduction only taking place during the operation of development.

The action of light upon the sensitive plate as it proceeds with time of exposure, and as it has been ascertained by Mr. Driffield and myself, is represented by the annexed diagram :—The curves represent the growth of metallic silver as, with a given time the intensity of the light increases; or as, with a given intensity of light, the time of exposure increases. The scale of exposures is a geometrical progression. Equidistant points do not indicate equal increments of light intensity or of time, but equal logarithms or equidistant terms of a geometrical progression. The vertical scale represents the amount of silver produced by the corresponding intensity of light or exposure. Each curve consists of three branches gradually merging into each other. The lower curved branch represents the period of under-exposure, the straight portion that of correct representation of light and shade (in which the silver grows arithmetically, while the exposure grows geometrically), and the upper curved portion represents the period of over-exposure.

Two curves are shown, and they are both characteristic of the same plate ; the difference between them merely represents a difference in length of time of development. As development is prolonged, every gradation grows, and the curve becomes more and more inclined ; but it does not change its position with respect to the exposure scale. When the straight portions of any number of the infinite group of curves which are all characteristic of one and the same plate, and which are decided by the length of time of development are produced, they all intersect, almost exactly, in the same point on the exposure scale. No method of development which has so far been tested alters the character of these curves ; it simply decides their inclination.

Much ridicule has been cast upon me and upon my colleague by photographers who pose as great authorities, but to whom a logarithm is an insurmountable obstacle, for having announced that the photographer has no power to alter, by development, the ratios of metallic silver on a negative, and that these ratios are alone decided by the laws which govern the action of light upon the sensitive plate. This assertion is true, nevertheless, and is equivalent to saying that the character of this curve cannot be altered by development. If, by development, one ordinate is altered, all the rest are altered with it, until the curve of maximum inclination is reached.

Dr. Emerson, who has taken a kind interest in our investigations, and who discerned from the first that some important truth might be concealed behind these awkward logarithms, gave us the following problem to consider :—Supposing, Dr. Emerson says, I want to photograph three houses, a white one, a grey one, and a black one. What is it you say I have to do to secure a truthful rendering of tone ; what is it you say I can alter by development, and what is it I cannot alter ?   As the reply we gave to Dr. Emerson may assist you also more clearly to grasp this subject, I think I cannot do better than give yon a few extracts from it.

In order to represent the three houses in their relatively correct tones, the first absolute essential is a thickly and evenly coated plate, and this we must assume we have.   Before long we hope plate-makers will realise the importance of attention to these points. It is entirely a mistake to suppose that a plate is sufficiently rich in silver because there is enough to yield the maximum density required. Our investigations show that great contrasts can only be truly rendered upon a liberally coated plate rich in silver compounds.

It will render the subject clearer to you if we proceed to discuss it under three heads—under, correct, and over-exposure. We will assume that we have taken three pictures of the houses

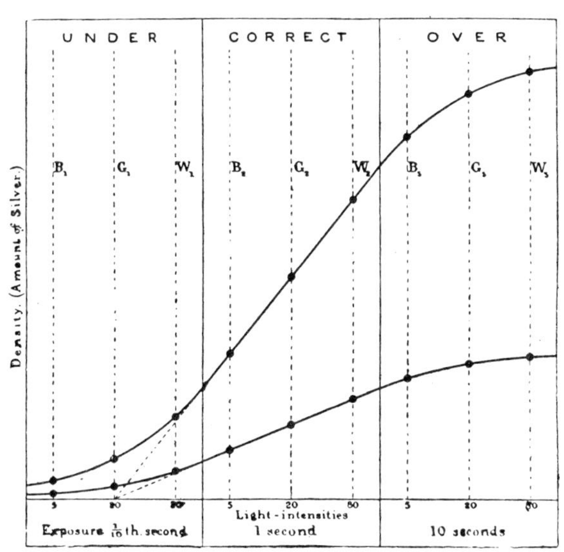


on three separate but similar plates, and that they have been exposed for $\frac{1}{10}$, 1, and 10 seconds respectively.   The three houses are represented on the diagram by dots.


## I.—Under-Exposure.

If the exposures given have been insufficient, the three equidistant lines, $B_1$, $G_1$, $W_1$, may mark the light intensities reflected by the three houses which, for the sake of argument, we will take as 5 for the black, 20 for the grey, and 80 for the white.   What we affirm is that any alteration, either in time of development or in constitution of the developer, will decide upon which of the system of curves the respective densities shall lie—whether, for example, on the lower or upper curve shown on the diagram.   It would be possible, even in a case of under-exposure, aided by an experienced eye, so to develop that something akin to a correct relationship between the two extreme densities might possibly result, but the density of the intermediate tone would be relatively false ; the density representing the grey house too closely approaching that of the black house.

If the degree of under-exposure have been very decided, the ratios of the amounts of silver deposited would be as $1 : 4 : 16$ (*i.e.*, as $5 : 20 : 80$), however long the development might be continued.   But, when the *amount of silver* is in the same ratio as the light reflected by the objects, the opacities of the images will produce prints false in tone, and this false relation being established by the peculiar form of the curve, the photographer has no power to alter it.

The opacity varies with the development, but it varies according to law ; the photographer cannot cause the opacity of the white house to grow without that of the black house growing with it in accordance with a fixed law indicated by the system of curves.

II.—CORRECT EXPOSURE.

If a longer (correct) exposure be given, the ratio of the silver deposited will be altogether different from that we have just considered.   Instead of the silver being deposited in the ratio of light intensities, $5 : 20 : 80$, it will be deposited in the ratio of the logarithms of these intensities.   With these particular intensities ($5 : 20 : 80$), this would mean that the difference between the amounts of silver representing the white and grey houses is the same as the difference between the amounts of silver representing the grey and black houses.

Different treatment in development would result in different amounts of silver deposited, though their ratio would remain undisturbed, but any increase of density in the white house would result in a corresponding increase of density in the black and grey houses in such a manner as to bring the three points on the lines $B_2$, $G_2$, $W_2$, simultaneously from a lower to a higher curve.   The photographer has the power to decide how far he will allow the density of the white house to proceed, but he cannot restrain the density of the black house while he allows the density of the white house to increase.

Among the infinity of curves which are intermediate between the axis of the abscissæ and the extreme curve, there is only one which would correspond to a negative from which a print true to nature could be obtained.   It is the decision of this curve which is the difficulty in development.   When this curve is reached, however, the *opacities* of the three gradations representing the three houses would be exactly as 5 : 20 : 80, the ratio of the light reflected by the houses.

If, however, development were stopped before this curve were reached, and if it happened that the plate were somewhat fogged, the negative would convey to the eye the impression of over-exposure. Such a negative could be remedied by intensification, and many experienced photographers would hence declare that they had corrected an over-exposed plate, whilst a measurement of the relative densities of the three houses would, at any stage of the development, have revealed the fact that it was a case of correct exposure after all, and that the real fault was under-development.

### III.—OVER-EXPOSURE.

In the case of unduly prolonged exposure, the images of the three houses would fall on the upper part of the curve, where intersected, say, by the lines $B_3$, $G_3$, $W_3$. The result of this would be that the tone of the grey house would too nearly approach that of the white house ; whilst in the case of under-exposure, it too nearly approached that of the black one. You might, by development, decide the density of one of the houses, but it would be out of your power to alter its relationship with respect to the other two.

*Exposure* decides within which of the three periods (under, correct, or over-exposure) the three houses shall lie.

*Development* decides which curve of the system shall be reached.

I have now explained in as elementary language as possible the action of light upon the sensitive film, and shown how a knowledge of these laws at once explains the phenomena of under, correct, and over-exposure, and how truth of gradation is only possible if the exposure be such that the amount of silver be proportional to the logarithm of the exposure.

I now pass to an entirely different question. What is the nature of the change which the light produces in the silver bromide, and which renders it capable of reduction by the developer ? I shall not enter into the historical aspect of the question, nor touch upon points which have recently been fully discussed in various papers on the latent image by Meldola, Brebner, Bothamley and others.[1] I shall only indicate what little I have myself done to elucidate this mysterious action of the light.

It is a well-known fact that when metallic silver combines with bromine, a great amount of heat is liberated ; molecular energy is transformed into heat, and is dissipated. Before silver combined with bromine can be separated

---

[1] *British Journal of Photography.*

therefrom, this energy must be again supplied. In the act of development, the heat produced by the oxidation of the developer may, and probably does, supply a portion of this energy ; but another portion must certainly be supplied by the light.

Another well-known fact is that different sensitive plates require very different exposures to produce the same quantity of metallic silver after development. At the last meeting of the Society of Chemical Industry an experiment was made by Mr. Driffield with Wratten " ordinary " and " instantaneous " plates, which showed that 1,200 seconds were required to produce the same result upon the " ordinary " plate as was produced in 87 seconds upon the " instantaneous " plate.[1]

This renders it almost certain that the halogen salts of silver exist in gelatine emulsion in different modifications, some requiring more, and some less, energy to render them capable of development. When a substance absorbs energy some molecular work is performed, which Professor Clausius termed " disgregation." Probably the work which the light does is disgregation also, and part of this work can evidently be done in the preparation of the sensitive emulsion ; the more energy thus supplied, the quicker is the plate.

Upon one of the most rapid plates in the market it is possible to produce a deposit of 15 milligrams of metallic silver on an area of 100 square centimetres by exposing the plate for 20 seconds to the light of a standard candle placed at a distance of one metre.[2]

If we imagine a sphere of one metre radius covered with the same sensitive emulsion, and, placed in the centre of this sphere, a standard candle, the whole sphere would, in 20 seconds, be affected to the same extent as the plate having an area of only 100 square centimetres, assuming the light to act equally in all directions. Such a sphere would have a surface of $100^2 \times 3\cdot14159 \times 4 = 125{,}664$ square centimetres, and upon this surface we should find, after development, $18\cdot849$ grams of metallic silver.

Now, when one gram of silver combines with bromine, heat equivalent to 211 units is developed, consequently the total separation of $18\cdot849$ grams of metallic silver from the bromine combined therewith would require a supply of energy equal to 3,977 units of heat.

Can this amount of heat be supplied by a standard candle ? Such a candle consumes 120 grains, or 7.77 grams of spermaceti per hour, and consequently in 20 seconds only $\frac{1}{180}$th of this amount, or $0\cdot043$ gram. One gram of spermaceti produces by its complete combustion 10,200 units of heat, and the candle would, therefore, only produce 438 units in 20 seconds. But most of

---

[1] See p. 174.      [2] H.N.—B., pp. 139–141, also paper of 1898.

this heat is carried away by the products of combustion as heat, and only about 15 per cent. of the total heat is converted into radiant energy ; of this again, only about 5 per cent. is capable of affecting the silver salts, so that the amount of useful energy derived from the candle is only equal to three or four units of heat in 20 seconds, whilst 3,977 units would be required to split up the whole of the silver bromide on the sensitive sphere. The energy supplied by the candle is therefore wholly inadequate to completely decompose an amount of silver bromide equivalent to 15 milligrams of metallic silver spread over an area of 100 square centimetres.

To me it has always been impossible to reconcile the short exposures necessary for the production of photographic images with any theory which demanded the absolute separation of the halogen, or part of it, from the silver. Nor would it account for the enormous discrepancy between the energy actually required and the energy supplied by the candle if we assumed that the halogen in some way combines with the gelatine, and so rendered it unnecessary, during the exposure, to supply the whole heat of combination between the halogen and the silver.

The work of my colleague, Mr. Driffield, and myself pointed out to us the possibility of so illuminating a sensitive plate that the whole of the halogen compounds of silver upon it should be so affected by the light as to be capable of development. The theory pointing to this fact was put to the test.

We chose a plate, a slow one, which would stand the action of ferrous oxalate for one hour without showing a trace of reduction. Such a plate was cut into two halves : one half served for a determination of the total quantity of silver upon the plate, and the other half was exposed to a standard candle, at a distance of half a metre, for 33 minutes. This half of the plate was developed with ferrous oxalate for 30 minutes, well washed, and fixed for 12 hours, the fixing bath being twice renewed during this time. After carefully washing for 24 hours the amount of metallic silver was determined.

I found upon an area of 100 square centimetres of the unexposed half 99·5 milligrams of silver, and upon the same area of the exposed half 52·0 milligrams of silver. The result showed that only 52·2 per cent. of the silver bromide had been changed by the light so far as to be capable of reduction by the ferrous oxalate.

The expedient was now adopted of illuminating the plate from both sides. A candle was placed on each side of the plate, and an exposure of 33 minutes was given, the development, fixing, &c., being carried out as before. The unexposed half of the plate gave 107·2 milligrams of silver on an area of 100 square centimetres, and the exposed half gave 102·2 milligrams of silver on the same area ; so that the experiment had succeeded, 95·3 per cent. of the silver bromide on the plate having been so changed by the light as to be capable of reduction by ferrous oxalate.

Having thus found a method of converting the whole, or nearly the whole, of the silver bromide on the plate into this peculiar condition, I thought it worth while to repeat the experiment, and to determine carefully what became of the bromine or the halogen.

A plate was, in the first place, washed with distilled water until all but the faintest trace of solubles, bromides, iodides and chlorides had been removed. It was then illuminated from both sides, and, after illumination, was again treated with distilled water. This water was tested for soluble halogen acids, but not a trace could be discovered by means of silver solution. It was clear no hydrobromic acid had been formed, and no substitution of bromine for hydrogen in the gelatine had consequently taken place.

The plate was next developed with a weak ammoniacal solution of pyrogallol, perfectly free from bromides, chlorides and iodides. After development, which was continued for half an hour, the plate was washed in distilled water, and the washings were added to the developing solution. This solution was strongly acidified with nitric acid, and the halogens were precipitated with silver nitrate and weighed as metallic silver, after reduction by hydrogen gas. The metallic silver thus weighed amounted to 197·7 milligrams.

The plate itself was fixed for twelve hours, washed for 24 hours, and the silver determined. I found upon it 194·4 milligrams of metallic silver.

As the area of this plate was 192 square centimetres, the amount of metallic silver on 100 square centimetres was 101·2 milligrams ; so that, in this case also, over 90 per cent. of the halogen salt had been reduced.

This experiment, which entirely corroborates the evidence afforded by the calculation of energy, clearly shows that during the illumination no bromine whatever was lost ; that no such decomposition had taken place as would correspond to a substitution of bromine for hydrogen in the gelatine ; and that, if the bromine had combined with the gelatine, the product thus formed yielded the whole of the bromine to the developer.

Here, then, is the outline of a method of quantitative research on the constitution of the latent image. The possibility of converting more than 90 per cent. of the silver bromide into this peculiar modification being thus demonstrated, I hope some member of the Liverpool Physical Society will further pursue this research, for the completion of which I fear I have no time in the immediate future.

[*Reprinted from the " Journal of the Society of Chemical Industry,"* 28th *February,* 1891. *No. 2, Vol. X.*]

# RELATION BETWEEN PHOTOGRAPHIC NEGATIVES AND THEIR POSITIVES.

BY

## F. HURTER, Ph.D., AND V. C. DRIFFIELD.

THE photo-chemical investigations which we had the honour to bring before this Section were undertaken with a view to render photographic operations more certain and reliable than they are at present, and by this communication we wish to direct the attention of photographers to the advantages of scientific procedure over rule of thumb manipulation. We propose to produce, by contact printing, a negative from a transparent positive, and from a negative two positives ; the three being produced upon three entirely different plates. We hope to prove that we can produce the best possible result upon these plates with certainty, without making any calculations, and that, although a knowledge of logarithms is necessary for the appreciation of our theory no such knowledge is required to carry out our practice, which, indeed, is simplicity itself.

In order to be successful in photographic operations it is essential to know exactly the properties of the plates we intend to use. We must know their sensitiveness to light, their behaviour during development, and their behaviour to negatives, if transparencies and secondary negatives are to be produced.

We think it well shortly to recapitulate as much as is necessary of what we have already published, so that the principles on which our operations depend may be properly understood.

We have shown that when light acts upon a sensitive film, the growth of the density of the resulting image (*i.e.,* the amount of reduced silver) is at first proportional to the intensity of the light, but, that owing to the decreasing amount of unaltered silver salt, the density grows less rapidly with prolonged exposure ; a period now supervenes when it ceases to grow at all, and at last it decreases if the exposure be unduly prolonged.   We have shown that for every plate there exists a range of exposures during which the growth of the density is proportional to the logarithm of the exposure, and this range we termed the " period of correct representation."

Now, what we aim at, in studying our plates, is to ascertain this range of exposures.   The method of doing so is simple.   We expose different portions of a plate to the light of a standard candle placed at a distance of one metre from the plate for various periods of time, every successive exposure being double the previous one.   After development we measure the amount of silver reduced by our photometric method.

The densities thus obtained, when plotted on a diagram, furnish the " characteristic curve " of the plate   We refer you to Diagram No. 6, which shows the characteristic curves of the Wratten " ordinary " and " instantaneous " plates, which we intend to use to-night.

### Relation between Photo-Negatives and their Positives.

The lower horizontal scale is a scale of exposures, the vertical scale the scale of densities.   The divisions of the exposure scale are similar to those of an ordinary slide rule.   The divisions of the vertical scale are all equal, and the

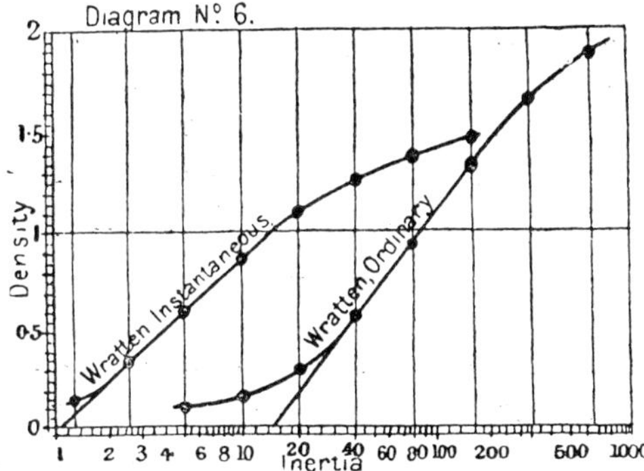


distance between 0. and 1.00 on this scale is exactly equal to the distance between 1 and 10 on the exposure scale.

In order to save trouble we have had skeleton diagrams with these scales lithographed, and members are welcome to copies.   They are exceedingly convenient for plotting characteristic curves and making other memoranda of experiments.

It will be seen that the two curves on this diagram are very similar, but they are situated on different portions of the exposure scale.   The one plate requires much shorter exposures for the production of the same density than the other. The more to the left of the exposure scale the curve is situated, the faster is the plate.

The curve itself consists of three distinct portions.   The lower strongly curved portion is the period of under-exposure ; the middle portion, almost a straight line, is the period of correct representation ; the upper curved end is the period of over-exposure.

The middle or straight line portion of this curve embraces the only useful range of exposures, and the only one which interests us to-night.   If we produce this straight line until it intersects the scale of exposures, the point of intersection marks a particular exposure, viz., the shortest, which will produce a density very nearly at the beginning of the period of correct representation.   We have shown that this point of intersection is practically independent of the length of time of development.

Diagram No. 7 shows the divisions of the characteristic curve into three periods more clearly.   The curves on this diagram are two of the infinite number which are all characteristic of the same plate, and which result from differences in the length of time of development.   The shorter the time of development the less inclined is the straight line, and as development is prolonged, the more inclined does the straight line become, but, whatever the inclination, it would still intersect the exposure scale at the same point.

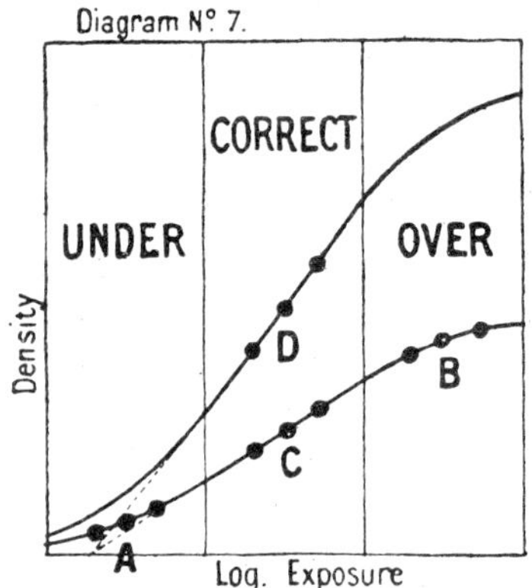


It is important to know what length of time development must last in order to reach any particular inclination of this straight line. We therefore develop the plate, when determining its speed, for an exact time at a specified temperature, and note the inclination of the line by drawing through the point 1,000 on the exposure scale, a line parallel to the straight part of the characteristic, noting its point of intersection with the density scale.   This gives us the value of the tangent of the angle of inclination, which value we term the " development constant."   Knowing the value of this constant for one time of development, we can approximately determine the time it would take to reach any other constant, but our results in this respect are not yet sufficiently complete for publication.[1]

We may here say that, in our first paper (9, 467), we gave a formula for the calculation of the development factor $\gamma$, which, we regret to say, was accidentally inverted.[2]

It should stand—

$$\gamma = \frac{D_2 - D_1}{\log. E_2 - \log. E_1}.$$

In our former publication we have shown how we utilise the information obtained by the simple experiment with a candle for the production of negatives

---

[1] See the paper of 1893.          [2] Corrected in this series of reprints.

in the camera ; we now proceed to show how we utilise it for the production of positive transparencies and secondary negatives.

The production of secondary negatives may not be considered by many as of importance, but other researches we have made have clearly shown to us that one and the same negative is not equally suitable for all printing processes, and that a negative yielding a good ordinary silver print is generally incapable of giving a first-class enlargement on bromide paper. There are therefore cases in which the production of secondary negatives of special qualities is most desirable.

Let us now imagine a sensitive plate behind a negative illuminated by a light of known intensity. For simplicity's sake, let the negative have only one or two different opacities. Let the opacities of the negative be 40, 20, and 10, then we should expect the plate to be illuminated behind the negative with $\frac{1}{40}$, $\frac{1}{20}$, and $\frac{1}{10}$, the original intensity of the light. Experiment reveals, however, that this is not so, but that the results of exposures to the light behind the negatives are greater than those which would be produced by $\frac{1}{40}$, $\frac{1}{20}$, and $\frac{1}{10}$ of the original light intensity. The reason for this is not far to seek. When the light shines on the plate directly, say about 70 to 80 per cent. of the light is reflected by the plate into space. When a negative is placed in front of the plate the light is similarly reflected by the sensitive surface, but a considerable portion of it is at once reflected back again by the two reflecting surfaces of the negative, so that behind a negative less of the light transmitted by it is lost by reflection from the sensitive film, and consequently more work is done on the film than would be the case if the same intensity of the light were to act upon a film free to reflect.

Suppose the naked film were exposed to light of unit intensity. It would reflect into space the fraction R of light. Of the rest ($1-R$) some would be absorbed, and some would pass through the plate. If, however, a negative be placed in front of the sensitive film, then the fraction R of the light cannot be reflected wholly into space ; a portion of it is reflected back again upon the film, and if the coefficient of reflection of the negative be $r$, the amount of light which is thus returned to the film is R $r$. Secondly, tertiary, &c., reflections add small amounts $R^2 r^2$, $R^3 r^3$, &c., to this. The result is that the effect of unit light coming through a negative is greater than the effect of unit light when the film can reflect freely, and is represented by the amount—

$$1 + R r + R^2 r^2 + R^3 r^3 + \ldots = \frac{1}{1 - R r}$$

or, what is the same thing, the opacity of the negative appears to be reduced by a fraction ($1 - R r$). It will therefore be seen that the same negative will give different results upon different printing surfaces, according to the amount of light which these surfaces reflect.

There is still another point to be considered.  When we measure the opacity of the negative, we measure it chiefly to the yellow rays of the lamp, whilst those rays are least active upon the plate.  The opacity of the negative to the blue rays is, in all cases we have tested, greater than the opacity to the yellow rays.

These considerations will explain why, when a negative is used for contact printing, its opacity must be considered as less than that indicated by our instrument ; and when it is used for enlargement the opacity must be considered as greater than that measured in our instrument, because, in the one case, the sensitive surface cannot reflect freely, whilst in the other it does do so.

The exact amount, therefore, by which we have to increase or decrease the value of the opacity of the negative depends upon the reflection of the film, upon its sensitiveness to different portions of the spectrum, and upon the colour of the negative.

If it were not for these corrections the relation between a negative and its positive could be at once deduced from the formula we gave in our paper for the calculation of the amount of silver deposited for a given exposure.  This formula was, for the period of correct representation—

$$D = \gamma \log. \left( \frac{I\,t}{i} \right)$$

We should have to consider that in this formula the intensity of the light I is reduced by the negative, and we should have to divide I by the opacity of the negative, which in logarithmic calculation means deducting the logarithm of the opacity from the logarithm of the intensity of the light.  But the logarithm of the opacity is the density as measured by our instrument, which density we simply subtract, and, in order to prevent confusion, we mark the densities of negatives, including the fog, by N, and the densities of positives by P.  The equation which results, if we introduce at the same time the correction $a$ of the negative density for the reasons just explained, stands thus:—

$$P = \gamma \left[ \log. \frac{I\,t}{i} - a\,N \right]$$

and this equation represents the general relation between a negative and its positive.  P is the density of the positive produced behind the negative of density N upon a plate of inertia $i$ by means of the light intensity I in the time $t$.

The coefficient $a$ which converts the density, as measured, into the printing density, is, for negatives developed by ferrous oxalate, usually a fraction ; for pyro-developed negatives it is generally nearly 1, if the negative be used for contact printing ; but when the negative is used for enlarging, the factor $a$ which changes the usual density of the negative into printing density, is always greater than 1, even for negatives developed with ferrous oxalate.

The method we have adopted as the simplest for finding the printing factor *a* is as follows, and is illustrated by Diagram No. 9.   We must assume that we have already made a speed determination of the plate of which we wish to determine the printing factor, and that we consequently know the extent and position of the straight line which indicates the period of correct representation. We proceed to make two more exposures which, so long as they fall within the correct period, should lie as widely apart as possible.   In our example we have given exposures of 5 and 40 C.M.S.   We next take a negative of a uniform density of, say, about 1·0.   Our object is, through this negative, to produce

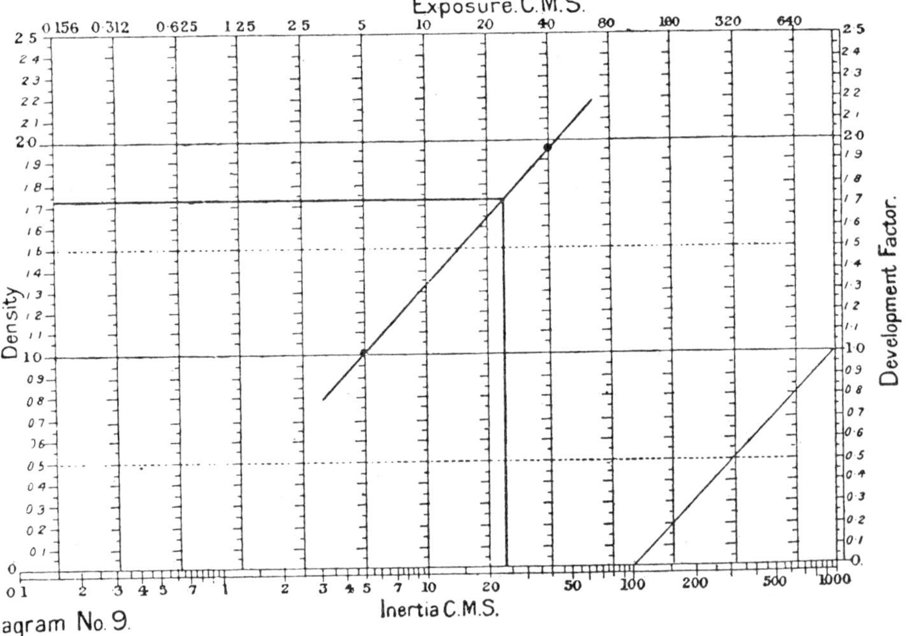


Diagram No. 9.

upon the plate under examination a density which shall lie somewhere between the densities which will result from the two direct exposures already given. The geometrical mean of 5 and 40 is, roughly, 15, and we therefore aim to produce a density behind the negative (the total density of which is, in our example, 0·985) equivalent to a direct exposure of 15 C.M.S.   We calculate the necessary exposure thus :—

$$\log. T = \log. 15 + 0·985$$
$$T = 145.$$

We now give this exposure of 145 C.M.S. through the negative and proceed to develop the resulting plate, together with that produced by the direct exposures of 5 and 40 C.M.S.   Having measured the resulting densities, we mark upon the exposure lines 5 and 40 of one of our skeleton diagrams those densities (exclusive of fog) which result from the two direct exposures in our example 1·010 and 1·965 respectively.   Through these two densities we draw a straight line which coincides with the correct period of the plate.   In our example the density produced through the negative is 1·730, exclusive of fog ; this we mark on the density scale, and draw through it a horizontal line intersecting the straight line we have already drawn.   Through this point of intersection we draw a perpendicular and mark the point of its intersection with the inertia scale.   This point of intersection gives the direct exposure to which an exposure of 145 C.M.S. through the negative is equivalent, in this example 24 C.M.S.   We have now merely to deduct log. 24 from log. 145 and divide the result by the density of the negative used, and we obtain the printing factor $a$ :—

$$\frac{\log. 145 - \log. 24}{·985} = 0·79$$

That this mode of converting the visual density into the printing density is correct practically, even for the errors caused by mutual reflection, is best proved by experiment.

Having measured in our instrument the densities of a negative with a number of different but uniform tints, and found the densities to be $N_1$, $N_2$, $N_3$, &c., we can calculate the time of exposure necessary to produce, behind each tint, exactly the same positive density if once we know the factor $a$.

The times of exposure are given by the equation—

$$\log. t - a N = \text{constant.}$$

We have made many such experiments, of which we quote one as an example.   Behind the negative densities N it was proposed to produce positive densities corresponding to 15 C.M.S. direct exposure upon a plate known as "Barnet ordinary," the printing factor for which is $a = 0·665$.   The following table shows the calculations and results, the time of exposure being calculated by the formula—

$$\log. T = \log. 15 + 0·665 N.$$

| N. | $a$N. | log. T. | T. | P. |
|---|---|---|---|---|
|  |  |  | Seconds. |  |
| 1·230 | ·8179 | 1·9939 | 98·6 | 1·300 |
| ·965 | ·6417 | 1·8177 | 65·7 | 1·310 |
| ·660 | ·4389 | 1·6149 | 41·2 | 1·330 |
| ·390 | ·2593 | 1·4353 | 27·2 | 1·285 |
|  |  |  | Mean | 1·306 |

It will be seen that the densities of the resulting positive were as nearly equal as they could possibly be made. Such experiments, of course, require an exact knowledge of the factor $a$.

The mode of correcting the visual density for mutual reflection and colour can, however, be proved correct in another way, which does not involve a previous knowledge of the factor $a$.

The formula $P = \gamma \left( \log. \dfrac{I\,t}{i} - a\,N \right)$ becomes by transposition $P + a\,\gamma\,N = \gamma \log. \dfrac{I\,t.}{i}$ Since when exposing a sensitive plate behind a negative, the intensity of the light I in front of the negative, the time of exposure and the inertia of the sensitive plate are all the same, the sum $P + a\,\gamma\,N$ must be the same for any corresponding points of the negative and positive. If, therefore, we print a positive from a negative, ensuring such exposures as fall within the period of correct representation, measure the resulting densities, and then form the sum $P + a\,\gamma\,N$, this sum must be constant. Since $P + a\,\gamma\,N = c$ is the equation of a straight line, we can show this property graphically without knowing $a\,\gamma$. We simply choose the densities of the negative as abscissæ, the densities of the positive as ordinates, and join the points which should form a straight line if the proposition is correct. We give a few experiments of this description.[1]

Experiments made in 1887. $P + 1\cdot6\,N = 3\cdot083$.

| Negative density, N. | Positive density, P. | P + 1·6 N. | Error. |
| --- | --- | --- | --- |
| 0·700 | 1·960 | 3·080 | − ·003 |
| 0·900 | 1·680 | 3·120 | + ·047 |
| 1·010 | 1·480 | 3·096 | + ·013 |
| 1·223 | 1·113 | 3·096 | + ·013 |
| 1·285 | 1·010 | 3·060 | − ·023 |
| 1·360 | ·850 | 3·020 | − ·063 |
| 1·550 | ·530 | 3·010 | − ·073 |
| 1·660 | ·417 | 3·073 | − ·010 |

[1] H.N.—A., p. 148. H.N.—B., p. 9.

[2] Experiment No. 2.   P + 1·5 N = 2·530.

| Negative density, N. | Positive density, P. | P + 1·5 N. | Error. |
|---|---|---|---|
| 0·700 | 1·470 | 2·520 | − ·010 |
| 0·900 | 1·140 | 2·490 | − ·040 |
| 1·010 | 1·007 | 2·562 | + ·032 |
| 1·223 | ·657 | 2·491 | − ·039 |
| 1·285 | ·547 | 2·474 | − ·056 |
| 1·360 | ·410 | 2·430 | − ·100 |
| 1·550 | ·270 | 2·595 | + ·065 |
| 1·660 | ·190 | 2·680 | + ·150 |

This experiment being made with a slow plate, the last few positive densities fell into the period of under-exposure. It must not be forgotten that all the formulæ so far given only apply to the period of correct representation.

The following more recent and more complete experiment has been made the subject of a diagram to illustrate the graphic mode of proving that the actual exposures a plate receives behind a negative are accurately represented by our formulæ.

To Diagram No. 8 the abscissæ are the densities of the negative, the ordinates the densities of the positive, and it will be seen that all the points can be joined by a straight line, which proves that the printing densities of the negative were absolutely proportional to the densities as measured by our grease-spot photometer; were it otherwise the points would have been situated on a curve. The plate

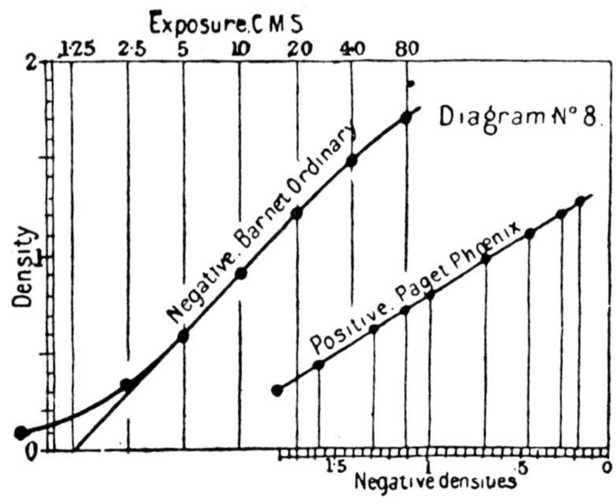


used for the positive was a Paget " Phœnix "; its constants had all been determined by special experiments, so as to make it possible to calculate beforehand the densities which ought to result. These constants were : Inertia = 6.11 C.M.S., printing factor $a$ = 0.577, development factor, for $4\frac{1}{2}$ minutes at 60° F., $\gamma$ = 1.03.  Behind a measured negative one of these plates was ex-

[2] H.N.—A , p. 155.

posed for 134 seconds to a standard candle at 1 metre distance.　The table shows the numerical results.　The calculated densities are obtained by the formula—

$$P = 1\cdot03\,[\log.\ \frac{134}{6\cdot11} - 0\cdot577\,N]$$

| [1] Negative density (observed). | Positive density (observed). | Positive density (calculated). |
|---|---|---|
| 0·165 | 1·270 | 1·285 |
| 0·255 | 1·225 | 1·230 |
| 0·440 | 1·120 | 1·120 |
| 0·670 | ·990 | ·982 |
| 0·98 | ·805 | ·800 |
| 1·28 | ·625 | ·620 |
| 1·57 | ·445 | ·450 |
| 1·81 | ·315 | ·300 |

These experiments clearly demonstrate the general relation between the negative and its positive, and show the truth of our formulæ for correct exposures.

But nothing will be so convincing of the truth of these formulæ and measurements than an ocular demonstration.　If, by carefully timing both the exposure and the development, we succeed in making the value of the product $a\,\gamma$ numerically equal to 1, then the formula becomes—

$$P + N = \text{constant.}$$

Since P and N represent the visual densities of the negative and positive, this formula really tells us that, if such a positive is placed in juxtaposition with its negative, the picture should vanish totally ; we ought to perceive nothing but a uniform tint all over the plate, since on every spot the sums of the positive and negative densities are alike.　We show here a negative and positive, at present fastened together, which will prove this special case of our formulæ, the only one which can be proved so readily.　But it must not be supposed that every positive and every negative will do this ; it is only when exposure and development have been carefully timed that this result is obtained.

We must now refer you again to Diagram 8.　If, on this diagram we produce the straight line until it intersects the scale of negative densities, the point of intersection would indicate the smallest negative density through which the standard candle, at one metre distance, would have been just unable to affect the plate in the 134 seconds given.

[1] H.N.—B., pp. 171, 176, 178.

This leads us to the rule by which we ascertain the exposure necessary to produce with certainty a good positive transparency upon a given plate.

We first of all measure the highest density of the negative which we then correct with the factor $a$ for the particular sensitive plate, and, knowing the inertia of the plate, we take care that the exposure shall be such that, behind the highest density of the negative, the plate shall receive an exposure at least equal to the inertia.   By our formula the necessary exposure would be—

$$\log. \text{T} = \log. i + a \text{ N}.$$

But we do not need to make the calculation at all.   Thanks to the arrangement of our diagrams, we need only take into a pair of compasses the printing density of the negative measured on the density scale, and measure from the inertia of the plate the same distance to the right on the exposure scale, and we read off at once the necessary exposure.

If the positive is to serve for the reproduction of a negative, it is absolutely necessary to continue development until the difference between two densities, say the extremes, is equal to the difference of the corresponding extremes in the negative.   If the development is too short the resulting positive may look better, but it will not yield a good secondary negative.

By variations in the time of development it is possible to produce secondary negatives in which the scale of tones is either contracted or extended, and this function of development is of the utmost value in the production of special negatives for special printing processes.

It is undoubtedly a difficulty that, with one and the same negative, we have to multiply its densities as measured photometrically with different factors according to the plates we use with it.   For negatives developed with ferrous oxalate the factor varies from about $0.6$ to $1.0$.   We find it, however, sufficient for practical purposes to use the factor $0.8$, but, of course, it is always better to ascertain the correct factor by experiment.

All this appears to be very complicated, but in actual practice it is very simple, as we shall now proceed to show.   At the last meeting we produced, from a positive, a secondary negative, and we ascertained the necessary exposure as follows :—The highest density of the positive, as measured in our instrument, was $2.70$, the printing factor $a$ for the plate we used (Barnet) was $0.665$, so that the highest printing density was $0.665 \times 2.70 = 1.7955$.   We measured the amount, $1.795$, or practically $1.800$, with the compasses on the density scale, and carried this distance off on the exposure scale from the point $1.3$ (the inertia of the Barnet plate).   This indicated an exposure of $81$ seconds, and this exposure we gave, the result proving it to have been correct.

To-night we propose to conclude our paper by producing two positive transparencies by contact printing on two plates of considerably different sensitiveness. The plates we shall use are Wratten " Ordinary " and " Instantaneous." The highest density of the negative we shall use is 2·385, and if you will refer to Diagram No. 6, you will see how, from this density, we arrive at the exposure necessary for the two transparencies. We first of all multiply the density 2·385 by 0·8, and this gives the effective printing density 1·90 for the Wratten plates. We measure with compasses 1·9 on the density scale, and applying the compasses to the inertia of each plate, we read off, on the inertia scale, exposures of 87 and 1,200 C.M.S. for the "instantaneous" and " ordinary " plates respectively.

We will expose the " instantaneous " plate first, but instead of giving the exposure of 87 seconds at a distance of 1 metre from the candle, we will, to save time, give 43½ seconds at a distance of 0·707 of a metre. Having made this exposure, we will proceed to expose the " ordinary " plate. The exposure indicated is 1,200 C.M.S., which amounts to 20 minutes, and, as we do not wish to tax your patience to this extent, we will show you how we curtail a too lengthy exposure. Instead of using a candle, we will take a paraffin lamp, and we will find the distance at which it must be placed from the plate to be equal to 100 candles at 1 metre distance. To do this we hold a piece of white cardboard in the place of the sensitive plate, and, by means of a simple shadow photometer, we adjust the position of the lamp until its light is equal in intensity to that of 100 candles at a distance of 1 metre. We view the shadows through a piece of green grass in order to obviate the colour difficulty. We have now increased our light one hundred-fold, and the exposure we must give is consequently 12 seconds.

[*Reprinted from the "Journal of the Society of Chemical Industry," 28th February, 1891. No. 2, Vol. X.*]

# THE SECTOR AND GREASE-SPOT PHOTOMETERS, AND THEIR RESULTS.

BY

## F. HURTER, Ph.D., and V. C. DRIFFIELD.

---

### (a) Reply to Captain Abney.

SINCE the last meeting we have constructed a photometer on the principle of Captain Abney's, and we are happy to be able to confirm every word he has said in his paper regarding the differences which result when one and the same negative is measured by his instrument and by our own. The density of the "fog," as we term it, is considerably smaller when measured by his instrument than when measured by ours, and we fully recognise that, although the higher densities measure only about 20 per cent. less by Captain Abney's photometer than by our instrument, his transparencies are much greater than ours.

The fact is, Captain Abney's transparencies are much too great and his densities too small. He can easily convince himself of this by measuring in his instrument the transparency of a piece of white paper, such as Rives, when he will find that it allows nearly 40 per cent. of the light to pass. We need not point out to him that this is far wide of the truth.

Such marked differences between the readings of Captain Abney's and our photometer must arise from causes which he ought to have had no difficulty in finding. He, no doubt, thought that these differences were entirely due to the scattering of the light, but, as we have shown, this is so trifling that it would never account for such discrepancies.

Whilst we measure the ratio of the amount of light which a given point (the grease spot) receives, first from the naked light and then through the negative, Captain Abney measures something entirely different.   He measures the alteration in the transparency of a piece of paper, which is brought about by placing a negative in front of it.   This alteration he takes to be the measure of the transparency of the negative, but herein he is entirely mistaken.   Had we thoroughly understood  the construction of his instrument at the last meeting, we could at once have pointed out the  cause of the differences, and could also have clearly shown his error.

We pointed out in our first paper that  the laws of absorption, as we there stated them, hold good only for  such substances as reflect but little light, and do not apply at all for other substances.   One substance, for which the law does not hold good, is white paper.   Now, Captain Abney's method of measuring actually assumes that  these laws do hold good for white paper, and that the density of a combination consisting of a piece  of white paper and a negative is the sum of the densities of  the paper and the negative taken singly.   He assumes the density of the paper as a constant, and takes the alteration produced by placing a negative in  contact with it as due to the density of  the negative only ; whereas, in reality, it is due to the density of the negative diminished by another very important factor, namely,  the alteration in the transparency of the paper  consequent upon the negative preventing reflection from its surface.

This law, which we have long known and which  applies to all bodies we have so far tested, black as well as white, is  the following :—If O is the opacity of one and $O_1$ of another substance, and if R and $R_1$ are their coefficients of reflection respectively, then the opacity of the combination of the two is—

$$O \times O_1 \times (1 - R\,R_1).$$

It is the last factor, the existence of which Captain Abney did  not recognise, which has led to the great differences in our results.   It is a very important factor, and it wholly accounts for these differences.

If we measure, in our  instrument, combinations of paper and negative, these differences vanish absolutely, and our readings are  in complete accord with Captain Abney's.   The order in which paper and negative are placed in our instrument is perfectly immaterial ; whether the light passes first through the paper and then through the  negative, or *vice versâ*, the density of the combination is exctly the same, and the formula given indicates this.

But when we combine *three* things—say, two pieces of paper and a negative, the opacity of  the combination differs according to  the order in which the three are used.   Suppose, for example, we use two pieces of paper and a negative.   Let O be the opacity of the paper (as  measured in our instrument) and $O_1$ that of the negative.   Let R be the coefficient of reflection of the paper, and $R_1$ that of the negative. The opacities of the three possible combinations will then be—

(1) Paper—paper—negative $= O^2 \times O_1 \times (1 - R^2) \times (1 - R\,R_1)$.
(2) Paper—negative—paper $= O^2 \times O_1 \times (1 - R\,R_1)^2$.
(3) Negative—paper—paper $= O^2 \times O_1 \times (1 - R\,R_1) \times (1 - R^2)$.

The first and the third are alike, but the second opacity is different. The reflective power of the negative being small compared with that of the paper, $1 - R\,R_1$ is greater than $1 - R^2$, and the opacity of the second combination is greater than that of the other two. The influence of mutual reflection can thus be readily shown without measurements by combining, in different ways, two pieces of paper and a negative.

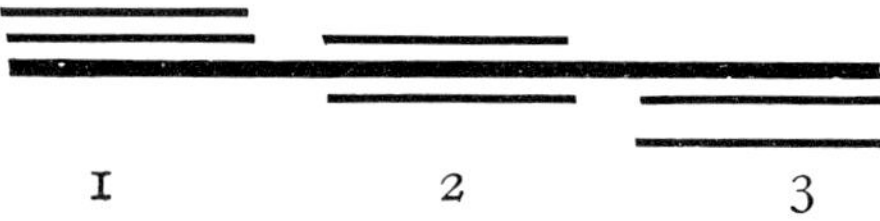
1       2       3

If, on a half-plate negative of uniform density we place two pieces of paper on one side (1), two pieces on the other side (3), and, between these one piece on either side (2), we then, in each case, look through two pieces of paper and a negative, but you will readily see that the combination (2), paper, —negative—paper, is very much darker than the other two combinations (1) and (3), the reason being that the powerful mutual reflection between two papers is absent in the second combination.

Captain Abney is therefore entirely mistaken when he thinks that his figures represent the true transparencies of the negative. They represent, in fact, the transparency increased by the mutual reflection between the paper and the negative.

But Captain Abney says that his experiment on platinotype paper shows that his figures are more nearly correct than are ours. To this we answer :— That is a mere coincidence. If he had made as many experiments in this direction as ourselves, he would have found that neither his nor our figures would suit all printing operations. Let the Captain, for instance, use the negative in an enlarging apparatus where it does not come into contact with the sensitive surface, and where mutual reflection is excluded, and he will find that the densities, as measured by his instrument, are absolutely useless and wrong by much more than 100 per cent. ; whereas ours are very nearly correct—not quite, because even the densities of negatives as given by our instrument are too small ; a ferrous oxalate developed plate even offering more resistance to the blue rays than to the others.

Captain Abney has evidently not studied the question as carefully as we have done, and he has not considered the mutual reflection at all.   The principle of his apparatus is wrong, and in attempting to avoid the trifling difficulty of " scattered light," he has fallen into the error of disregarding the much more important factor " reflected light."

We are certain that our instrument gives, as  nearly as it can be measured, the correct density of a negative free from all other  complications, and, so far, it is the only one which has proved  itself a reliable and handy substitute for a chemical balance in photographic researches.

### (*b*) Reply by Chapman Jones.

I have to thank Messrs. Hurter and Driffield for giving me this opportunity of replying to the  section of their paper that has an immediate reference to me.   I do not consider that they have correctly represented my position in the matter, nor the proper bearing of the particular  experiment which they deem of so much importance.

In a paper[1] by Messrs. Hurter and Driffield, published in the May number of the *Journal of the Society of Chemical Industry*, 1890, p. 455, the authors made several assertions concerning the development of photographic sensitive surfaces which are at variance with every-day experience.   Some of these I combated in a paper read before the  Photographic Society of Great Britain, and published in the November  number of that Society's *Journal*.   To this paper and Messrs. Hurter and Driffield's accompanying reply I  must refer those who are interested in the matter.   It is sufficient to state here that I showed evidence against Messrs. Hurter and  Driffield's assertions, and demonstrated that every experiment made by these  gentlemen that I knew of either confirmed or was agreeable with the views I upheld.   The particular experiment that they have just  criticised is a comparatively unimportant item in the argument.   I have dealt with this experiment in my paper, and have there met the hypothesis about the  inequalities of the coating of the plate, and quoted from Messrs. Hurter and  Driffield's correspondence what is practically an admission that there is such a difference  between the two plates as a partial remedying of over-exposure would effect.   The only new point now raised is the objection to my method of  averaging, based on the statement that all the highest ratios lie on one side of the  plate.   I would point out that the group that has been indicated as not  including any of the high marginal ratios, gives the same average as  the adjacent group, which includes two of these high ratios.   Messrs. Hurter and Driffield appear to have no objection to averaging in groups of four instead of five, as this gives  one high marginal ratio to each group, and  they state that the figures so obtained fail altogether

---

[1] p. 76.

to support my claim.  I had rejected this method as less impartial than the other.  Both series of figures show that the ratios rise as the densities increase :

Averages.

| In groups of five. | | | | | | | | In groups of four. |
|---|---|---|---|---|---|---|---|---|
| 1·48 | .. | .. | .. | .. | .. | .. | .. | 1·47 |
| 1·54 | .. | .. | .. | .. | .. | .. | .. | 1·51 |
| 1·54 | .. | .. | .. | .. | .. | .. | .. | 1·57 |
| 1·60 | .. | .. | .. | .. | .. | .. | .. | 1·58 |
| — | .. | .. | .. | .. | .. | .. | .. | 1·59 |

(c) REPLY TO MR. CHAPMAN JONES BY F. HURTER, PH.D., AND V. C. DRIFFIELD.

In reply to Mr. Chapman Jones's remarks, we much regret if we have in any degree misrepresented him ; but we are completely at a loss to understand in what way.  The growth of the density ratios, with which he is so deeply impressed, is fully accounted for by a thin place in one of the plates.  This place is marked by the lowest density ratio in square No. 3, from which point it will be seen the density ratios increase in all directions.  We have previously pointed out to Mr. Chapman Jones that a *thickly* coated plate does not, by any means, imply an *evenly* coated plate.

He has throughout professed to regard our results from the point of view of the practical photographer, and, granting that he has, in his experiment, remedied over-exposure to the full extent he claims, he has brought about a degree of improvement which the eye alone could never discover, and which, therefore, to the practical photographer would count for nothing.

[*Reprinted from the " Journal of the Society of Chemical Industry," 30th April,* 1891. *No.* 4, *Vol. X.*]

# THE SECTOR AND GREASE-SPOT PHOTOMETERS.

BY

## F. HURTER, PH.D.

WHILST paying a visit to Liverpool as judge of the Photographic Exhibition, Captain Abney kindly spent a few hours with Mr. Driffield and myself at Widnes. He inspected our instrument for measuring densities, and such other of our experimental work as we have exhibited before this Society. I shortly afterwards took advantage of an opportunity to pay a return visit to Captain Abney at South Kensington, and made some experiments with his own sector photometer. The results of both investigations I hasten to lay before the Society.

With respect to the experiments which Captain Abney made with our photometer at Widnes, they were confined to measurements of the densities of two plates, the mean densities of which were respectively 1·136 and 1·913. Three measurements were made of the first plate and six of the second. Captain Abney's extreme readings, at as different parts of the scale as possible, differed by 2·57 per cent. in the first plate and by 3·6 per cent. in the second plate, *i.e.*, the instrument gave a mean value ± 1·8 per cent.

We have received a letter[1] from Captain Abney, in which he bestows his unqualified praise upon our instrument, both for its handiness and for the consistency of its readings. In fact, there is only one point about which he now hesitates, and to which I shall presently refer.

The experiments made with the sector at South Kensington showed that, under the conditions as to speed of revolution, distance of screen from sector and lamp, &c., and within those limits between which it was tested, viz., with light intensities ranging from 1 to $\frac{1}{20}$, *the sector accurately agreed with the law of inverse square of distance.*

[1] Cor. 29th March, 1891, Abney—Hurter

Whilst we ourselves used the sector under conditions in which its errors are maxima, viz., with broad flames, and in very close proximity to the lamp and screen, Captain Abney uses the sector under conditions in which we have found that the error is very trifling, viz., with comparatively narrow flames considerable distances between screen, sector and lamp, and, more particularly, with a high number of revolutions. Captain Abney's sector has two openings, and makes upwards of 2,000 revolutions per minute, which is equal to a speed of 4,000 revolutions with a single opening, and if our diagram[1] (this Journal, 10, 21) be referred to, it will be found that for this number of revolutions our own experiments show the sector to be almost accurate, even with broad flames and relatively small distances.

We should be extremely sorry if any of our remarks have in the smallest degree detracted from the value of any of Captain Abney's beautiful researches on colour. He was good enough to show me some of these experiments, and I quite agree with him in saying that the revolving sector is the only instrument which could possibly be used in these particular investigations.

After my experiments with Captain Abney's sector, we have no hesitation whatever in stating that, as he uses it, it is a perfectly trustworthy instrument, and it certainly is, as we always considered it, an extremely beautiful device for rapidly varying the intensity of a given beam of light.

There is no longer, therefore, any difference of opinion between Captain Abney and ourselves as to the correctness of our respective instruments, but the Captain is not yet satisfied that our photometer gives the true optical density. As we ourselves know that it does not, and never held that any one particular number could possibly represent the true density, we shall have no difficulty in arriving at an understanding on this point, and we have pledged our word to settle this one remaining difference experimentally in conjunction with Captain Abney, and without any further controversial publications. We designed our photometer with a view to making it a substitute for chemical analysis, in order that its readings should be proportional to the weight of silver deposited, rather than give the true optical density, which, for the purpose of our research, is so far of secondary importance, and our last paper on the relation between positive and negative clearly shows that the density, however expressed, will need different corrections for different printing operations.

[1] p. 140.

[*Paper read at Photographic Convention, Plymouth. Reprinted from "Photography," 13th July, 1893.*]

# LATITUDE IN EXPOSURE AND SPEED OF PLATES.

BY

## F. HURTER, Ph.D., and V. C. DRIFFIELD.

---

IT is generally assumed, because our researches have led us to pronounce exposure, and not development, to be the determining factor in photography, that therefore the production of similar prints from a series of negatives which have received widely varying exposures, and have been submitted to widely different treatment in development, totally upsets the whole of our conclusions.

Our attention has been called, from time to time, to such series of negatives, and in all the instances which have come to our notice there has been no difficulty whatever in arranging the negatives in the order of their exposures ; nor has it been much more difficult, by mere inspection, to so arrange the prints. If, however, such negatives be measured, and their density ratios ascertained, the order of the negatives, with respect to the duration of exposure, is readily decided beyond all possibility of error.

As an instance of such a series of negatives, we give our measurements of four plates sent to us, two years ago, by a gentleman in Ireland, as an illustration of the latitude in exposure obtained by appropriate treatment during the operation of development.  The subject was the same in all four plates, and consisted of a field bordered by trees.  In the middle distance was a grey house, one side of which was illuminated by the diffuse light of the sky and the other side by the sun.  We measured the densities of the sky, the two sides of the house, the most transparent shadows in the trees, and a spot in the grass. In order to ensure the measurement of precisely the same spots in all four plates, masks with circular openings were fixed on each negative, so that the circles coincided when the subjects coincided. The four plates respectively received exposures of 1, 10, 30 and 60 seconds, and the resulting negatives yielded prints differing so little in quality that they were deemed to have completely demolished our contentions. The following table gives the results of the measurements :—

|  | Densities. | | | |
|---|---|---|---|---|
| Exposures. | $1''$ | $10''$ | $30''$ | $60''$ |
| Darkest shadow in trees .. | ·378 | ·553 | ·973 | 1·028 |
| House (shadow side) .. .. | ·833 | ·750 | 1·371 | 1·315 |
| Grass .. .. .. .. | ·930 | 1·005 | 1·706 | 1·581 |
| House (sunlit side) .. .. | 1·721 | 1·571 | 2·121 | 1·921 |
| Sky .. .. .. .. | 2·598 | 2·236 | 2·578 | 2·308 |

A glance at the densities of these negatives, particularly those indicating the extreme range (darkest shadow and sky), shows how widely they differ from each other ; whilst a glance at the negatives themselves surprises one, by revealing the inability of the eye to readily appreciate these differences. The eye is still less capable of appreciating the great alteration in the density ratios given in the next table :—

|  | Density Ratios. | | | |
|---|---|---|---|---|
| Exposures. | $1''$ | $10''$ | $30''$ | $60''$ |
| Darkest shadow in trees .. | 1 | 1 | 1 | 1 |
| House (shadow side) .. .. | 2·2 | 1·35 | 1·40 | 1·28 |
| Grass .. .. .. .. | 2·46 | 1·81 | 1·75 | 1·53 |
| House (sunlit side) .. .. | 4·55 | 2·84 | 2·17 | 1·86 |
| Sky .. .. .. .. | 6·87 | 4·04 | 2·65 | 2·24 |

These ratios decrease with increased exposure in perfect accordance with all our experiments. The negatives are very different indeed in this respect, and fully bear out our contention that the density ratios are a function of the exposure and not of modifications in development. We have no hesitation in asserting that such negatives may always be arranged in the order of their exposures by anyone acquainted with the subject. In printing quality, as regards time, these negatives also differ considerably.

It is clear, therefore, that these negatives do not illustrate in a very striking manner what they were intended to illustrate, namely, the great latitude in exposure. They do, however, illustrate another point, namely, the great latitude there is in the quality of prints acceptable to the eye, and the curious inability of the eye to judge numerical values of density differences. In this faulty perceptive power of the generality of eyes lies a great deal of the latitude of exposure.

Various authorities give wholly different limits for this latitude in exposures. Professor Burton has given it as 1 : 30, but states that he has succeeded with some plates with exposures ranging from 1 : 80. We ourselves stated in our original paper that the plates which we used in our experiments (Nos. 21 and 22) would have given good pictures of subjects with contrasts varying from 1 : 80, though the exposures had varied from 1 : 2—that is, the plates were capable of recording, *truly*, contrasts ranging from 1 : 160.

Latitude in exposure depends :—

(1) Upon the quality of the plate.
(2) Upon the range of contrasts in the subject.
(3) Upon the degree of truth with which the contrasts are to be presented in the positive print.

The quality of the plate is the most important question. There are some plates which have no latitude of exposure at all, or which are, at any rate, incapable of rendering any range of contrasts in this subject with any degree of truth, whatever exposure may be given. There are other plates capable of recording, *truthfully*, a comparatively wide range of contrasts, though exposures may vary from 1 : 5 or 1 : 6, and, if truthfulness of the intermediate tones be not absolutely demanded, such plates are capable of yielding useful negatives within such ranges as 1 : 20 or 1 : 30.

These different qualities of photographic plates are best represented graphically by the curve which we have termed the " characteristic curve " of the plate. The method of obtaining this curve will be presently described. Diagram No. 1 presents two characteristic curves of two well-known brands of plates, which we will call A and B. We at once perceive a characteristic difference between these two plates. While the curve belonging to plate A is nearly straight from exposure 0·625 cms. to exposure 80 cms., plate B yields a curve which has hardly any straight part in it. Now, we have shown that if a plate must truly represent the contrasts of the subject, it can only do so if it possesses a perfectly straight portion within its characteristic curve. The longer this straight part is the greater is the latitude of exposure for that plate.

Plate A would represent a subject with contrasts varying from 1 : 20 with a high degree of truth, though the exposures varied from 0·625 : 4, or from 1 : 6. If several exposures were made upon several plates, the exposures ranging from 1 : 6, they would yield negatives of very different appearance, giving, however, identical prints, though the negatives were all simultaneously developed in the same dish for the same length of time. But, though all these negatives yielded identical prints, the professional photographer would discard them all but one, which to him, at all events, would be the only really good negative. *There is one exposure, and only one, which yields a true representation with minimum density.*

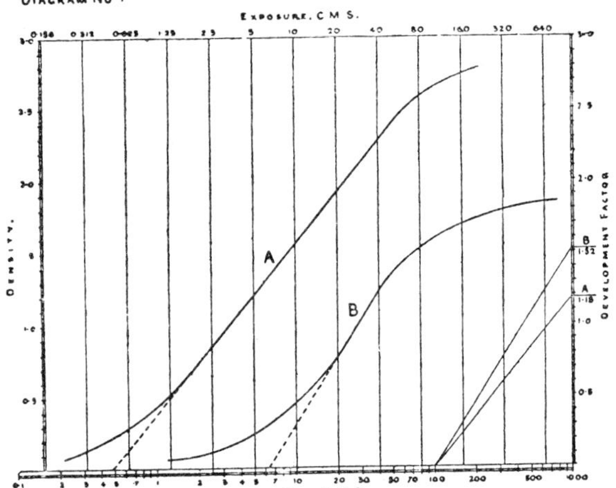


Plate B, on the other hand, would never give a correct representation of any subject. Such plates could not be sold or used if the eye were capable of readily detecting photographic untruth in prints. It is owing to this defect that such a plate can be used at all. But the unsatisfactory nature of the plate, as revealed by the characteristic curve, makes itself evident in practice by the very limited range of exposures which will yield satisfactory negatives. With such plates Professor Burton would have tried his art of altering density ratios in vain.

Next in importance to the quality of the plate is the question of range of light intensities which have to be recorded truly. Plate A is capable of representing light intensities lying between 1 and 70. If intensities had to be photographed embracing a greater limit than 1 : 70, it could only be done by sacrificing truth or proportionality to truth altogether. In the case of plate B the limit would lie between 1 and 2. The question arises, What are the usual variations in light intensities which have to be considered in photographic practice ? Many photographers appear to have highly exaggerated ideas upon this subject. We do not exactly know what Professor Burton's opinion is, but it would appear, from his remarks, that the power of altering density ratios by variations in the developers can only be exercised in the case of plates which have received light intensities varying from one to at least several hundred. From this we are led to assume that he supposed that the two prints he has recently published represent light intensities varying from one to at least several hundred.

Now it is an easy matter to ascertain the limits of light intensities which have to be dealt with in any given subject, and the following is the outline of the method we adopt in such an investigation. We cut a plate into two parts. Upon one part we make a series of exposures to the standard candles, so as to determine the characteristic curve. The other part of the plate is exposed in the camera to the object of which it is desired to ascertain the range of light intensities. We give such an exposure as will produce a correct negative, but it is not necessary to hit this very accurately. The two parts of the plate are then developed together for the same length of time, and with the same developer, and the highest and lowest densities of the negative and such others as are of interest are measured, as are also the densities resulting from the candle exposures. It will be evident that this graded plate, produced by exposure to the candle, serves as the scale wherewith to measure the light intensities actually at work in the camera, and which produced the densities of the negative. For such experiments it is, of course, desirable to select subjects which present sufficient areas of uniform density in the negative. A useful subject, because it comprises the entire range of tone, which a paper print admits of rendering truly, is an ordinary folding screen, upon each of two folds of which are fixed a sheet of white cardboard and a sheet of mat black paper. The screen is so placed that one fold is illuminated by direct sunlight and the other by the diffuse light of the sky, and so that the sky itself is included in the picture. This subject gives us five densities on the resulting negative, namely :—

> Sky.
> White, illuminated by the sun.
> White,      ,,      diffuse light.
> Black,      ,,      the sun.
> Black,      ,,      diffuse light.

The following are the details of such an experiment, and Diagram No. 2 illustrates graphically the method of ascertaining the equivalent of the light intensities in candlemetre seconds. A plate was cut into four parts. Three of them were exposed in the camera to a subject as just described, and the fourth was exposed to the standard candle, the exposures ranging from 0·312 cms. to 160 cms. The three exposures given in the camera were 0·8, 4 and 24 seconds respectively, and all four plates were developed together in one dish for the same length of time. The densities of the negatives and of the graded plate were found to be :—

DENSITIES OF NEGATIVES.

| Exposure. | 0·8″ | 4″ | 24″ |
|---|---|---|---|
| Sky    ..    ..    ..    .. | 0·940 | 1·695 | 2·260 |
| White in sunlight    ..    .. | 0·940 | 1·735 | 2·280 |
| White in shade  ..    ..    .. | 0·620 | 1·360 | 2·080 |
| Black in sunlight    ..    .. | 0·120 | 0·530 | 1·290 |
| Black in shade  ..    ..    .. | 0·060 | 0·320 | 1·025 |

DENSITIES OF GRADED PLATE.

| Exposure, cms. | Density. | Exposure,  cms. | Density. |
|---|---|---|---|
| 0·312 | 0·150 | 10 | 1·360 |
| 0·625 | 0·275 | 20 | 1·665 |
| 1·25 | 0·440 | 40 | 1·935 |
| 2·5 | 0·700 | 80 | 2·160 |
| 5·0 | 1·040 | 160 | 2·295 |

The densities of the gradations obtained by these ten exposures were plotted as a curve, the logarithms of the exposures as abscissæ, and the densities as ordinates.  Parallels corresponding to the densities of the three negatives were then drawn, and where they intersect the characteristic curve perpendiculars were drawn through the points of intersection.  These perpendiculars indicate at once the equivalent exposures in centimetres which produced the corresponding densities.

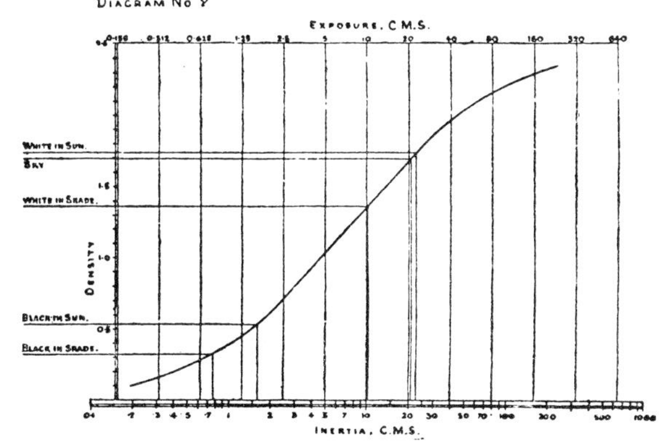


In Diagram No. 2 the densities of the negative which received an exposure of four seconds are thus plotted, and it will be seen that the respective equivalent exposures are :—

|  |  | Cms. |
|---|---|---|
| Negative, 4 secs. exposure. | Sky    ..    ..    ..    ..    .. | 20·80 |
|  | White in sun    ..    ..    ..    .. | 22·50 |
|  | ,,    shade  ..    ..    ..    .. | 10·20 |
|  | Black in sun    ..    ..    ..    .. | 1·62 |
|  | ,,    shade  ..    ..    ..    .. | 0·77 |

It will thus be seen that the whole range of light intensities, from mat black in the shade to the sky or white cardboard illuminated by the sun, is as 0·77 : 22·5, or as 1 : 29. Similar results were obtained with the other two negatives, and the following table gives their equivalents, the highest light being put = 30.

| Relative intensities of light emitted by | As shown by negatives exposed. | | | Mean. |
|---|---|---|---|---|
| | 0·8″ | 4″ | 24″ | |
| Sky  ..  ..  ..  .. | 30 | 27·7 | 29 | 28·9 |
| White in sun  ..  ..  .. | 30 | 30 · | 30 | 30 |
| ,,  shade ..  ..  .. | 15 | 13·6 | 13·0 | 13·8 |
| Black in sun  ..  ..  .. | 1·83 | 2·1 | 1·78 | 1·90 |
| ,,  shade ..  ..  .. | 1·16 | 1·02 | 1·01 | 1·06 |

We learn from this experiment that an object illuminated by direct sunlight is about twice as bright as the same object in the shade, and that the whole range between a mat black object in the shade and a brilliantly illuminated sky is about as 1 : 30. It will also be seen that the exposures given in the camera vary as 1 : 30, and yet the same relation as to light intensities is revealed by the shortest as by the longest exposure.

If we now examine Professor Burton's statements in the light of this, to him, evidently new knowledge, we have to point out that, according to his own confession, he cannot alter density ratios between limits of exposures 1 : 10, and he would not, we presume, undertake to seriously alter density ratios between such narrow limits as 1 : 30, since he says that " it is necessary to have ranges of exposures of at least several hundreds to one to be able readily to vary the density ratios."

Now, assuming certain conditions, *actually never present in photographic practice*, it seems, according to Professor Burton, true that it is possible to vary density ratios when the exposures vary between at least several hundred to one. Such variations do not occur in ordinary subjects ; the light intensities vary between limits of 30 : 1 at most. Professor Burton's faculty of producing negatives which yield similar prints is not due to his mode of development ; it lies wholly in the latitude of the plate and in the narrowness of the range of light intensities in his subject. He could have obtained identically the same result, and possibly a better, by means of *one* developer, and by simply varying the time of development for the shortest exposures.

Two negatives are alike in their printing quality when the density differences are alike throughout, whatever the density ratios may be. Two negatives may have totally different density ratios, and yet be equally true to nature and yield identical prints, whatever printing process may be employed, so long as it is the same in both cases. Thus, so long as the light intensities of a given subject lie within a certain limited range, and the time of exposure is such that the densities produced fall within the straight part of the characteristic curve, so long will the density differences for the same subject be independent of exposure, and alike.

Suppose the length of the straight part of the curve cover a range of exposures $1 : E$, and the light intensities to be photographed lie between the limits $1 : I$, the latitude of the exposure would then be $1 : \dfrac{E}{I}$, and within these two limits any exposure would produce negatives which, developed in the same developer for the same length of time, would yield negatives giving identical prints. Take the case of plate A. The straight part of its characteristic curve may be taken as extending from exposure 1 cms. to exposure 80 cms., *i.e.*, $1 : 80$. If a subject had to be photographed which was illuminated by diffuse light only, and in which the light intensities varied from mat black to white, or even more—say, a range of $1 : 20$—the plate would yield negatives with exposures varying from $1 : 4$ almost identical in printing quality, though they were all developed together. If a little deviation from truth is permissible, and the portion of the characteristic curve lying between exposures $0 \cdot 312$ cms. and 160 cms. (a range of $1 : 512$) be considered as sufficiently accurate, the same subject would permit of a latitude of exposure of $\frac{512}{20} = 25$, and there would still be very little difference in the negatives, particularly if development be prolonged in this case of the shorter exposures. For a sunlit landscape the latitude would be $\frac{512}{30} = 17$.

The experiment we have described was made on a plate, the straight part of which only extended from an exposure of about $1 \cdot 5$ cms. to one of 50 cms. For an ordinary sunlit landscape its latitude of exposure is, therefore, small, namely, $\dfrac{50}{1 \cdot 5 \times 30} = 1 \cdot 1$, and, consequently, if a correct negative be required on such a plate, the latitude of exposure would have to lie within 10 per cent. of its own value. The negative which was exposed for four seconds is the truest of the three ; the one which received one-fifth of this exposure renders the high lights correctly, but not the shadows, and the one which received six times the exposure of the first-named negative renders the gradations as far as white in diffuse light correctly, but not the highest lights. The following table shows the density differences for the various parts of the negatives, which would have to be all alike if the negatives must yield identical prints :—

| Exposure | 0·8″ | 4″ | 24″ |
|---|---|---|---|
| Density of clearest spot | ·060 | ·320 | 1·025 |
| Density difference—Black in shade and black in sun | ·060 | ·210 | ·265 |
| ,,　　,,　　,,　sun and white in shade | ·500 | ·830 | ·790 |
| ,,　　,,　White in shade and white in sun | ·320 | ·375 | ·200 |
| Total range of negative—Black in shade and white in sun | ·880 | 1·415 | 1·255 |

It will be seen that the negative which received four seconds, the correct exposure, gives for all parts of the subject, with the exception of the highest lights, practically the same density differences as the one which received 24 seconds' exposure. In prints from these two negatives all gradations lying between black in shade and white in shade would be exactly alike, though the exposure was, in the case of one negative, six times as much as in the other. The negative which received one-fifth the correct exposure only renders the high lights with equal truth. If, however, this negative had been developed for a longer time than the other two, its range could have been considerably improved ; the ratios remaining the same, the density differences would have altered, and it could easily have been brought to the following :—

| Exposure | 0·8″ | 4″ | 24″ |
|---|---|---|---|
| Density of clearest spot | ·100 | ·320 | 1·025 |
| Density difference—Black in shade and black in sun | ·100 | ·210 | ·265 |
| ,,　　,,　Black in sun and white in shade | ·830 | ·830 | ·790 |
| ,,　　,,　White in shade and white in sun | ·530 | ·375 | ·200 |
| Total range of negative—Black in shade and white in sun | 1·460 | 1·415 | 1·255 |

In this case the resulting prints would have differed little from each other, since all the main gradations lying between black in shade and white in shade would have been represented by the differences—

| 0·8″ | 4″ | 24″ |
|---|---|---|
| 0·930 | 1·040 | 1·055 |

which are so nearly alike that the eye could not detect the difference.  Only in the highest lights, beyond white in shade, would the difference be at all apparent.  The three negatives differ, however, very materially in the time they require to yield prints of equal depth in the shadows.  The last of the series (24 seconds' exposure) requires six times, and the second (correct exposure) nearly twice (five-thirds) the time which is needed for the first to print to the same depth.

From these experiments it is clear that latitude in exposure is not inherent in modifications of the developer, but in the plate itself, and in the comparatively narrow range of intensities which are ordinarily met with, combined with the inability of the eye to judge of the more or less truthful rendering of the various gradations.

As already pointed out, among the many negatives which may be produced by mere variations in exposure, there is only one which combines truthful rendering of tone with minimum density, and it is this one which the practical photographer aims to secure.  For the more accurate and certain production of this particular negative, it is necessary to ascertain the speed of the plate with tolerable accuracy, and we now propose to give a short,practical description of the method we have adopted for this purpose.  We believe that many amateur photographers would be glad to be in a position to determine speeds for themselves, and to obtain that knowledge of the properties of their plates which can only be derived from a study of the characteristic curve.

The course we pursued in our original investigations was to expose portions of the same plate consecutively to the light of a standard candle, doubling each successive exposure as we proceeded, and we naturally adopted this course when we came to make our first determinations of speed.  The errors to which we found the candle liable, however, when we had not the experience in its use which we have since gained, showed that much was to be desired in order to secure a constant ratio of illumination between the different exposures, and, in order to secure this, we adopted the plan of making our exposures, which we are about to describe, and which we believe to be the most satisfactory.  By this method the whole of the exposures are made simultaneously, so that any fluctuations taking place in the light of the candle proportionally affects all the exposures, and the determination is consequently more decisive and less liable to error than if fluctuations in the light were to take place during one or more of the individual exposures.  Moreover, the possibility of error arising from the difficulty of accurately timing very short exposures is wholly eliminated.

We will, in the first place, make a few remarks upon the standard candle as a unit of light.  While we candidly admit that the candle is by no means an ideal standard, we must say that we are not at present aware of any satisfactory substitute.  We adopted it, in the first instance, because it was ready to our hand, well known and recognised as a standard, and easily obtained. And we may perhaps be forgiven for entertaining a somewhat higher opinion of it than some of our friends, inasmuch as it was, at any rate, reliable enough to lead to the discoveries we have made.  It is asserted that the amyl-acetate lamp is a better standard than the candle, but the practical difficulties in its use are such that we can only say it has not proved itself so in our hands. Altogether, we know of nothing, as yet, better as a standard than the candle ; and if the suggestions for its use which we are about to make be adopted, we do not think it will lead to serious errors.  Two determinations of the inertia of this same plate which we have just had occasion to make on two different evenings differed only by 0·04 cms., a discrepancy of absolutely no practical moment.  We have unquestionably found that the standard candles of different makers do vary, and, for this reason, we think it well to say that the candles we have used throughout our investigations were supplied by Messrs. Sugg & Co., Vincent Works, Westminster.  The normal height of the flame of these candles, measured from the lowest point at which the wick blackens, is about 45 mm.

Our method of using the candle for the purpose of speed determination is as follows :—We will assume that the candle we are about to use has been used before.  We light it and then, with scissors, snip off the hardened tip of the wick.  The flame of the candle will now be found to grow steadily in height, and as soon as the distance from the tip of the flame to the lowest point at which the wick blackens has reached 45 mm. the exposure may commence. The candle flame may now be relied upon to remain sufficiently constant for about ten minutes, and this is amply long for our purpose.  If after this time, for any other purpose, the light is required, it will be well to again trim the wick and start *de novo*.  The height of the flame may be measured by a strip of cardboard, upon which two marks are made at a distance of 45 mm. apart. It is, of course, obvious that these experiments should be made in a room free from draught, and it is often a wise precaution to place the candle in a tall box, open on one side, and well blackened inside.  We are strongly in favour of keeping the candle well in view during the entire exposure, so that, should any fluctuation in the light take place, we may be aware of it.  If the candle be used in the open room, all white or bright surfaces capable of reflecting light should be removed.

We now come to a description of the apparatus we use for making speed determinations.  Diagram No. 3 shows the form in which we use it.  D is the candle, A is the dark slide containing the strip of plate of which the characteristic curve is to be determined, B marks the position occupied by the dark slide during exposure, and C is the revolving disc, by means of which the varying exposures are given, and, as this disc forms the most important part of the apparatus, we will proceed to describe it in detail.[1] The disc is preferably made of a sheet of metal, but may be cut out of cardboard. It is 11 inches in diameter, and Diagram No. 4 will serve to show how it is perforated in order to yield a series of nine exposures, each double the preceding one. The length of the strip we use for a determination is that of a quarter-plate, or $4\frac{1}{4}$ inches. This length, divided into ten equal parts, gives the width of

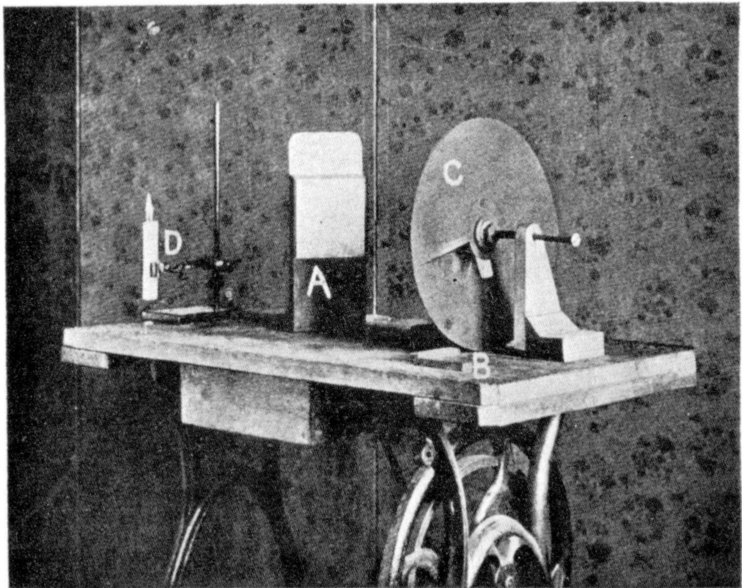

DIAGRAM NO. 3

each successive step in the perforations of the disc. Nine parts only are required for the exposures, the tenth being protected from light in the dark slide during the exposure, so as to provide what we term the " fog strips." It will be seen that the angular apertures of the first perforation is 180°, produced by cutting out two entire quadrants of the circle ; the next has an angular aperture of 90° or one quadrant ; the next of 45°, and so on, the angular aperture of each successive perforation being halved till the ninth is reached. These apertures, of course, require to be cut with the greatest accuracy, and the disc, when finished, should be coated with dead black paint. It should

[1] The original disc in the H. and D. collection at the R.P.S.

then be mounted on a central spindle, which can be caused to revolve with considerable rapidity by some suitable mechanical arrangement. We ourselves called into requisition for the purpose an old sewing machine stand, which permits the disc to be driven by the foot.

Having completed our description of the apparatus, we will next describe the actual operation of making this determination. First of all, as to the plate. If a plate be examined by placing it between the eye and the red lamp, it will be found that the opacity of the film falls off at the edges. The edges should, therefore, be scrupulously avoided, and the strip should be cut from

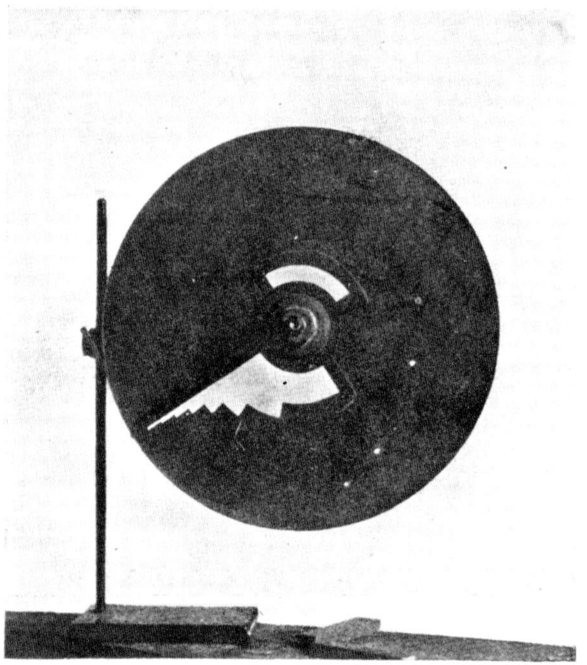

DIAGRAM No 4.

the centre of the plate, or, at any rate, well away from the margin. The operation of cutting the plate should be conducted as quickly as possible, and as far away as possible from the red light, so as to avoid all fogging action of the light upon the plate. The width of the strip may conveniently be made about 1 inch. When the plate is securely placed in the dark slide the latter is placed in its position behind the disc. The distance from the candle to the place occupied by the plate is carefully adjusted, and the candle is lighted and trimmed. When the flame has reached the requisite height the exposure may commence. The disc is caused to revolve, and, at a given moment, the slide protecting the plate is drawn, and the exposure continued for the requisite length of time.

Now, as to the best range of exposures to decide upon in the case of a plate of the speed of which we know nothing. We should advise a series commencing with 80 cms., down to $0 \cdot 312$ cms. This range will be found to include as much of the characteristic curve of the majority of commercial plates as is required for a speed determination. A little consideration of the revolving disc, however, will show that, in order to give an actual maximum exposure of 80 cms., it will be necessary to continue the exposure for twice 80, or 160, seconds, the candle being placed at a distance of 1 m. from the plate. The reason of this is that the actual maximum exposure only proceeds during half the revolution of the disc ; the light only reaching the plate during the passage across it of 180° out of the 360°. Though we prefer to work with the candle at a distance of 1 m. from the plate, it may be brought nearer to it if it be desired to curtail the exposure. At a distance of $0 \cdot 707$ m. the light of the candle is equal to 2 cms., and, at a distance of $\frac{1}{2}$ m., it is equal to 4 cms.

Having exposed the strip, we next proceed to develop it, and here we must say a word or two upon the subject of the developer. We do this knowing perfectly well that we shall meet with considerable opposition ; but we, nevertheless, again assert that, for all ordinary photographic work, there is no developer superior to ferrous oxalate. We prefer it because of the uniformity of the colour of the silver deposited by it, a point of very great importance when we come to the operations of printing and enlarging by the developing processes, in which the exposure is arrived at by calculation ; we prefer it because we never yet found a plate with which it disagreed, and this is more than can be said of other developers. It will also develop an old plate which may have been carelessly laid by for years, while, with another developer, it would be hopeless to obtain a passable result. We prefer ferrous oxalate because, of all developers, it is least liable to attack silver salts which have not been acted upon by the light, and because it will not lend itself to the production of foggy messes. We do not wish for a moment to imply that other developers may not have their special uses. On the contrary, for example, we have found rodinal of the greatest value in the case of certain plates, when dealing with extremely short shutter exposures, and also in flashlight work.

However, to proceed with the operation of development. It is advisable that this operation be conducted at a fixed temperature, and we find 65° Fahr. the best to adopt, as it is easily obtainable both in summer and winter. The developer itself should be brought to this temperature, and maintained at it by placing the developing dish in a water bath of the same temperature. The constituents of the developer are intimately mixed by stirring, and, at the moment of pouring on to the plate, the time is noted.  The dish should only be rocked for a few moments in order to expel any air bubbles from the surface of the plate, and should then be covered up, so as to expose the plate no more to the red light than is absolutely necessary.  Examination of the plate during development should be avoided as far as possible, as no red light whatever is safe in the case of even a fairly sensitive plate ; and we believe that too frequent examination, prompted by curiosity or impatience, is to some extent responsible for alleged alterations in density ratios.  About five or six minutes will, as a rule, be found the best length of time to continue development, in order to obtain that range of gradation most suitable for subsequent measurement.  But, however long development may be continued, the time occupied should be carefully noted.  The object of the fixed temperature, and the exact time a given plate takes to reach a certain development factor, is of the utmost importance if we afterwards desire, upon a similar plate, to produce another negative having a different range of density gradations.

After development, the strip is fixed and washed in the ordinary way, and, after washing, it is well to wipe the surface of the film gently with a plug of wetted cotton wool.  The plate may be treated with alum if desirable, and both the alum and fixing baths should be fresh and perfectly clean.  As the films of some plates are liable to loosen from the glass when submitted to the heat of the lamp in the photometer, it is sometimes well to soak the plates for a few moments in a weak solution of glycerine after washing and before drying.  When the plate is dry, and this may be hastened by means of alcohol if desired, the back of it should be thoroughly cleansed, and the film wiped with a silk handkerchief.  It will now be found advantageous to define the dividing lines of the smaller densities with a pen and ink on the film.  This will materially assist when we come to measure the plate, which operation may now be carried out.  We do not here propose to enter into any description of our photometer and the method of using it.  This will be found in our original paper in the *Journal of the Society of Chemical Industry*.[1]

The nine different densities and the " fog strip " having been measured, and having deducted, from each exposure density, the density of the incipient fog of the plate, and that due to the glass and film as given by the " fog strip," we proceed to plot the characteristic curve on one of the skeleton diagrams supplied for the purpose by Messrs. Marion & Co.  Assuming that our actual maximum exposure was 80 cms., we mark on the ordinate corresponding with this exposure this density, minus fog, due to the 80 cms. exposures, and so on till we reach the ordinate corresponding with exposure 0·312 cms.  Having thus plotted all the nine densities, we take a piece of black thread

---

[1] See pp. 79–86.

and stretch it along that part of the curve which practically forms a straight line, and which indicates the position and extent of the correct period. This enables us to decide upon the position of the straight line before we actually draw it on the diagram. We now draw the line, and continue it till it intersects the inertia scale at the bottom of the diagram. The point at which the intersection takes place gives the inertia of the plate, which is then converted into the speed by dividing it into the constant 34. For example, inertia 1 = speed 34. We may now join up to either end of the correct period curves passing through the remaining points of the determination. The curve at the upper end will represent a portion of the period of over-exposure, and that at the lower end of the period of under-exposure ; the whole representing the most important features of the characteristic curve. The details just described will be better understood by a reference to Diagram No. 1.

We should here like to express the importance we attach to obtaining, in every speed determination, distinct evidence of all three periods. It is only by so doing that we can be quite certain as to the position of the correct period. It would be quite possible for the higher densities in a series of under-exposure gradations to be mistaken for a portion of the correct period in the case of a high development factor—in fact, we have known this mistake to be made when, had there been evidence of all three periods, mistake would have been rendered impossible.

We generally have some idea whether the plate we are about to examine is a rapid or a slow one, and, after a little experience, it is easy to decide upon that range of exposures which will most probably yield evidence of the three periods ; but should we, in the case of a plate, of the speed of which we have no idea whatever, find that the exposures we have chosen yield a series of densities which leave room for doubt as to the position of the correct period, it will be necessary to make another determination, a more suitable range of exposures being chosen. The first determination will indicate whether a longer or a shorter exposure be desirable.

We must here call attention to a difficulty which may possibly arise ; but its occurrence is fortunately so rare as to speak well for the perfection of the machinery used for coating the plates. If, on plotting the densities, they are found to lie irregularly, so as to preclude the possibility of drawing through them a regular curve, there is serious reason to suspect an unevenly coated plate. In such a case as this the best thing to do is to cut another strip from the plate from which the first was taken, and running in the same direction of the plate as the first strip. The second strip should now be uniformly exposed to the candle and developed, the exposure and development being so timed as to produce an easily measurable density of, say, 1·0,

If the plate has been unevenly coated, the density of the second strip, when measured in different places, will be found to vary.  As an example, we have been able to lay our hands upon the record of a case which occurred in our own experience.  The irregular series of densities obtained in the first instance led us to make a second exposure as described, when we found that the density measured in different parts of the strip varied from 1·335 to 0·820.  When we remember that this means that one part of the strip transmitted more than three times as much light as another, the serious nature of such a fault as inequality in the thickness of the film will be apparent.

Reference has been made several times to the development factor.[1]  It is beyond the scope of this paper, however, to enter fully into this subject ; but as the numerical value of this factor is one of the data to be derived from every speed determination we will state how it is graphically ascertained. From the point 100 on the inertia scale of the skeleton diagram a line parallel to the straight portion of the characteristic curve is projected till it intersects the development factor scale.  The point of intersection gives the factor which expresses the extent to which the development of this particular plate was carried.  It is best for the purpose of speed determination to aim at reaching a development factor of 1·0 or a little more.  It will be seen, on referring to diagram No. 1, that the  development  factors  of the two plates A and B are 1·18 and 1·52 respectively.

We believe we have now explained the method of making a speed determination in sufficient detail to enable an amateur to carry out the operation. We trust, however, that any amateurs who take the matter up will not content themselves with plotting the characteristic curve of a plate for the sole purpose of ascertaining its speed, but will take an interest in tracing, in the conformation of the curve, the results which they  obtain in their photographic practice. It is a knowledge of this curve alone which can give the photographer complete control of the materials he employs.  On some other occasion we hope to show more fully than heretofore the part which the characteristic curve plays in the calculation of the exposure for transparencies and printing processes generally, as also in the production of negatives and positives having a special range of gradation.

[1] Generally referred to as γ (Gamma)

[*Reprinted from the " Journal of the Camera Club," July*, 1893, *Vol. VII, No.* 86.]

# " THE SPEED OF PLATES " AND " THE EFFECT OF LIGHT ON PLATES."

*Discussion at the Camera Club on Captain Abney's and Mr. Elder's Conference Papers.*[1]

(CAPTAIN ABNEY in the Chair.)

PAPER BY DR. HURTER.

DR. HURTER, on behalf of himself and Mr. Driffield (who could not attend), said :—It is said that there is no sincerer form of flattery than imitation, and we think no one can deny that both Captain Abney's method of speed determination and Mr. Elder's mathematical treatment of the effects of light on photographic plates are more or less close imitations of the methods we ourselves pursued when dealing with similar subjects in our well-known paper on " Photo-chemical Investigations, &c."[2]

We welcome the appearance of both papers, more particularly Captain Abney's, for several reasons. First of all, we are glad to find that Captain Abney endorses our view that the determination of the rapidity of a plate cannot be accomplished by any other means than the accurate measurements of the result of several successive exposures ; secondly, because he confirms, by his method, our statement that time of development has but little influence on density ratios, else his own method would be impossible, and, thirdly, because he now admits, for the first time, that the method of measuring densities by our photometer is, for the purposes of speed determination at all events, equivalent to his method of measuring transparencies.

Mr. Elder's paper deals with a number of hypotheses in a very able manner, and will always form an important addition to the scientific literature

---

[1] *Journal of the Camera Club*, Conference Number, July, 1893.
[2] pp, 76–122.

of photography. Mr. Elder divides his paper into two parts ; in the first part he recounts the formulæ already published, dealing with the effect of light on plates. He then develops the law of transparency for the purpose of showing the connection between our density D and Captain Abney's transparency T, a subject to which I shall presently return. He then formulates four hypotheses, *a*, *b*, *c* and *d*, and traces mathematically the relation between the density or transparency of the negative which would result if the hypotheses were correct. The whole of this part of his paper suffers from one serious defect. Mr. Elder tacitly assumes that every particle of silver throughout the film receives the same intensity of light. This is so manifestly opposed to the fact that I am afraid Mr. Elder must revise his formulæ to introduce this very essential condition.

In the second part of his paper Mr. Elder proposes certain tests which any law must satisfy in order to be worthy of recognition. These tests are three in number, but only two in substance ; but when discussing the law of error formulæ he points out that it fails to satisfy a condition which he ought to have stated as a fourth test. These tests are :—No. 1 and No. 2, that the law must agree with experimental data ; No. 3, that the law must indicate a maximum density or a minimum transparency, and, No. 4, that it must not lead to absurdities.

With Mr. Elder's permission, I will state what I consider, for the present, sufficient for practical photography by way of tests to be applied to such a law :—(1) The law must agree with experimental data fairly, if not accurately ; (2) it must be capable of explaining the phenomena of under, correct and over-exposure ; (3) it must not lead to absurdities.

Mr. Elder is no doubt aware that the formula we published, and which does take account of the difference of illumination at the front and back of the film, satisfies all the conditions I have just enumerated. It does not satisfy Mr. Elder's condition of a maximum density or minimum transparency, and Captain Abney draws attention to the same fact. We were, of course, fully aware of this when we concluded our paper with the remark, " It would not have been difficult to extend these considerations so as to include in them the reversing action," &c.

In order to include this reversing action it is, however, necessary to have very clear ideas as to what that action is. I have already published experiments which prove that the whole available haloid salt of silver (92 per cent.) can be obtained in the developable condition, and that reversal consequently only sets in after this has been accomplished. There is, in our opinion, no necessity that a law expressing the first action of light on the silver haloid in the plate should show anything beyond this, that the whole of the silver on the plate can be "reduced." Since reversal only sets in when the action indicated by this law ends, we hold that it need not indicate a maximum density or a minimum transparency. The formula published by us agrees fairly with experimental data, accounts satisfactorily for under-exposure, correct and over-exposure, and leads to no absurdities, and thus satisfies all that practical photography can at the present time demand of it.

Captain Abney begins his paper on the rapidity of plates by a reference to our own "*most serious attempt*" at a satisfactory solution of this question. He reviews our term "density" and our formula expressing the action of light on the sensitive film, which he says is open to criticism. Of course it is, but the criticism he applies seems to me altogether wide of the mark. Our reasoning was based on the amount of light entering the plate, and absorbed therein by unchanged silver haloid. Our equation is an energy-equation, connecting the amount of light with the effect produced. If the particles ever become so fine that they do not absorb blue light, then the constant $k$ of our equation becomes zero, and the formula shows that no effect is produced in that case. The Captain remarks that "there is difficulty in supposing that all particles are completely reduced." As we nowhere stated that they are so reduced —indeed, never intimated that we believe in any real reduction—we do not think ourselves called upon to answer the Captain's difficulty. He concludes this part of the subject by a candid admission "that our formula is one which fits measurements with a degree of accuracy, even for high densities, which is not to be passed over." We thank him for this admission.

Captain Abney goes on to state the "law of error" as he brought it forward at the Camera Club Conference in 1889, and then says :—"I would point out that it reduces itself to the following form" :—

$$T = \epsilon^{-\mu \{\log. I\, t + c\}^2}.$$

This form of the law of error is very important, since it shows the connection between the exposure and the resulting transparency, and thus permits a method of speed determination. This form of the law was communicated by us to Captain Abney in reply to a letter from him in November, 1889, and was first published by us in a paper in which we severely criticised the law. We have nothing to withdraw from that criticism, which has now been fully confirmed by Mr. Elder. We showed that the "law of error," when plotted on our system of densities, represents a parabola, and that such a parabola can be made to fit a short piece of any curve, having no singular point. Mr. Elder admits that the curve is such a parabola, and Captain Abney now claims no more for the law of error than that it fits a certain part of the range. Later on in his paper he attempts to prove that it does not differ much from a straight line, but the proof is, as, of course, it must be, a mistake.

This law Captain Abney proposes to utilise for the determination of the rapidity of plates.

Before we can examine the value of any process for the determination of the rapidity of a plate, we must clearly define what we mean by the rapidity of a plate, and we ought to choose that definition of rapidity which will be most serviceable to practical photography. Notwithstanding the opinion to the contrary expressed by Professor Armstrong, we hold that there are such phenomena as under-exposure and over-exposure, and it is, of course, desirable to be able to find as nearly as possible the correct exposure. Now, what is correct exposure ? We can only judge of it by results. A correct exposure is one which so renders the contrasts in the picture as to approach more or less nearly those which we see in the object itself. In under-exposure these contrasts are too great, in over-exposure they are too small.

We will ask ourselves the question, What must be the laws which govern the action of light on a sensitive film in order that the photographic positive representation may be exactly true ?[1]

Suppose that we know absolutely nothing of the laws involved in the process, and let us assume perfectly arbitrary laws. Say that the amount $(Q\,n)$ of silver on the negative produced after development by a given light intensity (I) is connected by an equation—

$$(1) \qquad Q\,n = F\,(I),$$

and that, in consequence of this silver, the negative has a transparency $T\,n$, which is an unknown function $f$ of the amount of silver $Q\,n$ such that—

$$(2) \qquad T\,n = f\,(Q\,n).$$

If through this transparency we allow light to fall upon another sensitive plate, the positive, then there will, after development, be an amount of silver in the positive $Q\,p$, which is connected with the light intensity $T\,n$ in the same way, $i.e.$, it is expressed by $F\,(T\,n)$, and we have :—

$$(3) \qquad Q\,p = F\,(T\,n).$$

On looking through this positive we perceive the transparency $T\,p$ which is expressed again as the function $f$ of $Q\,p$, and is—

$$(4) \qquad T\,p = f\,(Q\,p).$$

By suitably substituting the values of the various equations we can eliminate the intermediate negative, and arrive at the equation which directly connects the positive transparency $T\,p$ with the original light intensity I, viz. :—

$$T\,p = f\,F\,f\,F\,(I).$$

[1] See Lord Rayleigh's paper " On the general problem of photographic reproduction with suggestions for enhancing gradation originally invisible." (*Phil. Mag.*, XXII., p. 734 (1911), reprinted. *B.J.P.*, LVIII., p. 994 (1911).)

If we now make the assumption that photography is exactly true, then $T\,p$ must exactly represent the original light intensity I, and be equal or proportional to it.   In the case of equality (the case of proportionality makes no essential difference) we have—

$$I = f\,F\,f\,F\,(I),$$

from which follows the important conclusion that $f\,F$ must be $= 1$, or

$$f = F^{\,-1.}$$

In words this means that, if photographic truth is to be possible, the law F, which represents the action of light on the film, must be the exact inverse of the law $f$, which represents the law of transparency.

Now, whatever form these two laws may hereafter be discovered to have, the combination of equation (1) and (2), viz. :—

$$T\,n = f\,F\,(I)$$

will remain true, and considering that when I grows, the transparency of the negative diminishes, leads to the equation—

$$T\,n = \frac{m,}{I}$$

if $f = F^{\,-1}$;   that is, if photographic truth were a reality.

Now, we have defined the negative logarithm of transparency as the density, and we find, as the condition of the possibility of photographic truth, that—

$$D = (\log.\ I - \log.\ m).$$

Captain Abney holds that the law of transparency represented above by the letter $f$ is the " law of error."   We ourselves have proved experimentally, and most authorities hold that the formula given also by Mr. Elder in his paper is the correct formula ;  but whichever formula is correct—indeed, if any other law should be found in future to be the correct law, the equation just given remains unaffected thereby.   It represents the necessary relation between the density and the exposure which must be fulfilled if photography is to be true to nature.

It will readily be perceived that this equation is identical with the equation called the approximate equation in our paper, " Photo-chemical Investigations," and I hope that future critics of our approximate equation will not forget this meaning of it.   It represents the condition which must be satisfied if truthful rendering of an object by photography is to be possible.

But is this condition satisfied in practice ?

Captain Abney's " law of error " formula—

$$T = \epsilon^{\,-\mu\,(\log.\ I\,t)^2}$$

says, emphatically, No, it is not.   Our own formula—

$$D = y \log.\ \{O - (O - 1)\,\beta^{It}\}$$

says that in general the condition is not satisfied, but that there exists, for every plate, a series of exposures for which this conditional equation is so nearly satisfied that no human eye will ever discover the difference.

It follows from this that the best measure of the sensitiveness or rapidity of a plate is to be found in that exposure which forms the unit in that conditional equation—

$$D = y \, (\log. \, I \, t - \log. \, i)$$

for truthful representation. This unit $i$ and its inverse value, the speed, can be easily determined. Give to a plate a series of exposures, measure the densities free from fog, which can be done without a single calculation, thanks to a modification in our photometer, made by the able and energetic manager of Messrs. Marion & Co., Mr. Cowan. These densities are plotted as ordinates to the logarithm of the exposures as abscissæ and the points are connected by a suitable curve. If, in that curve, there be any portion very nearly straight, prolong that straight line until it intersects the axis of abscissæ, the point of intersection at once gives the exposure, which is the unit for the above conditional equation of truthful rendering.

This is our system of speed determination. It depends solely upon experiment, and upon no theory which can be upset. It matters not whether the laws which govern the action of the light on the sensitive film are known or unknown ; it is of no consequence whether Captain Abney's " law of error," or the law we stated, and which Mr. Elder stated again, be the true law of transparency, the system of speed determination has nothing whatever to do with it.

Let us now consult Captain Abney's definition of rapidity. He gives one on page 130, but when we pass on we find that the first definition is not quite correct. The real definition is contained in the words :—" The lantern plate is therefore $2^{1\cdot2}$, or about $2\cdot3$ times faster than the wet plate."

These words define the rapidity of a plate to be the inverse value of that exposure which, when introduced into the law of error formula, makes the transparency equal to 1, or the density equal to 0.

We therefore depend here entirely on the law of error. If that be true, the rapidity, by means of it, may be true also. If it be false, the rapidity may be erroneous. The position of this unit of rapidity is rendered more doubtful still by the fact that the law of error is inconsistent just in that part of the curve where the " zero " point lies, viz., the exposure for which the theory requires the transparency to be 100, whilst practice gives the value 100 to the film which received no exposure at all, a point which on the diagram would be situated at infinite distance to the left.

If the practical photographer only desires to know what exposure is just too short to give any deposit, then Captain Abney's speed determination would be sufficient ; but his " zero point " does not in the least assist us to find that least exposure which marks the beginning of correct representation. It has no relation whatever to the " zero point " found by the equation expressing the condition of correct representation.

To determine his " zero point," the Captain gives, like ourselves, a series of exposures, develops and measures the transparencies.   He then calculates these transparencies, referred to that of the " bare film " as 100, which is equivalent to our deducting the fog.   He plots these transparencies as ordinates to the logarithms of the exposures as abscissæ, draws the curve, and a tangent to the singular point.   Where that tangent intersects the 121st parallel there is to be found the " zero point " of the scale.   This singular point of the curve must not be supposed to be a singular point of the plate.   Its ordinate is now and for all time fixed at 60·6.   Its abscissæ (the log. of exposure) may be anything between two limits, which limits cannot be defined.   Thus the critical point of the curve, which determines the speed, is not the critical point of the plate.   Really any other point in the " law of error " is equally as good as this singular point.   The equation for the tangent at any point is—

$$t\, g = -\,2\,\mu\,x\,\epsilon^{-\mu\,x^2} = -\,2\,\mu\,x\,\mathrm{T}$$

from which the point of intersection with the " axis " of the curve (the " zero line ") can be found easily.   Its ordinate $y_1$ in the scale of transparencies is—

$$y_1 = \mathrm{T}\,(1 - 2\log.\,\epsilon\,\mathrm{T})$$

when T is the transparency to which the tangent is to be drawn.   As soon, therefore, as the transparency is mentioned we can at once say on which parallel the tangent to this given transparency will intersect the " zero line." Thus, for instance, to the transparency 28·46 on Abney's scale belongs the point of intersection on the parallel 100, quite independently of time of exposure or development ($x$ and $\mu$ in the law of error equation).

The diagram shows and compares the two methods of speed determination for Cowan's chloro-bromide plate.

The " law of error " curve for this plate is—

$$\mathrm{T} = \mathrm{T}\,a^{-\mu\,(\log.\,\mathrm{I}\,t - c)^2}$$

and $a = 10$, $\mu = 0\cdot406$, $c = 0\cdot506$.

There are two tangents drawn through the singular point at T = 60·6. The one corresponds to the calculated tangent, the direction of the other was simply dictated by appearances. It will be seen that the length of the straight line in this curve is very little.

The dotted curve in the diagram is the parabola represented by the equation—

$$D = 0 \cdot 406 \, [\log. \, I \, t - 0 \cdot 506]^2,$$

*i.e.*, it is the density curve calculated according to the law of error, and made to agree perfectly with the two exposures 10 seconds and 40 seconds, between

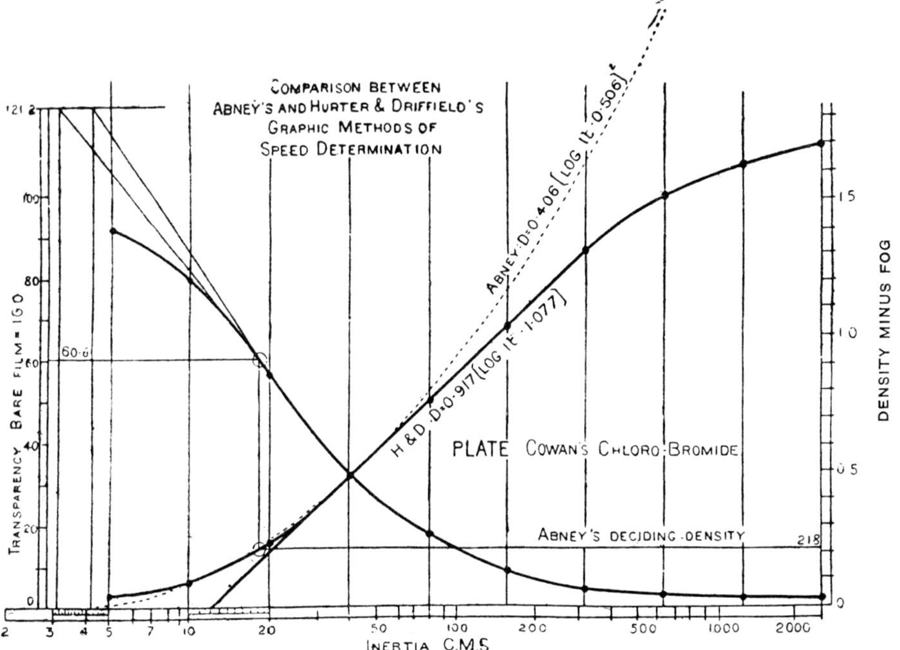


which the singular point of the transparency curve is situated. The density corresponding to this singular point is 0·218. It will be evident to those acquainted with this kind of work that it is not satisfactory to have to rely for a speed determination upon so low a range of densities.

The density curve, the parabola, may also easily be used to find the " zero point " of the law of error. The rules with respect to drawing tangents to a parabola are so well known and so simple that I believe this mode of proceeding would even be better than that involving the singular point of the transparency curve. It is clear that the tangent to any point of density D intersects the axis of the parabola (the zero line) at a distance below the axis of abscissæ equal to that density D.   Thus any point of the curve may easily be used, and the errors of experiments averaged by drawing several tangents.

The other curve on the diagram is simply the density curve as obtained by direct observation.   I append the values :—[1]

| Exposure, C.M.S. | | | Density. | Exposure, | | | Density. |
|---|---|---|---|---|---|---|---|
| $''$ | | | | $''$ | | | |
| 5 | .. | .. | .. | ·035 | 160 | .. | .. | .. | 1·040 |
| 10 | .. | .. | .. | ·100 | 320 | .. | .. | .. | 1·320 |
| 20 | .. | .. | .. | ·245 | 640 | .. | .. | .. | 1·510 |
| 40 | .. | .. | .. | ·490 | 1,280 | .. | .. | .. | 1·620 |
| 80 | .. | .. | .. | ·760 | 2,560 | .. | .. | .. | 1·690 |

Clearly the law of error curve, the dotted line, agrees with this only in what we have termed the period of under-exposure ; in the higher densities it rapidly gives too high values.   We draw attention to the long portion of the experimental density curve (which we have named the " characteristic curve " of the plate), which is as nearly straight as it can be, and more particularly we draw attention to the fact that the prolongation of this line intersects the axis of abscissæ at a considerable distance from the " zero point " found by means of the singular point of the transparency curve.   It will readily be granted, from a mere inspection of the diagram, that Captain Abney's " zero point " and our inertia point have nothing in common, nor have they any constant relation to each other.

In justice to ourselves I must point out that the photographic public will be misled if they accept the Captain's statement on page 131 :—" The zero point calculated from the formula I use should give close results to the zero point obtained by the method of densities.   Thus, in Experiment 22, Messrs. Hurter and Driffield state[2] that D $= 1·176$ (log. I $t - 0·579$), that is, when log. I $t = 0·579$, D $= 0$.   Using my formula, the zero point is $0·6$, that is, when log. I $t = 0·6$, which is practically the same."

Let us see what Captain Abney's constant for our Experiment No. 2[2] really is.   On page 127 we find the explanation :—" In my formula " (the Captain says) " $x$ is the number of successive exposures, and in the first one $x$ is $1·6$, No. 2 is $2·6$, No. 3 is $3·6$, and so on ; $\mu = 0·0237$, common logarithms being used."

The formula thus stands—

$$A_1 = A\, a^{-0·0237\, x^2}$$

<hr>

[1] H.N.—D., p. 132.                    [2] p. 111.

Now $x$ is really log. I $t + c$, and for the successive exposures, 1, 2, 4, &c., we have—

$$\text{Log. } 1 + c = 1 \cdot 6.$$
$$\text{Log. } 2 + c = 2 \cdot 6.$$
$$\text{Log. } 4 + c = 3 \cdot 6.$$

and so on.

We see that these terms differ by log. 2, and by subtraction we find that log. $2 = 1$. We are therefore in the system of logarithms to the base 2, and not in the common system. But whatever system we are in, the logarithm of 1 is always zero. Hence the Captain's constant is not, as he states, $0 \cdot 6$, but it is $1 \cdot 6$. And this constant is a logarithm to the base 2, and can only be compared with our constant, after changing the logarithmic system from the base 2 to the base 10. When that is done the result is $(1 \cdot 6 \times 0 \cdot 301) = 0 \cdot 48$.

But, whereas our constant $0 \cdot 579$ is negative, the Captain's constant $0 \cdot 48$ is positive, and thus the real difference in the rapidity of the plate, as found by the two methods, is expressed by the number, of which the sum $0 \cdot 48 + 0 \cdot 579 = 1 \cdot 059$ is the common logarithm, that is, $11 \cdot 4$.

The plate used in our experiment No. 22 is thus found to be 11 times faster by Captain Abney's method than by our own method, and the assertion that the speed found by the two methods ought to be the same is due to an error in stating the value of the constants. These constants have been wrongly stated in Captain Abney's paper in nearly every instance.

Owing to using several systems of logarithms in his paper the Captain has fallen into an awkward error also when comparing the " Seed plate " with the " Carbutt plate," one of which he states to be $4 \cdot 6$ times as fast as the other ; but it is not $3^{1 \cdot 4} = 4 \cdot 6$ times as fast, it is only $2^{1 \cdot 4} = 2 \cdot 6$ times as fast.

Whilst in our method of speed determination none of the constants depend upon the particular system of logarithms used, and the method itself is independent of any laws, the constants of Captain Abney's method all depend upon the particular logarithmic system employed, and the method itself depends upon the correctness of the " law of error." Moreover, it really gives as its result an exposure which just marks the beginning of under-exposure, whilst our method gives as its result an exposure which just marks the beginning of correct exposure for the particular plate.

[*Reprinted from " The British Journal of Photography," 1894, pp. 714, 724.*]

# THE PRINCIPLES INVOLVED IN ENLARGING.

## (WIDNES PHOTOGRAPHIC SOCIETY.)

THE enormous strides which have in late years been made in the production of sensitive materials have rendered the pursuit of this most interesting branch of photography comparatively easy. Not only can sensitive paper now be procured with various qualities of surface, but of varying degrees of sensitiveness, the slowest produced being very considerably quicker than the paper one used to prepare for oneself in the days before the advent of gelatino-bromide. Yet, years ago, I well remember how proud I was of some very poor productions obtained with an exposure of many minutes, the source of illumination being limelight. Now only a few seconds' exposure to the light of an oil lamp is required, and no trouble whatever in the preparation of the sensitive material. Nevertheless, there is a prejudice against an enlargement on bromide paper, many persons maintaining that satisfactory results cannot be produced on this material I am free to admit that the best possible results are probably obtained by a contact print in platinum or carbon from an enlarged negative ; but, at the same time, I maintain that very much more beautiful bromide enlargements can be produced than one very often sees, if only the conditions necessary for their production be observed. The failure to produce satisfactory enlargements on bromide paper is probably chiefly due to the fact that it is utterly impossible to produce a good enlargement from a negative which will yield a good contact print, and yet one negative is generally expected to serve both purposes.

There is also a general impression that the production of a good enlargement involves the use of a light of high intensity, preferably daylight, or, at any rate, such an illuminant as limelight. I believe that this impression is altogether a fallacy, and that, on the contrary, given a suitable negative and a correct exposure, a perfectly satisfactory result can be obtained with artificial light of extremely feeble intensity. I believe this mistake has arisen from attempting to produce enlargements from negatives of ordinary density with light of low intensity. The prolonged exposure necessary in such cases has not been realised and under-exposure has resulted; while, with daylight, it has been easy to secure a more adequate exposure, and the better result has been attributed to the higher illuminant. But neither daylight nor any other light will ever produce a satisfactory enlargement from an unsuitable negative. The only advantage that appertains to the use of daylight is that it does not necessitate the possession of an optical lantern ; but otherwise the balance of advantage is infinitely in favour of the lantern. Daylight is fickle and more difficult to gauge accurately than an oil lamp ; then, again, it is only available in the daytime, while enlarging by oil light can be conducted at any hour, day or night, a matter of considerable importance, to the amateur, at any rate.

The essential conditions to consider in connection with enlargement are, first, the quality of the negative required ; and, secondly, the estimation of the correct exposure, and to these points I shall almost exclusively confine myself. I intend to say very little about the use of the optical lantern, with which you are probably all familiar, and as I do not pretend to be able to convert an under or over-exposed bromide print into one correctly exposed by any mysterious compounding of the developer, I shall have very little to say about the extremely simple operation of development.

I will, therefore, proceed to consider the characteristics of a negative suited for the production of a bromide enlargement, and I will try to show you the grounds upon which these characteristics are based. The consideration which determines the character of the negative is the range of gradation which bromide paper is capable of yielding. The range of gradation of the negative must coincide with the range of gradation of the paper if a satisfactory result is to be looked for. By the range of the paper I mean the ratio existing between the two exposures, one of which just falls short of producing any deposit, and the other which just suffices to produce the deepest black which the paper is capable of recording when viewed by reflected light. Say, for example, that an exposure of five seconds just fails to produce a deposit, and that one of 160 seconds just produces maximum blackness, the range of the paper would be as 5 is to 160, or as 1 is to 32. Now, obviously, for a negative to exactly correspond with the paper range, its capacity for transmitting light must have the same ratio, that is to say, the ratio between the opacities representing the deepest shadow and the highest light must also be as 1 is to 32. Inasmuch, however, as we measure the densities of the negative, and not the opacities, and as the densities are, as you will remember, logarithms of the opacities, it amounts to just the same thing, and we find it much more convenient to express the range of the negative as the difference between its highest and lowest densities. But, in order to compare the range of the negative expressed in this way with the range of the paper, we must take the difference between the logarithms of the two exposures which produced the extreme paper range, thus :—

Negative.

| | | |
|---|---|---|
| Maximum density .. .. . .. | 1·735 |
| Minimum ,, .. .. .. .. | 0·230 |
| Range .. .. .. .. .. | 1·505 |

Paper.

| | | |
|---|---|---|
| Logarithm 160 .. .. .. .. | 2·204 |
| ,, 5 .. .. .. .. | 0·699 |
| Range .. .. .. .. .. | 1·505 |

In such a case the negative and paper ranges would absolutely agree, and the best possible result, subject to further considerations, would be obtained.

I do not propose to say anything about the way in which we measure the densities of our negative. With this you are all more or less familiar, many of you having seen the operation carried out at a previous meeting ; but we must go into the question of what may be taken as the range of bromide paper generally, and there is probably no material difference in the ranges of various papers. In order to decide this range, we made a series of exposures on a strip of bromide paper. On examining the gradations after fully developing out, we found that the extreme range did not coincide with that negative range which gave the best practical result ; the paper range, looked at in this way, was too extended, and an enlargement from a negative of a similar extended range produced a result of a strongly pronounced chalk and soot character, with which we are only too familiar. In order to discover the cause of this discrepancy, we measured

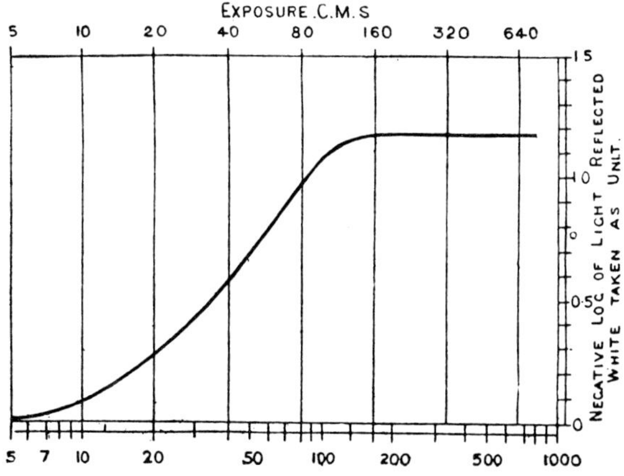


by reflected light, the gradations of the paper strip. For this purpose we employed a modification of our photometer, which I will not now occupy time in describing. Suffice it to say that we obtained a reading from each gradation.  The reading, however, in this case does not express density, but the fraction of light reflected by the gradation as compared with light reflected by the normal white of the paper.  A reading of $1\cdot3$ (log. 20) indicates that the gradation reflects $\frac{1}{20}$ of the light reflected by the pure white of the paper.  Having measured the gradations of the entire strip in this way, we proceeded to plot them just as in the case of the densities of a speed determination.  This diagram shows you the result, and you will at once see the strong resemblance of the paper scale to the " characteristic curve " of a plate ; but I want to call your attention chiefly to the upper part of the curve.  In the case of a plate this would merge from the straight line of the " correct period " much more gradually, but here you see that, when the ordinate 160 is reached, there is no further measurable difference in the degree of blackness, so that, though exposures beyond 160 C.M.S. have produced slight differences just discernible to the eye, comparatively large density differences in the negative would be represented by such trifling differences in the paper scale that we have simply to ignore the latter.  The same argument applies to the very faintest indications of deposit at the other end of the scale, so that you see the practically useful range of the paper is less than a mere inspection of the gradations would lead one to infer.  And you must remember that our test strip was practically developed out, while in picture-making this is generally not the case.  This diagram, therefore, teaches us that the practically useful range of bromide paper is capable of recording light intensities which are to each other as 5 : 160, or as 1 : 32 ; or, taking the difference between the logarithms of these  numbers, in order to compare directly with the negative densities, we at once learn that the density range of a negative suitable for enlargement must not exceed $1\cdot5$, and, as a matter of practical experience, a somewhat less range gives even better results.  An examination of this diagram further teaches that, as the more delicate intermediate tones of the negative correspond with the higher part of the paper curve where the gradations approach each other very closely, the small negative gradations should be kept as wide apart as possible.  This means that a negative for enlarging should be fully exposed, so as to bring its lower densities into the period of " correct exposure."

My reason for preferring a negative with a rather too contracted rather than a too extended range is that I think it far better to make quite sure of getting my delicate half-tones, even at some loss of the deepest black tones. In the finished print it is easy with the brush to strengthen the deepest shadows if desired, but it is a much more difficult matter to fill in half-tones which are wanting, and I need hardly point out the importance of taking all possible measures to reduce the necessity for hand work upon the finished enlargement to a minimum.

We have now considered the range a negative ought to have for the purpos of enlargement, and we have seen that the negative ought to be fully exposed. I also told you that a negative suitable for contact printing is utterly unsuited for enlarging. As most of our negatives are, however, specially taken for contact printing, the question arises what course we are to take if we wish to produce enlargements from them also. The answer is, we must make reproduced negatives having the density range we require. Fortunately, this is an easy thing to do, and I will indicate my own method of procedure. I first of all produce, by means of the camera, a transparency on a slow lantern plate, having all the qualities of a good lantern slide. From this again, also by means of the camera, a new negative is made on a  similar slow plate. The chief things to attend to are that the exposure for the new negative is decidedly ample, and that development be stopped  very early, as soon, in fact, as detail is generally visible by reflected light. By taking these two courses, we shall have no difficulty in procuring that narrow range, combined with adequate detail, which are requisite in a negative for the purpose of enlarging. With the plates I generally use I find that, if the exposure has been correctly timed, a development extending over from one to one and a-half minutes at a temperature of 65° F. will yield a negative having about the right range for the purpose of enlargement. I have purposely specified slow plates for the production of the transparency and the reproduced negative, because the grain of the deposit on a slow plate is much finer than on a rapid plate, and, of course, we must do all we can to obviate texture. It is perhaps hardly necessary to call attention to the importance of exercising the utmost care in the production of the transparency and the reproduced negative. They must be clean, and as absolutely free from faults of any description as possible, because it will be obvious to you that the enlarged print will bear the impress of any faults which may collectively exist in the original negative, the transparency, and the reproduced negative. But, on the other hand, to one expert in the use of the pencil or brush the removal of blemishes, and retouching generally, is assisted greatly by having three plates to work upon.

I now propose to show you a few negatives and rough unfinished enlargements produced from them, and I think you will agree that they bear out what I have said with regard to the production of half-tone. Here are five different portrait negatives of the same sitter, all as nearly as possible exposed for the same length of time, but the time of development varied in each case. The times of development were respectively one and a-half, two, two and a-half, three and a-half, and four and a-half minutes. You will see how the general density of the negatives increases from No. 1, a mere ghost, to No. 5, a strong, brilliant negative. I have marked upon these negatives their respective enlarging ranges, which, you will see, are 0·95, 1·37, 1·82, 2·19, and 2·37.   Now, from what has been said, you will have no difficulty in deciding which of these five negatives we must take if we want to produce the best enlargement.   The only question is, which range is nearest, but does not exceed 1·5 ?   This you will find to be No. 2, the enlarging range of which is 1·37.   No. 1 has a range of 0·95, which is too contracted ; and the range of No. 3, which is far too extended, and would never produce a pleasing result.   I now show you two enlargements produced from negatives Nos. 2 and 3.   You will at once see that No. 2 has produced a print full of half-tone, while the print from No. 3 is almost devoid of delicate intermediate tones, but has the well-known chalk and soot character. You may, therefore, easily imagine what an enlargement would be like made from negatives Nos. 4 and 5 ; yet even No. 5 would yield a good contact print. We thus see that totally different negatives are required for the two purposes. I now hand round a negative, which I must ask you to take special care of, as it has some historical value to me.   It has an enlarging range of 1·218, and it was produced about four years ago in order to confirm a conclusion Dr. Hurter and I had arrived at, on purely theoretical grounds, as to the special quality of negative required for enlarging purposes.   While it is capable of producing a good enlargement, as you will see, you will, I am sure, at once agree that it could, by no possibility, produce even a passable contact print.   I next show you a negative and a contact print taken from it.   The print shows the negative to have about the right range for a contact print on bromide paper ; but, as the enlarging range of the negative amounts to 1·95, you will see that it could not possibly yield a satisfactory enlargement.   Wanting an enlargement from it, however, I had to make a reproduced negative, which you may now see and compare with the original.   The new negative has an enlarging range of 1·09, which, though rather contracted, has produced the enlargement I now show you.   The next example is also an enlargement from a reproduced negative.   The original negative, a snap-shot, had far too wide a range, and a reproduction was a necessity.   You will see that I have, by double printing, introduced clouds, an operation not difficult to perform in enlarging.   As to timing the exposure for the clouds, I give them from one-fourth to one-half the exposure I should give for the picture itself, assuming the maximum density to be the same in both cases.   This serves to prevent the clouds becoming unduly heavy by the time the development of the rest of the picture is complete.

The last two examples I have to show you—one a portrait, and the other a landscape—are intended to illustrate the opinion I expressed that it is better to have a negative of too contracted rather than of too extended a range. These enlargements were produced from negatives having enlarging ranges of 0·952 and 0·896 respectively, and, when first produced, they appeared hopelessly flat and grey.   The high lights and half-tones were, however, there, and you see that, by accentuating the depth of the shadows with a few touches of the brush, the prints have become comparatively bright.   As I said, it is a very simple matter merely to strengthen shadows, but a work of great labour, and requiring considerable skill, to work in half-tones, which are lacking.

From these examples you will see what an assistance it is to know the range of your negative.   It enables one at once to decide whether it is possible to obtain a satisfactory enlargement from any given negative.

We have, I think, sufficiently considered the range and general quality of a negative suitable for the production of an enlargement.   We will now, there-fore, turn our attention to the second important essential, namely, the estima-tion of the correct exposure.   The first thing to be done is to ascertain the sen-sitiveness of our bromide paper, and, for this purpose, all we have to do is to discover what exposure just brings us to the commencement of the paper range ; that is to say, what is the maximum exposure we can give which will only just produce evidence of deposit with full development.   It is absolutely necessary, for reasons which I will point out, that this exposure be ascertained by the precise source of illumination we are going to employ for the production of our enlargement.   You will remember, when I gave you a demonstration on bromide printing by contact, that I explained how the sensitiveness of the paper was ascertained.   I told you that we proceeded to make a series of ex-posures on a strip of the paper to the light of a standard candle or to that of a paraffin lamp made equal to any desired multiple of the candle, and that each successive exposure was made double the preceding one.   Well, this is precisely the course we follow in order to ascertain the commencement of the paper range for the purpose of enlarging, excepting that in this case we employ the light emanating from our lantern as the source of illumination, instead of that given by a candle or a lamp.   The reason for this is that the relation between the chemical and visual rays is not the same in the case of a naked light as in the case of a light passing through the condenser and objective of the optical lantern.   In the latter case there is little or no obstruction to the visual rays, but the large masses of glass in the condenser and objective filters out certain chemically active rays of short wave-length which, in the case of the naked light, pass on and affect the sensitive paper.   You will also remember the method I showed you of producing a series of gradations on the paper by simultaneously making a number of exposures with a revolving disc.   I have here a small portable revolving disc which admits of my holding it against the screen upon which I fix the bromide paper when making an enlargement.[1]   This disc can be rotated by hand, and is precisely similar in principle to the one

[1] The disc now in the H. and D. collection at the R.P.S.

you saw before, excepting that, instead of producing exposures which progress by log. 2, the exposures progress by log. 1·41, thus providing an intermediate gradation, and so rendering the decision as to the commencement of the range more exact.   When making this determination, we simply project the light of the lantern upon the screen, having, of course, secured an accurate focus and a correct adjustment of the position of the light.   We then measure the amount of light falling upon the disc, as you will see me do when we make our enlargement ; we next place the revolving disc, with its sensitive strip, against the screen and proceed to make our exposure.   I hand round three gradation determinations made upon the same paper we are going to use to-night.   The first was produced with the light of an ordinary paraffin lamp, and the second also with the light of a paraffin lamp, but after passing through the condenser and objective of the lantern.   You will see that the lantern gradations are about one step behind the lamp gradations throughout the scale ; in the case of the simple lamp the first perceptible tint was obtained with an exposure equal to 2·5 C.M.S., while in the case of the lantern it required an exposure equal to 5 C.M.S. to yield the first perceptible tint.   This means that the light transmitted by the lantern is only half as rich in chemically active rays as the light emanating from the simple lamp, though in the two cases the light is visually equal.   The third gradation determination also gives 5 C.M.S. as the commencement of the range.   This last determination was made with the small portable disc, while the other two were made with the large fixed disc used for ordinary speed determinations.

It will be well to say here that a little difficulty may possibly be found in deciding which exposure must be regarded as marking the commencement of the range.   It is always better in case of doubt as to exactly where the range commences, to take too great rather than too small an exposure.   I always myself am guided by the earliest unmistakable deposit, ignoring a possible one or two gradations of an extremely faint and indecisive character.   And while about to ascertain this information regarding the paper, it is well to mask a small portion so as to be able to judge of the normal whiteness of the paper. If, after development, there is evidence of fogging on the part to which light has not had access, discard the paper altogether, it will never produce a satisfactory enlargement.   Such fogging may arise in the manufacture of the paper, or be the result of deterioration from long or careless keeping.

We have now, therefore, ascertained that the first evidence of deposit upon the paper we are going to use for our enlargement to-night is produced with an exposure to a light visually equal to 5 C.M.S., issuing from the lantern.   This is one factor required before we can calculate the exposure we must give for the enlargement we are about to make.   The other factor involves a consideration

of the negative we are going to use, and is simply its maximum density.   This
maximum density is 1·18.   This, however, you must remember, is the visual
density as measured in the photometer, and it has to undergo some modification
before it can be used to base the calculation of an exposure upon for the purpose
of enlarging.   Now, in order to make this clear to you, I have here a negative
having a uniform density of 1·05, the corresponding opacity being eleven.   If
I hold this negative up between my eye and a source of light, my  eye will
receive one-eleventh of the light it would receive without the interposition of
the negative.   But now imagine a piece of sensitive paper placed in the position
of my eye : it might be supposed  that an exposure of  eleven seconds with the
negative interposed would do the same chemical work on the paper as  an
exposure of one second to the naked light.   This is not so, however ; relatively
less work is done when the negative is interposed, and that because a large
fraction of the light reaching the paper through the negative is simply reflected
back into space, the amount of light actually absorbed by the paper being alone
left to do any work.   So large is the amount of light reflected by the paper that,
practically, instead of transmitting one-eleventh of the light it receives, we
should have to regard the negative as transmitting only about one-thirtieth of
the light it receives.   In other words, instead of regarding the density of this
negative for practical enlarging purposes as 1·05, we have to regard it as 1·4
times as great, or as 1·47.

From what we have just seen, you will understand the ground upon which
Dr. Hurter and I have always based our contention that there is no one number
which correctly expresses the density of a given deposit.   It is perfectly obvious that two deposits respectively developed with pyrogallol and
ferrous oxalate may have identical visual densities, and yet, owing to the wide
difference in their colour, their actinic densities will greatly differ ; but, further
than this, we now see that a given deposit has three distinct density values—
its visual value, its contact printing value, and its enlarging value.   The visual
density of a deposit, developed with ferrous oxalate, which measures 1·0,
becomes a contact printing density of 0·8, and an enlarging density of 1·4.

To return to the negative which more directly concerns us this evening,
and from which we are going to make our enlargement, I should like, before we
proceed to calculate our exposure, to consider its enlarging range, having regard
to the question we have just discussed.   The visual maximum and minimum
densities of this negative are 1·18 and 0·12, and the visual density range is
therefore 1·18 − 0·12 = 1·06.   When, however, these densities come to be
applied in the operation of enlarging, we have just seen that they require to be
respectively multiplied by 1·4.   This converts the visual densities 1·18 and
0·12 into the enlarging densities 1·652 and 0·168, thus making the enlarging

range of the negative we are about to use 1·484.   From what we saw when we considered the question of range generally, this negative, the enlarging range of which is so nearly 1·5, ought to produce a satisfactory enlargement ; but of this you must judge for yourselves, when, having caught our hare, we have cooked him.

We will now proceed to calculate our exposure for the enlargement we are about to make.   All we have to keep in view is that the exposure must be so timed that the action of the light passing through the maximum density of the negative shall just bring us to the commencement of the paper range ; or, in other words, the exposure must be so timed that the light passing through the maximum density of the negative shall produce the same effect as an exposure, without the interposition of the negative, of 5 C.M.S.   The maximum enlarging density of our negative is 1·052, and as this density only transmits about one-forty-fifth of the light it receives, it is obvious that, in order to produce the same result upon the paper as would be produced by an exposure of 5 C.M.S. to the naked light, we shall have to multiply 5 C.M.S. by 45, the opacity corresponding to our maximum density.   Five times 45 gives us 225, and this is our required exposure in C.M.S.

This calculation is more conveniently made as follows :—

Maximum enlarging density of negative   ..    ..    1·652

Log. 5, exposure marking commencement of range    0·699

—————

2·351

The number corresponding to this logarithm is 224·4, or, say, 225, the exposure required in C.M.S.

Having ascertained our exposure, we will now turn our attention to the practical production of the enlargement.   The lantern I am about to use is an excellent form of instrument made by Mr. Hume, of Edinburgh, and known as the " Cantilever."   The optical parts of the lantern are extremely satisfactory, and the illumination afforded by the lamp is very even, and free from any image of the flame.   The lantern runs on rails, thus permitting of easy adjustment, and the bellows are removable so as to permit of the lantern being used for the demonstration of physical and chemical experiments.   The objective is fitted with a cap containing orange glass, so as to provide non-actinic light for the adjustment of the sensitive medium.

We will now focus the image upon the screen, and adjust the lamp so as to give a perfectly evenly illuminated disc.   The next thing to do will be to ascertain the value of the disc in candle metres.   For this purpose I have here a portable photometer bar, provided at one end with a wire rod, which is held against the screen in such a way as to cast two shadows side by side, one thrown by the light of the lantern, and the other by the light of a candle, so arranged as to slide backwards and forwards upon the bar. The bar is marked with a scale which indicates the value of the disc in candlemetres when the two shadows are of equal intensity. As these shadows vary considerably in colour, the difficulty in comparing their intensities is overcome by viewing them through a piece of green glass. Applying this bar, we learn that the value of our disc is four and a-half candlemetres, and as our exposure was calculated to be 225 seconds to one candlemetre, we shall actually have to give an exposure of 225 divided by four and a-half, or 50 seconds.

Our enlargement is now before you, and I must leave the judgment in your hands as to whether I have been justified in laying the stress I have done upon the important parts played by the range of the negative and the exposure. I think it will be well for you to see the negative which produced the enlargement before you, and I will therefore hand it round. The question is, Does our print fairly utilise the entire range of the paper and give a satisfactory rendering of the half-tones ? If you answer " Yes," I think we may conclude that neither the range of the negative nor the exposure were far wrong. A very old maxim applied to the production of negatives in the camera was, " Take care of the shadows, and let the high lights take care of themselves." In the case of enlargements on bromide paper I would say, " Take care of the half-tones, and let the shadows take care of themselves."

I daresay you have expected me to say something on the subject of the development of bromide paper. I have not done so because the operation is so very simple that it can hardly go wrong. The negative and the exposure are the potent factors, the question of development resolving itself into the individual characteristics of different reducing agents. This question I may have something to say about on some other occasion ; but, for the present, you will not do wrong in using, as I have done to-night, ferrous oxalate. All I would say on the development of bromide paper is, Observe the strictest cleanliness, use plenty of yellow light, and wash well with water acidulated with acetic acid immediately after development.

With regard to the factor $1\cdot4$ for converting the visual into the enlarging density, this strictly only applies in the case of negatives developed with ferrous oxalate. In the case of negatives very yellow in colour as from development with unpreserved pyrogallol, this factor will be somewhat greater ; how much will be easily decided by an experiment or two.

I much regret that time did not allow me to prepare a more imposing series of examples, both as to number, size, and finish ; but I trust that those I have been able to show you have, at any rate, been sufficient to demonstrate the chief points which it has been my object to lay prominently before you. Had I contemplated that this demonstration would be given in this large room, I should certainly not have been satisfied to confine myself to the comparatively narrow limits of a 12 × 10 enlargement ; but when it was decided to hold our meeting here, it was too late for me to change my plans.

I cannot but feel that, in these days of snap-shots, and the consequent production of small negatives, enlargement has a special importance. It is true that, to produce a good enlargement, we must have an adequately exposed negative, and it is, unfortunately, also true that an enormous percentage of snap-shots are made almost regardless of exposure, and result, of course, in under-exposed negatives, totally unfit for the purpose of enlargement. This is not as it should be, and not as it need be. There is no valid reason why we should not obtain good enlarged copies of our hand-camera negatives if we so wish.

I have to-night had another opportunity of demonstrating to you the scientific as opposed to the rule-of-thumb method ; and, though some of you may take a conservative view of the case, and prefer to cling to the good old-fashioned ways, I think you will agree that, at any rate, there is something in scientific procedure. Though the measurements and calculations we have considered may at first sight appear to be a circuitous course to take as compared with rule of thumb, I assure you that a very little familiarity with them would cause you to think differently, and, having once tasted the pleasure of working by pre-calculation, I am certain you would never care to go back. I can hardly hope that you will all go home vowing never again to use a negative of which you have not ascertained the maximum and minimum densities ; but if we have learnt nothing else this evening, we may at least have gained a general idea as to the quality a negative ought to possess if we want it for the purpose of enlargement. I sincerely hope the members of our Society may be induced to take up the practice of enlarging, particularly as, owing to the munificence of Mr. Gossage, we are now the possessors of a lantern.

In conclusion, I will only express my thanks to you all for your patient hearing, and I trust that while I may have interested some of you I have at least not wearied others.

V. C. Driffield.

[*Reprinted from the " Photographic Journal," 1898.*]

# THE LATENT IMAGE AND ITS DEVELOPMENT.

BY

FERDINAND HURTER, Ph.D., AND VERO C. DRIFFIELD.

---

## (*a*) THE LATENT IMAGE.

### I.—INTRODUCTORY AND RETROSPECTIVE.

IN a paper[1] read before the Liverpool section of the Society of Chemical Industry in May, 1890, entitled "Photo-chemical Investigations and a New Method of Determination of the Sensitiveness of Photographic Plates," we endeavoured to show the connection existing between the intensity of the light acting upon a photographic plate, the time during which it acted, and the amount of metallic silver deposited per unit area of the plate after development. We further showed how the experimental knowledge thus obtained might be practically applied to determine the sensitiveness of any given plate, and how that exposure in the camera might be ascertained which would result in a technically perfect negative, that is, one combining with minimum density the greatest approach to truthful representation.

In order to arrive at these results it was necessary to investigate to some extent the influence of variations in development, and to assure ourselves that a developer existed which could be relied upon to yield constant results.

We gave it as our experimental experience that a developer might be so constituted as (1) to develop metallic silver from bromide of silver which had never been exposed to light; (2) to so retard development that the latent image impressed upon the plate should not become visible within the limits of the ordinary time of development, and (3) that a developer might be so "well balanced" that, within a given considerable period, it would not affect unexposed bromide of silver, while, readily, in course of time, developing the latent image of such light impressions as were capable of development.

[1] p. 76.

The outcome of this enquiry was the adoption of ferrous oxalate for the purpose we had in view, on the ground that this developer was the least liable to attack unexposed bromide of silver ; that its action least varied with its composition, and that it was least affected by variations in the amount of bromide used in conjunction with it.

We found that generally, on prolonged development, the latent image tended towards a maximum density, and we gave the law connecting the various densities with the length of time of development as—

$$D_t = D \, (1 - a^t),$$

where $D_t$ is the density after $t$ minutes' development, D the maximum density possible, and $a$ a constant which, for the plates we then used, had the numerical value 0·9015.

With "well balanced" developers we studied the relation between the amount of silver reduced and the exposure which produced the deposit, and we found that the relation was complicated and could not be readily expressed in its entirety by any simple formula.

Represented graphically, however, choosing, as abscissæ, logarithms of exposures, and as ordinates, the amount of silver deposited per unit area of the plate (densities), the effect of prolonged exposure showed itself as a curve of double flexure, which we named the "Characteristic Curve" of the plate. We then showed, from considerations of the laws of absorption of light, now generally accepted, that truthful representation can only be expected if the exposures are such that they fall within the straight portion of the characteristic curve.

The sensitiveness of the plate we found to depend upon the general position of the characteristic curve with reference to the scale of exposures. For practical purposes it was necessary to find a simple method of deciding and numerically expressing the position of the characteristic curve on the scale of exposures, so as to provide a numerical expression for the speed of the plate. Several methods suggested themselves. One was to take the value of the longest exposure which the plate could bear without producing any deposit on development. This method was found to be practically useless, as slight alterations in the constitution of the developer seriously affect this point. Next in importance was the position of maximum density, but experiments made to ascertain this point led to the discovery of the curve of reversal and showed that the position of the point of maximum density was even more difficult to decide than the zero point. The best point of all to adopt would probably have been the point of double flexure, but the difficulty of deciding this also rendered it impracticable.

Thus we abandoned all methods of deciding the speed of the plate from the position of any one single peculiar point of the characteristic curve, and we adopted the method now in general use, viz., that of deciding the position of the characteristic curve on the scale of exposures by means of the point of intersection of the straight portion of the curve with the axis of abscissæ, *i.e.*, the exposure scale. This proceeding seemed to be further justified by our experimental results, which indicated that, for those exposures which resulted in densities belonging to the straight portion of the curve, the density ratios did not materially alter with length of time of development.

The results thus obtained gave values for the sensitiveness of plates which might differ within 20 per cent. to 30 per cent. from each other, but such differences are of no practical importance whatever, for, whether an exposure be given of 10 seconds or one of 13 seconds, its influence upon the general qualities of the resulting negative would be inappreciable.

Our general conclusion was that the density of the latent images is a function of the sensitiveness of the plate and of the exposure only ; that so long as developers are employed which are capable of developing, within a reasonable time, the whole of the latent image, without attacking unexposed bromide of silver, the relation between the resulting gradations cannot be altered by development, and that the density ratios, at any rate in the straight portion of the characteristic curve, are practically unalterable.

Since the publication of our research, our general method of experimenting, of measuring and recording results, and of expressing the speed of the plate, has been adopted by eminent firms of plate makers both in this country and abroad. Photographers in general have, however, taken exception to our use of the term " density," and our conclusions as to the constancy of density ratios have been rejected as not founded upon fact.

We must point out, however, as we have done before, that the photographic public altogether failed to realise the object we had in view when we carried out our investigation. Our object was to discover a method of speed determination, and it was not, as the public seemed to infer, to deal finally and exhaustively with the subject of development. This subject was purely incidental and was merely investigated as far as was necessary for the real object of our enquiry.

The facts which we then recorded were, nevertheless, as carefully ascertained as are those we shall presently quote ; but owing to the greater accuracy and ease with which we are now able to impress a series of exposures upon a series of plates, at a single operation, and owing to the greater accuracy and rapidity with which the photometric measurements of the resulting densities can now be made, our more recent experiments generally embrace a wider range of gradation than our previous experiments did.

Our work still points to the conclusion that what we have termed the " density of the latent image " (that is, the quantity of silver bromide rendered amenable to development) is a function of the exposure (intensity of light $\times$ time) and of the sensitiveness of the plate. Our work, at the same time, indicates that if all possible variations in concentration and in composition of developing solutions are to be taken into consideration, the density ratios of the visible image cannot be said to be constant, and our demand that the developer shall be so " well balanced " that it shall not attack unexposed silver bromide, while capable of developing the latent image within a reasonable time, limits the choice of developers, and with it the applicability of the law of constant density ratios.

We see, however, more and more clearly that the law of constant density ratios is, so to speak, the fundamental principle of photography, and that deviations from it find a ready explanation in the peculiar properties of gelatine and the diffusive and other properties of the chemicals used.

The principle of constant density ratios enables us to pre-calculate photographic phenomena, and, by the knowledge acquired in the course of the present investigation, we hope to show how to pre-calculate, to some extent at least, deviations from this fundamental principle which are due to the behaviour of gelatine and to the laws of diffusion, &c.


## II.—Thermochemistry of Development.

The process of development consists in the decomposition of bromide of silver into metallic silver and bromine, the latter combining with one of the constitutents of the developer itself.

The decomposition of bromide of silver (or other halogen compound) demands the supply of a certain amount of energy, and the question arises whether this necessary energy can be entirely supplied by the chemical changes taking place in the developer, or whether any material part of it must be supplied by the action of the light.

The chemical change which takes place in the developer consists in the formation of an alkaline bromide and of an oxidation product. Development by alkaline pyrogallol, for instance, may be represented by the following equation :—

$$2AgBr + 2NH_4HO + Pyro. = Ag_2 + 2NH_4Br + H_2O + (Pyro. + O)$$
$$\text{Oxidation Product}$$

The energy required for the decomposition of the silver haloids, and that produced by the formation of the corresponding alkaline haloids, is given in the following table :—

TABLE I.—*Energy Developed per Gramme-molecule of Compounds in Calories.*
1 *Cal.* = 1,000 *Grammes Water* × 1° *C.*

|       | Cl. | Br. | I. | OH. |
|-------|-----|-----|-----|-----|
| Ag    .. .. ..  | 29·0  | 20·7–23·7 | 14·3 | — |
| K     .. .. ..  | 101·2 | 90·4  | 74·7 | 117·1 |
| Na    .. .. ..  | 96·6  | 86·4  | 70·1 | 112·5 |
| NH$_4$ .. .. .. | 72·8  | 62·9  | 47·1 | 90·0 |
| H     .. .. ..  | —     | —     | —    | 69·0 |

From this table it will be seen that the formation of potassium bromide will produce 90·4 calories, and, conversely, that the dissociation of the same compound demands a supply of 90·4 calories.

With the values given in this table the energy equation for any development may be calculated as follows :—

Taking the equation given above as an example, we calculate the heat of formation for both sides of the equation, leaving out of the question the heat produced by the oxidation of the pyrogallol, thus :—

$$2AgBr + 2NH_4HO + Pyro. =$$
$$2 \times 23·7 + 2 \times 90 + ?$$

227·4 Cal. to be supplied.

$$Ag2 + 2NH_4Br + H_2O + (Pyro + O)$$
$$—\quad 2 \times 62·9 + 69·0 + ?$$

194·8 cal. produced.

The difference between the energy required for the decomposition on one side, and the energy produced by the formation on the other side, amounts to 227·4 − 194·8 = 32·6 cal. for 2 Ag or 16·3 cal. for Ag, and represents the amount of energy which must be furnished either by the formation of the oxidation product or by the light.

In a similar manner the following values have been calculated :—

TABLE II.—*Calories Required for the Reduction of* 108 *Grammes of Metallic Silver.*

| Reduction of | Hydrates. | | | Carbonates. | | |
|---|---|---|---|---|---|---|
| | K. | Na. | NH$_3$. | K. | Na. | NH$_3$. |
| AgCl .. .. | 10·3 | 10·4 | 11·7 | 13·9 | 14·0 | 13·5 |
| AgBr .. .. | 15·9 | 15·3 | 16·3 | 19·5 | 18·9 | 18·1 |
| AgI .. .. | 22·2 | 22·4 | 22·7 | 25·8 | 25·8 | 24·5 |

From this table we learn that the decomposition of silver chloride requires the least, and that of silver iodide the most, energy for alkaline development, but that there is no material difference in the amount of energy required whichever alkali be employed. There is, however, a material difference of about 3 cal. between the carbonates and the hydrates.

Since the particular reducing agent employed, pyrogallol, for instance, would produce nearly the same constant amount of heat when yielding the same oxidation product, whichever alkali be employed, the result of this thermo-chemical consideration is that, with any given reducing agent, such as pyrogallol, the amount of energy to be furnished by the light is also nearly constant, and the speed of the plate will not be materially affected by the particular alkali employed.

Unfortunately, the oxidation products of most of the organic developers are not well known, nor is the heat determined which they develop on oxidation in alkaline solutions. If, however, the heat developed is to be sufficient to supply all the energy required, the absorption of one atom of oxygen by the developer must produce from 30 cal. to 32 cal. in order to reduce 2 molecules of silver bromide ; or, from 44 cal. to 45 cal. in order to reduce 2 molecules of silver iodide to metallic silver in alkaline solutions.

The few oxidation phenomena which have been studied lead us to believe that, for one atom of oxygen absorbed, the amount of heat (30 cal.) would be easily supplied by the oxidation of pyrogallol ; but nothing certain is known about it. It may be pointed out, however, that the oxidation of an iron protosalt into its persalt in aqueous solution by bromine produces 48·9 cal. for Br$_2$, or suffices to supply the whole heat necessary for the decomposition of 2 AgBr (47·4 cal.). Hence, if ferrous oxalate, which is admittedly a less energetic developer than alkaline pyrogallol, can supply the whole energy required for the reduction of the silver, it is highly probable that the oxidation of pyrogallol will more than provide the energy wanting.

These considerations lead us to the conclusion that the light need not supply any material amount of energy. This conclusion is further supported by the fact that bromide of silver, which has never been exposed to light at all, is yet capable of development ; fairly easily by the alkaline, less readily by the iron developer.

### III.—Constitution and Properties of the Latent Image.

The application of thermo-chemical data to the theory of development having shown that the whole of the energy required for the decomposition of silver bromide may possibly be, and probably is, derived from the changes which the developer undergoes during development, it would appear to be possible to dismiss the old theory of the constitution of the latent image long held by many authors.

The idea that some portion of the silver bromide is decomposed by the light into a sub-bromide and free bromine, is not necessary for the explanation of the phenomenon of development. It is quite sufficient to assume that the light causes some change in the molecular structure of silver bromide ; that it changes, for instance, a complex molecule $Ag^nBr^n$ into simple ones. We may assume that the light does some work of disgregation, as Clausius would say ; not involving a complete change in chemical composition, such as the formation of a sub-bromide, but work, such as is done during the change in the crystalline structure of sulphur or of calcium carbonate ; work which requires a much smaller amount of energy than the complete separation of atoms of bromine from the molecule of silver bromide would involve.

There is absolutely no experimental proof that the change which silver bromide undergoes when exposed to light of such small intensity, and for such small periods of time, as suffice for the production of photographic negatives, produces any visible effect or any measurable chemical transformation. All that can be proved is that exposed silver bromide is more rapidly attacked by the developer than unexposed silver bromide ; but the character of the change (whatever its nature) and its progress in course of time are identical for the exposed and for the unexposed silver bromide.[1]

When silver bromide is treated with a solution of potassium iodide, chemical decomposition takes place, the bromine and the iodine are exchanged, and we then have silver iodide. This reaction takes place also in the case of silver bromide in the sensitive film. If silver bromide which has been exposed to light (*i.e.*, impressed with a latent image) consisted of sub-bromide, this sub-bromide would either remain as such, when treated with potassium iodide, or it would yield a sub-iodide. In either case it ought to yield, upon development, a visible image ; but the treatment of a latent image with potassium iodide completely destroys the image, and we must therefore conclude that the latent image consists of bromide of silver, possibly in an allotropic modification.

If a film containing exposed silver bromide be treated with potassium bromide, no effect whatever is produced ; the latent image can be developed in its full vigour after the potassium bromide has been washed out.

Again, if a sensitive gelatino-bromide plate be treated with a dilute solution of bromine in water, the film loses its sensitiveness to light, that is, the plate becomes exceedingly slow.　If the sensitive plate had a latent image impressed upon it by suitable exposure to light before it was treated with bromine, this latent image would no longer be capable of development ; the difference in rapidity of attack by the developer on the exposed and unexposed silver bromide would have vanished.

This peculiar behaviour of the film, under the influence of free bromine, shows that if the action of the light upon the sensitive film were continued so long as to bring about actual decomposition, and so produce a certain amount of free bromine, the bromine thus liberated would efface the latent image, and render the film almost insensitive.　This is exactly what happens when the exposure is continued so long as to produce the phenomenon of reversal.

That any ordinary camera exposure is inadequate to produce a material decomposition of the silver bromide on the plate can be shown by other experiments and considerations.[1]　A standard candle consumes 120 grains, or $7 \cdot 77$ grammes of spermaceti per hour, or about $0 \cdot 0021$ gramme per second.　The energy evolved by the combustion of $0 \cdot 0021$ gramme spermaceti (1 gramme $= 10,000$ units of heat) is 21 gramme-units (small calories).　If the whole of this energy were produced in the form of chemically active light and evenly distributed over a sphere of 1 metre radius $= 125,663$ square cm., the amount of energy per 100 square cm. of surface would be $\dfrac{21 \times 100}{125,663} = 0 \cdot 016$ gramme-units of heat.

While it is possible on a sensitive plate to produce a deposit of $26 \cdot 5$ milligrammes of metallic silver per 100 square cm. area by an exposure of 10 C.M.S., the amount of energy received by this area, assuming the whole energy yielded by the candle to be taken into consideration, as in the above calculation, is $10 \times 0 \cdot 016 = 0 \cdot 16$ units in 10 seconds.

Now, the decomposition of silver bromide, equivalent to 108 milligrammes of silver, requires energy amounting to 23 gramme-units, and the energy necessary for $26 \cdot 5$ milligrammes of silver is $5 \cdot 6$ units, so that the candle, even if the whole of its energy of combustion were active in decomposing silver

---

[1] H.N.—B., p. 139.

bromide, could only decompose 2·9 per cent. of the amount which experiment shows can be actually rendered amenable to development.

As a matter of fact, however, only a small fraction of the energy of the candle is transformed into radiant energy, and, again, a very small fraction of the radiant energy constitutes etherial waves of sufficiently short wave length to affect silver bromide.

It is thus rendered quite evident that the candle can only furnish an infinitesimal part of the energy necessary to produce 26·5 milligrammes of metallic silver per 100 square cm. with an exposure of 10 C.M.S., and that the whole of this energy is, in all probability, provided by the developer.

We have, moreover, furnished the proof, as far as this can be done, that the composition of the latent image is, as nearly as possible, AgBr, and, in a paper published in February, 1891, we showed that no bromine is liberated in the course of development. As this paper[1] may not be readily accessible, we will briefly repeat our experience therein recorded.

A gelatino-bromide plate ($6\frac{1}{2}$ inches by $4\frac{3}{4}$ inches) was exposed to the light of two standard candles, one on either side of the plate, at a distance of half a metre, for 33 minutes. The plate was then well washed with pure distilled water to remove any bromine which might either have become free as such or which might, by action on the gelatine, have formed hydrobromic acid.

The result was that no soluble bromine could be detected in the wash water.

The plate was then developed with ammoniacal pyrogallol for 30 minutes and washed. The developing solution and the wash water were together oxidised with nitric acid and the bromide precipitated, washed, filtered and weighed as metallic silver. The weight found was 197·7 milligrammes.

The plate was then fixed in pure thiosulphate, well washed, and the film stripped. The amount of metallic silver contained in the film was determined and found to be 194·4 milligrammes.

The amount of bromine found in the developer was thus slightly more than the equivalent of the metallic silver found in the developed plate. Hence we must conclude that the chemical composition of the latent image is AgBr, and this conclusion is further strengthened by the fact that almost the whole of the bromide of silver on the plate had been brought into a readily developable form.

The behaviour of exposed silver bromide to a solution of potassium iodide only furnished qualitative results.

---

[1] *See Photography*, 19th **February**, 1891, *see* p. 151.

The behaviour of exposed silver bromide to a solution of potassium bromide is shown by the following experiment. A plate which had received a series of graduated exposures was cut into two parts. One part was soaked for 20 minutes in a solution of potassium bromide, and then washed for 40 minutes. The other part was soaked in water for 60 minutes. Both parts were then developed and gave the following result :—[1]

*Experiment* 1.

| Exposure. C.M.S. | Density. Plate $D_2$. | |
| --- | --- | --- |
| | Soaked in KBr. | Soaked in water. |
| ·625 | ·065 | ·060 |
| 1·25 | ·360 | ·385 |
| 2·5 | ·870 | ·910 |
| 5 | 1·305 | 1·365 |
| 10 | 1·740 | 1·820 |
| 20 | 2·190 | 2·230 |
| 40 | 2·515 | 2·510 |

That, in course of time, the rate of action of the developer upon unexposed silver bromide is the same as upon exposed is shown by the following comparative results :—

TABLE III.

| | | Time of development. | | |
| --- | --- | --- | --- | --- |
| | Plate. | 2 min. | 4 min. | 8 min. |
| Unexposed .. .. .. | $D_2$ | ·745 | 1·165 | 1·765 |
| ,, .. .. .. | $D_6$ | ·760 | 1·370 | 2·140 |
| ,, .. .. .. | $D_2$ | ·790 | 1·290 | 1·890 |
| Exposed 2·5 C.M.S. .. .. | G | ·660 | 1·095 | 1·600 |
| ,, 10 ,, .. .. | $H_2$ | ·505 | 1·260 | 1·965 |
| ,, 20 ,, .. .. | $D_7$ | ·650 | 1·270 | 1·945 |

In the case of the unexposed plates the developer contained no bromide, while bromide was used in the case of the exposed plates. It will be seen, however, that the growth of density with time is nearly the same in both cases.

[1] D.N.—Ng., p. 46.

When unexposed and exposed silver bromide are developed together, this equal rate of growth is not so easily detected, since the action of the developer upon the unexposed silver bromide is then comparatively small, but the ratio does approximate to equality, as is shown by the following experiments, in which the exposed and the unexposed plates were developed together.

TABLE IV.

| Plate $D_2$. Developed. | 2 min. | 4 min. | Ratio. |
|---|---|---|---|
| Unexposed    ..    ..    .. | ·175 | ·300 | 1·71 |
| Exposed.   1·25 C.M.S.    .. | ·370 | ·615 | 1·66 |
| ,,    2·5    ,,    .. | ·725 | 1·100 | 1·51 |
| ,,    5    ,,    .. | 1·040 | 1·520 | 1·46 |

These experiments show that the difference between unexposed and exposed silver bromide is of the same character as the difference between two successive exposures ; it is a difference of degree only, and not of kind.[1]

### IV.—Speed of Plates Dependent on Physical Properties of the Sensitive Film.

Our previous experiments and calculations indicate that it is highly probable that the difference in the amount of energy contained in the exposed and unexposed silver bromide is very small, and that the rapidity with which the developer attacks the unexposed films of plates, varying considerably in speed, is almost identical, showing that there is but a trifling difference, if any, in the amount of energy contained in the unexposed silver bromide, whatever the speed of the plate. The rapidity of attack of unexposed silver bromide in plates varying in speed is shown in the following table :—

TABLE V.

| | H. and D. Speed. | Plate. | Density developed in | | |
|---|---|---|---|---|---|
| | | | 2 min. | 4 min. | 8 min. |
| Unexposed    .. | 24 | $D_2$ | ·790 | 1·290 | 1·890 |
| ,,    ..    .. | 96 | $D_6$ | ·760 | 1·370 | 2·140 |
| ,,    ..    .. | 83 | $D_5$ | ·745 | 1·165 | 1·765 |

[1] Corr. Hurter—Driffield, 22nd August, 1897. See p. 39.

If, then, the silver bromide in rapid plates is of the same composition and contains the same amount of energy as that in slow plates, the difference in the speed of gelatino-bromide plates must be due more to their physical constitution and optical properties than to any difference in the silver bromide.

In our original paper we developed a theory of the action of the light upon the sensitive film, in which we assumed that the amount of work done upon the film, at any moment of the exposure, was proportional to the useful light only, and we showed that the light reflected from the surface of the film and the light transmitted were useless.

In the course of the development of this theory we introduced the term "inertia," which we denoted by the symbol $i$. We wrote $i = \dfrac{e}{k\,(1 - a)}$ where $e$ was the small amount of energy needed to bring the particle of silver bromide into the developable condition, $k$ the coefficient of absorption of light of the silver bromide, and $a$ a fraction indicating the amount of light reflected by the plate. These coefficients referred, of course, to light of that wave-length which alone is capable of affecting the particular haloid salt of silver.

It became interesting to investigate whether any relation exist between the optical properties of the plate and its speed as ascertained by our method. Unfortunately, it is almost impossible to measure the reflected light of that particular part of the spectrum to which the plate is sensitive, and we had to content ourselves with measurements of the reflected white light of the lamp of our photometer.

For the purpose of this investigation we have examined 16 different samples of plates produced by 10 different manufacturers. We ascertained the speed with reference to ferrous oxalate, the light reflected, the light transmitted, and the amount of silver bromide, from pieces of one and the same plate, and we may here point out that, in making these measurements, the edges of the plate, from which the emulsion has receded on drying, should be scrupulously avoided. If a half-plate be taken, a piece the size of a quarter-plate may be cut out of the centre of it, and this will more than suffice for the examination.

Our method of procedure is as follows :—In order to ascertain the light reflected by the plate, we make use of our photometer, which for the purpose must be provided with a Schmidt and Haensch indicator, which lends itself admirably to our object. The plaster disc with which this instrument is provided must be removed, and it must be replaced with a thin piece of timber. On the right-hand side of the photometer a piece of pure white cardboard must be glued on to the timber, and a mask of mat black paper, with an opening $\frac{5}{8}$ inch diameter, glued on to the cardboard. The left-hand side of the timber must be covered with mat black paper. Against this the back of the plate to be measured rests, the plate being supported by strips of cardboard, into which it slides. In front of the plate, and attached to the cardboard strips, is also a mask of mat black paper, with an opening $\frac{5}{8}$ inch diameter, and exactly similar to the one on the other side of the timber. As the area of the plate actually used for measuring is only that of a circle $\frac{5}{8}$ inch diameter, the plate itself is conveniently cut $\frac{3}{4}$ inch square.

In order to ascertain the neutral point of the photometer before commencing to measure plates, a strip of cardboard of precisely similar quality to that on the right-hand side of the timber must be inserted behind the mask on the left-hand side. The neutral point being ascertained, the strip of cardboard on the left-hand side is withdrawn and the plates to be measured are substituted, one after the other.

It should be here remarked that the photometer[1] we use for this purpose is 20 inches long from diaphragm to diaphragm. A shorter photometer than this cannot be advantageously used with the Schmidt and Haensch indicator.

The readings which we obtain by the method indicated above are the logarithms of the light reflected by white cardboard, the light reflected by the plate being taken as unit. By deduction the readings obtained from 2·0 (log. 100), the result is the log. of the percentage of light reflected by the plate measured. (White cardboard = 100.)

In order to ascertain the light transmitted, the same pieces of the plates just used for reflected light measurements may be again employed. The plates are placed film side towards, and directly against, the diaphragm at the left-hand end of the photometer. The measurements are then made just as in the case of speed determination. It is, however, necessary to take two precautions. First, a piece of yellow glass must be inserted between the lamp and the diaphragm at either end of the photometer, otherwise the intense light of the lamp will so darken the silver salt on the plate as to render measurement uncertain, if not impossible. Secondly, it is necessary to mask the plate inside the photometer by covering it with a metallic mask having an aperture just a shade larger than the diaphragm of the photometer. If this be not done, the whole area of the plate becomes luminous and the readings are inaccurate.

The readings in this case are, of course, densities, and by deducting them from 2·0 (log. 100) the result is the log of the percentage of light transmitted.

In order to obtain the amount of silver salts present upon an area of 100 square cm. of the plates under investigation, we have adopted the following

[1] This photometer in H. and D. Collection at R.P.S.

method as sufficiently accurate, and as occupying far less time and labour than would be involved in an actual chemical analysis. A strip of the plate is taken, which should measure not less in area than from 20 to 25 square cm. This strip, after drying, is accurately weighed on a fine chemical balance to a tenth of a milligramme, the plate is then very thoroughly fixed in thiosulphate, thoroughly washed and dried. It is now weighed again and the difference between the two weighings is, of course, due to the silver salts dissolved out by the thiosulphate.

A further strip of the same plate receives a series of exposures with the revolving disc. It is then developed with standard ferrous oxalate and the speed determined in the usual way.

The following table gives the results we obtained with the 16 plates we examined :—

TABLE VI.—*Speed from Physical Properties of Sensitive Plates.*

| Group. | Plate. | H. & D. Speed to Ferr. Ox. | Light, per cent. | | | Silver salt. Mgrms. per 100 sq. cm. | Product Ag × (100−a). | Speed from physical properties. |
|---|---|---|---|---|---|---|---|---|
| | | | Reflected a. | Transmitted. | Absorbed. | | | |
| I | A | 1·2 | 86·1 | 2·18 | 11·72 | 132 | 1,833 | 2·15 |
| | B | 2·8 | 91·2 | 1·62 | 7·18 | 215 | 1,892 | 2·55 |
| | C | 3·0 | 83·1 | 1·69 | 15·21 | 115 | 1,943 | 2·90 |
| | D₁ | 12 | 71·6 | 2·45 | 25·95 | 122 | 3,464 | 15·70 |
| | D₂ | 24 | 79·4 | 1·99 | 18·61 | 183 | 3,769 | 19·20 |
| | E | 27 | 75·8 | 1·73 | 22·47 | 187 | 4,525 | 28·8 |
| | F | 31 | 69·1 | 2·66 | 28·24 | 155 | 4,789 | 32·8 |
| | D₄ | 63 | 63·8 | 2·63 | 33·58 | 179 | 6,579 | 64·0 |
| | D₅ | 83 | 66·0 | 2·72 | 31·28 | 206 | 7,004 | 72·3 |
| | D₆ | 96 | 58·8 | 2·75 | 38·45 | 194 | 7,993 | 97·0 |
| II | H₁ | 44 | 70·8 | 2·60 | 26·60 | 157 | 4,584 | 29·8 |
| | I | 50 | 67·7 | 2·75 | 29·65 | 136 | 4,392 | 27·2 |
| | J | 53 | 69·9 | 2·54 | 27·56 | 165 | 4,966 | 35·6 |
| | D₃ | 56 | 66·0 | 3·27 | 30·73 | 146 | 4,964 | 35·6 |
| III | G | 40 | 75·8 | 2·13 | 22·07 | 128 | 3,097 | 12·0 |
| | H₂ | 64 | 69·1 | 2·66 | 28·24 | 134 | 4,131 | 23·6 |

$$\text{Speed} = \left(\frac{(100-a) \times \text{Silver}}{800}\right)^2 - 3.$$

In considering the probable connection between the physical properties and the speed of the plate, it will be evident that, with the above method of measurement, the transmitted light refers to yellow light only, but that, as this plays no part in the production of the image, the figure so ascertained is of but little importance. The light reflected will be more or less coloured yellow, according to the colour of the plate, but it is clear that the amount of reflected light given in the table will represent the maximum of light reflected of that particular quality which will affect the plate, and, consequently, that 100 — $a$ will represent the minimum of active light which enters that particular plate, part of which light may and does pass through the plate unabsorbed.

It must also be mentioned that the figures indicating the percentage of reflected light are relative only and not absolute. They give the percentage of light reflected compared with white cardboard, taken as 100.

The rapidity of the plate may be assumed to be, in some way, proportional to the amount of light which enters the plate, and to the amount of silver haloid which is spread over a given area of the plate. In the last column but one of the table are given the products obtained by multiplying the percentage of light entering the plate (100 — $a$) with the number of milli- grammes of silver per 100 square cm. The speed of the plate, if dependent upon its physical properties only, should be some function of this product.

It will be noted that the plates given in this table are divided into three groups, representing respectively 10, 4 and 2 plates, the grouping being arranged according to the closeness with which the speed, calculated from the physical properties of the plate, accords with the actual speed.

The speed of the plate to ferrous oxalate is calculated from its physical properties by the approximate empirical formula given at the bottom of the table. For instance, if the reflected light is 69·1 per cent., the light entering the film is 100 — 69·1 = 30·9 ; then, if there are 155 milligrammes of silver per 100 square cm. of the plate—

$$\left(\frac{30\cdot9 \times 155}{800}\right)^2 = \left(\frac{4{,}789}{800}\right)^2 = 5\cdot98^2 = 35\cdot8.$$

Deducting the constant 3 gives 32·8 as the speed of the plate to oxalate.

Group 1 of this table clearly demonstrates that the speed of the plate is really determined by its physical properties. In Group 2 the calculated and actual speeds do not correspond so well, and in Group 3 the discrepancy is still more marked. Groups 2 and 3 indicate that the calculation of the speed of a plate from its physical properties requires more knowledge than we at present possess ; probably a knowledge of the relative amounts of bromide and iodide in the film.

Nevertheless, for 14 out of the 16 plates examined, the investigation of the plate for reflecting capacity and for the amount of silver contained in the film, has given speeds which would be quite sufficiently accurate for practical purposes.

If the speeds of these plates as obtained by our method of speed-determination be taken as abscissæ, and the products of the light entering the film and the silver present be taken as ordinates, the plates arrange themselves as shown in Diagram No. 1.

In this diagram 10 of the 16 plates examined, and which form Group 1, can be joined by a parabolic curve and relatively correspond with the speeds of the plates.

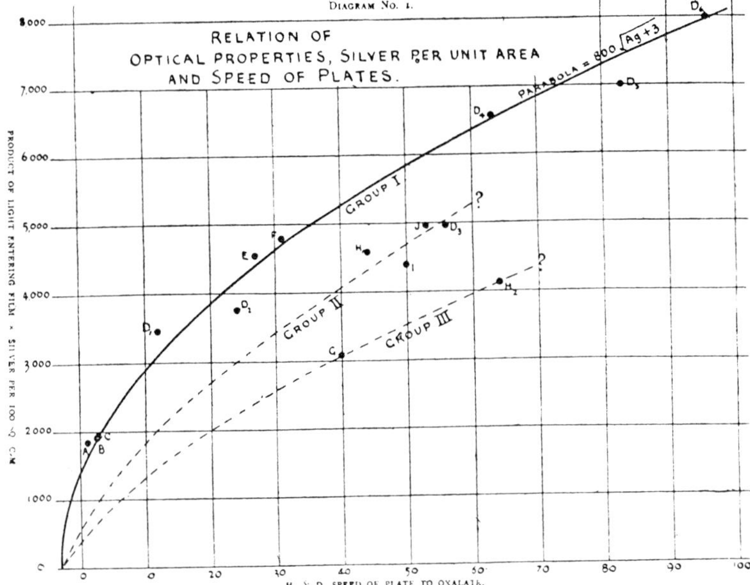


While these investigations have not given us a method of speed determination which can offer the same accuracy of result, or supply the same amount of information concerning the plate as our original method, yet they are extremely interesting and important, as pointing strongly to the probability that speed is purely a function of the physical properties of the plate. The table clearly indicates that a fast plate is one which is rich in silver and reflects a minimum of light.

We must now leave this subject to the attention of plate manufacturers. The evidence we have just laid before you has only been completed in time for this paper, and, though much further investigation is needed, we think enough has been done to indicate clearly wherein lie the essential conditions of speed. It is almost impossible by chemical analysis to ascertain, with a sufficient degree of accuracy, the relative amounts of silver bromide and of silver iodide on small pieces of plates, whilst the plate maker has, of course, the advantage of knowing precisely the proportion he employs.

## (b) THE DEVELOPMENT.

### V.—Properties of Gelatine and of the Sensitive Film.

The conclusions we have so far arrived at are :—

(1) That the energy needed for the production of the visible image from silver bromide may be wholly supplied by the developer ;

(2) That the energy supplied by the light during an ordinary photographic exposure is too small to account for any complete separation of bromine from silver bromide ;

(3) That the composition of the exposed silver bromide in a photographic film still corresponds to the formula $AgBr$, and

(4) That the amount of energy required to render silver bromide developable appears to be the same for all plates ; the rapidity of the plate depending upon its physical properties ; mainly upon the amount of light reflected by the film.

These conclusions point to the probability that the behaviour of various plates to various developers will not differ much, since such differences as exist in the exposed silver haloids of the various plates cannot be very great. The exposures are generally proportioned to the rapidity of the plate, so that the energy stored in the latent images of different plates is almost the same in amount.

The differences which manifest themselves in the behaviour of various plates to the same developer are chiefly due to differences in the amount and quality of the gelatine employed in the manufacture of the plates. These differences are generally confined to the time required to reach a given development factor upon a correctly exposed plate.

The rapidity of the chemical change which constitutes the development depends upon the facility with which the reagents of the developer can approach and come into contact with the silver bromide in the film. The gelatine of the film may rapidly absorb sufficient of the developing solution to supply the whole amount of reducing agent required, and, in that case, development will be complete after the process of absorption has proceeded a comparatively short time. On the other hand, if the gelatine be incapable of absorbing sufficient reducing agent to complete development, a process of diffusion takes place and continues till the reduction is complete.   It is evident from these considerations that, in order to thoroughly understand the process of development, it is necessary to study the properties of gelatine.

The gelatine used in our experiments was in the form of thin sheets and was supplied to us by a well-known firm of platemakers.

0·8665 gramme air-dried gelatine absorbed the following amounts of water :—

TABLE VII.

In 15 minutes 2·999 grms. or 3·45 water per 1 gelatine.
,, 30   ,,        3·177   ,,      3·66   ,,        ,,
,, 12 hours   4·468   ,,      5·16   ,,        ,,
,, 24   ,,        5·148   ,,      5·95   ,,        ,,
,, 48   ,,        5·447   ,,      6·30   ,,        ,,
,, 60   ,,        5·864   ,,      6·77   ,,        ,,

It will be seen that the absorption is very rapid at first, and proceeds very slowly at last.   Thus, if the water absorbed in 60 hours be taken as 100, we have :—

TABLE VIII.

In 60 hours    water absorbed = 100 per cent.
,, 24   ,,        ,,        ,,        88   ,,
,, 12   ,,        ,,        ,,        76   ,,
,, 30 minutes   ,,        ,,        54   ,,
,, 15   ,,        ,,        ,,        51   ,,

This absorption depends, however, much on the temperature at which the experiment is made.   For instance, the following absorptions were observed in 15 minutes at 50° Fahr. and at 70° Fahr.

0·1317 grm. gelatine absorbed 0·4222 grm. water at 50° Fahr., or 3·22 water per 1 gelatine.

0·1309 grm. gelatine absorbed 0·5740 grm. water at 70° Fahr., or 4·35 water, per 1 gelatine.

While gelatine absorbs of water and of dilute solutions from three to seven times its own weight, according to length of time and temperature, more concentrated solutions are not so readily absorbed.   Thus, we found that 1 grm. of gelatine absorbed the following amounts of various saline solutions in 15 minutes :—

TABLE IX.

(1) Pure water .. .. .. ..    3·8 to 3·5 grms.

(2) Potassium oxalate (neutral)—
     36° twaddle .. .. .. ..    0·89 to 0·75 grms.
     27°  ,,   .. .. .. ..    1·48 grms.
     21°  ,,   .. .. .. ..    2·57  ,,
     11°  ,,   .. .. .. ..    4·35  ,,

(3) Dilute ammonia .. .. ..    5·70  ,,

(4) Sodium carbonate—
     4° twaddle .. .. .. ..    5·70  ,,

(5) Sodium thiosulphate—
     33° twaddle .. .. .. ..    1·73  ,,
     17°  ,,   .. .. .. ..    4·75  ,,

(6) Sodium chloride—
     41° twaddle .. .. .. ..    1·91  ,,
     22°  ,,   .. .. .. ..    5·40  ,,

(7) { 5 per cent. solution sodium carbonate / 5  ,,   ,,   ,,   sulphite }   3·60  ,,

A glance at this table indicates that a half-saturated solution of thiosulphate is more efficient for fixing purposes than a saturated solution ; that very little concentrated ferrous oxalate developer will enter the film, and, generally, that dilute solutions enter the film much more rapidly than do concentrated.

A strong saline solution will deprive a wet gelatine film of the water it had previously absorbed, as is shown by the following experiment :—

0·3139 grm. gelatine, soaked in water for 15 minutes, absorbed 1·225 grms. of water, or 3·9 times its own weight. After immersion in a strong solution of potassium oxalate the gelatine contained 0·478 grm. of solution, or only 1·5 times its own weight. Hence a considerable quantity of the water (at least twice the weight of the gelatine) had passed from the gelatine into the oxalate solution.

The question as to whether the solution absorbed by the gelatine has the same composition as the solution into which it is immersed is also of importance. Experiment shows that in the case of common salt, caustic soda and ammonia (with which it is comparatively easily performed) that the solution absorbed by the gelatine is identical in composition with that surrounding the gelatine. The method of making such experiments is very simple, and may be illustrated by the two following examples :—

1·082 grm. of air-dried gelatine was submerged for 5 minutes in a solution of sodium hydrate containing 80 grms. NaHO per litre. The gelatine was rapidly freed from adhering solution by means of blotting paper and was again weighed. It was found to weigh 5·598 grms., and had thus absorbed 5·598 — 1·082 grms. = 4·516 grms. of solution. The specific gravity of the solution is 1·08, hence the gelatine had absorbed $\dfrac{4\cdot516}{1\cdot08}$ = 4·18 c.c. of the solution. The gelatine was next dissolved in water and the solution titrated with normal nitric acid, using methylorange as indicator. The amount of acid consumed was 9·7 c.c., indicating 0·38 grm. NaHO in 4·18 c.c., or 90 grms. NaHO per litre. The solution, therefore, within the gelatine was richer in sodium hydrate than that in which the gelatine was immersed.

In the case of a solution of common salt containing 234 grms. per litre (1·15 specific gravity), in which 0·415 grm. gelatine was submerged for 15 minutes, it was found that the gelatine had absorbed 1·491 grms. of solution, or 1·3 c.c., yielding, on titration with silver, 0·303 grm. NaCl = 233 grms. NaCl per litre. In this case the solution entering the gelatine had the same composition as the solution in which it was placed.

If, however, gelatine be first immersed in water and then in a salt solution, the water previously absorbed is rapidly displaced. 0·508 grm. gelatine immersed first in water and then in a salt solution for 7 minutes absorbed 2·49 grms. = 2·16 c.c. of solution containing 0·508 grm. salt = 235 grms. per litre. Hence, in a very short time, the gelatine had exchanged its water for salt solution.

These properties of gelatine are, of course, shared by photographic plates ; indeed, almost exactly the same figures are obtained for the absorption of liquids, if the amount of gelatine upon the plate be known. A certain quarter-plate, for instance, absorbed in 15 minutes 0·968 grm. of water, but only 0·296 grm., or not quite one-third as much of a strong potassium oxalate solution. Another plate, of different make, absorbed 0·803 grm. of water, but only 0·175 grm. of strong oxalate solution.

The rate at which any particular plate absorbs either water or other solution differs very much with the quality of the gelatine and the relative quantity of it upon the plate. A soft gelatine absorbs readily, a hard gelatine very slowly. The following table shows the difference in the absorbing capacity of some different brands of plates :—

TABLE X.—*Grammes Water Absorbed per 100 square cm. area.*

| Time. Min. | Plates. | | | | | | |
|---|---|---|---|---|---|---|---|
| | $D_2$. | $E_1$. | $H_3$. | $H_1$. | C. | $D_6$. | K. |
| 2·5 | 1·045 | 0·715 | 0·632 | 0·535 | 0·572 | 1·12 | 0·580 |
| 5 | 1·42 | 0·899 | 0·780 | 0·627 | 0·670 | 1·62 | 0·661 |
| 10 | 1·86 | 1·03 | 0·805 | 0·661 | 0·765 | — | 0·691 |
| 15 | 2·12 | 1·12 | 0·810 | 0·670 | 0·790 | — | 0·712 |
| 25 | — | — | — | — | — | 2·65 | — |

In studying the properties of a plate it is worth while to make the following experiments so as to learn (1) the quantity of water absorbed in a given time, say, 15 minutes, and (2) the approximate composition of the film.

A quarter-plate, which has been carefully dried, is weighed on a fine chemical balance and then plunged into pure water for exactly 15 minutes. Adhering moisture is then rapidly removed by means of blotting paper from the film and from the back of the plate, and the plate is re-weighed. The difference in weight gives the amount of water absorbed.

The plate is next thoroughly fixed, washed, dried and weighed again. The difference between the first and this third weight gives the amount of silver haloids on the plate.

Finally, the plate is washed in hot water, so as to entirely remove the film, and, when quite dry, the plate is weighed a fourth time. The difference between the last two weighings gives the amount of gelatine on the plate.

In this way the following results have been obtained :—

TABLE XI.[1]

| Plates .. .. | $E_1$. | $H_4$. | $D_2$. | L. | K. | H. |
|---|---|---|---|---|---|---|
| Grammes emulsion on ¼-plate | ·461 | ·282 | ·527 | ·290 | ·254 | ·398 |
| „ silver haloid „ .. | ·210 | ·108 | ·140 | ·098 | ·065 | ·181 |
| Silver haloid ⎱ in 100 emul- ⎰ | 46 | 38 | 26·5 | 34 | 26 | 47 |
| Gelatine ⎰ sion ⎱ | 54 | 62 | 73·5 | 66 | 74 | 53 |
| Water absorbed in 15 min., ¼-plate .. .. .. | ·968 | ·803 | 1·861 | ·975 | ·626 | ·710 |
| Water absorbed per 1 gramme emulsion .. .. .. | 2·10 | 2·86 | 3·54 | 3·35 | 2·46 | 1·78 |
| Water absorbed per 1 gramme silver salt .. .. .. | 4·57 | 7·50 | 13·40 | 9·85 | 9·50 | 3·80 |
| Water absorbed per 1 gramme gelatine .. .. .. | 3·90 | 4·60 | 4·80 | 5·10 | 3·34 | 3·35 |
| Per cent. silver required for density 2·0 .. .. .. | 18·5 | 36 | 28 | 40 | 60 | 20 |



[1] H.N.—I., pp. 105–108.

TABLE XI.—*continued.*

| Plates | H$_1$. | C. | D$_6$. | G. | I. | Dry collodion. |
|---|---|---|---|---|---|---|
| Grammes emulsion on ¼-plate | ·301 | ·276 | ·517 | ·300 | ·421 | ·278 |
| „　　silver haloid　„　.. | ·149 | ·098 | ·177 | ·098 | ·114 | ·052 |
| Silver haloid ⎱ in 100 emul- ⎰ | 49 | 34 | 34 | 33 | 27·5 | — |
| Gelatine　　⎰　　sion　　⎱ | 51 | 66 | 66 | 67 | 72·5 | — |
| Water absorbed in 15 min., ¼-plate　..　..　.. | ·588 | ·693 | 2·120 | 1·15 | 1·629 | — |
| Water absorbed per 1 gramme emulsion　..　..　.. | 1·96 | 2·52 | 4·07 | 3·45 | 3·75 | — |
| Water absorbed per 1 gramme silver salt　..　..　.. | 4·02 | 7·40 | 11·90 | 11·20 | 15·20 | — |
| Water absorbed per 1 gramme gelatine　..　..　.. | 3·85 | 3·82 | 6·15 | 5·70 | 5·06 | — |
| Per cent. silver required for density 2·0　..　..　.. | 26 | 40 | 22 | 40 | 34·5 | 76 |

These results explain much of the different behaviour of plates as regards rapidity of development and facility of developing high densities.

Whilst some plates are so poor in silver that from 60 per cent. to 70 per cent. of the silver present has to be reduced in order to obtain a sufficiently dense sky in a landscape negative (say, density 2·0), others are so rich that 20 per cent. only of the silver present is utilised to yield the required density.

Plates which absorb from 4·8 to 6 grms. of water per 1 grm. gelatine in 15 minutes develop rapidly, while plates which only absorb 3 to 4 grms. of water develop slowly.

We may here call attention to variations we have incidentally found in the amount of emulsion on plates taken from the same packet. Our conclusions, with regard to the physical properties of plates, render it clear that these plates would vary in speed. Absolute uniformity of speed in the 12 plates contained in a single packet is therefore not to be expected.

TABLE XII.[1]—*Emulsion, in Milligrammes per Quarter-plate, on Plates taken from the same packet.*

| Plate H$_4$. | | Plate E$_1$. |
|---|---|---|
| (1) 273　..　..　..　..　..　..　.. | | (1) 414 |
| (2) 283　..　..　..　..　..　..　.. | | (2) 452 |
| (3) 295　..　..　..　..　..　..　.. | | (3) 403 |
| (4) 271　..　..　..　..　..　..　.. | | (4) 420 |

[1] H.N.—I., p. 70.

VI.—QUANTITATIVE CHEMISTRY OF DEVELOPMENT.

The result of the development of the latent image is said to be a deposit of metallic silver in the film.   This deposit is the denser the less light it permits to pass through, that is, the more silver there is deposited per unit area of the film.   We have defined the density of a plate as the logarithm of its opacity, a number which is proportional to the weight of metallic silver per unit area, and which is also proportional to the sensation produced upon the eye.   The eye, in judging gradation, is influenced by the amount of silver which produces the gradation, and it calls that a perfect gradation in which the amount of silver per unit area uniformly increases in arithmetic progression ; such a gradation as is observed on looking through a wedge of coloured glass.

The amount of metallic silver corresponding to any given density, as measured in our photometer, varies with the colour of the precipitated silver, and may be approximately ascertained, for a sufficiently large plate, by chemical analysis.   The smallest area which will yield satisfactory results is that of a quarter-plate.   The sensitive plate is exposed to light so as to produce approximately the required density uniformly all over the plate.   After development, fixing, washing and drying the density is measured in at least nine places (preferably in more) and the mean of the measurements is taken as the density.

The film of the plate is next removed by immersion in water acidulated with a few drops of hydrofluoric acid, and is then transferred in one single piece, by means of a camel-hair brush, into a small beaker.   It is next washed with distilled water and drained.   A small quantity of strong nitric acid is now added, which generally produces sufficient heat to liquefy the gelatine, and which dissolves the metallic silver.   When solution is complete (assisted, if necessary, by warming in a waterbath), water, together with sufficient hydrochloric acid to precipitate the whole of the silver, are added.   The liquid is allowed to remain on the water bath until the precipitate has completely settled and the supernatant fluid is perfectly clear.   Occasional stirring assists. The chloride of silver is then filtered, washed, dried and transferred to a weighed porcelain crucible.   The filter is burnt and the crucible allowed to cool.   A drop of nitric acid is dropped into the crucible to re-dissolve any metallic silver, which is again transformed into chloride by the further addition of a drop of hydrochloric acid.   Moisture is now expelled by gently heating the crucible (carefully avoiding spurting), and the temperature is then raised till the silver chloride is just brought to fusion.

We published a series of such determinations in 1891,[1] which we here repeat :—

*Experiment 2.*

| Optical density. | | | | | | | Grms. AgCl. |
|---|---|---|---|---|---|---|---|
| 0·525 | .. | .. | .. | .. | .. | .. | 0·0163 |
| 0·960 | .. | .. | .. | .. | .. | .. | 0·0299 |
| 1·470 | .. | .. | .. | .. | .. | .. | 0·0450 |
| 1·970 | .. | .. | .. | .. | .. | .. | 0·0611 |
| 4·925 | .. | .. | .. | .. | .. | .. | 0·1523 |

The ratio $\dfrac{0·1523}{4·925}$ gives the amount of silver chloride which corresponds to density 1·00. The area of the plates was 192 square cm., hence the amount of metallic silver per 100 square cm., corresponding to the optical density 1·00, was found to be—

$$\frac{0·1523}{4·925} \times \frac{100}{192} \times \frac{108}{143·5} = 0·01212 \text{ grm.}$$

Since these determinations were made our photometer readings have gained in accuracy, and the following new determinations have been recently made :—

*Experiment 3.*

| Optical density. | | | | | | | Grms. AgCl. |
|---|---|---|---|---|---|---|---|
| 0·757 | .. | .. | .. | .. | .. | .. | 0·0115 |
| 2·535 | .. | .. | .. | .. | .. | .. | 0·0388 |
| 3·292 | .. | .. | .. | .. | .. | .. | 0·0503 |

The area of these plates was 87·2 square cm., hence the amount of metallic silver, per 100 square cm., corresponding to unit density, is—

$$\frac{·0503}{3·292} \times \frac{100}{87·2} \times \frac{108}{143·5} = 0·0131 \text{ grm.}$$

The above plates were all developed with ferrous oxalate. The density of plates differs, however, with the colour of the precipitated silver, pyro-developed negatives requiring less silver to yield the same optical density.

A plate developed with pyro-soda gave the following results (Experiment 4) :—

Density 2·356 = ·0547 grm. AgCl.

[1] See p. 146, and H.N.—B., p. 167.

The area of this plate was 168 square cm., hence the amount of metallic silver per 100 square cm., corresponding to unit density, is in this case—

$$\frac{\cdot 0547}{2 \cdot 356} \times \frac{100}{168} \times \frac{108}{143 \cdot 5} = 0 \cdot 0104 \text{ grm.}$$

The mean of these results (having due regard to the number of experiments made) gives, as the amount of silver per 100 square cm., corresponding to density $1 \cdot 00$, $0 \cdot 0121$ grm., or, say, 12 milligrammes.

The densities of good ordinary pictorial negatives range between the limits 0 and $2 \cdot 5$. The extreme density of a landscape negative is usually that due to the sky, which amounts to about $2 \cdot 0$. The highest density in a studio portrait is frequently about $1 \cdot 5$.

The following table gives the amount of chemical changes which occur during development, expressed as milligrammes of the substances produced and consumed per 100 square cm.:—

TABLE XIII.—*Metallic Silver and Potassium Bromide Produced, and Ferrous Sulphate ($FeSO_4 + 7H_2O$) and Pyrogallol Required, for the Development of Different Densities.*

| Optical density. | Milligrammes per 100 sq. cm. sensitive film area. | | | |
|---|---|---|---|---|
| | Metallic silver. | Potassium bromide. | Ferrous sulphate. | Pyrogallol. |
| $0 \cdot 50$ | $6 \cdot 05$ | $6 \cdot 67$ | $15 \cdot 55$ | $1 \cdot 78$ |
| $1 \cdot 00$ | $12 \cdot 10$ | $13 \cdot 35$ | $31 \cdot 10$ | $3 \cdot 57$ |
| $1 \cdot 50$ | $18 \cdot 15$ | $20 \cdot 02$ | $46 \cdot 65$ | $5 \cdot 35$ |
| $2 \cdot 00$ | $24 \cdot 20$ | $26 \cdot 70$ | $62 \cdot 20$ | $7 \cdot 14$ |
| $2 \cdot 50$ | $30 \cdot 25$ | $33 \cdot 37$ | $77 \cdot 75$ | $8 \cdot 92$ |
| $3 \cdot 00$ | $36 \cdot 30$ | $40 \cdot 05$ | $93 \cdot 30$ | $10 \cdot 71$ |

The pyrogallol required is calculated from experiments which are detailed below. The ferrous sulphate required is calculated on the basis that 108 milligrammes Ag correspond to 278 milligrams ($FeSO_4 + 7H_2O$).

This table enables us to judge more correctly the quantitative aspect of the process of development, and we will now proceed to discuss some points in connection with the developers we most frequently use. We here give our standard formula for ferrous oxalate :—

*Ferrous Oxalate.*

|              | A. | | | |              | C. | | | |
| --- | --- | --- | --- | --- | --- | --- | --- | --- | --- |
| | | | Parts. | | | | | | Parts. |
| Potassium oxalate | | .. | I | | Potassium bromide | | .. | | I |
| Water | .. | .. | .. | 4 | Water | .. | .. | .. | 100 |

|              | B. | | | |              | | | | |
| --- | --- | --- | --- | --- | --- | --- | --- | --- | --- |
| | | | | | For use take : | | | | |
| Ferrous ulphate | | .. | I | | A .. | .. | .. | .. | 100 |
| Citric acid | | .. | .. | 0·01 | B .. | .. | .. | .. | 25 |
| Water | .. | .. | .. | 3 | C .. | .. | .. | .. | 10 |

Development to be conducted at a temperature of 65° Fahr.

### (I) *Ferrous Oxalate.*

The ferrous oxalate developer, compounded as above, contains in—

|              |              | Parts. |
| --- | --- | --- |
| | potassium oxalate .. .. .. | 185 |
| 1,000 parts | ferrous sulphate .. .. .. | 61·5 |
| | citric acid .. .. .. .. | 0·61 |
| | potassium bromide .. .. .. | 0·74 |

From previous experiments (see Tables IX and X) we have learnt that the plate with the highest absorption capacity absorbs, in 15 minutes, 2·12 grms. of water per 100 square cm., and that it would only absorb a quarter of this amount of strong oxalate solution—that is, about 0·53 grm. or c.c. of solution.

Since 1,000 parts of standard ferrous oxalate developer contain only 61·5 parts of ferrous sulphate, 530 milligrammes of developer will contain 32·5 milligrammes of ferrous sulphate. As we learnt from Table XIII that 31·1 milligrammes of ferrous sulphate are required to produce an optical density of 1·0, it will be quite evident that the most absorbent plate is quite incapable of absorbing, in 15 minutes, sufficient ferrous oxalate solution to develop anything like a sky density of 2·0. In this case development depends upon exchange of reagents between the film and the mass of the developer by a process of diffusion.

Remembering that the film absorbs relatively much more of a dilute than of a concentrated solution, it will be readily seen that the dilute solution will actually introduce more ferrous sulphate into the film in a given time than a concentrated solution ; thus the rapidity of development does not depend very much upon the concentration of the developer.

It will also be perceived that for other plates which absorb less than 2·12 grms. of water in 15 minutes development will depend almost entirely upon diffusion of the reagents from the mass of the developer into the film, and that the amount of the developing solution absorbed by the film is utterly inadequate to produce such densities as are obtained and required.

### (2) *Pyrogallol.*

It is easy to calculate the quantitative changes which happen within the film when ferrous oxalate is the developer employed, since one atom of iron reduces one atom of silver. It is not so, however, with pyrogallol. Its formula and constitution are very well understood, but its behaviour on oxidation is still very obscure, and no literature at our disposal enabled us to obtain even an approximate idea of the relative amount of metallic silver which one part of pyrogallol might reduce. We had therefore to appeal to direct experiment. After many failures the following method gave approximately constant results.

A carefully weighed quantity of pyrogallol is dissolved in distilled water. A quantity of silver nitrate (from eight to twelve times the weight of the pyrogallol) is also dissolved in distilled water, and dilute ammonia is carefully added until the brown precipitate of silver oxide is just re-dissolved.

To this ammoniacal silver solution the solution of the weighed quantity of pyrogallol is added, well mixed and allowed to settle. The yellow-coloured solution containing the excess of silver is passed through filter paper (Schleich and Schüll's), and the precipitate is washed by decantation with very little water. The precipitate is then transferred to the filter paper and again washed with a small quantity of water. The washing must be interrupted immediately the precipitate begins to pass through the paper.

The dark grey precipitate is now dried and ignited in a porcelain crucible and weighed. It appears then as an almost white powder, which on polishing in an agate mortar, assumes the metallic lustre. It is pure metallic silver after ignition, but it is not wholly so before the drying operation. The precipitate when treated with potassium bromide yields silver bromide and a strongly-coloured solution. Double decomposition also takes place on the addition of thiosulphate, and it would appear as if an organic salt of silver were present in the precipitate.

The following results were obtained :—

(1) 0·2214 grm. pyrogallol and 1·8308 grm. silver nitrate. Pyro solution poured into ammoniacal silver solution.

Obtained 0·8285 grm. silver.

(2) 0·1855 grm. pyrogallol and 2·0214 grm. silver nitrate. Ammoniacal silver solution poured into pyro solution.

Obtained 0·6349 grm. silver.

(3) 0·1560 grm. pyrogallol and 2·0541 grm. silver nitrate. Ammoniacal silver solution poured into pyro solution.
Obtained 0·5673 grm. silver.

The molecular weight of pyrogallol, $C_6H_3(OH)_3$, is 126. The above results calculated on 126 of pyrogallol give the following amounts of silver reduced per molecule of pyrogallol :—

| | |
|---|---|
| (1) .. .. .. .. .. .. .. | 472 |
| (2) .. .. .. .. .. .. .. | 429 |
| (3) .. .. .. .. .. .. .. | 457 |
| Mean .. .. .. .. .. | 452 |

The atomic weight of silver being 108, we find that one molecule of pyrogallol can reduce, under the most favourable circumstances, about four atoms of metallic silver from ammoniacal solution. Upon this basis the figures given in Table XIII have been calculated.

Applying this knowledge, we find that it is possible to compound a pyrogallol developer so that the quantity of solution absorbed by the film shall contain sufficient pyrogallol to readily develop any density.

On again consulting Tables IX and X we find that the least absorbent plate absorbs, in $2\frac{1}{2}$ minutes, 535 mgrms. of water per 100 square cm., and as much or more of a dilute alkaline solution such as is employed in conjunction with pyrogallol.

Since the production of a sky density of 2·0 on 100 square cm. area requires 7·14 mgrms. of pyrogallol, it is evident that a developer containing this amount in 535 mgrms. will, even with the least absorbent plate in our table, produce a density of 2·0 in $2\frac{1}{2}$ minutes. Such a developer would contain about 6 grains of pyrogallol to the ounce.

Alkaline pyrogallol thus differs from ferrous oxalate. While the former is able to produce the necessary density without the process of diffusion, the latter cannot, and depends essentially upon diffusion for the production of the necessary density.

It will be noticed that the concentration of the pyrogallol developer in the example just given is such as is seldom used, and from this it may be inferred that, with developers containing less pyrogallol, we also depend upon the process of diffusion for the supply of a further amount of pyrogallol.

As a further example we will take the same plate again. In 15 minutes this plate absorbs 670 mgrms. of solution. If the developer were to contain only one part of pyrogallol in 1,000, there would enter the film, with the 670 mgrms. of solution, 0·67 mgrm. of pyrogallol, and this would produce a density of only 0·185. It is evident that the production of any larger density than this would depend upon the process of diffusion for the necessary further supply of pyrogallol to the film. Even with the most favourable plate, which absorbs 2·12 grms. of solution in 15 minutes, the density due to the pyrogallol entering the film would only be 0·59.

These examples will illustrate the difference in the behaviour of different plates towards the same developer, and of different concentrations of the same developer towards the same plate.

We have purposely separated in imagination the two processes by which the reducing agent obtains access to the silver haloid. These processes of absorption and diffusion proceed, of course, simultaneously, and we have already seen that the process of diffusion in gelatine is fairly rapid. Indeed, it is well known that the process of diffusion is quite as rapid in gelatinous masses as in pure water. Nevertheless, the imaginary separation of the two processes assists in understanding some peculiarities of pyro-development, which are indicated by the following experiments :—

A plate ($D_2$) was given a series of exposures, cut into strips, and each strip developed with a different amount of pyrogallol. The developer contained :—

*Experiment* 4.[1]

|  |  |  | Parts. |
|---|---|---|---|
| | potassium bromide | ..    .. | 2·0 |
| In 1,000 parts | ammonia ($NH_3$) .. | ..    .. | 1·56 |
| | pyrogallol    .. | ..    .. | 1 to 4 |

| Pyrogallol 1 in 1,000. | | 2 in 1,000. | 4 in 1,000. |
|---|---|---|---|
| Time developed 2½ min. | 5 min. | 2½ min. | 2½ min. |
| C.M.S. | | | |
| 1·25     ·150 | ·315 | ·160 | ·180 |
| 2·5     ·405 | ·645 | ·515 | ·580 |
| 5     ·600 | ·890 | ·880 | 1·060 |
| 10     ·760 | 1·120 | 1·185 | 1·530 |
| 20     ·920 | 1·310 | 1·425 | 1·925 |
| 40     1·065 | 1·460 | 1·665 | 2·215 |

The rate of absorption for this plate is—

1·06 grms. in 2·5 minutes ; and

1·45   ,,    5      ,,

[1] D.N.—Ng., pp. 38, 39, also Charts Driffield to Hurter, 16th March, 1897.

The amount of pyrogallol entering the film by absorption alone would, therefore, be in a developer containing :—

| Pyrogallol 1 in 1,000. | | 2 in 1,000. | 4 in 1,000. |
|---|---|---|---|
| Mgrms. pyro. | | | |
| In 2·5 minutes .. .. .. | 1·06 | 2·12 | 4·24 |
| In 5 ,, .. .. .. | 1·45 | — | — |

To these amounts of pyrogallol would correspond the following densities as the highest which would be obtained were the process of diffusion absent :—

| Pyrogallol in developer. | Time of development. | Highest density possible by developer absorbed. | Density obtained for 40 C.M.S. exposure. |
|---|---|---|---|
| | Mins. | | |
| 1 in 1,000 | 2·5 | ·300 | 1·065 |
| 1 ,, | 5 | ·410 | 1·460 |
| 2 ,, | 2·5 | ·600 | 1·665 |
| 4 ,, | 2·5 | 1·200 | 2·215 |

It is again evident from this experiment that by far the larger amount of reducing agent is introduced into the film by the process of diffusion, but the influence of the richer developer shows itself in the more rapid growth of those densities which require the larger amount of reducing agent. The smaller densities are nearly the same in magnitude for all three developers, because the reducing agent necessary to develop them is fully contained in the solution absorbed, whilst the higher densities show marked differences of about density 0·600, which differences are almost entirely due to the larger supply of pyrogallol introduced by the process of absorption, since doubling the time, to allow for longer diffusion, does not produce the same result.

VII.—INFLUENCE OF THE QUANTITATIVE COMPOSITION OF THE DEVELOPER ON THE DENSITY OF THE IMAGE AND ON THE CHARACTER OF THE NEGATIVE.

We have shown that, if a negative is to be true to nature, its densities, when plotted as ordinates to the logarithms of the exposures as abscissæ, must lie on a straight line, and if the visual densities, as obtained by photo-metric measurements, were equivalent to the printing densities, this straight line would be inclined at an angle of 45°, the tangent of which angle is = 1.

We have also shown that, when the densities of a negative, graded as required in our method of speed determination, are plotted as indicated above, a certain curve results, a considerable portion of which is practically a straight line.

We further proved that, by alterations in the time of development, it is possible to cause this straight line to assume different angles of inclination, or, as we express it, the development factors (the tangents to these angles) can be caused to assume values greater or less than 1. We have also introduced, as a measure of the sensitiveness of the plate, the numerical value of the exposure corresponding to the point of intersection of the straight line with the axis of exposures ; the greater the exposure at which the straight line intersects the slower is the plate, and *vice versa*, and we have termed the particular exposure at the point of intersection the " inertia " of the plate. The greater this value, the more inert is the plate.

Variations in the composition of the developer may affect (1) the general aspect of the characteristic curve ; (2) the development factor (the inclination of the tangent to the singular point) and (3) the inertia.

Since, however, the length of time of development with the same developer may also affect these three qualities, it is necessary, for all comparative experiments made to ascertain the influence of alterations in the composition of the developer, to restrict the development to a suitable definite time for all the experiments of one series.

One constituent, namely, an alkaline bromide, is usually employed in all developing solutions, in which it exerts such a peculiar influence that we shall discuss its properties separately after we have considered the variation of the other constituents.

### I.—*Ferrous Oxalate.*

This developer is not capable of much variation. For convenience it is compounded of ferrous sulphate and potassium oxalate in excess, in order that the resulting ferrous oxalate (itself insoluble in water) may be retained in solution by the potassium oxalate. The relative quantities of potassium oxalate and of ferrous sulphate are not, therefore, capable of great variation, and we have not thought it necessary to make experiments in this direction.

The greater or less dilution of the ferrous oxalate developer causes more or less ferrous salt to enter the film in a given time. The four solutions with which we made absorption experiments, for instance (see Table IX), would introduce the following relative quantities of ferrous salt into the film :—

TABLE XIV.

| Relative quantity in solution. | Twaddle. | Relative quantity in film. |
|---|---|---|
| | Deg. | Parts. |
| 4 | 36 | 69 |
| 3 | 27 | 86 |
| 2 | 21 | 100 |
| 1 | 11 | 84 |

We see from this table that most ferrous oxalate would be introduced into the film by the solution of 21° Tw., *i.e.*, the strong solution diluted with an equal bulk of water. The effect of even this dilution is comparatively trifling. We give the following experiment as an example of what may be expected :—

*Experiment* 5.   PLATE M.

| Exposure, C.M.S. | Developed 7 mins. in saturated solution. | Developed 7 mins. in half saturated solution. |
|---|---|---|
| 0 | ·080 | ·085 |
| 5 | ·390 | ·385 |
| 10 | ·660 | ·675 |
| 20 | ·965 | 1·050 |
| 40 | 1·230 | 1·405 |

It will be noticed that the larger quantity of ferrous salt introduced into the film by the weaker solution has made itself felt in the higher densities. This is exactly what might be expected. A reaction depending upon two reagents (in this case affected silver bromide and the ferrous salt), proceeds with a velocity proportional to the one reagent if the other is in large excess. Were the ferrous oxalate in the film in large excess, the reaction in the various parts of the negative would proceed in proportion to the affected silver salt present, and the negative would show a uniform growth all over. But if the ferrous oxalate were in excess in one part and deficient in another part, then the density ratios would be disturbed, and the higher densities would grow too slowly. The clear understanding of the influence of the concentration of the developer on the characteristic curve of a plate could only be arrived at by an appreciation of the quantitative chemistry of development, in conjunction with the absorptive properties of gelatine.

The tendency of the ferrous oxalate developer is to stunt the growth of the higher densities ; hence the upper portion of the characteristic curve is curved too much, and the straight, or useful portion, is shortened owing to this retarded growth of the higher densities, which depend upon diffusion chiefly for their supply of reducing agent, while the lower densities obtain sufficient from the solution actually absorbed by the film.

No important variation in the results of development can be produced by variation in the composition of this developer except as regards the employment of bromide, which we shall fully discuss later on.

### II.—*Alkaline Pyrogallol.*

The usual constituents of this developer are (1) either ammonia or an alkaline carbonate, (2) sodium sulphite, (3) pyrogallol, and (4) potassium or ammonium bromide. The influence of these constituents we will proceed to consider.

### (1) *Variation in the Amount of Alkali.*

We have confined our investigation to the ammoniacal and sodium carbonate-pyrogallol developers.

The following experiment shows the variation which the densities of a negative undergo by reason of variations in the amount of ammonia only :—

[1] *Experiment* 6.—Ammoniacal pyrogallol. Plate $D_2$.

Composition of solution. In 1,000 parts $\begin{cases} \text{Pyro. 4} \\ \text{KBr 4} \\ \text{NH}_3 x \end{cases}$

All developed 2·5 minutes. Densities inclusive of fog.

| Exposure, C.M.S. | NH$_3$ in 1,000 parts developer. | | | |
|---|---|---|---|---|
| | 1·56. | 3·12. | 6·24. | 12·48. |
| 0 | ·090 | ·335 | ·905 | 1·375 |
| 0·625 | ·110 | ·390 | ·975 | 1·395 |
| 1·25 | ·235 | ·785 | 1·315 | 1·555 |
| 2·5 | ·645 | 1·375 | 1·835 | 1·890 |
| 5 | 1·160 | 1·915 | 2·280 | 2·230 |
| 10 | 1·650 | 2·405 | 2·605 | 2·550 |
| 20 | 2·080 | 2·810 | 2·920 | 2·765 |
| Negative No. .. | I | II | III | IV |

[1] H.N.—E., p. 35.

The irregularity of the growth of the densities due to different exposures is readily seen from the diagram. The unexposed film is attacked by the developer to such an extent that the fog grows from 0·090 to 1·375. The rapid attack of the unexposed silver bromide by this developer causes irregularities which render ammoniacal pyrogallol quite inapplicable for any accurate work.

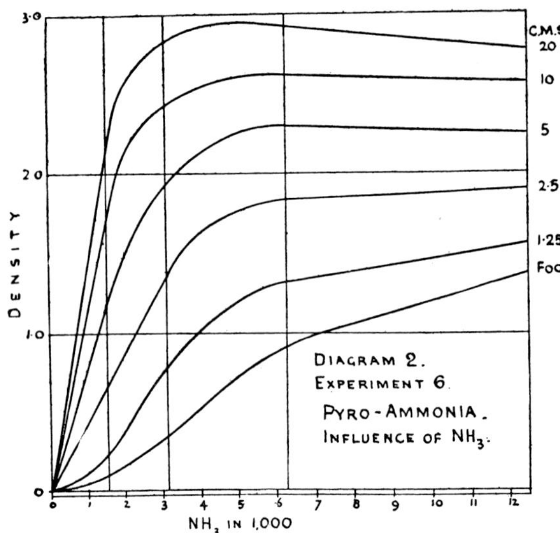


To the practical photographer the following results are perhaps interesting, it being an old belief that under-exposed negatives can be remedied by a plentiful use of the accelerator, ammonia.

| Negative No. | Density difference for extreme exposures. | Density of fog. | Relative time for printing. | Range of negative. |
|---|---|---|---|---|
| I | 1·970 | ·090 | 1 | 1 : 93·3 |
| II | 2·425 | ·335 | 1·75 | 1 : 266·1 |
| III | 1·945 | ·905 | 6·53 | 1 : 88·1 |
| IV | 1·370 | 1·375 | 19·2 | 1 : 23·4 |

These figures have the following meaning :—The actual range of exposures given is from 1 to 32. Assuming, however, that an ordinary printing paper be capable of differentiating between exposures ranging from 1 to 90, it will be seen that, while this range is practically obtained in negative No. 1, and approximately so in negative No. 3, the range in negative No. 2 is far too extended, while, in negative No. 4, it is far too contracted. The irregularity in the growth of the densities with increased additions of ammonia is such that no control whatever can be exercised over the printing range of the negative, while this is the only real control the photographer has, and hence one of vital importance. It will also be seen how the time occupied in printing from these four negatives would vary. If the time necessary to print from negative No. 1 were, say, 30 minutes, the time required to give the same depth of shadow in negative No. 4 would be 9 hours 36 minutes.

Far more regular results are, however, obtained by increasing the amount of carbonate of soda in the pyro-soda developer, as is shown in the following experiment :—

*Experiment 7.*—Pyro-soda.    Plate $D_2$.

Composition of solution.    In 1,000 parts $\left\{\begin{array}{lll} \text{Pyro} & .. & 8 \\ \text{KBr} & .. & 2 \\ \text{Na}_2\text{CO}_3 + \text{10 Aq.} & & x \end{array}\right.$

All developed 3 minutes.    Densities inclusive of fog.

| Exposure, C.M.S. | Parts of carbonate of soda in 1,000 of solution. | | | |
|---|---|---|---|---|
| | 25. | 50. | 100. | 200. |
| 0 | ·090 | ·095 | ·135 | ·205 |
| 0·625 | ·090 | ·095 | ·160 | ·265 |
| 1·25 | ·125 | ·205 | ·360 | ·595 |
| 2·5 | ·375 | ·580 | ·885 | 1·240 |
| 5 | ·710 | 1·065 | 1·555 | 1·985 |
| 10 | 1·065 | 1·560 | 2·245 | 2·730 |
| 20 | 1·430 | 2·060 | 2·880 | 3·455 |
| 40 | 1·770 | 2·540 | — | — |
| Negative No.    .. | I | II | III | IV |

The great difference between the use of sodium carbonate and of ammonia is, first of all, marked by the very much slower attack of the unexposed silver bromide in the case of the former alkali.    The fog has only increased from 0·090 to 0·205.    The 200 parts of sodium carbonate are equivalent to no less than 34 parts of ammonia, and yet the soda developer has hardly attacked the unexposed film.    A further marked difference in the use of the two alkalis is the great regularity in the growth of density for each exposure in the case of sodium carbonate, as is clearly shown by the diagram.

We also tabulate, as follows, the printing ranges of these four negatives and give the relative times which would be occupied in printing from them :—

| Negative No. | Density difference for exposures 1·25 to 20 C.M.S. | Density of fog. | Relative time for printing. | The range of exposure 1 : 16 is represented by the range. |
|---|---|---|---|---|
| I | 1·305 | ·090 | 1 | 1 :   20 |
| II | 1·855 | ·095 | 1·01 | 1 :   71 |
| III | 2·520 | ·135 | 1·11 | 1 : 331 |
| IV | 2·860 | ·205 | 1·30 | 1 : 724 |

It will be seen that in this case the range of the negative regularly increases for every further addition of soda. Though the numbers do not absolutely agree, the diagram clearly points to the existence of constant density ratios

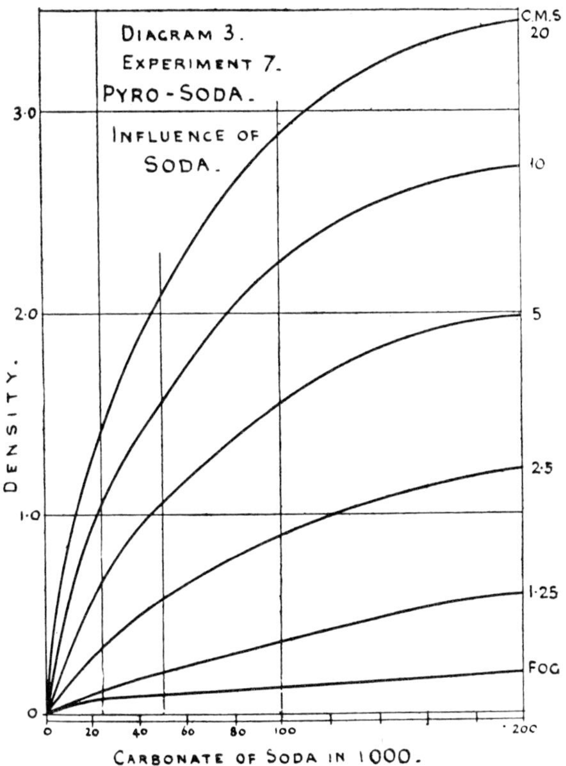



among these four negatives. It will be seen that negative No. 4 would only require 30 per cent. more time for printing than negative No. 1, so that the fog is hardly of any consequence.

(2) Variation in the Amount of Sodium Sulphite.

Sodium sulphite appears to have little or no influence on the density of the image, and serves simply to correct the colour of the deposit. We have not considered it necessary to make many experiments in this direction, but the following suffices to show how very trifling the influence of this reagent is :—

*Experiment* 8.—Densities inclusive of fog—

|  | Plate D$_2$.  Slow. Pyro-soda. | | Plate D$_6$.  Rapid. Pyro-ammonia. | |
|---|---|---|---|---|
| Sulphite in 1,000. | 0. | 120. | 0. | 50. |
| Time developed. | 3 min. | 3 min. | 6 min. | 6 min. |
| 0 | ·170 | ·160 | ·310 | ·235 |
| 1·25 C.M.S. | ·450 | ·570 | ·930 | ·860 |
| 2·5 ,, | ·890 | 1·010 | 1·315 | 1·265 |
| 5 ,, | 1·235 | 1·390 | 1·665 | 1·660 |
| 10 ,, | 1·740 | 1·740 | 1·965 | 1·980 |
| 20 ,, | 2·130 | 2·075 | 2·185 | 2·145 |
| 40 ,, | 2·490 | 2·385 | — | — |

Whether sodium sulphite be used with pyro-ammonia on a rapid plate or with pyro-soda on a comparatively slow plate, the very great variation from total absence of sulphite to the presence of 10 per cent. on the solution has no material influence on the densities.

### (3) *Variation in the Amount of Pyrogallol.*

If, to a developer containing a given amount of alkali (be it ammonia or soda) we add increasing quantities of pyrogallol, the effect is that the densities increase with the pyrogallol at first, but, after a certain amount of pyrogallol has been added, not only is there no further increase, but a decrease takes place in the density attained in a given time. This result we pointed out in our original paper, and also that the maximum activity of ammoniacal pyrogallol was reached when the solution approximately contained, upon one molecule of pyrogallol, three molecules of ammonia. The following experimental evidence appears to confirm this observation. The figures given in this experiment are graphically represented in diagram No. 4.

*Experiment* 9.—Pyro-ammonia.    Plate D$_2$.

Composition of solution.    In 1,000 parts $\left\{ \begin{array}{l} NH_3 \ 1·52 \\ KBr \ 2 \\ Pyro \ x \end{array} \right.$

All developed 2½ minutes.    Densities inclusive of fog.

| $x =$ | I. | 2. | 4. | 8. |
|---|---|---|---|---|
| 0 | ·155 | ·150 | ·130 | ·120 |
| 1·25 C.M.S. | ·305 | ·310 | ·310 | ·225 |
| 2·5  ,, | ·560 | ·665 | ·710 | ·615 |
| 5  ,, | ·755 | 1·030 | 1·190 | 1·115 |
| 10  ,, | ·915 | 1·335 | 1·660 | 1·600 |
| 20  ,, | 1·075 | 1·575 | 2·055 | 2·050 |
| 40  ,, | 1·220 | 1·815 | 2·345 | 2·390 |
| Negative No. .. .. | I | II | III | IV |

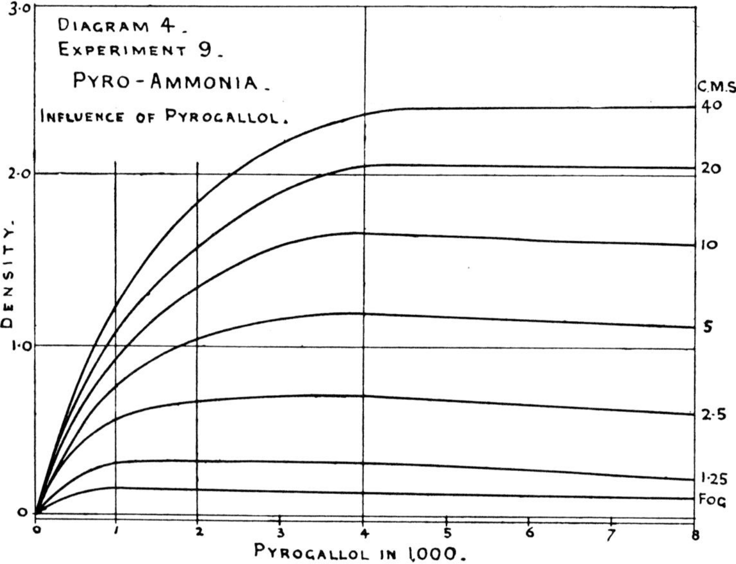



It will be seen that the results are again somewhat irregular, but it is evident that the maximum density was reached when the developer contained, upon 1·52 parts of ammonia, about four parts of pyrogallol. If the maximum were reached when the pyrogallol has exactly three molecules of ammonia associated with it, the maximum ought to have been reached when 3·75 parts of pyrogallol had been added.

That the increase in pyrogallol, when the soda developer is used, appears to follow a similar rule, is shown by the following experimental results graphically represented in diagram No. 5.

*Experiment* 10.—Pyro-soda.   Plate $D_2$.

Composition of solution.   In 1,000 parts $\begin{cases} Na_2 CO_3 + 10\ Aq. & 50 \\ Na_2 SO_3 & \ldots\ 50 \\ KBr & \ldots\ \ldots\ 1 \\ Pyro & \ldots\ \ldots\ x \end{cases}$

All developed $2\frac{1}{2}$ minutes.   Densities inclusive of fog.

| $x =$ | 1 | 2 | 4 | 8 | 16 | 32 | 64 |
|---|---|---|---|---|---|---|---|
| 0 | ·065 | ·070 | ·070 | ·080 | ·085 | ·075 | ·085 |
| 1·25  C.M.S. | ·065 | ·070 | ·120 | ·235 | ·260 | ·195 | ·095 |
| 2·5  ,, | ·065 | ·070 | ·305 | ·585 | ·650 | ·515 | ·245 |
| 5  ,, | ·065 | ·120 | ·585 | 1·025 | 1·145 | ·985 | ·605 |
| 10  ,, | ·065 | ·220 | ·900 | 1·435 | 1·620 | 1·435 | 1·010 |
| 20  ,, | ·065 | ·390 | 1·230 | 1·900 | 2·190 | 1·945 | 1·485 |
| 40  ,, | ·145 | ·620 | 1·565 | 2·360 | 2·675 | 2·450 | 2·005 |
| Negative No.   .. | I | II | III | IV | V | VI | VII |

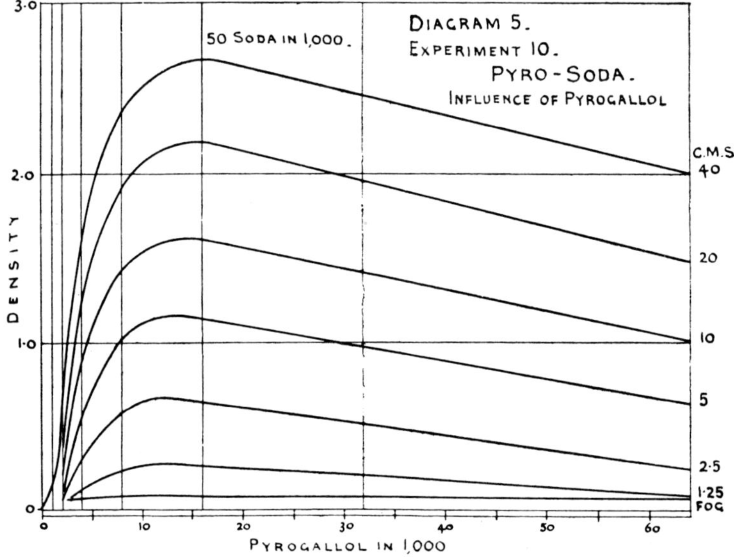


Diagram No. 5 again indicates greater regularity than results in the case of ammoniacal pyrogallol. The curves indicate that maximum density is reached when about 14 parts of pyrogallol were present. The molecular weight of crytallised sodium carbonate is 286, the amount of soda containing 3 atoms of sodium is 429, and the proportion—

$$429 : 126 :: 50 : 14·7,$$

indicates that, upon 50 parts of soda, there ought to be present 14·7 parts of pyrogallol if, for each molecule of pyrogallol, there were present 3 atoms of sodium. The above experiment seems to agree fairly with this proportion. There is not, however, any good chemical reason for supposing that this must be so, and, consequently more experiments were needed to ascertain whether this proportion was accidental or was really based upon some interesting fact.

For this purpose further experiments were made with solutions of higher and lower concentrations of sodium carbonate in order to ascertain whether the amount of pyrogallol required to produce maximum density bore a constant proportion to the soda employed.

Experiments 11 and 12, represented by Diagrams 6 and 7, give the results obtained. The sodium carbonate, in the first experiment, amounted to 25 parts in 1,000 of developer, and, in the second, to 100 parts, *i.e.*, one-half and double the amount used in Experiment 10.

*Experiment* 11.—Pyro-soda.   Plate $D_2$.

Composition of solution.   In 1,000 parts
$$\left\{\begin{array}{lll} Na_2CO_3 + \text{10 Aq.} & & 25 \\ Na_2SO_3 & .. & .. & 25 \\ KBr & .. & .. & 1 \\ Pyro & .. & .. & x \end{array}\right.$$

All developed 4 minutes.   Densities inclusive of fog.

| $x =$ | 2 | 4 | 8 | 16 |
|---|---|---|---|---|
| 0 | ·075 | ·075 | ·085 | ·085 |
| ·625 C.M.S. | ·075 | ·115 | ·135 | ·115 |
| 1·25 ,, | ·100 | ·255 | ·340 | ·305 |
| 2·5 ,, | ·230 | ·560 | ·750 | ·675 |
| 5 ,, | ·450 | ·990 | 1·215 | 1·155 |
| 10 ,, | ·735 | 1·390 | 1·715 | 1·635 |
| 20 ,, | 1·050 | 1·810 | 2·180 | 2·095 |
| 40 ,, | 1·335 | 2·200 | 2·615 | 2·505 |
| Negative No. .. | I | II | III | IV |

The curves show the maximum to be probably situated at about 7 parts of pyrogallol, so that here, again, the same ratio between soda and pyrogallol appears to produce maximum density in the given time. The regularity of the curves and their similarity to the previous ones are also striking.

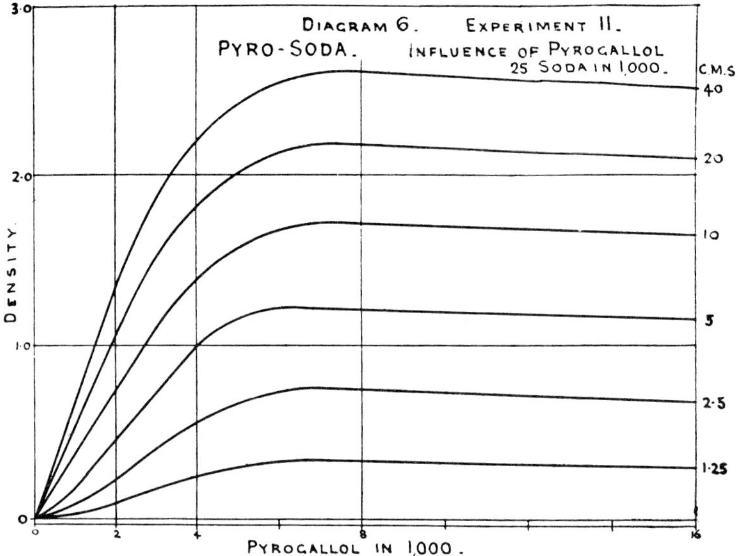



*Experiment* 12.—Pyro-soda.    Plate $D_2$.

Composition of solution.    In 1,000 parts
$\begin{cases} Na_2CO_3 + 10 \text{ Aq.} & 100 \\ Na_2SO_3 & \ldots \quad \ldots \quad 100 \\ KBr & \ldots \quad \ldots \quad 4 \\ Pyro & \ldots \quad \ldots \quad x \end{cases}$

All developed $2\frac{1}{2}$ minutes.    Densities inclusive of fog.

| $x =$ | 8 | 16 | 32 | 64 |
|---|---|---|---|---|
| 0 | ·080 | ·100 | ·090 | ·080 |
| ·625 C.M.S. | ·095 | ·110 | ·100 | ·085 |
| 1·25 ,, | ·190 | ·280 | ·215 | ·160 |
| 2·5 ,, | ·500 | ·685 | ·575 | ·335 |
| 5 ,, | ·935 | 1·255 | 1·105 | ·810 |
| 10 ,, | 1·335 | 1·795 | 1·630 | 1·255 |
| 20 ,, | 1·810 | 2·325 | 2·220 | 1·770 |
| 40 ,, | 2·280 | 2·855 | 2·765 | 2·265 |
| Negative No. .. | I | II | III | IV |

The curves indicate that the maxima here lie between 16 and 32 parts of pyrogallol, probably at about 20 parts.    In this case, therefore, the previous proportion is not maintained.    Owing to the determined points not lying very close to the summits of the curves in any one of these experiments, the experimental maximum value is not absolutely and accurately determined.  It is, however, evident that the maximum has no relation to the constitution of the pyrogallol (*i.e.*, the three hydroxyls, $C_6$, $H_3$ $(OH)_3$ ).   The chemical

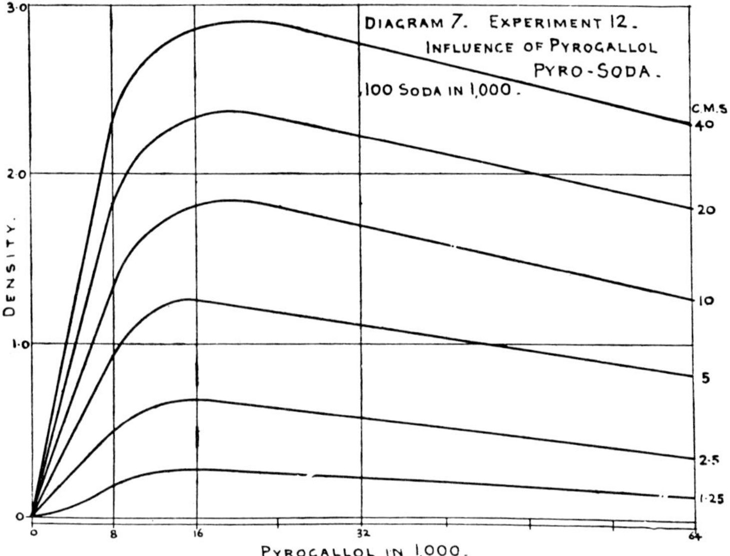


explanation of the composition of pyrogallol developers is, however, very likely given by the following equation, based upon the experiments detailed in Part VI, where we show that one molecule of pyrogallol decomposes four molecules of silver bromide.

$$4AgBr + C_6H_3 (OH)_3 + 2Na_2CO_3 =$$
$$4Ag + \text{Oxidation product} + 4NaBr + 2 CO_2.$$

It is clear then that we must have sufficient alkali to take up the liberated bromine, *i.e.*, 4 atoms of sodium, or 4 molecules of ammonium must be present for every 1 molecule of pyrogallol.

In this case, maximum development ought to have taken place with—

|       |       |       |       |       |       |       |
|-------|-------|-------|-------|-------|-------|-------|
| 25 soda and | 5·5 | pyrogallol, instead of | 7 | pyrogallol; |  |  |
| 50 | ,, | 11 | ,, | ,, | 14 | ,, |
| 100 | ,, | 22 | ,, | ,, | 20 | ,, |

but the curves, as already said, are hardly sufficiently defined to determine this point.

It will be well to remember that the soda ought to be about four or five times the weight of the pyrogallol in order to yield maximum density in a given time.   A larger proportion of pyrogallol acts as a restrainer, and the objection to restrainers will be pointed out later on when discussing the influence of bromide.

Diagram 8 has been drawn in order to give an idea of the average meaning of the last three experiments. The densities reached by exposures 40 C.M.S. and 2·5 C.M.S. are plotted for each of the three developers. The ordinates are densities as usual, and the abscissæ are molecules of pyrogallol per one atom of sodium in the developer. The diagram shows that it is highly probable that the true maximum lies at about 0·25 molecules of pyrogallol per atom of sodium, or per molecule of ammonia.

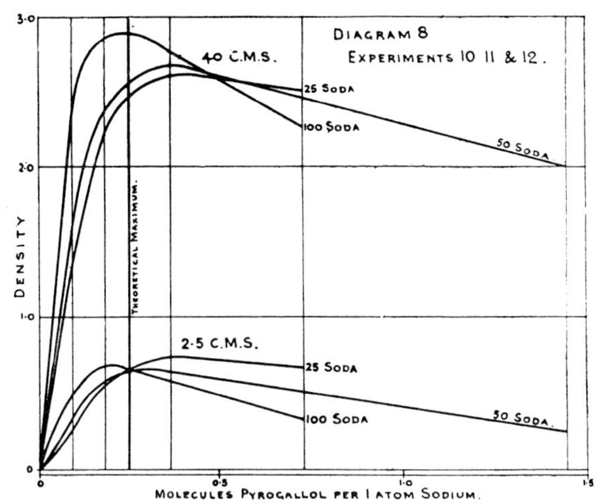


On the strength of these experiments we have decided to employ as our standard pyro-soda developer a solution containing, in 1,000 parts, 8 parts of pyrogallol (sufficient to readily allow high densities to grow), 40 parts of soda, and the same amount of sodium sulphite.

So far we have only dealt with the influence of variations in the composition of the developer on single densities. We have now to consider the influence upon the whole of the negative as affecting its printing qualities and its truthfulness. This is best done by considering the variations produced in the position and curvature of the characteristic curve of the plate.

In the previous experiments we have given the densities inclusive of fog, since we wished to present the action of the developer in its entirety. In plotting the characteristic curve it has been our rule to deduct the fog (*i.e.*, the amount of silver reduced by the developer from the unexposed silver bromide) from the total density, and to consider the difference as due to the action of light. Whilst this proceeding is perfectly correct as far as the printing values of the negative are concerned, it is open to question whether this procedure is otherwise justifiable in ascertaining the speed of a plate. We therefore made a few experiments to satisfy ourselves upon this point. A dense fog can only be produced by inadvertent exposure to light, by a faulty emulsion, or by a badly-balanced developer, notably the ammoniacal developer.

Three strips of plate $D_2$ were exposed as for a speed determination. One (A) was developed in a well-balanced pyro-ammonia developer ; the second strip (B) was fogged by light, and the third (C) was fogged by the application of a developer containing an excess of free ammonia and no bromide. The developers employed were as follows :—

|  | I | II |
|---|---|---|
| In 1,000 $\left\{\begin{array}{l}\text{NH}_3 \\ \text{KBr} \\ \text{Pyro}\end{array}\right.$ .. .. .. .. | 1·01 2 3 | 2·53 0 3 |

The following densities were observed :—

*Experiment* 13.

| Exposure, C.M.S. | Strip A. Developer I. | Fogged by | |
|---|---|---|---|
|  |  | Exposure. | Developer. |
|  |  | Strip B. Developer I. | Strip C. Developer II. |
| 0 | ·100 | ·860 | ·845 |
| 1·25 | ·205 | ·925 | 1·045 |
| 2·5 | ·510 | 1·030 | 1·465 |
| 5 | ·870 | 1·200 | 1·855 |
| 10 | 1·240 | 1·460 | 2·155 |
| 20 | 1·570 | 1·710 | 2·470 |
| 40 | 1·870 | 1·950 | 2·675 |

These results are plotted in Diagram 9 as in the case of a speed determination, and give rise to the three curves A, B and C.

If the straight portions of these curves be produced, they intersect the exposure scale as follows :—

Curve A at 0·96 C.M.S.. corresponding to speed  35
  ,,   B  ,, 0·18   ,,    ,,    ,,  190
  ,,   2  ,, 0·21   ,,    ,,    ,,  162

It is therefore quite evident that when a plate is seriously fogged, whether by light or in development, and the densities inclusive of fog are plotted, the speed becomes absolutely false.

If, however, instead of taking the point of intersection with the exposure scale itself, we take the intersection with a line drawn through the value of the fog density and parallel to the exposure scale, this line is then intersected by—

Curve B at 2·0 C.M.S. corresponding to speed 17
  ,,   C ,, 0·9   ,,       ,,       ,,    37

In the case of curve C, therefore, the subtraction of the fog would so change the position of the curve as to make no material alteration in the speed. In the case of curve B, however, this is not so. As a matter of fact, after the intentional gradations of exposure had been given to the plate in this experiment, an additional uniform exposure of 5 seconds to the same light was given to represent an accidental exposure to light. Each density ought, therefore, to be plotted by 5 C.M.S. in advance of the exposure to which it actually was plotted, *i.e.*, the exposures were, in reality—

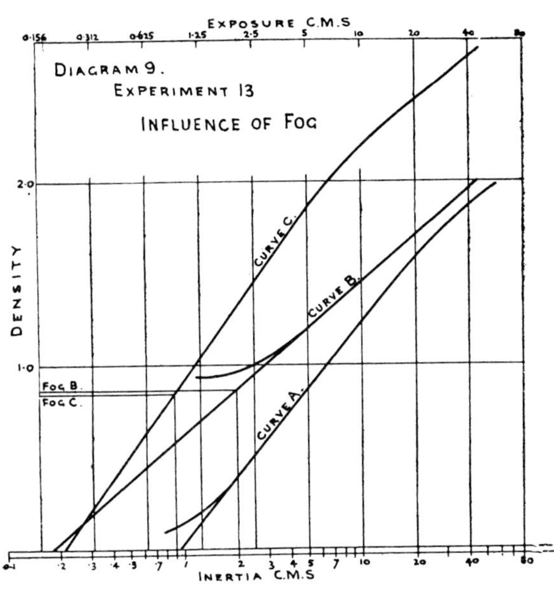


| Not | 1·25 | 2·5 | 5 | 10 | 20 | 40 |
| --- | --- | --- | --- | --- | --- | --- |
| But | 6·25 | 7·5 | 10 | 15 | 25 | 45 |

When this is done, it will be found that the curve, so constructed, coincides absolutely with the normal curve A, and, of course, gives the same speed.

We have therefore this rule : When fog is produced by the developer only the density plotted exclusive of fog will give an approximately correct speed. When, however, fog is produced by inadvertent exposure to light, either in the manufacture or in the manipulation of the plate, the curve cannot be corrected, because the value of the exposure is unknown, and the speed determination is consequently useless.

In presenting, therefore, our previous experiments in the form of diagrams to show the influence of variations in the developer upon the general character of the negative and upon the speed of the plate, all densities are plotted exclusive of fog.

*Variation of Alkali.*

The influence of the variation of ammonia is represented in Diagram 2A, and the influence of the variation of soda in Diagram 3A.

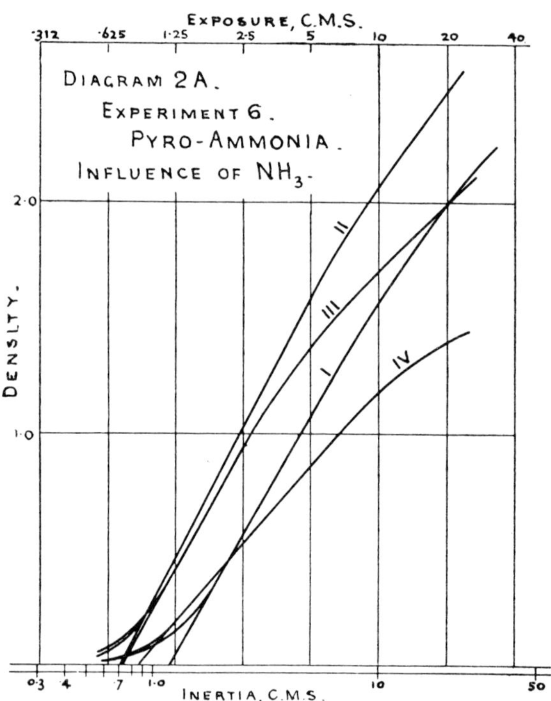


The character of the negatives has already been discussed, and it only remains to point out the very unsatisfactory nature of the negatives obtained by the pyro-ammonia developer, as revealed by the curvature of the characteristic. On the other hand, with, of course, the exception of the period of under-exposure, the four characteristics representing the pyro-soda developer are all distinguished by straight lines.

With respect to the development factor (which measures the degree by which the gradations of the negative deviate from the gradations of the object photographed), the increase in the amount of ammonia has exercised but a small influence upon its value, whilst the increase in the relative amount of soda produced a marked and regular effect.

| Pyro-ammonia. | | Pyro-soda. | |
| --- | --- | --- | --- |
| Relative amount of NH₃. | Development factor. | Relative amount of soda. | Development factor. |
| 1 | 1·7 | 1 | 1·2 |
| 2 | 1·9 | 2 | 1·65 |
| 4 | 1·75 | 4 | 2·2 |
| 8. | 1·1 | 8 | 2·45 |

With respect to the influence of these various developers upon the speed of the plate, the alterations in the inertia are as follows :—

| Pyro-ammonia. | | Pyro-soda. | |
| --- | --- | --- | --- |
| Relative amount of $NH_3$. | Inertia. | Relative amount of soda. | Inertia |
| | C.M.S. | | C.M.S. |
| 1 | 1·18 | 1 | 1·50 |
| 2 | 0·70 | 2 | 1·25 |
| 4 | 0·73 | 4 | 1·15 |
| 8 | 0·86 | 8 | 0·93 |

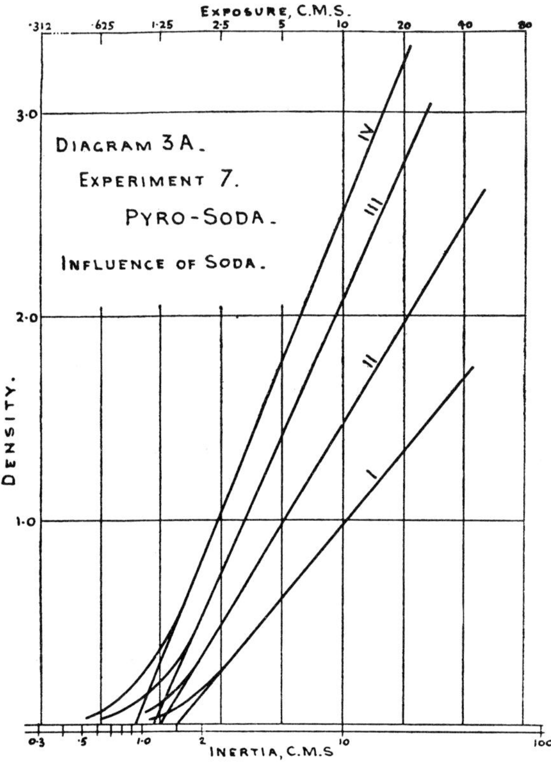


Here, again, the influence of ammonia is irregular, whilst that of soda is regular, the inertia decreasing, or the speed increasing, as the amount of alkali increases.  It would, however, be premature to ascribe this alteration to the influence of the increased alkali, the rule being that when the developer contains a bromide, an increasing development factor is always associated with a decreasing inertia, even when the alteration in the development factor is due to a different time of development with the same developer.  There is little doubt that the alteration in the speed would not have shown itself had the developer been compounded without bromide.

*Variation of Pyrogallol.*

Casting another glance at the curves in Diagrams 4, 5, 6 and 7, which represent the growth of the densities, we see that the curves spread at first like a fan until the maximum activity is reached.  After this the curves

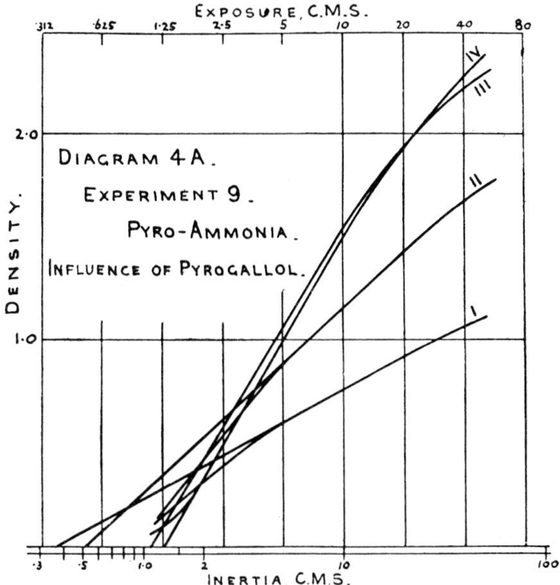


become parallel straight lines.  We have, therefore, two distinct laws before us.  So long as the pyrogallol is less than the necessary amount for maximum activity, we have a law closely approaching the law of " constant density ratios," whilst, when the necessary amount of pyrogallol has been exceeded, we have a totally different law, whch might be termed the law of " constant density differences."  In the first instance pyrogallol is an accelerator ; in the second, it is a restrainer, and we shall see that the chief restrainer, namely, alkaline bromide, behaves almost identically with pyrogallol when in excess of the quantity necessary for maximum activity.

The general character of pyro-ammonia negatives is represented by their characteristic curves in Diagram 4A.

The curves are again very irregular. The general character of pyro-soda negatives, with varying amounts of pyrogallol, are plotted in Diagram 5A, in which negatives 2, 3, 4 and 5 are represented.

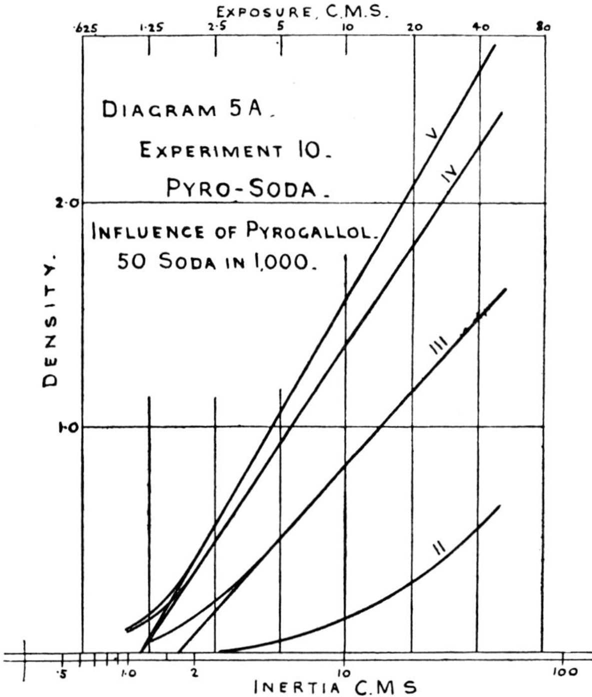


We notice that, until maximum density is reached, the negatives are good, and differ chiefly in the development factor. The curve No. 2 is unsatisfactory, the amount of pyrogallol being insufficient to allow of full development without calling into requisition the process of diffusion.

Diagram 5B represents the negatives 5, 6 and 7 obtained on and after reaching the maximum activity of the developer. The further increase of pyrogallol does not practically change the development factor at all, but it materially changes the inertia. Numerically the results are as follows :—

*Experiment* 10.

| Negative No. | Relative amount of pyro molecules per 1 soda. | Development factor $\gamma$. | Inertia. $i$. |
|---|---|---|---|
| II | ·045 | (?) | (?) |
| III | ·09 | 1·10 | 1·65 |
| IV | ·181 | 1·50 | 1·12 |
| V (Max. density) | ·362 | 1·70 | 1·12 |
| VI | ·725 | 1·60 | 1·40 |
| VII | 1·45 | 1·60 | 2·70 |

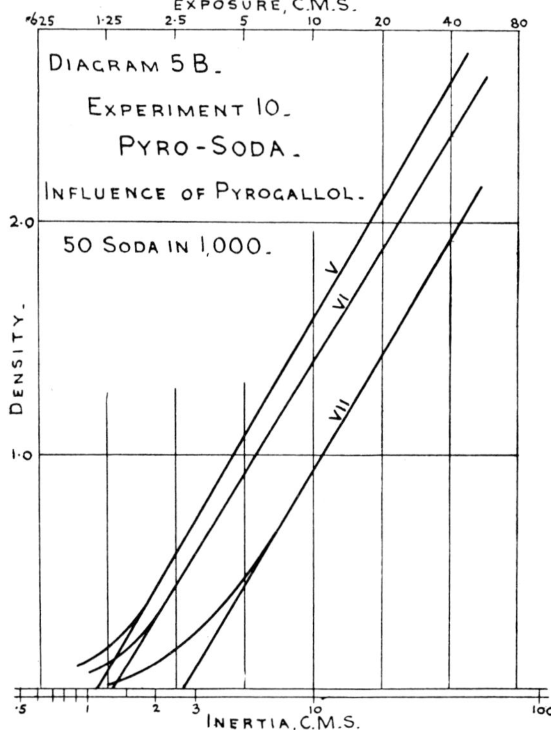


This very material change in the inertia, not associated with a change in the development factor, is characteristic of the restraining action of an excess of pyrogallol over the necessary quantity. Diagrams 6A and 7A represent the several negatives of Experiments 11 and 12. The straight lines show all the negatives to be good. The following table shows the influence of variation in the amount of pyrogallol upon the development factor and upon the inertia of the plate :—

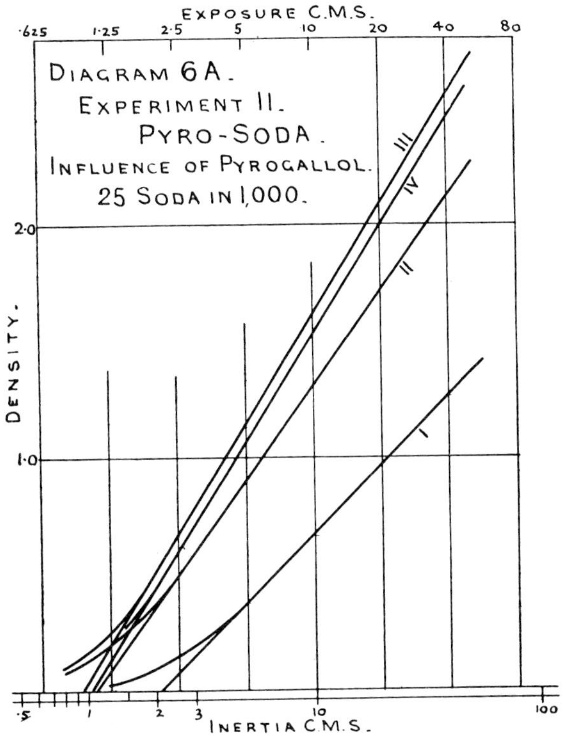


| Negative No. | Molecules pyro per 1 soda. | Experiment 11. | | Experiment 12. | |
|---|---|---|---|---|---|
| | | $\gamma$ | $i$ | $\gamma$ | $i$ |
| I | ·090 | 0·97 | 2·05 | 1·42 | 1·30 |
| II | ·181 | 1·35 | 1·10 | 1·78 | 1·15 |
| III | ·362 | 1·57 | 0·95 | 1·70 | 1·30 |
| IV | ·725 | 1·55 | 1·05 | 1·55 | 1·70 |

Influence of the Variation of Bromide in the Developing Solution.

Whilst the pyrogallol and the alkali are absolutely necessary reagents for the development of the image, the alkaline-bromide is a product of the reaction, which can and does go on perfectly well in its absence.

A developer which contains no alkali does not develop at all.  A curve representing the influence of the variation in the amount of alkali starts, as we have seen, from zero density, and the densities increase as more and more alkali is added (*see* Diagram 3).  The general effect upon the characteristic curve is shown by the growth of the inclination of the straight line, that is, by the rapid growth of the development factor $\gamma$ (*see* Diagram 3A).

Similarly, in the absence of pyrogallol, no development can take place. Curves which represent the influence upon the density of increasing amounts

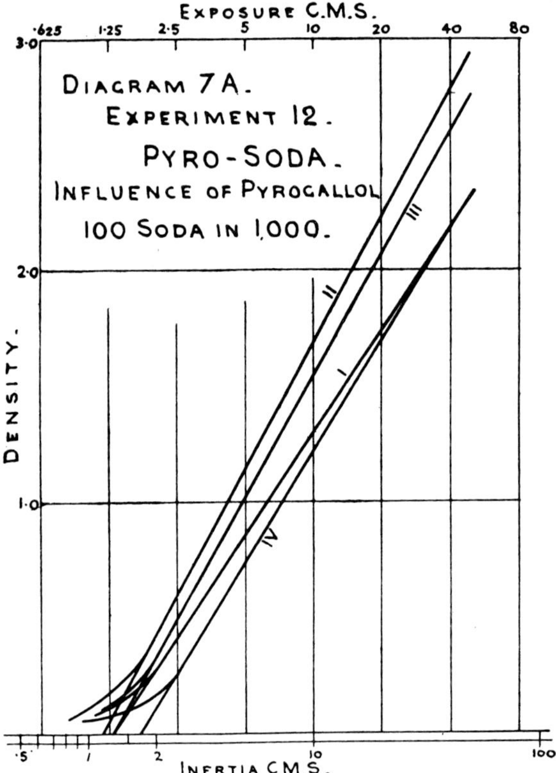


of pyrogallol, start from zero density and rapidly increase to a maximum (*see* Diagram 5).  The effect of the increase upon the characteristic curve makes itself felt, just as in the case of alkali, by an increase in the development factor, until a certain ratio between alkali and pyrogallol is attained, when a further increase of pyrogallol no longer affects the development factor, but begins to change the inertia of the plate (*see* Diagrams 5A and 5B).

Thus the *essential* constituents of the developer affect, almost entirely and exclusively, the development factor.

Bromide, on the other hand, is one of the products of the chemical change which takes place in the process of development. It is well known in chemical dynamics that the products of a reaction generally retard the process—that is, the speed of the reaction, and, in so-called reversible reactions, the reaction may entirely cease when a certain amount of the products have accumulated The addition of a bromide to the developing solution very seriously retards the reaction—that is, the development. We have tested the influence of the addition of potassium bromide, both with ferrous oxalate and with alkaline pyrogallol, up to a 12 per cent. solution, but we have not found that the reaction ceases. It is simply retarded, and, if sufficient time be allowed, the image will make its appearance in full force.

The retarding action of the bromide is not, however, its only action. As more and more bromide is added to the developer, the image changes in colour from the usual black to a fawn colour. The effect of this change in colour is such that photometric measurements are no longer a reliable indication of the amount of silver present in the image.

A uniformly exposed plate was developed with pyro-soda containing 128 parts of potassium bromide in 1,000 parts of developing solution (12·8 per cent.). Its colour was a yellowish grey (fawn colour) and its density was found to be 2·628. Analysis gave 0·0632 gramme of metallic silver on an area of 81·6 square cm. Hence, on 100 square cm., there were 77·4 milligrammes of silver, or, for density 1·0, there were 29·4 milligrammes of silver per 100 square cm. This is more than twice (2·43 times) as much silver as we find for the same density when the deposit is black. The silver deposit is formed very slowly in the presence of these large amounts of bromide, and is evidently of a totally different physical character, which gradually alters as the bromide in the solution is gradually increased.

We attempted to determine the gradual change in the optical properties of the deposit by converting the silver into the black modification in the film itself. For this purpose, negatives developed with varying amounts of bromide were, after having been measured, treated with a dilute solution of potassium bichromate and hydrochloric acid, in order to convert the silver into chloride. The chloride was then re-developed with hydrochinon or pyrogallol, and the densities were again measured. It was found, in all cases, that the density had increased fairly regularly by 25 per cent.—that is, density 1·0 became 1·25, and so on. This increase in density did not, however, appear to have any relation to the amount of bromide present in the original developer, and the same increase was found to occur when no bromide at all had been used in the first development. It would therefore appear that the reduction of silver chloride furnishes a blacker precipitate than the reduction of silver bromide and the process becomes useful when feeble intensification is required, the densities growing by about one-fourth their amount.

*Experiment* 14.

|  | Original densities, inclusive of fog. | | | | | Re-developed densities, inclusive of fog | | | |
|---|---|---|---|---|---|---|---|---|---|
| KBr in 1,000. | 0 | 32 | 45(a) | 64 | 90 | 0 | 32 | 64 | 90 |
| Time developed. Mins. | 3 | 8 | 9 | 10 | 15 | Pyro. | Hydrochinon. | | |
| 0 | ·160 | ·100 | ·100 | ·100 | ·130 | ·205 | ·145 | ·125 | ·265 |
| 1·25 C.M.S. | ·565 | ·130 | ·135 | ·155 | ·265 | ·685 | ·195 | ·205 | ·350 |
| 2·5 ,, | 1·045 | ·335 | ·330 | ·390 | ·535 | 1·335 | ·410 | ·480 | ·665 |
| 5 ,, | 1·530 | ·785 | ·755 | ·775 | ·950 | 1·945 | ·965 | ·955 | 1·220 |
| 10 ,, | 1·940 | 1·395 | 1·330 | 1·260 | 1·450 | 2·410 | 1·720 | 1·565 | 1·915 |
| 20 ,, | 2·255 | 1·985 | 1·920 | 1·760 | 1·930 | 2·780 | 2·455 | 2·185 | 2·650 |
| 40 ,, | 2·500 | 2·510 | 2·270 | 2·270 | 2·425 | 3·130 | 3·130 | 2·865 | (?) |
| Negative No. | I | II | III | IV | V | | | | |

A glance at the corresponding columns of the original and re-developed densities shows that, with 90 parts of potassium bromide, for instance, density 1·930 became 2·650, or increased as 1 : 1·37, whilst, when no bromide was used in the development, the increase was from 2·50 to 3·13, or as 1 : 1·25. Thus the addition of a very large amount of bromide has but slightly altered the ratio of density after re-development, and this indicates that the increase in density on re-development is not due to the bromide originally used in development.

It will be seen that the densities of the negatives could be brought to almost equal values by suitably varying the time of development. While, in 3 minutes, with no bromide, density 2·50 was obtained, a density of 2·425 was reached in 15 minutes with 90 parts of bromide. Thus the retarding influence of bromide can be fully compensated by time of development, and the character of the negative is not materially altered in the end. Nor is the speed of the plate really altered by the addition of bromide.

The following experiment shows the very great retardation produced by the addition of large amounts of bromide :—

(a) In the MSS. this column is marked :—" To be left out, as re-development experiment failed."

*Experiment* 15.—Pyro-soda.   Plate $D_2$.

Composition of solution.   In 1,000 parts
$$\begin{cases} Na_2CO_3 + 10\ Aq... & 50 \\ Na_2SO_3 & \quad .. \quad .. & 50 \\ Pyro & \quad .. \quad .. & 6 \\ KBr & \quad .. \quad .. & x \end{cases}$$

All developed 3 minutes.   Densities inclusive of fog.

| $x =$ | 0 | 2 | 8 | 32 | 128 |
|---|---|---|---|---|---|
| 0 | ·160 | ·090 | ·065 | ·060 | ·060 |
| 1·25  C.M S | ·565 | ·120 | ·065 | ·060 | ·060 |
| 2·5  ,, | 1·045 | ·375 | ·085 | ·060 | ·060 |
| 5  ,, | 1·530 | ·790 | ·145 | ·060 | ·060 |
| 10  ,, | 1·940 | 1·250 | ·330 | ·090 | ·060 |
| 20  ,, | 2·255 | 1·700 | ·705 | ·170 | ·070 |
| 40  ,, | 2·500 | 2·020 | 1·190 | ·290 | ·100 |
| Negative No. .. | I | II | III | IV | V |

It will be seen that a developer containing 128 parts of potassium bromide in 1,000 of solution almost entirely prevented development in 3 minutes, and that the addition of 2 parts of bromide reduced the highest density from 2·5 to 2·0.

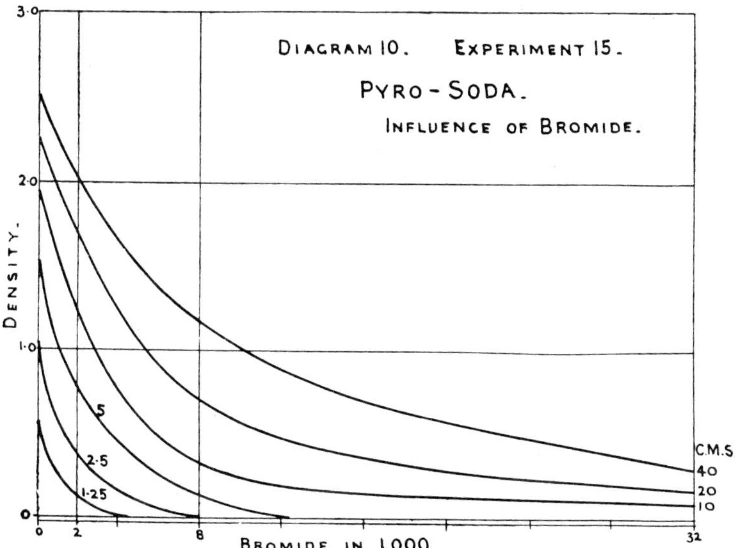


The retarding influence of bromide upon the single densities of a negative is shown as a series of more or less parallel curves in Diagram 10, which graphically represents Experiment 15.

(8731)

S 2

The following experiment shows this a little better, within narrower limits :—

*Experiment* 16.—Pyro-soda.    Plate $D_2$.

Composition of solution.    In 1,000 parts $\begin{cases} Na_2CO_3 + 10 \text{ Aq.} & .. & 50 \\ Na_2SO_3 & .. & .. & 50 \\ Pyro & .. & .. & 6 \\ KBr & .. & .. & x \end{cases}$

All developed 4 minutes.    Densities inclusive of fog.

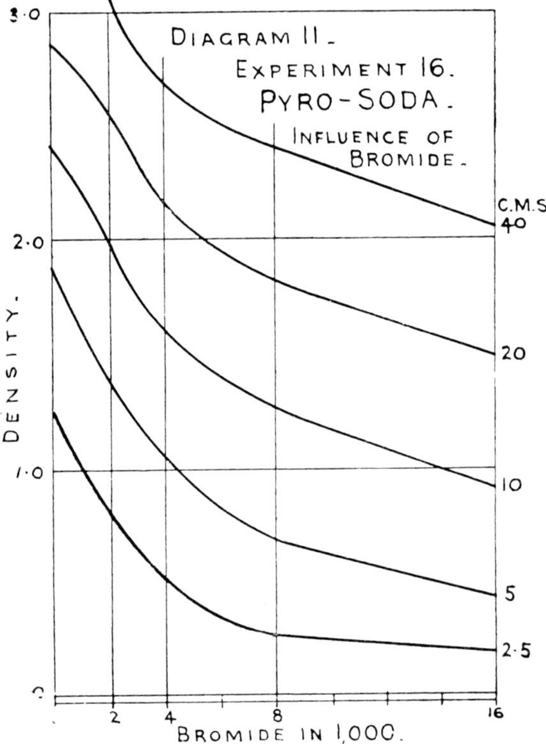


| $x =$ | | 0 | 2 | 4 | 8 | 16 |
|---|---|---|---|---|---|---|
| 0 | | ·280 | ·065 | ·065 | ·065 | ·065 |
| 0·625 | C.M.S. | ·335 | ·080 | ·065 | ·065 | ·065 |
| 1·25 | ,, | ·685 | ·255 | ·170 | ·095 | ·065 |
| 2·5 | ,, | 1·255 | ·825 | ·505 | ·265 | ·180 |
| 5 | ,, | 1·865 | 1·395 | 1·045 | ·695 | ·435 |
| 10 | ,, | 2·395 | 1·965 | 1·595 | 1·255 | ·905 |
| 20 | ,, | 2·850 | 2·550 | 2·145 | 1·815 | 1·448 |
| 40 | ,, | (?) | 3·065 | 2·665 | 2·380 | 2·055 |
| Negative No. .. | | I | II | III | IV | V |

These results are graphically represented in Diagram 11, from which it will be observed that the higher densities remain more or less accurately equidistant, as if the addition of increasing amounts of bromide reduced the densities by equal amounts.

A precisely similar effect shows itself in the case of the ammoniacal-pyrogallol developer, and is exemplified in Experiment 17 and Diagram 12.

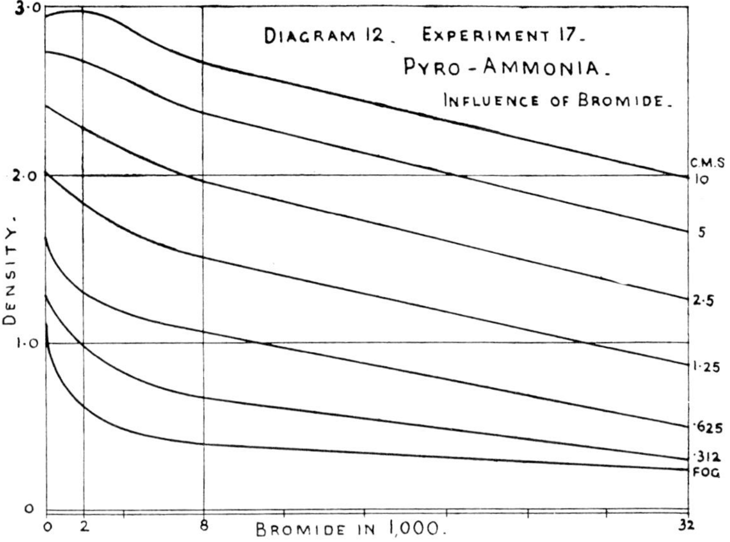


*Experiment* 17.—Pyro-ammonia.  Plate $D_6$.

Composition of solution.  In 1,000 parts $\left\{\begin{array}{l} NH_3 \quad .. \quad .. \quad 1\cdot52 \\ Na_2SO_3 \quad .. \quad .. \quad 25 \\ Pyro \quad .. \quad .. \quad 6 \\ KBr \quad .. \quad .. \quad x \end{array}\right.$

Developed 6 minutes (excepting V).  Densities inclusive of fog.

| $x =$ | 0 | 2 | 8 | 32 | 128 |
|---|---|---|---|---|---|
| 0 | 1·140 | ·600 | ·390 | ·235 | ·420 |
| 0·312 C.M.S. | 1·280 | ·980 | ·660 | ·295 | ·530 |
| 0·625 ,, | 1·645 | 1·395 | 1·060 | ·485 | ·680 |
| 1·25 ,, | 2·020 | 1·840 | 1·510 | ·860 | ·870 |
| 2·5 ,, | 2·400 | 2·270 | 1·960 | 1·265 | 1·115 |
| 5 ,, | 2·745 | 2·675 | 2·450 | 1·660 | 1·345 |
| 10 ,, | 2·945 | 2·970 | 2·670 | 1·980 | 1·500 |
| 20 ,, | (?) | (?) | 2·760 | 2·145 | 1·640 |
| Negative No. .. | I | II | III | IV | V |

Negative No. V was fawn-coloured, and was developed for 60 minutes.

The parallelism of the curves for the single densities is very striking in this diagram.

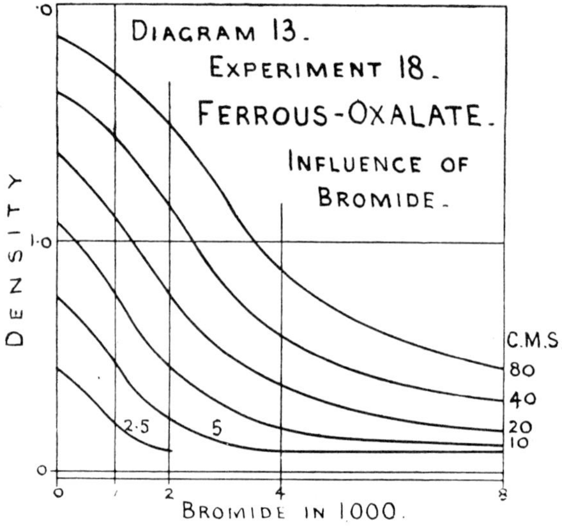


The addition of bromide to the ferrous oxalate developer has a similar effect. Again, the curves representing the variation of each density with increasing amounts of bromide, appear to have an equidistant course, but their form is totally different from that of the curves yielded by the alkaline developers, as will be seen from Experiment 18, graphically represented in Diagram 13.

*Experiment* 18.—Ferrous oxalate.  Plate $D_2$.  Inclusive of fog.

| Developed. | 3 min. | | | | | 60 min. |
|---|---|---|---|---|---|---|
| KBr in 1,000. | 0 | 1 | 2 | 4 | 8 | 128 |
| 0 | ·115 | ·100 | ·095 | ·095 | ·095 | ·095 |
| 1·25 C.M.S. | ·225 | ·100 | ·095 | ·095 | ·095 | ·095 |
| 2·5 ,, | ·445 | ·205 | ·095 | ·095 | ·095 | ·195 |
| 5 ,, | ·755 | ·465 | ·225 | ·095 | ·095 | ·375 |
| 10 ,, | 1·075 | ·785 | ·455 | ·195 | ·120 | ·620 |
| 20 ,, | 1·365 | 1·095 | ·785 | ·375 | ·180 | ·940 |
| 40 ,, | 1·630 | 1·430 | 1·140 | ·595 | ·310 | 1·255 |
| 80 ,, | 1·865 | 1·715 | 1·500 | ·880 | ·445 | 1·465 |
| Negative No... | I | II | III | IV | V | VI |

Negative No. VI is fawn-coloured.

The difference in the course of the curves in Diagram 13 is probably due to the fact that, in the case of ferrous oxalate, a ferric salt is produced which has itself a tendency to cause the reaction to reverse, and is therefore an additional retarding agent.

The general tendency of these various curves to become equidistant is indicative of the fact that the addition of bromide to any developer has but little influence on the development factor. Whenever an agent affects this factor it shows itself in the diagrams by the fan-like spreading of the various curves (*see* Diagrams 2 and 3). The influence of bromide makes itself felt chiefly by the apparent increase in the inertia of the plate. This influence is apparent only, because it can be compensated by time of development.

These peculiarities of bromide have given rise to considerable difficulty in the determination of the speed of plates, and they are mainly responsible for the great difference of opinion which exists as to the value of bromide in correcting over-exposure. We therefore enter somewhat more deeply into a discussion on the influence of this reagent.

The effect of the addition of bromide to the developer upon the inertia of the plate is best shown by the characteristic curves

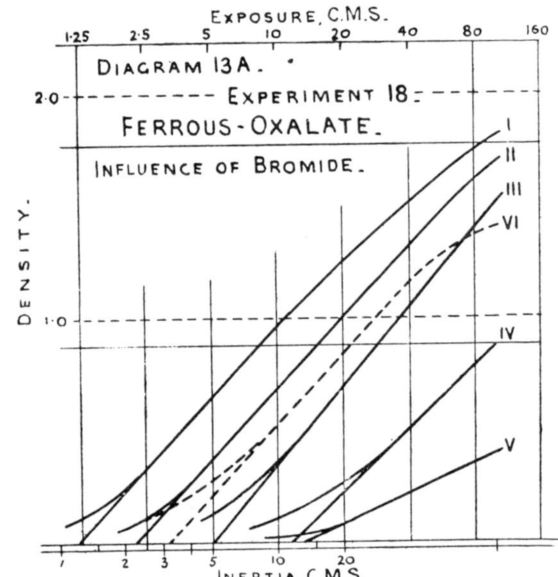


of the various negatives, the densities of which are given in the above experiments.

Referring first to Diagram 13A, which represents the six negatives obtained by ferrous oxalate development, plotted exclusive of fog, we have the following results as regards the values of the development factor and the inertia.

*Experiment* 18.—Ferrous oxalate.

| Negative No. | Time developed. | KBr in 1,000. | Development factor. $\gamma$ | Inertia. $i$ |
|---|---|---|---|---|
| | Min. | | | |
| I | 3 | 0 | 1·05 | 1·20 |
| II | 3 | 1 | 1·06 | 2·22 |
| III | 3 | 2 | 1·17 | 5·20 |
| IV | 3 | 4 | 0·94 | 11·50 |
| V | 3 | 8 | 0·45 | 13·30 |
| VI | 60 | 128 | 1·06 | 3·20 |

It will be seen that, with the same time of development, negatives I to IV have hardly changed the development factor, while the inertia has increased from $1 \cdot 2$ to $11 \cdot 5$, the speed of the plate having apparently become one-tenth of what it originally was. The low development factor $0 \cdot 45$ only occurs in the case of negative V, which hardly developed any density. That the inertia of the plate when bromide is used is only apparent and not real, and that bromide does not really reduce the speed of the plate, is shown by negative VI, in which, in spite of the large amount of bromide (128 parts in 1,000), the inertia is only $3 \cdot 2$, and the development factor has again assumed the value 1. This series strikingly shows that the influence of bromide may be compensated by time of development ; that it hardly affects the development factor, but very seriously affects the inertia, though temporarily only, since, if sufficient time be given, the negative will finally come back to the real inertia of the plate.

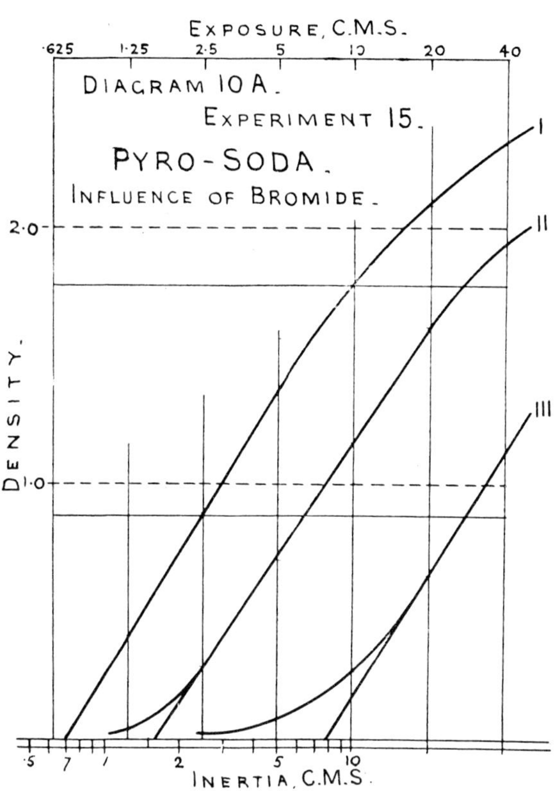


Similar results are shown in Diagrams 10A and 11A by the two series of negatives obtained with the pyro-soda developer, and detailed in Experiments 15 and 16. The densities are plotted exclusive of fog.

*Experiment* 15.—Pyro-soda.

| Negative No. | Time developed. | KBr in 1,000. | $\gamma$ | $i$ |
|---|---|---|---|---|
| | Min. | | | |
| I | 3 | 0 | $1 \cdot 57$ | $0 \cdot 70$ |
| II | 3 | 2 | $1 \cdot 60$ | $1 \cdot 47$ |
| III | 3 | 8 | $1 \cdot 57$ | $7 \cdot 70$ |

*Experiment* 16.—Pyro-soda.

| Negative No. | Time developed. | KBr in 1,000. | $\gamma$ | $i$ |
|---|---|---|---|---|
| | Min. | | | |
| I | 4 | 0 | 1·8 | 0·7 |
| II | 4 | 2 | 1·9 | 1·0 |
| III | 4 | 4 | 1·8 | 1·4 |
| IV | 4 | 8 | 1·85 | 2·2 |
| V | 4 | 16 | 1·9 | 3·5 |

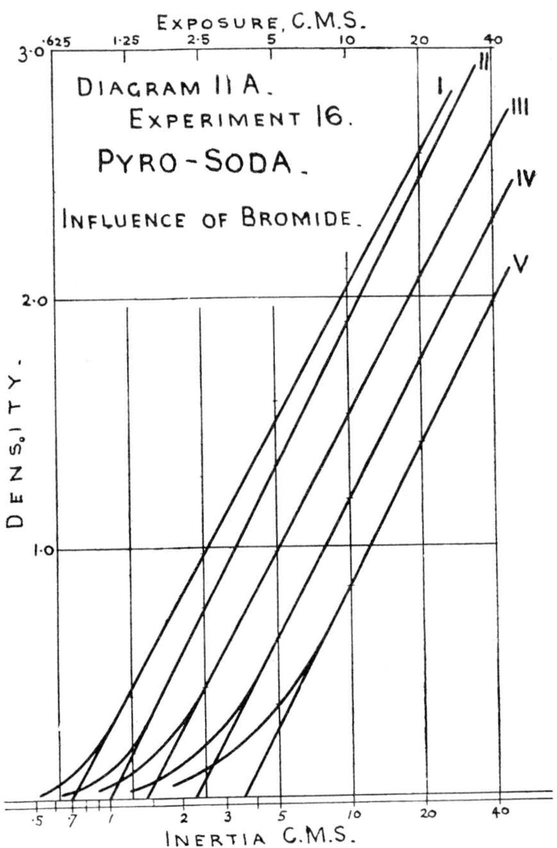



Comparing these results, the difference of 3 minutes' against 4 minutes' development shows itself in the lower development factor, but in the higher inertia reached.

Diagram 14 shows how closely alike negatives may become if the varying amounts of bromide used in their development be compensated by time, so that, to the eye, their densities are similar.   The curves represent the negatives II, III, IV and V of Experiment 14, plotted exclusive of fog.

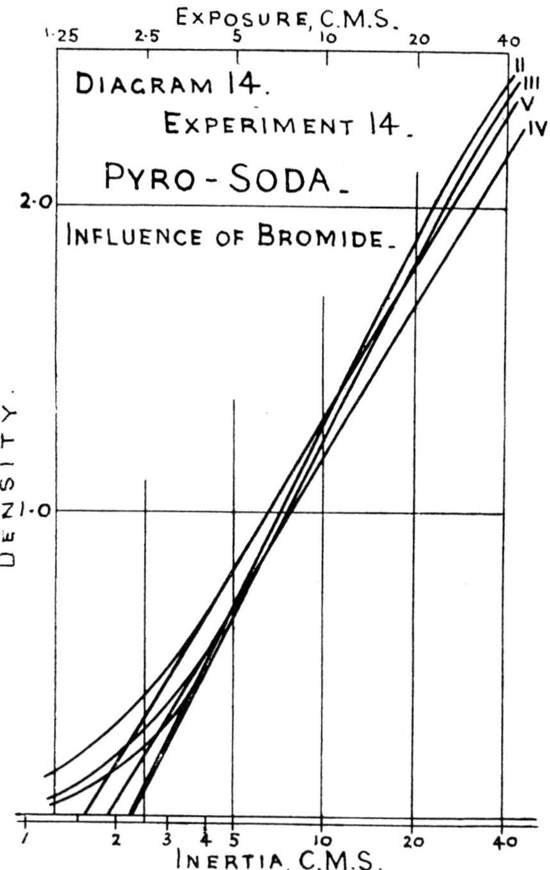


*Experiment* 14.—Pyro-soda.

| Negative No. | Time developed. | KBr in 1.000. | $\gamma$ | $i$ |
|---|---|---|---|---|
| | Min. | | | |
| I | 3 | 0 | 1·55 | 0·7 |
| II | 8 | 32 | 2·0 | 2·2 |
| III | 9 | 45 | 1·9 | 2·25 |
| IV | 10 | 64 | 1·6 | 1·8$_7$ |
| V | 15 | 90 | 1·6 | 1·6 |

Practically there is little difference in the speed of the plate, as shown by the four last negatives, and very trifling differences in the development factor. Time evidently compensates for bromide.

The same results show themselves in negatives developed by ammoniacal pyrogallol, as will be seen in Diagram 12A, which represents the negatives I, II, III and IV of Experiment 17, plotted exclusive of fog.

*Experiment* 17.—Pyro-ammonia.

| Negative No. | Time developed. | KBr in 1 000. | $\gamma$ | $i$ |
|---|---|---|---|---|
| | Min. | | | |
| I | 6 | 0 | 1·23 | 0·24 |
| II | 6 | 2 | 1·45 | 0·17 |
| III | 6 | 8 | 1·46 | 0·22 |
| IV | 6 | 32 | 1·28 | 0·40 |

The development factor undergoes very little change, and the inertia only changes from 0·17 to 0·40. The inertia of the first negative is too high, simply because, in this case, the correction for fog is so very large, amounting to 38·7 per cent. of the total highest density. Such corrections render the results very doubtful. It is worth mentioning that, in the case of the pyro-ammonia developer, the influence of bromide is much less marked than in the case of pyro-soda or ferrous oxalate. Hence in our original paper it was overlooked.

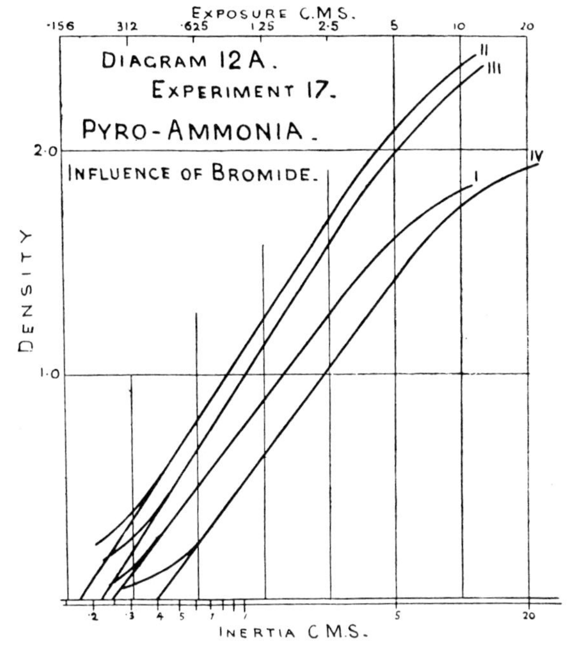


The general results of these experiments may thus be stated :—

|  |  |  |
|---|---|---|
| Increase of alkali increases the development factor | .. | $\gamma$ |
| Increase of pyro increases the development factor | .. | $\gamma$ |
| Excess of pyro increases the inertia    ..    .. | .. | $i$ |
| Addition of bromide increases the inertia ..    .. | .. | $i$ |

The effect of bromide upon $i$ vanishes if the time of development be prolonged, but in that case the development factor continually increases as the inertia decreases.

Owing to the importance of the apparent change of inertia consequent upon the use of bromide in the developing solution, both in practical photography and in the determination of the speed of the plate, we submit the following further considerations which lead to an approximate graphic representation of the influence of bromide.

The following results are taken from Experiment 16, the densities being inclusive of fog :—

*Experiment* 16.—Pyro-soda.   4 minutes' development.

| Negative No. | I | II | III | | |
|---|---|---|---|---|---|
| KBr = | $\frac{0}{1000}$ | $\frac{2}{1000}$ | $\frac{8}{1000}$ | Difference I and II | Difference I and III |
| 0·625 C.M.S. | ·335 | ·080 | — | ·255 | — |
| 1·25 ,, | ·685 | ·255 | ·095 | ·430 | ·590 |
| 2·5 ,, | 1·255 | ·825 | ·265 | ·430 | ·995 |
| 5 ,, | 1·870 | 1·395 | ·695 | ·475 | 1·175 |
| 10 ,, | 2·395 | 1·965 | 1·255 | ·430 | 1·140 |
| 20 ,, | 2·850 | 2·550 | 1·815 | ·300 | 1·035 |
| | | | Mean equal difference .. | ·441 | 1·086 |

It will be seen that negatives I and II differ, for a certain number of densities, by the mean amount of 0·441, and that the negatives I and III differ by the amount 1·086.   Hence we conclude that the use of eight parts of bromide, or four times the amount of bromide used in the first case, has depressed the densities by rather more than twice as much as they were depressed by the use of two parts of bromide, thus :—

Density with $\frac{2}{1000}$ bromide = density with o bromide $- 0·441$.

Density with $\frac{8}{1000}$ bromide = density with o bromide $- 1·086$.

A similar relation is shown by the following results, obtained with a more rapid plate :—

Densities inclusive of fog.

*Experiment* 19.—Pyro-soda.   6 minutes' development.

| Negative No. | I | II | III | | |
|---|---|---|---|---|---|
| KBr = | $\frac{0}{1000}$ | $\frac{2}{1000}$ | $\frac{8}{1000}$ | Difference I and II. | Difference I and III. |
| 0·312 C.M.S. | ·645 | ·310 | ·150 | ·335 | ·495 |
| 0·625 ,, | ·990 | ·600 | ·275 | ·390 | ·715 |
| 1·25 ,, | 1·320 | ·940 | ·520 | ·380 | ·800 |
| 2·5 ,, | 1·615 | 1·275 | ·850 | ·340 | ·765 |
| 5 ,, | 1·835 | 1·580 | 1·165 | ·255 | ·670 |
| 10 ,, | 2·030 | 1·880 | 1·490 | ·150 | ·540 |
| 20 ,, | 2·220 | 2·100 | 1·735 | ·120 | ·485 |
| Mean equal difference .. | | | | ·361 | ·737 |

It is therefore evident that the depression of the densities is not directly proportional to the amount of bromide added, but that it grows much more slowly, being only about twice as great when four times the amount of bromide is used.   Within these, and much wider limits, we may assume, as a first approximation, that the depression of the straight part of the characteristic curve is proportional to the square root of the amount of bromide added to the developer, if the development extends over the same time.

From Experiment 14, in which, with very different amounts of bromide and different times of development, several negatives were obtained which differed little from each other, we can obtain some clue as to how far, and in what ratio, the time of development counteracts the effect of the bromide added.

This experiment shows that with :—

| $n$ Bromide in 1,000. | $t$ minutes' development. | Exposure 40 C.M.S. gave density. | $\sqrt{n}.$ | $\dfrac{\sqrt{n}.}{t.}$ |
|---|---|---|---|---|
| 32 | 8 | 2·510 | 5·66 | 0·707 |
| 45 | 9 | 2·470 | 6·71 | 0·745 |
| 64 | 10 | 2·270 | 8·00 | 0·800 |
| 90 | 15 | 2·425 | 9·5 | 0·633 |
| Mean .. | | | | 0·721 |

These nearly constant quotients make it appear likely that the depression in the density is inversely proportional to the time of development, so that we have, in the case of Experiment 16, $\dfrac{1 \cdot 086 \times 4}{\sqrt{8}} = 1 \cdot 5$, and, as a rough approximation to the truth, we may write the depression of density $= \dfrac{1 \cdot 5 \sqrt{n}}{t}$.

If the density in the straight part of the characteristic curve be represented, when no bromide is used, by the formula—

$$D = \gamma \log. \frac{E}{i}$$

(E $=$ exposure and $i =$ inertia), then, with $n$ parts of bromide, the formula for the new straight part of the curve becomes—

$$D = \gamma \log. \frac{E}{i} - \frac{1 \cdot 5 \sqrt{n}}{t}$$

for the plate under consideration.

We have defined the exposure at which the straight portion of the characteristic curve intersects the axis of abscissæ as the "inertia," but it is evident that, when bromide is used, the inertia so found is not the true inertia of the plate. If, in the above formula, we put the density $= 0$, we have as the resulting exposure for this point—

$$\text{Log. E} = \frac{1 \cdot 5 \sqrt{n}}{t \cdot \gamma} + \log. i$$

or, passing from logarithms to numbers—

$$E = i \times 31 \cdot 6^{\left(\frac{\sqrt{n}}{\gamma \cdot t}\right)}$$

Thus it will be seen how much slower a plate appears to be when bromide is used than in its absence.

As an example, take the time of development as four minutes, the bromide as 16 per 1,000, and the development factor as $1 \cdot 9$ (circumstances of Experiment 16) and we have—

$$\frac{\sqrt{n}}{t \cdot \gamma} = \frac{\sqrt{16}}{4 \times 1 \cdot 9} = 0 \cdot 52, \text{ and } 31 \cdot 6^{0 \cdot 52} = 6$$

so that the apparent inertia is six times as great by the formula as the real inertia, or the apparent speed of the plate is one-sixth of the real speed.

As a matter of fact, the inertia of the plate, without bromide, was found to be $0 \cdot 7$; with 16 parts of bromide, a development factor of $1 \cdot 9$ was reached in four minutes, and the apparent inertia was found to be $3 \cdot 5$, or five times as great as the real inertia, while the formula shows six times.

The influence of bromide upon other plates developed with pyro-soda may have different values. Upon a plate, the inertia of which, without bromide, is found to be 0·15 (Experiment 19) the difference in the density between 0 part and 8 parts of bromide was found to be 0·737. The plate was developed for 6 minutes, and thus we have—

$$\frac{\cdot 737 \times 6}{\sqrt{8}} = 1 \cdot 56$$

so that, for this plate, we have—

$$D = \gamma \log. \frac{E}{i} - \frac{1 \cdot 56 \sqrt{n}}{t}$$

Whether the constant 1·5 applies to other plates we have not at present sufficient material to decide, but it is very possible that different plates will have different constants, since different plates behave very differently as regards the time necessary to reach a given density under the influence of one and the same developer.

We here give a graphic representation of the application of this formula :—

Assume that only one part of bromide had been added to the developer, and that the development factor reached, after 2 minutes' development, was 0·8 (to which corresponds the angle of inclination 38·5°), then the value $\dfrac{1 \cdot 5 \times \sqrt{1}}{2} =$ 0·750 represents the depression of the densities. Assuming the real inertia of the plate to be 1, log. $i = 0$, we measure perpendicularly downwards the density 0·750. Through this point we draw, at an angle of 38·5°, the line representing the negative resulting from a

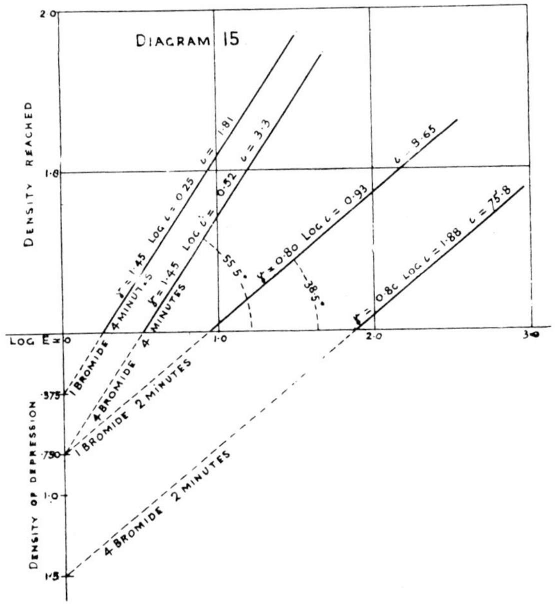


development of two minutes with pyro-soda containing 1 part of bromide in 1,000.

Similarly, a line is drawn to represent development for four minutes with four parts of bromide.

The diagram shows exactly what the experiments themselves showed, and it illustrates in a peculiar way an important fact which the practical photographer cannot neglect, namely, that if a good negative is to result with a developer containing bromide, the time of exposure must be adjusted both to the amount of bromide used and to the development factor which it is required to reach.   It is not possible to convert an over-exposed into a true negative by the indiscriminate addition of bromide to the developer.   The character of the negative depends upon the exposure, upon the bromide in the solution, and upon the time of development, and, in order to control the result, all three factors must be accurately known.   This, however, introduces such a serious complication that the difficulty is best overcome by the total omission of bromide in the developer, to which we shall further allude.

Diagram 15 further suggests a method for finding, when bromide is used in the developer, the true inertia of the plate.   For this purpose two strips of the same plate are simultaneously exposed, as in the case of a speed determination. The strips are then developed in the same developer, but one strip is developed for twice as long as the other.   Since the depression of the density in time 2 is one-half of that in time 1, we draw the straight line representing the negative developed for the shorter time.   We prolong this line below the line of exposures, and anywhere draw an ordinate downwards.   This ordinate we bisect, and through the point thus found and the apparent inertia we draw a line. Where this line cuts a produced line representing the negative developed for the longer time, we erect another ordinate.   This ordinate passes through the real point of inertia.

This method of finding the true inertia is illustrated by Experiment 20 and Diagram 16.   We should, however, wish it to be understood that we regard this method as of scientific rather than practical value, and that we do not advise its application in the case of speed determination.

*Experiment* 20.—Densities exclusive of fog.

| KBr in 1,000 = | 0 | 2 | 2 |
|---|---|---|---|
| Time developed. | 3 min. | 3 min. | 6 min. |
| 0·625 C.M.S. | ·120 | — | ·040 |
| 1·25  ,, | ·405 | ·055 | ·305 |
| 2·5  ,, | ·735 | ·300 | ·930 |
| 5  ,, | 1·155 | ·660 | 1·620 |
| 10  ,, | 1·575 | 1·125 | 2·300 |
| 20  ,, | 1·930 | 1·580 | 2·990 |
| 40  ,, | 2·165 | 1·975 | — |
| Negative No.  ..  .. | I | II | III |

Referring to Diagram 16, the straight line of negative II is produced downwards. At any point A an ordinate is drawn, and this is bisected in point B. A straight line is drawn through point B to the apparent inertia at C, and the straight line of negative III is produced. Where this intersects the line B C an ordinate is drawn which indicates the true inertia of the plate.

The results are as follows :—

Apparent inertia, 3 minutes, 2 bromide .. .. .. 1·75
,, 6 ,, 2 ,, .. .. .. 0·95
True inertia found by construction .. .. .. 0·7
,, ,, development without bromide .. 0·72

Our experiments do not permit us, even approximately, to represent by means of a formula the influence of bromide in the pyro-ammonia developer. Apparently the greatest effect is produced by bromide in the case of ferrous oxalate. The depression of the densities by a given amount of bromide increases very rapidly with the amount of bromide, and is almost proportional to it, but we have not followed the subject sufficiently far to give decisive results. However, the general law in all developers is that bromide does not affect the development factor. It affects the inertia of the plate only, and does so very materially, though only temporarily.

It will have been noted that, in the earlier part of this chapter, we gave a formula for a standard pyro-soda developer. In the light of our latest investigations we are satisfied

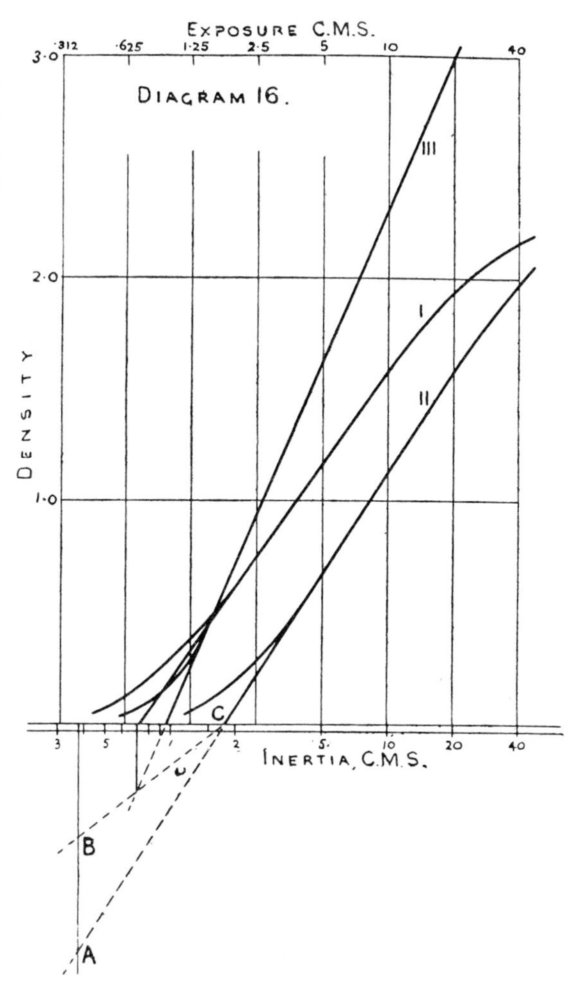




T

that this is the best developer we have so far investigated, and we have decided to adopt it as our standard in preference to ferrous oxalate. If we dare hope for uniformity on the part of those plate manufacturers who use our system, we should strongly urge them to quote the speed of their plates as ascertained by this developer, and we trust that our adoption of this standard may, at any rate, overcome the objection which some plate manufacturers have to ferrous oxalate, and so do something to establish uniformity among those who have adopted or who may adopt our system.

While our standard pyro-soda gives the maximum speed of a plate, it at the same time makes the utmost of the plate as regards its capacity for truthful representation, and it is a developer in very general use. Ferrous oxalate, on the other hand, is by no means popular, in this country at any rate. It does not yield, as a rule, more than half the maximum speed of a plate, and, owing to its acting by diffusion, it causes the period of correct exposure to merge prematurely into that of over-exposure, so curtailing the capacity of the plate for truthful representation, and, hence, reducing latitude in exposure.

At first sight exception may be taken to the entire omission of bromide in our standard pyro-soda developer, but to this we attach the utmost importance. It may be advanced that the omission of bromide will lead to the production of fog, but we have satisfied ourselves that as some of the most rapid plates on the market, when developed without bromide, yield no undue amount of fog, plates which are not amenable to development without the use of bromide should simply be avoided. We have, however, only come across one brand of plates which yielded an undesirable amount of fog on development with pyro-soda without bromide.

As we have frequently pointed out, the real control which the photographer has it in his power to exercise lies in deciding what development factor he will reach. By this means he determines the range of gradation of his negative, and adapts the range of light intensities in his subject to the range capacity of the material upon which he prints. He also modifies the range of his negative in order to adapt it to the printing method he means to employ. He may, for example, require a low development factor, as in the case of a delicate portrait negative for the purpose of producing an enlargement, or he may require a comparatively high development factor, as in the case of a landscape negative for contact printing. Assuming a correct exposure, which must be regarded as an absolute necessity, the suitability of the negative for the particular purpose in view is decided by the development factor reached, and this, again, by the time occupied in development.

Now, it is equally necessary that the exposure be correct, whether the development factor of the resulting negative be high or low—that is, whether the time occupied in development be long or short—and this means that the time occupied in development must not affect the inertia of the plate. We have, however, shown that, as soon as bromide enters into the composition of the developer, the time of development does influence the inertia ; in other words, the speed of the plate is less for a low development factor than for a high. Hence, when bromide is used, the correct exposure depends upon the development factor it is desired to reach, and this introduces a most serious and unnecessary complication.

In making investigations on the development factor we had long been troubled with the difficulty of obtaining, on the same plate and with different times of development, a series of tangents which intersected the exposure scale at the same point. As the development factor increased the inertia always moved from the right to the left hand. This we have now traced to the presence of bromide in the developer. We have, therefore, been forced to the conclusion that the practice of photography by methods of pre-calculation renders it imperative to employ a developer compounded without bromide.

The omission of bromide in a developer used for the purpose of speed-determination is also of the utmost importance. Only by omitting bromide altogether will different operators ever agree as to the speed of a plate ; for even if the same amount of bromide be used by different operators, varying speeds will result unless identically the same development factor be reached in each case.

We hope that the importance of the development factor, as the only scientific means the photographer has of controlling the gradations of his negative will soon be recognised. It is quite clear that density ratios can be disturbed by developers too poor or too rich in pyrogallol, and particularly by the use of bromide, but we are convinced that quantitative photography can only be conducted by recognising, as a fundamental principle, the law of constant density ratios, and by working under conditions in harmony therewith. We are further satisfied that the certain and truthful correction of unknown errors in exposure is not within the power of the photographer.

We look forward to the time when the vital importance of correct exposure shall be insisted upon rather than that of corrective development. We can imagine nothing more detrimental to the photographic student than to teach him that exposure is comparatively unimportant, and that his energies should be directed to learning how to compound his developer so as to remedy errors in exposure.

It appears to us that the chief glory of photography lies in its power to truthfully represent natural objects, and, in the attainment of this end, we are ourselves quite content. It may, of course, be necessary to somewhat compress or extend the range of gradation of the negative in order to bring the range of intensities in the subject and the range capacity of the printing material into agreement, but we maintain that the tone values should be *relatively* true, and this can only be brought about by a correct exposure.

With those photographers who deliberately aspire, by means of irregularities in exposure and development, to interpret nature other than as she is, we have nothing in common, and we expect no sympathy from them.

Our aim throughout has been to banish rule-of-thumb, to remove any necessity for correction in development, to render the production of the negative a matter of certainty, and to place photography in its proper position as a quantitative science.

*    *    *    *    *    *    *

My pen has now recorded the last work which it has been my privilege to carry out in conjunction with my lamented friend and colleague Dr. Hurter. Nevermore shall I have the advantage of his masterly co-operation, and no longer will photography benefit by his rare attainments and natural gifts. I would take this opportunity of placing upon record the profound admiration I had for Dr. Hurter as a scientist, and the deep regard I had for his character as a man. To have been associated with him in his work was to receive an invaluable training in scientific methods, and to have claimed him as a friend was to possess one of sterling worth.

It had been our intention to have added two further chapters to this paper, one on the influence of time in development, or the control of the development factor, and the other on the bearing of our investigations on practical photography. With some views on which we were agreed with regard to the latter subject, I have brought the last part of our paper to a conclusion. I long considered whether I ought myself to supply, to the best of my ability, the two remaining chapters, but, under the circumstances, I felt it more fitting to conclude at the point reached when Dr. Hurter was taken from us, especially as the publication of our paper had already extended over a long period, and much further experimental work was needed to cover the ground we had intended.

At a later period I trust I may be able to deal with those parts of the subject upon which we had together intended to treat, but when all is done, we both felt that our work has only paved the way for further investigation, and that much still remains to be done before any finality can be reached.

V. C. D.

[*Reprinted from " The Photographic Journal," January,* 1903.]

# CONTROL OF THE DEVELOPMENT FACTOR AND A NOTE ON SPEED-DETERMINATION.

By

VERO C. DRIFFIELD.

---

IN a paper recently read before the Society of Arts by Mr. Alfred Watkins, he says, alluding to our introduction of the term " development factor," that " it was a weak point that the development factor was merely a record of a result attained, and not a help towards the attainment of the same result another time."

My object in this communication is to remove this " weak point," and to show, not only how the same development factor may be obtained at any time and upon any plate capable of yielding it, but how the development factor may be modified in order to adapt the negative to different classes of subject and to different printing processes, or to give expression to the artistic perceptions of the photographer.

It has long been my intention to deal with this matter ; but in order to render it more complete, I deferred doing so until I was prepared to show not only how to control the development factor, but how the considerations which determine its value are amenable to calculation. Unfortunately time has not permitted me to complete the necessary investigations ; but Mr. Watkins' allusion has determined me to deal at once with the first part of the subject.

It has been with great satisfaction that I have noted a growing tendency to abandon mere ocular examination of the negative during the course of development for some more scientific and certain mode of procedure. More especially, the want of scientific method appears to have made itself felt in the case of colour-photography ; the sensitiveness of the plates employed for this purpose being such, that no light is admissible in the dark room which will permit of adequate examination of the negative during development. I also gather that, in order to secure the three negatives, representing the three fundamental colours, in relatively correct relationship, the importance attaching to correct exposure, and to securing the correct development factor, is becoming more and more recognised ; and evidence is not wanting that the old idea of correcting errors in exposure by modified development is fast waning. While, however, the necessity of a scientific means of controlling the degree of development, and the paramount importance attaching to correct exposure, are fast making themselves felt in the more technical branches of photography, I believe that their recognition in ordinary pictorial work will speedily follow.

I shall now proceed to describe the method of controlling the development factor which I have adopted in my own practice.   I need hardly point out, to begin with, the necessity of observing standard conditions as regards the developer itself and the temperature at which development is conducted.

In our paper on the latent image we gave, as our standard pyro-soda developer, a solution containing, in 1,000 parts : 8 parts of pyrogallol, 40 parts of sodium carbonate (crystallised) and 40 parts of sodium sulphite.   On no account must a bromide be added.   For the purpose of speed-determination by plate manufacturers, as also for experimental work generally, this standard should be used as here given ; but, as this developer is very energetic in the case of some plates, and as it may be considered more convenient to prolong the time of development, the photographer may, if he think fit in his ordinary practice, reduce the strength to one-half that of the standard given above. Beyond this, however, the strength should certainly not be reduced or the higher densities of the negative will materially suffer.

The standard temperature at which development should take place is 65° Fahr., a temperature which can be readily commanded either summer or winter.   My own developing dishes are constructed of ordinary tinned iron plate, the bottom of the dish itself resting on the surface of water at the necessary temperature, and contained in a fairly large outer bath, also constructed of tinned plate, which may, with advantage, in very cold weather, be protected by some non-conducting material.   The dish is supported at its two ends by projecting flanges, which rest upon the edges of the outer bath, and this allows the dish to be gently rocked during the progress of development.   The exposed plate should be placed in the dish and covered up sufficiently long before the developer is applied, to allow it to assume the proper temperature, and I need hardly say that the developer itself, as well as the vessels containing it, must also be allowed, by immersion in a water bath, to acquire the requisite temperature.

We will now assume that we have procured a large stock of plates coated from the same batch of emulsion, and that, before commencing to use them in the camera, we are about to make a thorough investigation of their characteristics. In addition to determining their speed, their capacity for truthful representation, or, in other words, their latitude, their inherent fog, and so forth, we wish to ascertain how the growth of the development factor progresses, in order that we may make such modifications in the time of development as are demanded for different classes of subject—say, landscape, portrait and interior.

In the ordinary procedure of speed determination we have hitherto only regarded it as necessary to make a series of exposures in geometrical progression upon a single strip of plate. In order, however, to obtain data to enable us to control the development factor, it is necessary to simultaneously expose two or more strips of the same plate. In ordinary photographic practice, however, two strips will be found to be sufficient, as the two development factor values which they provide, together with the zero point, afford us three points through which we may draw a curve representing the growth of the development factor with time of development.

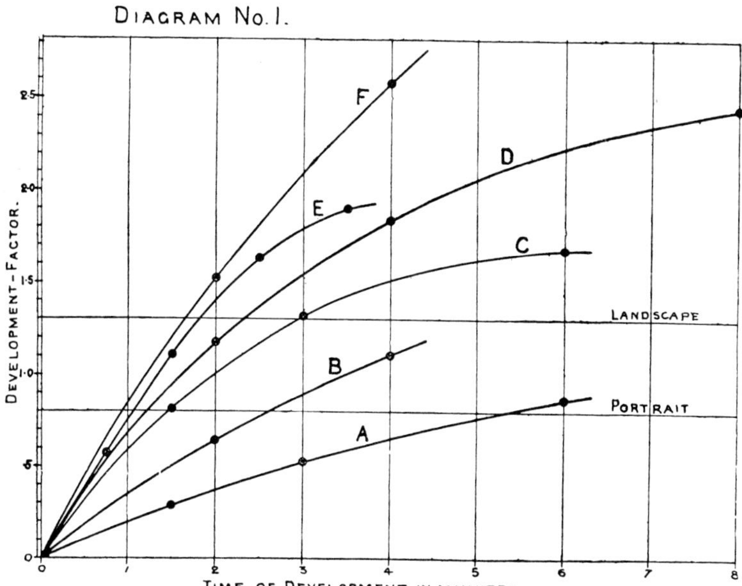



Diagram No. 1 shows the development factor curves of six different plates, the times of development in minutes being taken as abscissæ and the development factors as ordinates. The points marked indicate the values of the factors ascertained, which, with the zero point, determine the course of each curve. I have chosen these six curves as illustrating the great difference which exists in different plates as regards the growth of the development factor. The numerical data determining the curves are given in the following table, and the relative times of development required in each case for a portrait and a landscape are also indicated :—

I had perhaps better here remark that I have assumed that those whom I now address are familiar with the graphic method of determining the value of the development factor as explained in our original paper.

| Plate. | Strips developed. | Development factors obtained. | Time of development for | |
|---|---|---|---|---|
| | | | Portrait. | Landscape. |
| | Mins. | | Mins. | Mins. |
| A | 1½, 3, 6. | 0·29, 0·52, 0·85. | 5·5 | — |
| B | 2, 4. | 0·64, 1·10. | 2·6 | 5·2 |
| C | 1½, 3, 6. | 0·8, 1·32, 1·675. | 1·5 | 3 |
| D | 2, 4, 8. | 1·17, 1·83, 2·44. | 1·25 | 2·3 |
| E | ¾, 1½, 2½, 3½. | 0·57, 1·09, 1·63, 1·9. | 1·1 | 1·8 |
| F | 2, 4. | 1·52, 2·58. | 0·95 | 1·65 |

Taking the two extreme curves A and F, it will be seen that while, in the case of A, a portrait would require 5½ minutes' development, the same result would be obtained on plate F in rather less than 1 minute, and, as the curve A clearly approaches its limit, the plate it represents would probably be useless for landscape work or for any subject requiring a more materially extended range of opacities than a portrait.

As a rough guide to the development factors required for different classes of subject, I may indicate the following values :—

| | |
|---|---|
| Ordinary landscape .. . . .. .. .. | 1·3 |
| Interior .. .. .. .. .. .. .. | 1·0 |
| Portrait .. .. .. .. . .. .. .. | 0·8 |

But it must be clearly understood that these values can only be absolutely determined by a knowledge of the range of light intensities reflected by the subject photographed, and of the range of luminosities which the printing medium employed is capable of rendering. The artistic perceptions of the photographer also enter into consideration, as, in order to obtain a certain desired effect, he may deem it necessary to compress or to expand the opacity range of a particular negative. I feel very confident that when the practical photographer learns to associate with a particular quality of negative a definite numerical value, he will find this in itself a great boon. It is quite time that such crude generalisations as " thin " and " dense " should give way to definite numerical expressions.

In order to determine the development factor curve of a plate it is only really necessary, as I said before, to develop two simultaneously exposed strips for different lengths of time. Though it is not material what the lengths of time chosen may be, so long as they are accurately known and sufficiently far apart, I find it most convenient to develop one strip for exactly twice as long as the other.

The time occupied in the development of the first strip must be determined by the facility with which the plate develops, but the longer the time the better, so long as the second strip, on receiving twice the time of development, does not become too dense to be readily measured. The strip should be removed from the developer a second or two before the time is up, and, the moment the time has expired, the strip should be rapidly passed through a dish of water and then straight into the fixing bath. In timing the development I make use of a stop chronograph provided with two hands, one indicating seconds and the other minutes.

Having determined the development factors of the two strips, we have only to mark them on a skeleton diagram and draw through them and the zero point a curve representing the growth of the factor with time of development. This curve then enables us to determine the time of development necessary to reach any factor desired, and to attain the same result as often as we wish.

The employment of two strips in order to ascertain the growth of the development factor when determining the speed of a plate has a further very important advantage, to which I wish to take this opportunity of calling attention.

In our paper on the latent image we, for the first time, clearly indicated the influence of bromide in the developing solution. We pointed out that this reagent is not an essential constituent of the developer, but that it is a product of the chemical change which takes place in the process of development, and hence leads to retardation. We showed that while an increase in the amount of pyrogallol or of alkali affects the development factor, it has no influence upon the inertia, but that, on the contrary, the mere presence of bromide disturbs the inertia, though only apparently, as its influence may be compensated by time of development.

The presence of free bromide has a seriously disturbing effect upon speed determination, is accountable for much of our earlier difficulty, and explains why the inertiæ of simultaneously exposed strips of the same plate developed for different lengths of time were in some cases coincident, while in others the inertia decreased with time of development. Clearly a single strip developed in the presence of free bromide cannot determine with absolute certainty the speed of a plate.

It is for this reason that I wish to impress the importance of employing a developer containing no free bromide, and, as plates of the highest rapidity can be and are manufactured which do not yield an undue amount of fog when developed without bromide, I am forced to the conclusion that a plate which compels the use of bromide may justly be condemned.

But while the photographer is in a position to secure immunity from free bromide as far as the developer is concerned, he has no control over its presence in the plate he employs. If free bromide exist in the plate itself a single determination of its speed will be more or less misleading, unless the strip be allowed to reach a very high development factor.

The further advantage gained by making use of two strips in determining the speed of a plate is that we thus obtain a clue as to whether the plate contains free bromide or not. If, after measuring the strips and plotting the characteristic curves, we find the inertiæ practically coincident, we may infer the absence of free bromide ; but if the inertia decrease with time of development it presumably indicates the presence of more or less free bromide.

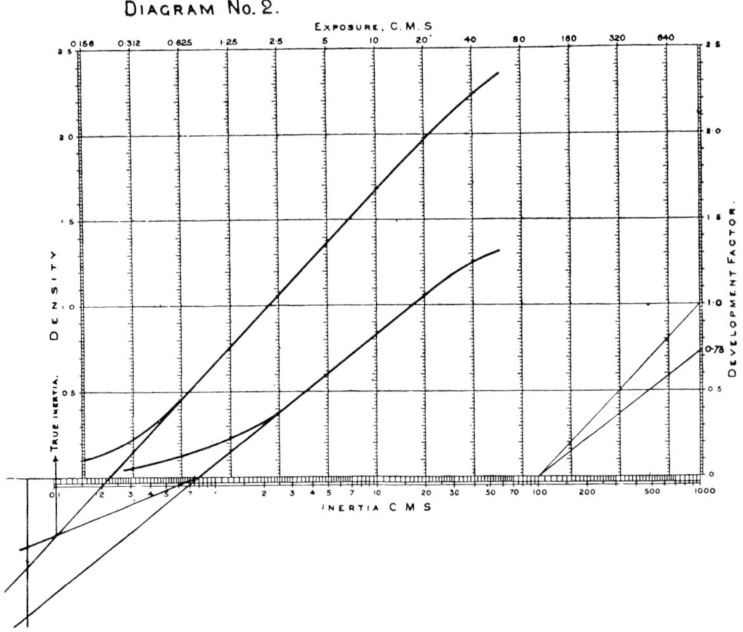



Diagram No. 2 affords a practical example of decreasing inertia with time of development. The two strips were developed for two and for four minutes respectively, the development factors obtained being 0·73 and 1·0. The resulting inertiæ were 0·75 C.M.S. and 0·22 C.M.S., which correspond with speeds of 45 and 155. If we apply to these determinations the graphic method of correction described in our paper on the latent image and indicated on the diagram we find the true inertia of the plate to be 0·103, which corresponds with a speed of 330. It will, however, be found, on plotting the development factor curve of this plate, that it is incapable of attaining a higher development factor than 1·0. From this example it will be seen how utterly misleading a single determination of the speed of such a plate as this would be, because its speed is dependent upon the development factor attained.

I trust, however, that plate manufacturers will give their attention to this matter, and that they will see their way to provide us with plates containing no trace of free bromide. I further hope that it will come to be recognised as a characteristic of a really good plate that it shall, unlike plate A on Diagram No. 1, be capable of attaining the highest development factor demanded in practical photography.

[*Reprinted from "The Photo-Miniature," Vol. V., No. 56, November,* 1903.]

# THE HURTER AND DRIFFIELD SYSTEM: BEING A BRIEF ACCOUNT OF THEIR PHOTO-CHEMICAL INVESTIGATIONS AND METHOD OF SPEED DETERMINATION.

---

IT was a source of considerable disappointment to my late colleague, Dr. Hurter, and to myself, that the primary object we had in view when we published our photo-chemical investigations, was not more fully realised. Our immediate object was to provide amateur photographers, like ourselves, with a method of determining the speed of the plates they used, and to lead them to substitute methods of scientific precision for the rule-of-thumb empiricism so generally practised. That our system has not been more generally adopted by amateur photographers is probably due to the somewhat abstruse mathematical treatment which the subject necessitated in the first instance, and to the fact that our publications were so widely distributed over the various journals as to render them difficult of access.

The desirability of publishing a short and concise account of our investigations, and their practical application, in a popular form, and as free as possible from the mathematical considerations involved, has often presented itself to my mind ; and the cordial invitation of the editor of *The Photo-Miniature* to provide such a treatise, as a contribution to this excellent series of photographic handbooks, seemed to indicate that the opportunity had arrived. I therefore propose, in this little monograph, to explain, in as simple language as possible, our discovery of the law which expresses the action of light upon the sensitive plate, its bearing upon the functions of exposure and development, and the method of speed determination which was the outcome of this discovery.

Our investigations date from the period when we first made the acquaintance of the gelatine dry plate. Accustomed, as we were, to the uniform rapidity of the old collodion wet plate, the wide variation in the speed of gelatine plates was, to us, a serious embarrassment. We were, accordingly, strongly impressed with the importance of discovering a means of determining the speed of these plates by some more satisfactory method than that of trial in the camera, and one which would enable us to apply strictly proportional numerical values to the results obtained.

Further, we had long felt that art in photography ceased to play any part the moment the cap was removed from the lens, and that every subsequent operation, whether exposure, development, printing or enlarging, was strictly a matter of science, and amenable to calculation. While we quite realised that the artist will always produce the best *picture*, we contended that the scientist will produce the best *negative*. The photographer, therefore, who combines scientific method with artistic skill is in the best possible position to produce good work. Hence, our aim was to raise technical photography from an empirical art to a quantitative science.

*The Technically Perfect Negative.*—It always appeared to us that the most valuable distinction of photography lies in its capacity to truthfully represent natural objects, both as regards delineation and light and shade. The truthful representation of light and shade, however, involves the production of a technically perfect negative, of which it is necessary to give a definition.

We define a technically perfect negative as one in which the opacities of its gradations are proportional to the light reflected by those parts of the original object which they represent. It will be well to keep this definition in mind, as we shall have to refer to it again when we come to consider the action of the light. If photography is to be capable of rendering gradations truly, this relationship, and no other, between the opacities and the light-intensities which produced them, must exist. Our investigations show that such a relationship does exist, but only when a plate has received what we term a correct exposure.

*The Definition of " Opacity."*—This definition demands another, namely, the meaning we attach to the term " opacity." Opacity is simply the optical property of a substance (in our case silver) to impede the passage through it of light. " Transparency " is the inverse of this, and is measured by that fraction of the original light which a substance transmits. The opacity of a deposit of silver, which transmits one-half the original light, is 2.

*" Density."*—In seeking to ascertain, for the purpose of our investigations, the connection between the exposure or the light-intensity, and the opacity, we found that this relation is of a very complicated nature ; while that which exists between the exposure and the actual weight of silver, representing a given opacity, is comparatively simple. To the relative quantity of silver deposited per unit area we applied the term " density " ; and as the relation between the density and opacity is also of a simple character, the density forms a connecting link between the exposure and the opacity.

The relation which exists between density and opacity is expressed by saying that the former is the logarithm of the latter. An opacity of 10, which transmits one-tenth of the light it receives, is therefore represented by a density (weight of silver) of 1, because 1 is the common logarithm of 10.

Having regard to the density, the law which alone would produce absolutely true tones in photography would be expressed by saying that the quantity of silver reduced on the negative is proportional to the logarithm of the light-intensity.

*"Density" and "Opacity" Confused.*—Unfortunately the terms "density" and "opacity" have hitherto been used indiscriminately by photographers, and have, in consequence, produced confusion and led to misunderstanding of our publications. Photographic authorities of eminence, indeed, have seriously complained of our making the distinction at all, and of the great importance we attach to the density of the deposit, rather than to its opacity. Had they grasped the subject in all its bearings, they would have seen good reason for the course we took.

*An Explanation.*—By the application of a factor, the density of a deposit is at once converted into the weight of silver per unit area ; and, consequently, a measurement of the density affords a ready means of estimating quantitatively the amount of silver present, even in such minute quantities as to entirely defy the finest analytical balance. The important part which the density plays in all calculations of exposure for printing processes by development, fully justifies the prominence we gave to it ; and, further, had our investigations been based upon the opacity instead of upon the density, we should never have discovered the law which expresses the action of light upon the sensitive plate. For the purpose of measuring the density of a deposit, we devised a special photometer. This instrument is extremely simple in principle, can be readily constructed by any amateur, and will be fully described at a later stage.

## ACTION OF LIGHT UPON THE SENSITIVE PLATE. THE "CHARACTERISTIC CURVE."

The reader will now be in a position to follow the procedure by which we traced the action of light upon the photographic plate, and which, in turn, led to the discovery of what we termed the "characteristic curve."

Our earliest investigations were conducted upon thickly-coated plates, especially manufactured for the purpose. Upon one of these plates we made a series of exposures, doubling each exposure as we proceeded. This course had the advantage of enabling us very rapidly to trace the action of light through a large range of exposures, and, at the same time, led us to discover that the relationship between opacity and exposure which our definition of a perfect negative demands, does actually exist. After development, etc., the density resulting from each exposure was carefully measured and its value plotted on the ordinate, or exposure line, representing the corresponding exposure, as shown in Fig. 1. The points thus obtained were then joined, and resulted in a peculiar curve which we styled the " characteristic curve " of the plate. It will be noted that the vertical scale of this diagram indicates

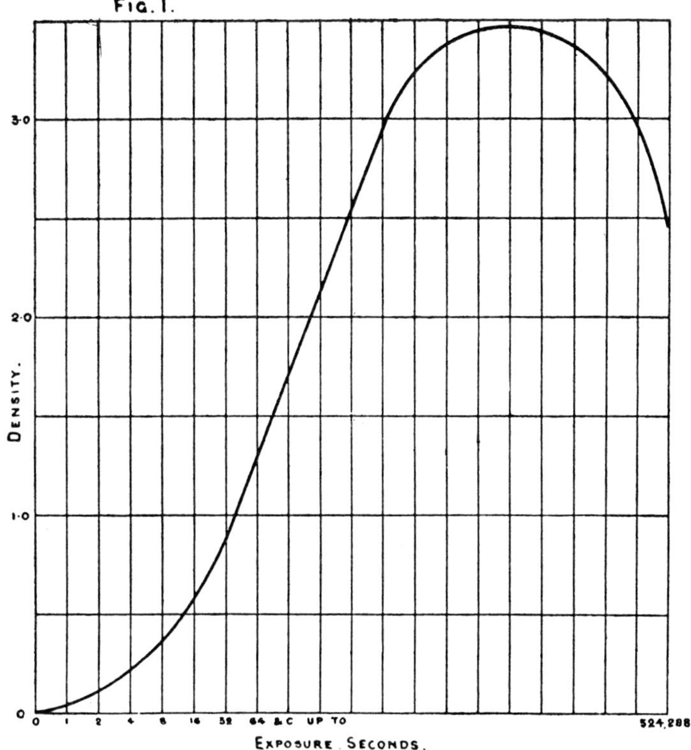


density, or amount of silver ; while the horizontal scale indicates exposure, or light-intensity. It will also be observed that the horizontal scale progresses in geometric series, each successive exposure (equidistant on the scale) being double the preceding exposure; the horizontal scale is thus the logarithmic scale of the ordinary slide-rule.

An examination of the characteristic curve shows that it consists of four distinct branches, gradually merging from one into the other. It commences with a strongly bent portion, which then merges into a straight line. This gradually assumes a curvature in the opposite direction until it reaches a maximum density, when the curve takes a downward course. The four distinct branches of this curve correspond with the phenomena of under-, correct-, and over-exposure, and of reversal, with which the practical photographer is familiar.

These distinctive periods in the action of the light upon the sensitive plate are due to the fact that the work done by the light, at any moment of the exposure, is proportional to the amount of energy received at that moment by the *unaltered* silver bromide, and as the silver bromide is gradually altered the amount of unaltered silver bromide grows gradually less and less. Were this not so, the density, and not the opacity as demanded, would be, throughout the entire range of exposures, proportional to the light-intensities. Every picture would appear what we call under-exposed, and truth in photography would be an impossibility

We shall now proceed to consider the subject of

## EXPOSURE,

and, in doing so, it will probably assist the reader if, instead of illustrating the relationship between density and light-intensity, or exposure, by means of a curve, we do so by a series of steps, which may be collectively taken to represent a peculiarly constructed staircase. This staircase (*see* Fig. 2) is, in a more or less modified form, common to all plates.

*Correct Exposure Imperative.*—While many photographers attach very little importance to accuracy in exposure, and maintain that errors may be readily corrected by suitable modifications in the composition of the developer, we have always strongly insisted that a correct exposure is an essential foundation if we aim to produce a technically perfect negative. It must, however, be clearly understood that, by a correct exposure we do not imply that there is necessarily one exposure, and one only, which will yield a negative answering to our definition. Fortunately, most plates admit of some latitude in this respect, a matter which we shall further consider at a later stage.

When we make an exposure in the camera we impress upon the sensitive plate a latent range of gradations. If our exposure be correct this latent image bears a truthful relationship to the light-intensities which produced it; if our exposure fall outside the limits which the latitude of the plate permits, this relationship will accordingly be false. Our contention is that a latent image, false in its gradations, cannot, by modifications in the constitution of the developer, be made to yield a visible image true in its gradations. The practice of photography, by methods of scientific predetermination, imperatively demands a correct exposure as a fundamental condition.

Returning now to the staircase depicted in Fig. 2, and having regard to the "rise" of the individual steps, we note that three distinctly different conditions exist which represent the periods of under-, correct-, and over-exposure respectively. Under these heads we shall discuss them. The period of reversal may be dismissed, for, though of considerable scientific interest, it has little or no bearing on practical photography.

FIG. 2.

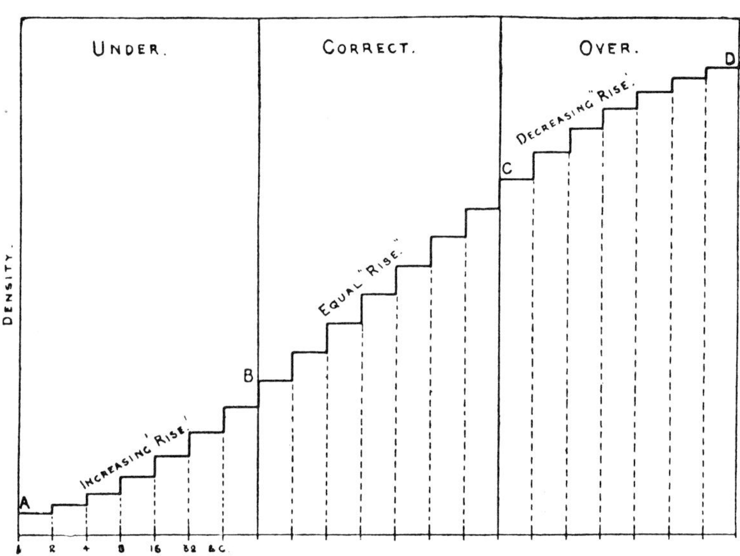


*Period of Under-exposure.*—Commencing at A and proceeding as far as B, we notice that the steps are marked by a gradually *increasing* rise ; but, at the very commencement, this rise is proportional to the exposure, or light-intensity. Bearing in mind that the rise of each step means growth in density, and keeping in view our definition of a perfect negative, it will be seen that we have here an altogether false relationship. In this case proportionality exists between exposure and density, instead of between exposure and opacity. A negative the gradations of which fall within this period would yield prints which have been characterised as of the "chalk and soot" variety, and, by the practical photographer, would be recognised as under-exposed. The characteristic of this period is a negative in which the shadows, and nearly all the half-tones, are indiscriminately represented by almost bare glass; the high-lights being marked by relatively extreme density. From this period we pass imperceptibly into the period of correct exposure.

*Period of Correct Exposure.*—From the point B, and extending to C, the steps of the staircase are all of equal rise; that is to say, each doubling of the exposure is represented by an equal increment of density. While the density grows arithmetically, the exposure progresses geometrically; and, as the mathematician calls each term of an arithmetic series the logarithm of the corresponding term of a geometric series, it will be seen that we have secured in this period that logarithmic relationship between density and exposure which truthful representation demands. The following ratios will serve as an example of this relationship :—

Light-intensities (exposure)    ..     1 : 4 : 16 (geometric).

Silver deposited (density) ..    ..     0 : 0·6 : 1·2 (arithmetic).

Opacity    ..    ..    ..    ..     1 : 4 : 16 (geometric).

Thus we see that a photographic plate is capable of truly rendering a series of light-intensities, *i.e.*, of yielding a range of opacities proportional to the light reflected by the different parts of the object represented, but only on the condition that all its gradations fall within that portion of the staircase (Fig. 2) in which the steps are of equal rise; or, in the case of the characteristic curve (Fig. 1), within that portion which is represented by a straight line. Of course, there is the further condition that the plate must have a sufficiently extended correct period to include the required range of light-intensities. This will be further considered under the head of latitude in exposure.

A study of this period will show that the deepest shadow of a correctly-exposed negative is necessarily represented by a certain deposit of silver. The presence of bare, or almost bare, glass would be an indication of the inclusion of the commencement of the period of under-exposure. In ordinary pictorial photography, however, it is quite admissible to include a few of the steps of unequal rise at either end of, but immediately contiguous to, the correct period, because of the inability of the eye to readily appreciate small deviations from truthful rendering.

*Period of Over-exposure.*—This period commences at C and continues till the highest step in the staircase is reached, and the period of reversal sets in. It is marked by a gradually *decreasing* rise in the steps, which finally becomes almost imperceptible. A negative the gradations of which fall within this period would be equally as false, but in the opposite direction, as if its gradations fell within the period of under-exposure. The characteristic of under-exposure is too great contrast; in this period the contrasts are too small The tendency of the gradations in the case of over-exposure is to approach one uniform density. Hence, the flat results with which the photographer is familiar, in which the high-lights and the half-tones are represented by almost similar opacities. Obviously, if a negative is to be capable of yielding a print absolutely true to nature, it must include no steps in the under- and over-exposure portions of the staircase.

We shall now turn our attention to the subject of

## DEVELOPMENT.

Having, by means of a correct exposure, established a true relationship between the latent gradations and the light-intensities, the function of development is to reduce the latent image to metallic silver. Something more than this is, however, involved in the process, because the time occupied in development materially influences the result. The photographer would say that, as development proceeds, the negative becomes denser. In order to make what really occurs quite clear, we will revert to the staircase as an illustration.

Fig. 3 represents two staircases, but, as we now assume that we are dealing with correctly-exposed negatives, the steps in both are shown of equal rise. The two series of gradations are representative of two strips of the same plate equally and simultaneously exposed, and developed together, but for different lengths of time. The one series represents a development extending over, say, four minutes, and the other a development of, say, two minutes. Relatively, the two strips represent what the photographer would term a " dense " and a " thin " negative. It

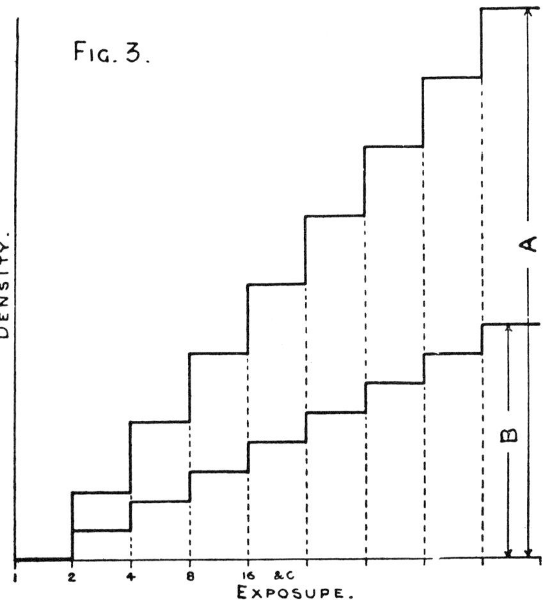


will be noticed that the maximum height (A) of one staircase is considerably greater than that (B) of the other; and, as the number of steps in each is equal, the rise of each individual step is greater in one case than in the other. The equal rise in the steps of each staircase indicates that the relationship between the densities is identical in the two cases ; in other words, that the density ratios are constant and independent of the time of development. But while the relationship between the densities is constant, that existing between the corresponding opacities increases as the time of development is prolonged.   Hence, the range of light-intensities transmitted by the series of densities A would be far greater than that transmitted by the series of densities B.   Between and beyond the two staircases shown, an infinite number of others may be considered to lie ; but while, in each case, the densities would be correctly related to the light-intensities, there is only one staircase which would fulfil the conditions laid down in our definition of a perfect negative by yielding a series of opacities proportional to the light-intensities.

*Time of Development and Density.*—The following illustration will further help to elucidate the influence of time of development upon the densities of a negative.   Suppose we submit three portions of a sensitive plate to the action of a standard light for 5, 20 and 80 seconds respectively, and that the plate is of that degree of sensitiveness that the resulting densities are rendered in their true proportionality (correctly exposed).   It will be found that the densities are related to each other as 1 : 2 : 3.

If we take a piece of elastic, represented by the line A B, secured at the end A, and if we stick through it three pins at distances of 1, 2 and 3 inches from A, the three pins will represent our three densities after a development of, say, 2 minutes.   If we now stretch the elastic, the pins will move further apart, as indicated at C D and E F, which may be considered to represent

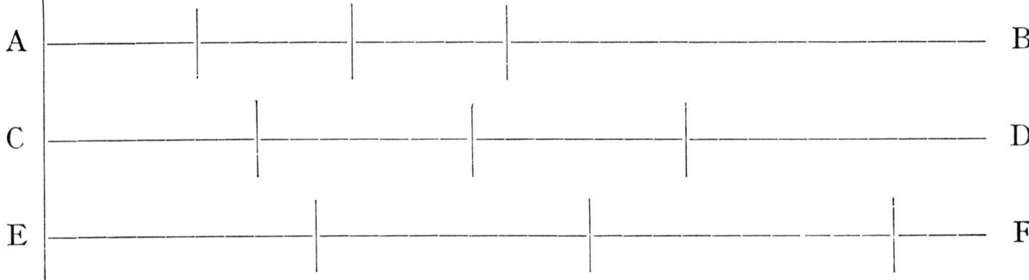

developments of 4 and 6 minutes respectively.   It will be seen from this that while by increased development we have increased the distance apart of the extreme densities, we have in no way interfered with the relationship existing between the three.

In the case of under-exposure, these densities would not be related to each other as 1 : 2 : 3, but more nearly as 1 : 4 : 16, and the light transmitted by them would consequently be false in gradation.   Prolonged development would merely stretch the densities further apart, but they would always retain their false relationship.   The same remark applies to over-exposure, though the false relationship would be different.   The experiment with the elastic and the pins will serve to illustrate the influence of time of development upon under-exposure by fixing the pins at distances of 1, 4 and 16 inches respectively from the point A.

These considerations lead to the conclusion that the function of exposure is to determine the relationship which shall exist between the densities and the light-intensities they represent; in other words, to determine into which portion of the characteristic curve the gradations of the negative shall fall. The function of development is, then, to determine, by its duration, the extreme range of opacities which the negative shall include.

*The Logical Conclusion.*—Our investigations forced us to the conclusion that the relationship existing between the densities and the light-intensities is, once for all, determined by the exposure, and remains unalterable by modifications in the constitution of the developer, or by the time occupied in development, and so led us to recognise the law of " Constant Density Ratios."

This conclusion, perhaps, did more than anything else to bring us into conflict with practical photographers. It had ever been held that errors in exposure could be corrected by judicious modifications in the constitution of the developer, or, in other words, that development could be made to usurp the function of exposure. Such views are, however, based upon empiricism, and entirely unsupported by quantitative methods of research. What gave rise to this popular opinion was, on the one hand, the employment of ammonia; and, on the other, the use of a soluble bromide in the developer. To the solvent action of ammonia upon silver bromide, and the facility with which it lends itself to the production of "fog," together with the apparent retarding action of a soluble bromide, the doctrine of corrective development is no doubt due ; but the disturbing effect of these reagents (especially of ammonia) upon the density ratios is altogether irregular, and does not admit of scientific control.

## THE LAW OF " CONSTANT DENSITY RATIOS "

has such an important bearing upon quantitative photography that it is very important that the reader should clearly grasp the subject. To this end the following practical example, taken from one of our earliest experiments, will probably be of assistance.

Three separate exposures were made upon different parts of a plate extending across its width. The exposures given were equivalent to $1\frac{1}{4}$, $2\frac{1}{2}$ and 5 seconds, the light used being that of a standard candle placed at a distance of 1 metre from the plate. The plate was then cut lengthways into three strips, each of them being impressed with the same three exposures. The three strips were next developed in the same solution for 4, 8 and 12 minutes respectively.

The second column gives the densities as measured by our photometer, the density due to glass and gelatine and any fog inherent in the film being deducted. It will be seen that the density increased for the same exposure as the time of development was prolonged. But the third column, which

| | 1 | 2 | 3 | 4 | 5 |
|---|---|---|---|---|---|
| | Exposure, C.M.S. | Density. | Density ratio. | Opacity. | Opacity ratio. |
| Strip No. 1 .. Developed .. 4 minutes .. | 1·25 2·5 5·0 | ·310 ·520 ·725 | 1·0 1·67 2·33 | 2·04 3·31 5·30 | 1·0 1·62 2·59 |
| Strip No. 2 .. Developed .. 8 minutes .. | 1·25 2·5 5·0 | ·530 ·905 1·235 | 1·0 1·70 2·33 | 3·38 8·03 17·18 | 1·0 2·37 5·08 |
| Strip No. 3 .. Developed .. 12 minutes .. | 1·25 2·5 5·0 | ·695 1·140 1·625 | 1·0 1·64 2·33 | 4·95 13·80 42·17 | 1·0 2·78 8·51 |

gives the ratio of the densities, shows that, within trifling errors of observation, the relationship between the three densities of each strip is identical ; that is to say, prolonged development caused each density to grow, but in such a manner that the amounts of silver on the different strips still bear the same ratio to each other.

It is this unalterable relationship which we refer to when we speak of " constant density ratios."

*An Important Difference.*—But, though the density ratios are constant, the opacities, which appeal directly to the eye, do alter, not only in amount, but in ratio also, as is shown by columns 4 and 5. In the first strip, for instance, the extreme opacities were 2·04 and 5·30 respectively, while, after 8 minutes' more development, the opacities became 4·95 and 42·17 respectively. The lightest shade in strip No. 3 is almost as opaque as the darkest in strip No. 1. The opacity ratios have also increased from as 1 : 2·59 to as 1 : 8·51.

It is this great difference in the *opacity* ratios, with which the practical photographer is so familiar, which led him to contradict our statements with respect to the constancy of the *density* ratios. The great mistake the photographer makes is in assuming that the opacity ratios are alterable at will. This is not so ; the opacity ratios alter in accordance with fixed laws, just as surely as, by the same laws, the density ratios are unalterable. All the control the photographer can therefore exercise in development must result from intelligibly working in obedience to these laws, and so rendering them subservient to his own ends.

*Control in Development.*—That control of the utmost importance exists in development has already been indicated, but such control is confined altogether to the length of time the developer is allowed to act, during which no modification whatever should be made in the constitution of the developer with the object of correcting an apparent error in exposure. If, owing to erroneous exposure, the gradations are false, no alteration in the constitution of the developer can make them true. Photographers, instead of striving to make their reagents play the part of light, should take more pains to expose their negatives correctly, and leave to development its legitimate function. Were it not that some of the most eminent photographers have so long accustomed us to the idea that errors in exposure admit of correction in development, it is probable that our conclusions would be regarded as a common-sense view of the subject. It must be borne in mind that photographers have formed their conclusions on this subject from mere ocular inspection of their negatives—generally negatives of objects produced in the camera in the ordinary way. We have, on the other hand, made all our investigations by submitting parts of a sensitive plate to the direct action of a standard light. This has permitted us to measure our results, and so provided us with numerical data wherewith to compare and estimate them. It has also enabled us to discriminate between action on the plate due to light and mere fog resulting either from the action of the developer or inherent in the plate itself.

*Dr. Emerson's Problem.*—The publication of our first paper awakened the interest of the well-known photographer, Dr. Emerson, who submitted the following problem to us for consideration, and, as it may still further assist the reader to grasp the distinction which exists between the functions of exposure and development, I propose to state the question propounded, and to give a few extracts from our reply :—

" Supposing," said Dr. Emerson, " I want to photograph three houses —a white one, a grey one and a black one. What is it you say I have to do to secure truthful rendering of tone ? What is it you say I can alter by development, and what is it I cannot alter ? "

*Its Solution.*—In reply, we proceeded to discuss the subject under the three heads of under-, correct- and over-exposure, and we assumed that we had taken three negatives of the houses on separate but similar plates, and that they had received exposure of $\frac{1}{10}$, 1 and 10 seconds respectively. The subject was illustrated by Fig. 4, on which the three houses are represented by dots.

## I. Under-exposure.

If the exposure given have been insufficient, the three equidistant lines B1, G1, W1, may mark the light-intensities reflected by the three houses, which, for the sake of argument, we will take as 5 for the black, 20 for the grey and 80 for the white. What we affirm is that any alteration, either in time of development or in constitution of the developer, will decide upon which of the system of curves the respective densities shall lie—whether, for example, on the lower or upper curve shown on the diagram. It would be possible, even in a case of under-exposure, aided by an experienced eye, so to develop that something akin to a correct relationship between the two extreme densities might result, but the density of the intermediate tone would be relatively false, the density representing the grey house too closely approaching that of the black house.

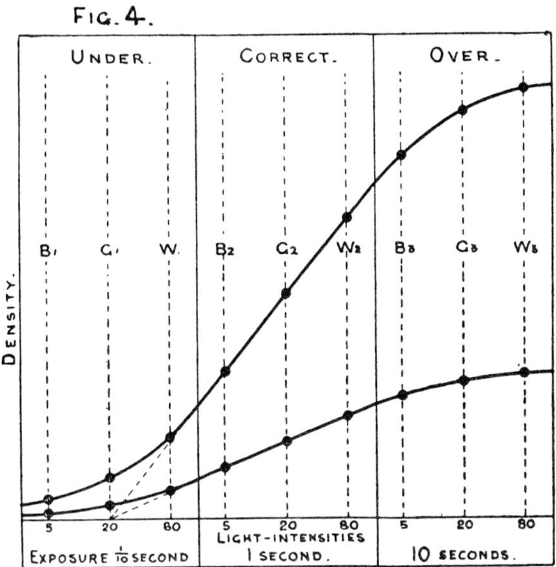


If the degree of under-exposure has been very decided the ratios of the amounts of silver deposited would be as $1 : 4 : 16$ (*i.e.*, as $5 : 20 : 80$), however long development might be continued. But when the amount of silver is in the same ratio as the light reflected by the objects, the opacities of the images will produce prints false in tone, and this false relation being established by the peculiar form of the curve, the photographer has no power to alter it.

The opacity varies with the development, but it varies according to law. The photographer cannot cause the opacity of the white house to grow without that of the black house growing with it, in accordance with a fixed law indicated by the system of curves.


## II. Correct Exposure.

If a longer (correct) exposure be given, the ratio of the silver deposited will be altogether different from that we have just considered. Instead of the silver being deposited in the ratio of the light-intensities $5 : 20 : 80$, it will be deposited in the ratio of the logarithms of these intensities. With these particular intensities ($5 : 20 : 80$), this would mean that the difference between the amounts of silver representing the white and grey houses is the same as the difference between the amounts of silver representing the grey and black houses.

Different treatment in development would result in different amounts of silver deposited, though their ratio would remain undisturbed, but any increase in density in the white house would result in a corresponding increase of density in the black and grey houses, in such a manner as to bring the three points on the lines B2, G2, W2, simultaneously from a lower to a higher curve. The photographer has the power to decide how far he will allow the density of the white house to proceed, but he cannot restrain the density of the black house while he allows that of the white house to increase.

Among the infinity of curves which are intermediate between the axis of the abscissæ and the extreme curve there is only one which would correspond to a negative from which a print true to nature could be obtained. It is the decision of this curve which is the difficulty in development. When this curve is reached, however, the opacities of the three gradations representing the three houses would be exactly as 5 : 20 : 80, the ratio of the light reflected by the houses.

### III. OVER-EXPOSURE.

In the case of unduly prolonged exposure the images of the three houses would fall on the upper part of the curve where intersected, say, by the lines B3, G3, W3. The result of this would be that the tone of the grey house would too nearly approach that of the white house ; whilst, in the case of under-exposure, it too nearly approached that of the black one. You might, by development, decide the density of one of the houses, but it would be out of your power to alter its relationship with respect to the other two.

EXPOSURE decides within which of the three periods (under-, correct- or over-exposure) the three houses shall lie.

DEVELOPMENT decides which curve of the system shall be reached.

### THE DEVELOPMENT FACTOR.

To the exact amount of development a negative receives we apply a numerical value. This value we term the " development factor," and it is determined by the inclination of the straight portion of the characteristic curve.

The importance of expressing the degree of development by a definite numerical value, and the advantage of such a system over the present method of comparison by crude generalisations, can hardly need pointing out. It is surely more scientific to state that the development factor of this negative is 0·8, and of that, 1·5, than to speak of them as being relatively " thin " and " dense," and, besides, there are all the possible degrees of development within and beyond these limits which call for differentiation. As the desired development factor is reached simply by controlling the time occupied in the operation, there is no occasion whatever to examine a negative during the progress of development. It may straightway be fixed the moment the time has expired. This consideration is of special importance in the case of orthochromatic plates, during the development of which examination by any serviceable light is unsafe.

*Modifying the " D.F."*—The method of assigning a numerical value to the degree of development will be explained later on, but it may be here stated that when this value is 1·0 the gradations of the negative are absolutely true to nature. This statement, however, requires some qualification in practical photography. Inasmuch as the negative is not the ultimate object we have in view, but the print which it is intended to yield, the nature of the desired print exercises considerable influence upon the development factor of the negative. Photographers have learned by experience that a certain negative will yield a more satisfactory print by the carbon or platinum process than it will, say, on a silver paper. This is because different papers vary in the range of gradation which they are capable of rendering. A silver print on highly-enamelled paper is more brilliant and has a more extended range of gradation than a silver print on matt paper, owing to the greater transparency of its image. By the range of gradation of a particular paper is meant the extreme difference of tone, ranging from the normal tint of the paper itself to the deepest shade it is capable of assuming, beyond which no deeper can be differentiated by reflected light. The range of the paper upon which we intend to print is therefore a factor in determining the degree of development of the negative, and this is further influenced by the range of light-intensities reflected by the subject we wish to photograph. This latter range varies considerably, that of an ordinary open landscape being probably the least, and that of a dark interior, including a window in the picture, probably the greatest met with in ordinary practice. The development factor, therefore, for an interior requires to be less than that for an open landscape, in order to adapt their respective light-intensities to the range of the paper upon which the print is to be made. It is probable that the positive which most truthfully reproduces the gradations of the negative, particularly when the range is extensive, is a transparency on a glass plate.

The question as to whether a negative is required for the production of contact prints, or for the purpose of enlarging, say, on bromide paper, also affects the development factor. For reasons which cannot be fully explained here the optical value of a given density is totally different under the two conditions. In the case of an enlargement much of the light passing through the negative is lost by reflection from the surface of the paper and consequently does no work at all, while in the case of a contact print a considerable portion of the light reflected from the surface of the paper is at once reflected back again by the two reflecting surfaces of the negative. For the purpose of enlarging, the densities of a negative are practically much greater than for the purpose of contact printing, and a less development factor is consequently demanded. Roughly a photometric density of $1 \cdot 0$ corresponds with a contact printing density of $0 \cdot 8$ and an enlarging density of $1 \cdot 4$.

Another matter which materially affects the development factor is the artistic aspect of the question. We cannot look around the walls of our photographic exhibitions without being struck with the straining after effects, which certainly cannot be characterised as true to nature. It is not my province to criticise work of this kind, but to point out that a scientific knowledge of the functions of exposure and development, and a determination of the characteristic curves of the plates he uses, will place the photographer who wishes to produce abnormal results in a position to do so, with the certainty of achieving the end he has in view. If he desire a false gradation he may deliberately include portions of the periods of under or over-exposure in his negative, and the effect produced by a departure from correct exposure may be further influenced by the development factor employed.

It is not within the scope of this work to show how the range of different printing papers and of the light-intensities reflected by different classes of subjects enable one to calculate the exact development factor required in any given case. My immediate object is to impress the photographer with the great advantage of being able to express and compare the degree of development of his negatives by definite numerical values ; to show how the development factor may be controlled, and thus assist him to produce negatives of the precise quality he desires.

As a rough initial guide to those about to put our system into practice, the following values may be indicated for the development factors of negatives for the production of contact prints :—

| | |
|---|---|
| Ordinary landscapes | $1 \cdot 3$ |
| Interiors | $1 \cdot 0$ |
| Portraits | $0 \cdot 8$ |

### STANDARD LIGHT AND UNIT OF EXPOSURE.

When we commenced our investigations we adopted as our unit of light the intensity of the light yielded by a standard candle acting at a distance of one metre, and, as our unit of time, the second ; our unit of exposure is therefore the product of the intensity of the light of a standard candle at a distance of one metre and of the second, and this unit we termed one " candle-metre-second " (C.M.S.).   While we quite recognised that the candle is by no means an ideal standard, we adopted it, in the first instance, because we were not aware of any better substitute, because it was ready to our hand, recognised as a standard and readily obtained.   It is necessary, however, to exercise control over the height of flame of the candle.   The height should be exactly 45 millimetres from the tip of the flame to that portion of the wick where blackening commences.   This height of flame is readily obtained by judicious trimming of the wick, and, when once attained, it will remain constant sufficiently long for any ordinary experiment.

Our adoption of the candle as our standard light does not at all imply that no other standard light may be employed.   Any source of light may be adopted for the purpose of speed determination ; but, as the candle-metre-second is the unit of exposure decided upon, any source of light other than the candle will require to be carefully standardised to the candle itself.   This must not be done by ordinary photometric means, but by actual measurement of the work done upon a sensitive plate by the two lights to be compared, otherwise speed determinations made by different operators would not yield comparable results.   In my own practice I frequently find it more convenient to use an amyl-acetate lamp than the candle ; but in this case a correction has to be applied, my amyl-acetate lamp being $1\cdot4$ times less actinic than the candle.   The Dibdin standard pentane lamp has also been adopted by some plate manufacturers in this country (England).

Another obvious precaution to be taken in using the candle, or, indeed, any other standard light, is that it must be carefully protected against draughts.

### STANDARD DEVELOPER.

As the activity of the various reagents employed as developers differs considerably, it is necessary to adopt a standard developer for the purpose of speed determination, if the results obtained by different operators are to be comparable.   To the amateur, however, who employs our system simply for his own guidance, it is quite open, of course, to employ any developer he thinks fit, but he must clearly understand that the speeds he obtains will not necessarily correspond with those obtained with our standard.

*Pyro-soda.*—As the result of our earlier investigations we decided in favour of ferrous oxalate as our standard developer, and an excellent standard it is from many points of view. It has, however, never been a popular developer, and it has the drawback of being considerably less energetic than alkaline pyrogallol. After further investigation, therefore, we decided to employ a pyro-soda developer as our standard, satisfying ourselves that it possessed the requisite qualifications. At the same time we found it necessary to reprobate as strongly as possible the use of pyro-ammonia. Owing to the solvent action of ammonia upon silver bromide the behaviour of this developer is so irregular as to render it altogether inapplicable for work of a scientific character.

The formula of our standard pyro-soda developer is as follows :—1,000 parts of developer contain

|  | Parts. |
|---|---|
| Pyrogallol.. | 8 |
| Sodium carbonate (recrystallised) | 40 |
| Sodium sulphite | 40 |

Perhaps the best way of compounding this developer is to keep the sodium carbonate and sulphite in a solution of convenient strength, and to add the pyrogallol dry immediately prior to development, together with the requisite amount of water over and above that in which the carbonate and sulphite are dissolved. If preferred, however, the pyrogallol may be made up in solution together with the sulphite, the carbonate being kept in solution by itself. In any case the best plan is to keep the solutions in small bottles, each containing, say, 4 ounces, filled up to the neck and tightly corked.

It will probably be remarked that the quantity of pyrogallol is much larger than the quantity usually recommended. The amount given was, however, decided upon after careful investigation. Developers act in two ways—by direct absorption into the film and by a process of diffusion. Unless there be present in the quantity of developer directly absorbed by the film sufficient of the reducing agent to reduce the whole of the silver salt necessary to form the image, the higher densities will fall short and the correct period of the plate will be, in consequence, curtailed. The quantity of pyrogallol recommended, therefore, is calculated to make the best of the plate. Ferrous oxalate is a developer which acts by diffusion, the film being incapable of directly absorbing sufficient of this reagent to complete the operation of development. From this point of view it is inferior to pyro-soda containing the amount of pyrogallol prescribed. As, however, our standard pyro-soda developer is very energetic in the case of some plates, and as it may be considered desirable to prolong the time of development, the photographer may, if he think fit in his ordinary practice, reduce the strength to one-half that of the standard given.  Beyond this the strength should certainly not be reduced, or a serious falling-off in the higher densities will result.

*Free Bromide in the Developer.*—It will be noted that our standard formula does not include a bromide as one of its constituents.  This omission is of the utmost importance, and must be insisted upon, at any rate, when determining the speed of a plate.   While the pyrogallol and the alkali are essential elements of the developer, a bromide is altogether unessential.  It is a product of the chemical change which takes place during the process of development, and it is well known in chemical dynamics that the products of a reaction generally retard the speed of the reaction.  This is precisely what occurs when development takes place in the presence of free bromide—an apparent retardation in the speed of the plate ; but that this retardation is only apparent is shown by the fact that it can be compensated by time of development.  The result of this is that a plate developed in the presence of a bromide has practically different speeds, depending upon the length of time the plate is developed. Hence bromide has a seriously disturbing effect upon speed determination, and interferes considerably with the practice of photography by quantitative methods.  I shall have occasion to say more upon the influence of bromide when we come to consider the subject of speed determination.

*Standard Temperature.*—It is hardly necessary to point out that development must be conducted under standard conditions as regards temperature. As a temperature which may be readily commanded both summer and winter, we decided upon 65° Fahr.  The development dishes I recommended may be conveniently constructed of ordinary tinned iron plate, and made to suit the dimensions of any plate desired.  The dish has flanges at either end, which rest upon the edges of an outer water-bath, also of tin plate, and which may, with advantage in very cold weather, be protected by some non-conducting material. In use the outer bath is filled up with water at 65° to such a level as to allow the bottom of the developing dish to rest upon the surface of the water. The exposed plate should be placed in the dish and covered up sufficiently long before the developer is applied to allow it to assume the requisite temperature.   The vessels containing the developer must likewise be allowed, by immersion in a water-bath, to acquire the standard temperature.   During development the dish should be gently rocked.  As we are no longer dependent upon ocular examination to determine when development is complete but decide this all-important question by time alone, the plate should be removed from the developer a second or two before the requisite time has elapsed, and the moment the time has expired it should be rapidly passed through a dish of water and then straight into the fixing-bath.

*Special Apparatus.*—Before we proceed to determine the speed and other characteristics of a plate it is necessary to provide ourselves with two special instruments—one for exposing strips of the plate to be examined and one to measure the densities of the deposits developed on the strips. In their essentials these instruments are exceedingly simple, and may readily be constructed by any amateur at all accustomed to the use of tools.

### THE EXPOSING APPARATUS.

When, in our original researches, we wished to make a series of exposures upon a plate, we made them successively. As, however, eight or nine exposures are necessary in determining the speed of a plate, we found that to make a separate exposure for each gradation involved a considerable amount of time, and, not only so, but any trifling variation in the luminosity of the candle flame made itself felt. We overcame these objections by employing a revolving disc, so perforated as to yield, with a single exposure, the whole series of gradations required. By this means also any trifling fluctuation in the light proportionately affects all the gradations.

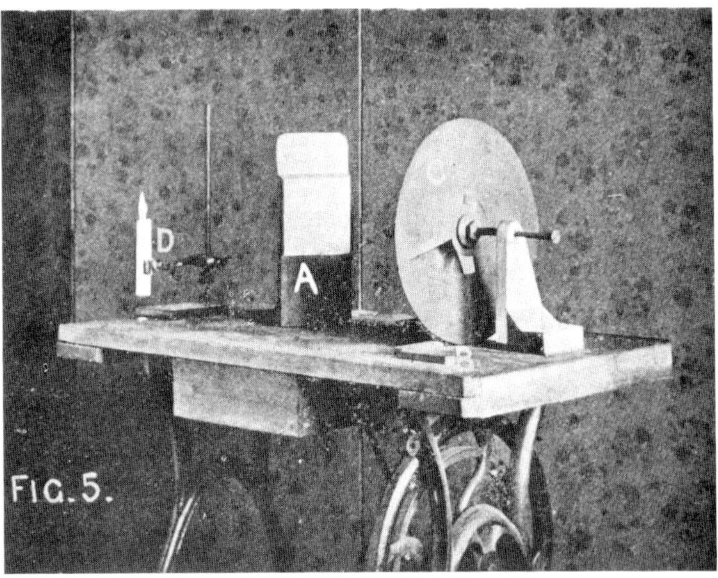


Fig. 5 represents the first revolving disc apparatus we constructed. It will be seen that an old sewing machine table was called into requisition so as to permit the disc to be driven by foot, thus leaving the hands free to operate the shutter of the dark slide containing the strips of sensitive plate. The front of the dark slide is shown at A, the shutter being constructed of thin metal so that when the slide is placed in position at B the sensitive strips will be as close as possible to the revolving disc C.  D is the standard candle fixed at a distance of one metre from the surface of the sensitive strips.

The dimensions we adopted for the strip of plate to be used for the purpose of speed determination are $4\frac{1}{4}$ by $1\frac{3}{16}$ inches, being the length of a quarter-plate by one-fourth of its width, a quarter-plate thus cutting into four strips.   The dark slide is constructed to take two such strips, lying, of course, horizontally.

It may be here mentioned that if one of the edges of a quarter-plate show a falling off in the coating of emulsion the strip including such an edge should always be discarded ; indeed, the best possible course is to cut the strips from the centre portion of a larger-sized plate.

We must now consider the most important detail of the apparatus, namely, the revolving disc.  This is separately represented in Fig. 6, which is a photograph of a disc constructed of a piece of cardboard, 11 inches in

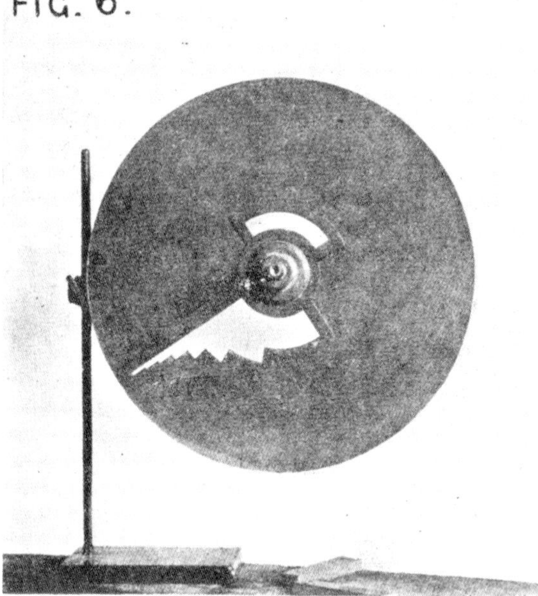



diameter.  The length of the strip ($4\frac{1}{4}$ inches) divided into ten equal parts, gives the width of each successive step in the perforations of the disc.  Nine parts only are, however, required for the exposures, the tenth being protected from light in the dark slide during the exposure, so as to provide what we term the " fog strip." It will readily be seen how the angular apertures of the perforations are arranged to yield a series of exposures, each being double the preceding one. The longest exposure is represented by an angular aperture of 180°, obtained by cutting out two entire quadrants of the circle ; the next by an angular aperture of 90°, or one quadrant ; the next of 45°, and so on, the angular aperture of each successive perforation being halved till the ninth is reached.

The apertures in the disc, of course, require to be cut with the greatest precision, as any inaccuracy in the angular openings would necessarily disturb the ratio of the exposures. The disc itself may be constructed of any suitable material, of which sheet zinc and ebonite may be mentioned. Such a material is undoubtedly superior to cardboard where frequent use is demanded or rough handling is incurred. Nevertheless, the cardboard disc shown in the illustration has been in use for upwards of ten years, and is still in perfect order. Should cardboard be decided upon, the simplest way of cutting the perforations is to cut in the cardboard itself two openings decidedly larger than the finished dimensions of the apertures. The apertures themselves are accurately cut in two pieces of stiff paper or very thin cardboard of fine, hard texture, and these pieces are then fixed by means of an adhesive in their proper positions over the openings already cut in the disc.[1] The disc, when finished, should be coated with dead-black paint and mounted upon a central spindle. The rapidity at which the disc is caused to revolve is not of material importance, but 500 revolutions per minute may be indicated as a convenient speed.

## THE PHOTOMETER.

This instrument, which is illustrated in Figs. 7, 8 and 9, consists essentially of a small Bunsen photometer, and is based upon the relationship existing between density and opacity. We measure the opacity of the deposit, but, in order to avoid calculations and references to tables of logarithms, the scale of the instrument is so arranged as to read directly the logarithm of the opacity, which is the density.

The body of the instrument consists of a box constructed of timber, the front side being open and splayed outward at the top and two sides so as to protect the eyes from light while making measurements. Convenient internal dimensions of the box itself are 12 inches long, 9 inches high and 7 inches deep. At either end of the box is a diaphragm of 6 millimetres diameter, and outside. as close as possible to the diaphragm, is a powerful duplex paraffin lamp.

---

[1] The disc and Photometers are in the H. and D. Collection at the Royal Photographic Society.

The two lamps may be, with advantage, attached, as shown, to the same oil-container, which passes beneath the baseboard of the instrument, the height

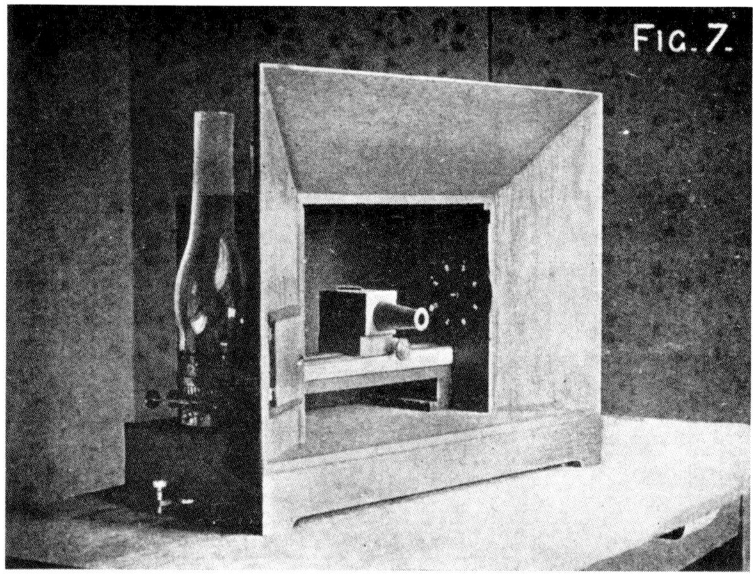


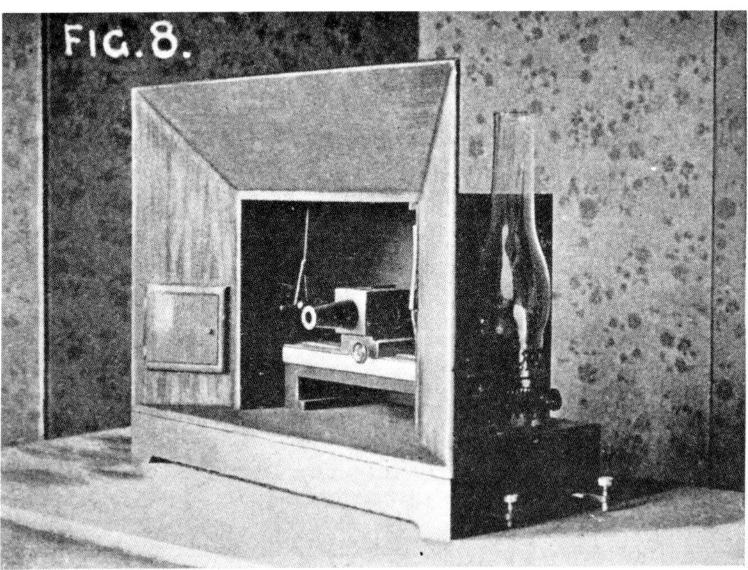


of the container admitting of adjustment by means of three levelling screws. The diaphragms, which must be exactly in the line of the axis of the instrument, are drilled in sheets of copper, which fit inside the ends of the instrument. As the heat evolved by the lamps is considerable, it is necessary to protect

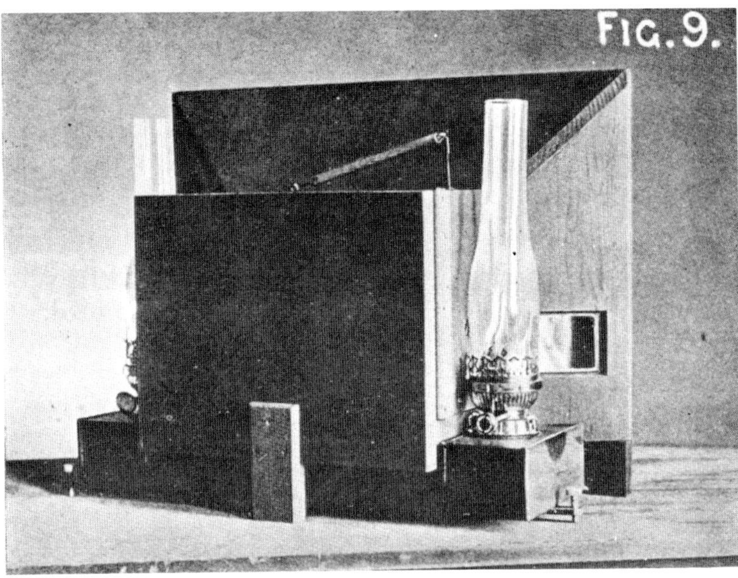


the woodwork by means of asbestos millboard. The method of doing this is shown in Fig. 10, which is a section through the axis of the photometer. As much as possible of the timber at the ends of the box should be cut away and the openings filled in with the millboard, thinner pieces of the same material entirely covering the outside of the ends, and also the splayed front on the lamp side. The whole of the instrument, excepting, of course, the scale, should be painted dead-black.

Should the intending constructor be disposed to substitute for the duplex paraffin lamp any other source of illumination, it will be well here to caution him against the use of burners of the argand type. A circular flame, such as an argand burner has, would give utterly erroneous results. The whole principle of the photometer depends upon the use of a flat sheet of flame of such a size that, at whatever distance the indicating grease spot may be from the lamp, the angle determined by the diameter of the diaphragm, with the grease spot as the apex, must be uniformly covered by the flame. It is therefore very necessary that the lamp wicks be kept carefully trimmed, and this is best done by wiping away the charred wick with a piece of rag, the corners of the wick being rounded off with scissors. The lamps should always be allowed to burn about ten minutes before any readings are taken, so as to allow them to become steady.   In adjusting the flames of the lamps the operator should always view them through a piece of green glass, as gazing at the naked light would unfit the eye for the delicate work of deciding the grease spot indications.

The construction of the small chamber containing the indicating grease spot is clearly shown on Fig. 10.   The chamber itself is a small box measuring 2 inches by $1\frac{1}{2}$ inches inside.   The grease spot is inserted through a slit in the centre of the upper side of the chamber, at the back of which are cemented, at a suitable angle, two small mirrors, in which reflections of the grease spot from either side may be viewed through an eye-piece fitted to the front of the chamber.   The eye-piece may be with advantage provided with a simple magnifying lens of suitable focal length, but this is not essential.   On either side of the chamber a circular hole is bored of about $\frac{3}{4}$-inch diameter, these

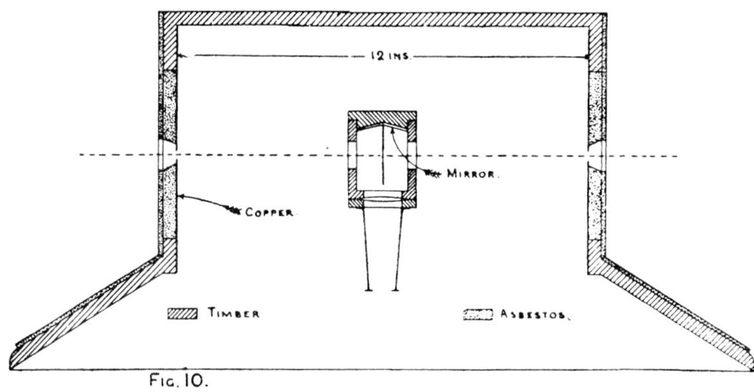


Fig. 10.

holes and the grease spot lying, of course, in the axis of the instrument.   The back of the chamber carrying the mirrors should be made detachable.   The chamber is carried upon a small block of timber which slides upon a carriage extending the whole length of the instrument.   This block may be conveniently moved backward and forward (as shown in Figs. 7 and 8) by a rack fixed on the carriage and a pinion on the block, or, if preferred, the motion may be obtained by a cord fixed to the block and passing over pulleys at either end of the carriage, the pulley at the right-hand side being fitted with a spindle provided with a milled head.   The block carrying the grease-spot chamber is provided with a pointer fixed in the centre and reaching downward to the divisions on the scale of the instrument.

We must now proceed to consider two very important details of the photometer, namely, the grease spot and the scale.

*The Grease Spot.*—To make a satisfactory grease spot requires a little practice and the selection of a suitable paper. The paper should be fairly thin and unglazed, and while it should not be too bibulous, it should not be too hard and impervious. Having found a satisfactory quality, melt a little solid paraffin wax in a suitable vessel; next warm the end of a fine wire in the flame of a spirit lamp, dip it quickly into the melted paraffin, and just touch the paper with it. This should produce a spot about one millimetre in diameter. It is just as well to produce a number of such spots—say, one inch apart—over the surface of the paper, and afterward to select the best spots for the purpose in view. As it is necessary that the appearance of the spot on both sides of the paper shall be similar, the paper must now be turned over and dots of melted paraffin placed exactly over the first spots.

It may here be explained that the less pronounced the grease spot the more sensitive it is ; but, on the other hand, the less capable it is of indicating high densities. The reverse holds good in the case of a very translucent grease-spot. While it is quite possible to hit a happy mean, it will often be found convenient, in the case of very high densities, to resort to the use of a specially translucent spot. If a superabundance of paraffin has been deposited upon the spot, or if it be desired to render the spot less pronounced, the paper bearing the spot may be placed between two sheets of blotting paper and a warm flat-iron lightly applied.

Having selected the most satisfactory grease-spots, they should be cut out of the sheet of paper, each spot being the centre of a disc of, say, one inch in diameter. Each disc must now be gummed in between two pieces of matt black paper, into both of which a circular opening of about $\frac{3}{8}$ inch diameter has been cut. The grease-spot, of course, occupies exactly the centre of the openings in the matt black paper, and the whole must be so trimmed as to bring the grease-spot accurately into the axial line of the photometer when placed in position in the little chamber.

*The Scale.*—Before discussing the scale of the instrument it must be clearly understood that its divisions are absolutely determined by the distance between the diaphragms in the ends of the photometer. The data here given are for an instrument of which this dimension is 12 inches. It will, therefore, be seen that this measurement must be most accurately adhered to.

The zero point of the scale is exactly midway between the diaphragms in the two ends of the photometer, or exactly 6 inches from either diaphragm. On either side of the zero point the scale is symmetrical. For the purpose of constructing the scale the distances from the zero point to the chief divisions (·1, ·2, ·3, ·4, etc.) lying symmetrically on either side of it are given in the following table :—

| Value of division. | Distance from zero point. | Value of division. | Distance from zero point. |
|---|---|---|---|
| | Inches. | | Inches. |
| 0·1 | 0·342 | 1·0 | 3·114 |
| 0·2 | 0·684 | 1·1 | 3·360 |
| 0·3 | 1·026 | 1·2 | 3·594 |
| 0·4 | 1·356 | 1·3 | 3·804 |
| 0·5 | 1·680 | 1·4 | 4·002 |
| 0·6 | 1·992 | 1·5 | 4·188 |
| 0·7 | 2·292 | 1·6 | 4·356 |
| 0·8 | 2·580 | 1·7 | 4·512 |
| 0·9 | 2·856 | 1·8 | 4·656 |

The values of the divisions may be marked on the scale as here given, but in this case the values to the right hand of the zero point must be considered as negative and those to the left as positive. It will, however, simplify reading the densities if the division 1·8 at the extreme right-hand of the scale be regarded and marked as 0 (zero), the succeeding divisions being marked ·1, ·2, ·3, ·4, etc., proceeding up to 3·6 for the final division on the left-hand of the scale. In this case the true zero of the scale will be marked 1·8. This plan being adopted, we have merely to deduct the smaller from the greater reading in order to determine the density. The main divisions of the scale should be further divided into five equal parts, the value of each subdivision being 0·02.

At the right-hand end of the instrument it will be seen that a rotating disc is provided which is perforated with a number of supplementary diaphragms, gradually increasing in diameter from that of the fixed 6 millimetre diaphragm in the end of the photometer itself. In practice, however, three additional diaphragms will be found quite sufficient. They should be approximately equal in reducing the light to densities of 0·5, 1·0 and 1·5. If the diameter of the fixed diaphragm be accurately 6 millimetres, the diameters of the three diaphragms in question will be 3·37, 1·90 and 1·07 millimetres respectively. To these dimensions the diaphragms should be as nearly as possible drilled, but their absolute accuracy is immaterial, as their real values will be determined by trial in the photometer itself, as will be explained later.

At the left-hand end of the photometer is a forked clip, for the purpose of holding the strip of plate during measurement. This clip is pivoted on the top of the photometer, and the necessary pressure is applied by a spiral spring. On the left-hand side of the splayed front of the instrument, and on about the same level as the scale, a small hinged door is provided, a mirror being attached thereto on the lamp side. The object of this mirror is to illuminate the scale by opening the door when observing the readings.

*The Photometer in Use.*—Having described the photometer, it will be well at this point to indicate the manner of its use. We will therefore assume that we are about to measure the densities of two gradations developed upon a strip of plate. The lamps having been lighted and allowed to become quite steady, we adjust the position of the grease-spot chamber till the two images of the grease-spot reflected in the small mirrors are exactly similar. The pointer now indicates on a scale the neutral or equality point from which all measurements are calculated. If the diaphragms in the end of the photometer be of exactly equal value, and the two lamps of exactly equal luminosity, the neutral point will be the true zero of the instrument, marked 1·8 on the scale. This is, however, very unlikely to be the case and is quite immaterial ; indeed, it is distinctly desirable to make the diaphragm in the left-hand end of the photometer a shade larger than that in the right, purposely to bring the neutral point nearer the right-hand side. This gives a longer range of direct readings, and avoids unnecessary recourse to the supplementary diaphragms. Suppose, therefore, that we find the neutral point, indicating the position of the grease spot when equally illuminated on both sides, to be 1·4. We next slightly warm the strip of plate and bring the gradation we wish to measure opposite the diaphragm on the left-hand side of the instrument, where it is held by the forked clip. If we now examine the images of the grease-spot, we shall find that they are dissimilar and that it is necessary to move the little chamber over to the left in order to restore equality. The point indicated on the scale at which equality is restored gives us a second reading, say, 2·9, and all we have to do to determine the density is to deduct the first from the second reading : thus, 2·9 — 1·4 = 1·5, which is the total density of the gradation measured.

We next bring the second gradation opposite the left-hand diaphragm, and we will assume that its density is materially greater than that of the former gradation. We now find that, though we move the grease-spot chamber to the left as far as it will go, we are unable to restore equality. In this case we make use of the largest supplementary diaphragm (value, say, 0·5) at the right-hand end of the photometer, when we are enabled to restore equality by turning the grease-spot chamber back again to the right. Taking 1·4 as the neutral point as before, and supposing that, on inserting the supplementary diaphragm, we obtain a reading on the scale of 3·4, we again deduct the smaller from the greater reading, but, in this case, we must add the value of the diaphragm. Thus, 3·4 — 1·4 + 0·5 = 2·5, the total density of the gradation. Of course, in the case of still higher densities, it will be necessary to resort to the use of the smaller diaphragms.

The determination of the value of the supplementary diaphragms is made as follows :—Ascertain the neutral point on the scale when the grease-spot is illuminated by light passing through the fixed diaphragms of the photometer ; then bring one of the supplementary diaphragms into position and take the reading when equality is restored by moving the chamber to the right. The difference of the two readings is the value of the diaphragm. In finally deciding the value, it will be well to take the mean of, say, half a dozen readings.

While the photometer, as described, is quite sufficient to meet the requirements of the amateur, the plate-manufacturer employing our system of speed determination may with advantage substitute the Schmidt and Haensch indicator for the grease-spot. Owing to its greater sensitiveness, it expedites the work of reading, but its adoption necessitates a photometer 20 inches instead of 12 inches long.

SPEED DETERMINATION.

*Exposure.*—We are now in a position to determine the speed and other characteristics of a plate. Having cut a strip of the plate to be tested and placed it in the dark slide, we proceed to make the exposure behind the revolving disc. If we have a rough clue as to whether the plate be rapid or slow, a little experience will guide us in determining the best exposure to give ; but in the case of a plate of which we have no clue to the speed, 40 C.M.S. may be taken as the longest exposure of the series. A little consideration of the revolving disc will, however, show that, in order to obtain an effective maximum exposure of 40 C.M.S., it will be necessary to continue the exposure for twice 40, or for 80 C.M.S. The reason for this is that the effective exposure only proceeds during half the revolution of the disc, the light only reaching the plate during the passage across it of 180° out of the 360°. An actual exposure of 80 C.M.S. will therefore give us a series of nine effective exposures, ranging from 40 C.M.S. to 0·156 C.M.S. Though it is preferable to work with the candle at a distance of one metre from the plate, it might be desirable, in order to curtail the exposure, in the case of a very slow plate, to place the candle at a distance of 0·707 of a metre from the plate, the light of the candle at this distance being equal to that of two candles at one metre, and thus halving the exposure. The exposure is made by drawing and closing the shutter of the dark slide, the disc being caused to revolve before the exposure commences and kept steadily revolving during its continuance.

*Development.*—Having impressed the strip of plate with its series of nine exposures, we next proceed to develop it, carefully observing the precautions already laid down. A little experience will be required to judge the best time for continuing development, which varies, of course, with different plates. While the densities of the gradations should be well marked, the higher densities should not be allowed to grow too dense, otherwise there will be difficulty in measuring them. A good development factor to aim at is $1 \cdot 0$ or thereabouts. However long the time occupied in development, it should be carefully noted. After development the strip is fixed and washed in the ordinary way, and it is well to wipe the surface of the film gently with a plug of wetted cotton wool. If time be an object, a very short washing will suffice, and the drying of the strip may be hastened by means of alcohol. When dry the back of the strip should be thoroughly cleansed from any emulsion marks and the film wiped with a soft cloth. The dividing lines between the gradations should be strengthened with a pen and ink, as this will materially assist the operator in adjusting the strip in the photometer afterwards.

*Measuring and Recording Densities.*—Following the instructions already given, there will be no difficulty in measuring the densities of the series of gradations. In the examples of measurements submitted, however, it was expressly stated that they represented the *total* densities. By this is meant not only the density of the deposit resulting from the exposure, but also the density due to the glass and gelatine, and to any incipient fog. For our purpose it is necessary to ascertain the density of the deposit due to the exposure alone. We must, therefore, eliminate from each measurement such amount of density as is due to glass, gelatine and fog. It is with this object that we protect one-tenth of the strip from light. This portion of the strip we term the " fog-strip." In order to obtain the net densities resulting from the exposures alone we proceed as follows :—The neutral or equality point having been ascertained, we bring the fog strip over the left-hand diaphragm of the photometer, and restore equality by moving the grease-spot chamber to the left, the difference between the readings giving the density due to glass, gelatine and fog.

The following practical example taken from my note-book will show the method of recording the readings obtained in the photometer, and make what has been said more readily understood. In this example it will be noted that the exposures given ranged from $0 \cdot 312$ C.M.S. to 80 C.M.S. and that the developer used was ferrous oxalate :—

| | |
|---|---|
| Neutral point | $1 \cdot 740$ |
| Fog point | $1 \cdot 960$ |
| Fog (difference) | $0 \cdot 220$ |

| Exposure, C.M.S. | Reading. | Net density. 1·960 deducted. | |
|---|---|---|---|
| 0·312 | 2·110 | 0·150 | |
| 0·625 | 2·235 | 0·275 | |
| 1·25 | 2·400 | 0·440 | |
| 2·5 | 2·660 | 0·700 | |
| 5· | 3·000 | 1·040 | |
| 10· | 3·320 | 1·360 | |
| 20· | 3·090 | 1·665 | 0·535 added |
| 40· | 3·360 | 1·935 | ,,　,, |
| 80· | 3·220 | 2·160 | 0·900 added |

Developer : Standard ferrous oxalate. Developed : 7 minutes at 65° Fahr. Development factor : 1·06. Inertia : 0·54. Speed : 63.

In measuring the densities due to the 20 and 40 C.M.S. exposures it was necessary to resort to a supplementary diaphragm (value 0·535), and the density due to the 80 C.M.S. exposure required a still smaller diaphragm (value 0·900).

It will be seen that the density due to glass, gelatine and incipient fog (all included in the term " fog ") is obtained by deducting the neutral from the fog reading. The first column gives the series of effective exposures resulting from a single actual exposure of 160 C.M.S. The second column gives the reading of each gradation as indicated on the scale of the photometer, and the third column is the difference between the values given in the second column and the value of the fog point, or the net density resulting from the exposure alone.

*Obtaining the Characteristic Curve.*—The next step is to plot the measurements thus obtained, and so determine the characteristic curve of the plate. For this purpose the best plan is to employ lithographed skeleton diagrams or charts as illustrated in Fig. 11, but, if preferred, the skeleton form may be scratched on a piece of slate, and the curve plotted with a slate pencil. Fig. 11 is produced from one of our lithographed charts, and the curve resulting from the measurements just given is plotted thereon. The horizontal or " inertia " scale of the chart may be constructed from the scale of an ordinary slide rule, the scale, however, being repeated four times instead of twice. The density scale on the left-hand, and the development factor scale on the right, are precisely alike as regards their divisions and values. The vertical measurement of these scales from 0 to 1·0 should exactly correspond with one length of the inertia scale, say, from 10 to 100, or from 100 to 1,000 ; the graphic determination of a development factor of 1·0 will then be represented by an angle of 45°. Vertical equidistant exposure lines are drawn at the points 0·156, 0·312, 0·625, 1·25, &c., and they are conveniently divided so as to facilitate the plotting of the densities.

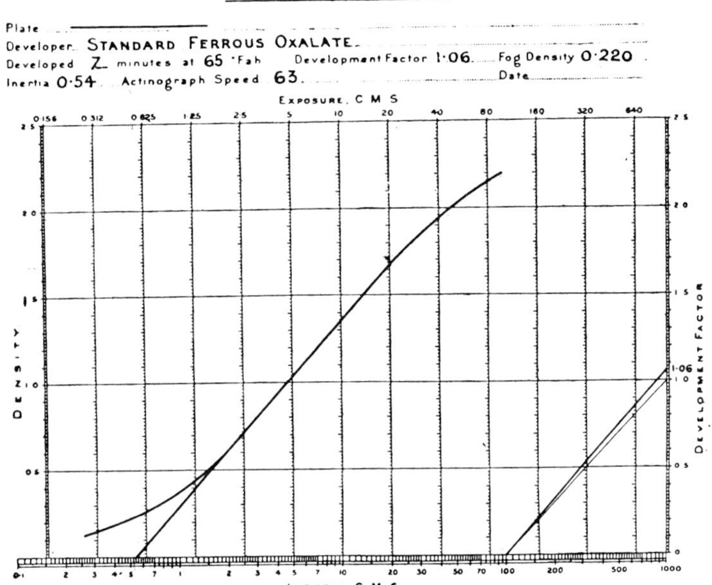



Upon each of the vertical exposure lines we mark the density corresponding to the exposure it represents, and we must then carefully consider the course and position of the straight part of the curve upon which the speed of the plate depends. By holding a piece of thread tightly stretched over the points marked on the exposure lines, the position of the straight line will be readily decided, and it may then be drawn on the chart, the line being continued till it intersects the inertia scale. Occasionally it may be found that one or more of the plotted points do not lie evenly in the path of the curve. This may arise either from an error in measuring the density or from a false density due to an inequality in the coating of the plate ; but, unless in a very extreme case, there will be little difficulty in determining the course of the curve.

The point at which the continuation of the straight line intersects the horizontal scale indicates an exposure which we termed the " inertia," and which is a measure of the slowness of the plate—the greater the inertia the slower the plate. The most important practical application of the inertia is that it indicates that exposure which just marks the commencement of the period of correct exposure. This is not absolutely true, but sufficiently so for all practical purposes, no better means having been found of deciding and expressing the position of the characteristic curve with regard to the exposure scale.

In the example under consideration the inertia is 0·54. The speed of the plate, which is the inverse of the inertia, is obtained by dividing the factor 34 by the inertia 0·54, and hence is 63. The factor 34 is, of course, only applicable when the source of light employed is the standard candle used under the conditions previously laid down. The substitution of another source of light would involve the use of another factor.

We thus see how the position of the characteristic curve on the chart enables us to assign a definite numerical value to the speed of a plate. A value is similarly assigned to the development factor as follows :—From the point 100 on the exposure scale draw a line parallel to the straight portion of the characteristic curve, and the point at which it intersects the development factor scale indicates the value required. In the example before us the development factor is 1·06.

## LATITUDE IN EXPOSURE.

The characteristic curve of a plate thus obtained further teaches us what capacity the plate has for truthful representation, or, in other words, the amount of latitude in exposure of which the plate admits. In the example under consideration it would be quite admissible, in ordinary photographic practice, to consider the range of the correct period as extending from 0·54 C.M.S. (the inertia) to 80 C.M.S., the plate being thus capable of registering a series of light-intensities ranging from 1 to 148. This is, of course, not absolutely true, because we have included slight deviations from the straight line both in the under- and over-exposure periods ; but these deviations are unimportant, and their influence would never be felt in ordinary pictorial work.

Taking the length of the practically straight part of the curve as including a range of exposures 1 : E, and the light-intensities to be photographed as lying between the limits 1 : I, the latitude in exposure would be $1 : \dfrac{E}{I}$, and within these two limits the negatives resulting from any exposure would, if developed together and for the same length of time, yield identical prints. Applying the figures given as representing the range of exposures covered by the straight part of the curve, and taking the light-intensities of an ordinary open landscape as 1 : 30, the latitude of exposure permissible would be $1 : \dfrac{148}{30}$, or, roughly, 1 : 5 ; that is to say, whether the plate received an exposure of 1 second or of 5 seconds, it would be immaterial. But two negatives of the same subject exposed for these lengths of time and developed together would be very different in appearance. The latter would be generally the denser, and would take three to four times as long to print as the former, but the resulting prints would be practically indistinguishable.

I have in my possession two negatives of the same subject taken upon the same plate and developed together for the same length of time, but the latitude of the plate used was such as to permit of one negative being exposed for ten times as long as the other. While one of the negatives has every indication of a perfect exposure, the other gives to the eye the impression of heavily-fogged over-exposure ; yet they yield identical prints. The time occupied in printing, however, while quite normal in one case, amounts to two or three days in the other. My object in mentioning this is to point out that a photographer who might inadvertently produce such a negative as the denser of these would, from its behaviour in the developer, probably conclude that he had enormously over-exposed. He would at once stop development, reconstitute his developer, and, on taking a print from the finished negative, flatter himself that the result was due to his skill in development, while, as a matter of fact, the gradations of his negative were true from the outset. In the instance referred to the image of the denser negative flashed up in the developer far more rapidly than that of the other, and by the time development was completed it was lost in an apparently impenetrable deposit of high density. From this it is obvious that a system of timing development by the first appearance of the image is fallacious, and, had it been resorted to in this instance, the two negatives would never have yielded identical prints. When two negatives, such as those described, yield identical prints, their density differences are alike throughout, though the density ratios differ.

On the ground of economy of time occupied in printing the photographer will, of course, always aim at so exposing that the gradations of his negatives shall commence at the lowest part of the straight line representing the correct period. The best possible negative is one which combines truthful representation with minimum density ; but owing to the difficulty of attaining to absolute accuracy in exposure, the photographer must often be content if he succeed in bringing the gradations of his negatives anywhere within the period of correct representation. The extent of the correct period varies very greatly in different plates, and as the more limited it is the more absolute accuracy of exposure is demanded the importance of this characteristic will be appreciated. The latitude of exposure is generally greater in a slow than in a rapid plate, and it is largely dependent upon the amount of silver haloid upon the plate.

### RANGE OF LIGHT-INTENSITIES.

The range of light-intensities reflected by a particular class of subject may be readily determined by the following method :—Cut from the centre of, say, a half-plate a piece (A) the size of a quarter-plate and a strip (B) of the size prescribed for the purpose of speed determination. Upon A take a photograph in the camera of the subject of which it is desired to determine the range of light-intensities, and expose B behind the revolving disc to the standard light. A and B must then be developed together for exactly the same length of time. When fixed, washed and dried we proceed to measure the densities of the strip B and to plot them upon a skeleton chart, just as in the case of a

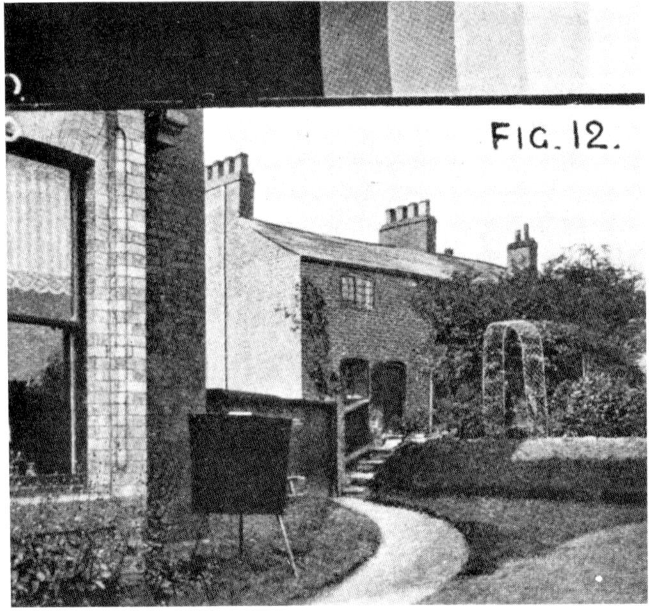


speed determination. We also very carefully measure the densities of the highest light and the deepest shadow yielded by the negative A, and mark their position on the curve representing the densities of the strip B. From these two points we draw vertical lines till they intersect the horizontal exposure scale. The ratio of the two exposures thus indicated is the range of light-intensities in the subject photographed. Fig. 12 is produced from the negative of a subject which may be regarded as typical of a landscape with a decidedly wide range of light-intensities. The sky affords the highest light and the dark reflection in the window the deepest shadow. As the window is illuminated only by diffused light, and is in close proximity to the camera, its dark reflection represents a dark object in the close foreground. The gradations shown on the upper side of the photograph are printed simultaneously with the picture itself from the strip exposed to the standard candle. The densities of this strip, being produced by known exposures or light-intensities, provide a scale which enables us to assign a value to the intensity of

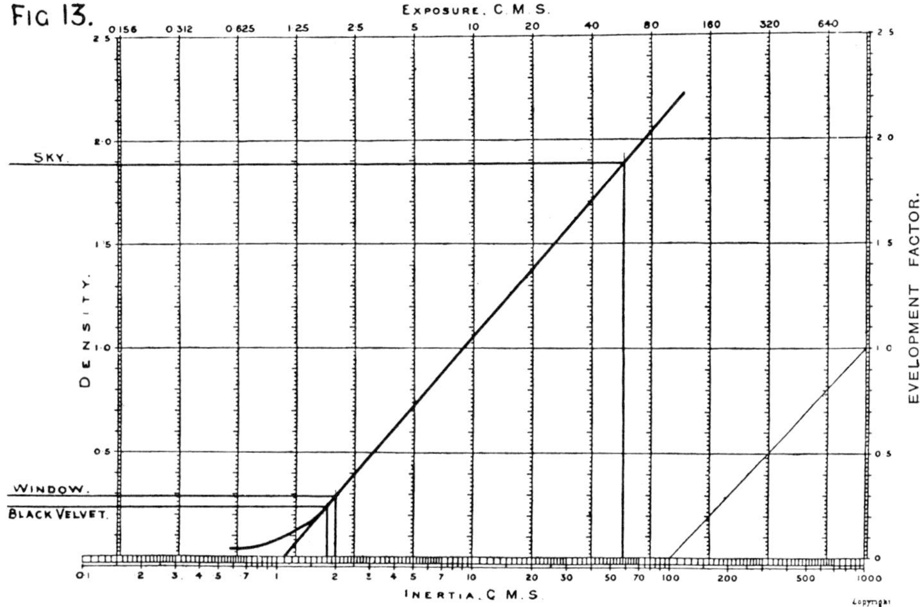


the light which yielded any particular density upon the picture negative itself. Fig. 13 shows the plotting of the densities of the strip B. The densities representing the sky and the reflection in the window are indicated by horizontal lines, and the vertical lines intersecting the exposure scale show the equivalent exposures to be 2 C.M.S. and 58 C.M.S. respectively. The extreme range, therefore, in this subject is only as 1 : 29.

In seeking to determine the range of light-intensities in a particular subject it sometimes happens that it is difficult to secure a patch of the highest light or deepest shadow of sufficient area to admit of being readily measured in the photometer. In such a case we proved experimentally that a sheet of pure white cardboard and a sheet of matt black paper, or a piece of black velvet, suitably disposed with regard to illumination and to distance from the camera, may be safely introduced. A piece of pure white cardboard, for instance, illuminated by direct sunlight, and placed at a distance from the camera of not less than, say, 100 times the focal length of the lens, would yield a density equal to that produced by the sky under the same condition of illumination ; while a piece of black velvet, at close quarters and illuminated by diffused light, would adequately represent the deepest shadow which would occur in an object similarly situated.   In Fig. 12 a piece of black velvet is included on the left-hand side, and a measurement of the density it yielded is equivalent to a light-intensity of $1 \cdot 8$ C.M.S., or to a slightly less intensity than that of the dark reflection in the window.   The extreme range, therefore, from the sky to the black velvet is as 1 : 32.   In making experiments of this kind it is necessary to employ slow plates having as extended a period of correct exposure as possible.

Exception has several times been taken to our statements as to the range of light-intensities in an ordinary open landscape.   While, however, we have submitted proof of the accuracy of our contention, our critics have been satisfied to advance mere opinions.   If the exaggerated views they hold upon the subject were correct, truthful representation by photographic means would be an impossibility.   There are many plates upon the market which would be taxed to the utmost in truthfully representing even so narrow a range of light-intensities as 1 : 30.

## FREE BROMIDE IN THE FILM.

We have thus far only considered it necessary to expose and develop a single strip of plate in order to determine its speed.   In the case of an unknown brand of plates, however, there is always the possibility of the presence of a disturbing element in the film which would cause a single determination to be more or less misleading.   This disturbing element is free bromide, the influence of which is to cause the inertia to decrease with time of development until a certain development factor is reached, when it is no longer felt.   While, however, it rests with ourselves to avoid the use of bromide in the developer, its presence in the film is beyond our control, and, in view of the serious objection to its presence, it is greatly to be desired that plate makers will realise the importance of securing the elimination of free bromide from their emulsions.

In Fig. 4 it will be noted that the two characteristic curves resulting from different times of development have exactly the same inertia.   The speed of the plate might consequently have been accurately determined by the measurements of either strip alone.   If free bromide were present in the film, however, the inertiæ of the two strips would not be coincident ; in other words, the speed of the plate would vary, more or less, with the development factor reached.   For this reason it is always better to simultaneously expose *two* strips of the same plate, developing one, preferably, for exactly twice as long as the other. If, on plotting the measurements of the two strips, we find the inertiæ practically coincident, we may infer the absence of free bromide in the film and regard the speed as determined. If, on the other hand, the inertiæ do not coincide, the presence of free bromide would be indicated, and the speed of the plate would be dependent upon the development factor reached. In the latter case it would probably be sufficiently accurate for all practical purposes to take, as the true inertia, the mean of the two determinations, though, should the discrepancy be very marked, it might be advisable to modify the speed according to the development factor to be reached.

The time occupied in the development of the first strip must be determined by the facility with which the plate develops, but the longer the time the better, so long as the second strip, on receiving twice the time of development, does not become too dense to be readily measured.

In an extreme case the influence of free bromide in the film is so marked as to absolutely necessitate a recognition of the varying speed of the plate as dependent upon the development factor to be reached. It will therefore

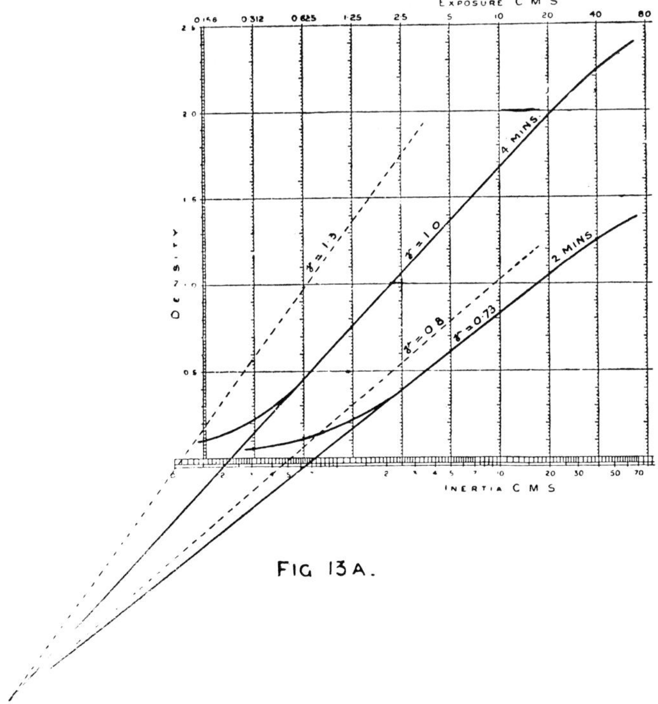


be useful to indicate how the variations in the speed of such a plate may best be determined for any desired development factor. Fig. 13A represents one of the most marked cases met with by the writer. The two strips simultaneously exposed, but developed for two and for four minutes respectively, gave development factors of 0·73 and 1·0. Had there been no free bromide present, the inertiæ yielded by the two strips would have been coincident, and the speed in consequence constant ; but in this instance the inertiæ are 0·75 and 0·22 respectively, so that the speed varies from 45·3 to 154·5 for the two development factors obtained. In the instance under consideration the straight portions of the curves, instead of originating from a point upon the exposure scale, originate from a point marked A, considerably below it. The point A is, of course, obtained by producing the straight portions of the two curves until they intersect.

Let us now consider how the speed of this plate would vary accordingly as it might be required for the production of a portrait, an interior or a landscape, to be developed respectively, say, to factors 0·8, 1·0 and 1·3. As it happens, the inertia for development factor 1·0 is already determined, and we obtain the inertiæ corresponding to the factors 0·8 and 1·3 by drawing lines, as dotted, from the point A at angles corresponding to the two development factors in question. The points at which these lines intersect the exposure scale give the respective inertiæ, which, divided into 34, give the speeds required. The speeds and their ratios corresponding to the three development factors are therefore as follows :—

| Nature of subject. | Development factor. | Inertia. | Speed. | Speed ratio. |
|---|---|---|---|---|
| Portrait    . .    . . | 0·8 | 0·52 | 65 | 1·00 |
| Interior    . .    . . | 1·0 | 0·22 | 154 | 2·36 |
| Landscape   . .    . . | 1·3 | 0·11 | 309 | 4·72 |

From this it will be seen that the plate is nearly five times as rapid for a landscape as for a portrait. It may be well, however, to remark that, as a matter of fact, this particular plate is incapable of reaching a higher development factor than 1·0, but it serves to illustrate the principle and method to which it is my object to call attention.

## CONTROL OF THE DEVELOPMENT FACTOR.

Apart from the reason just advanced, another very important object is attained by the simultaneous exposure of two, instead of a single strip. By this means we obtain data for the control of the development factor ; that is to say, we learn how to modify the time of development so as to adapt the range of our negatives to the subjects photographed and to the particular effect we wish to produce.

In order to determine the time required to reach any desired development factor we have only to ascertain the development factors yielded by the two strips. These factors are then plotted upon another skeleton chart, as illustrated in Fig. 14, the two development factor values, together with the zero

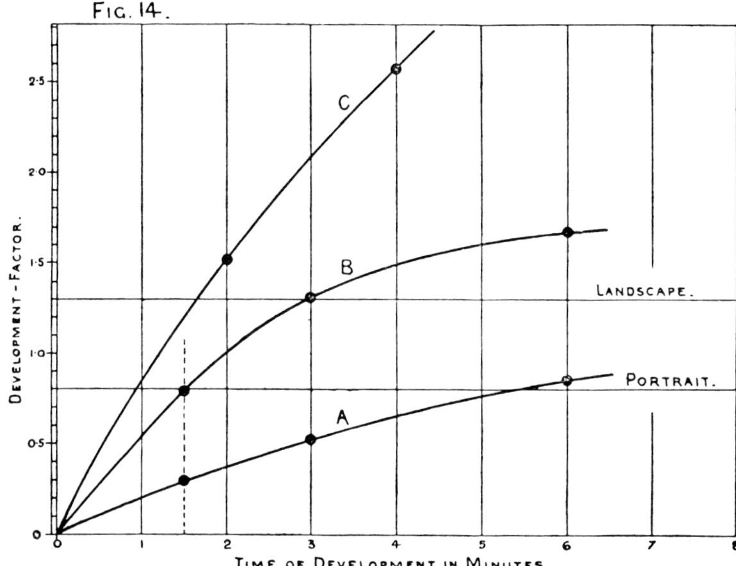


point, affording us three points through which a curve is drawn which represents the growth of the development factor with time of development. This curve then enables us to ascertain the time required to reach any desired factor.

In Fig. 14 three development-factor curves, A, B and C, are plotted, and they serve to show the great difference which exists in different plates as regards the growth of this factor. The numerical data determining the curves are given in the following table, and the relative times of development required in each case for a portrait and an ordinary open landscape are also indicated. The development factors indicated for these two classes of subjects are, of course, given quite provisionally. The dots marked on the curves indicate the values of the factors ascertained, which, with the zero point, determine the course of each curve :—

| Plate. | Strips developed. | Development factors obtained. | Time of development for | |
|---|---|---|---|---|
| | | | Portrait. | Landscape. |
| A | Mins.<br>1½, 3, 6. | 0·29, 0·52, 0·85. | Mins.<br>5·5 | Mins.<br>— |
| B | 1½, 3, 6. | 0·8, 1·32, 1·675. | 1·5 | 3·0 |
| C | 2, 4. | 1·52, 2·58. | 0·95 | 1·65 |

Taking the two extreme curves, A and C, it will be seen that while in the case of A a portrait would require 5½ minutes' development, the same result would be obtained on plate C in rather less than 1 minute, and, as the curve A clearly approaches its limit, the plate it represents would probably be useless for landscape work or for any subject requiring a more extended range of opacities than a portrait. It is to be hoped that it will come to be recognised as a characteristic of a really good plate that it shall, unlike plate A, be capable of attaining the highest development factor demanded in practical photography.

The photographer who elects to work in accordance with the principles laid down in this little work is advised to decide upon a really good brand of plates, and, having done so, to obtain a sufficient supply, say, for a season's requirements, taking care that the whole are coated from the same batch of emulsion. A single careful determination of the characteristics of his plates will then provide him with data which will enable him to apply them in practice to the best advantage.

The ground which I proposed to traverse in this monograph is now covered, and I trust that the principles underlying our quantitative system of photography, and the directions for their practical application, have been sufficiently clearly laid down to enable any photographer who may desire to do so to put our system into practice. Opposed we have always been by photographers who prefer to attain their ends by empirical methods rather than pursue a scientific course, which, if faithfully followed, leads directly to success. It has, however, been gratifying to note a growing tendency to adopt scientific methods. This has been especially marked in connection with colour photography, in which it is of such vital importance to secure the three fundamental negatives in relatively correct relationship. If accuracy in the exposure and development of negatives for colour and other branches of technical photography be found to be essential, it is essential also, though perhaps in a less degree, in ordinary photographic practice.

The production of a photograph is governed by natural laws, and a definite effect must result from a definite cause. The same cause, under the same conditions, always produces the same effect. The law which governs the action of light upon the sensitive plate teaches us that only a limited range of such action is available in photography if truthful representation be demanded, and hence the necessity of accuracy in exposure. Having by means of a correct exposure produced a latent image true in the relationship of its gradations, the developer enables us to produce a metallic image, of which the gradations shall be equally true. The developer employed, however, must be so constituted that its exact effect can be predetermined, and no developer will comply with this demand which does not act in conformity with the law of ".constant density ratios." Only by clearly grasping and working in harmony with the laws governing the action of light and the action of the developer can we really become masters of technical photography.

I earnestly hope that this little work may be the means of inducing some amateur photographers to take up the scientific method, and I feel very confident in assuring any who may do so that they will discover a new field of unexpected pleasure in the pursuit of photography.

VERO C. DRIFFIELD.

Widnes, Eng.,
    *November 15th*, 1903.

# BIBLIOGRAPHY.

## ABBREVIATIONS.

| | |
|---|---|
| Hurter, F., and Driffield, V. C. | H. and D. |
| Amateur Photographer | Am. P. |
| Apollo | Apollo |
| Archives für wissenschaftliche Photographie | Arch. Wiss. P. |
| British Journal of Photography | B. J. P. |
| Bulletin de la Société Belge de Photographie | Bull. Soc. Belge P. |
| Bulletin de la Société Française | Bull. Soc. Fr. P. |
| Bolletino della Societa Fot. | Boll. So. Fot. It. |
| Camera Club Journal | C. C. J. |
| Chemical News | Chem. N. |
| Chemische Zeitung | Chem. Zeit. |
| Dry Plates | Dry Plates |
| Eders Jahrbuch | Eders. J. |
| Journal of Society of Chemical Industry | J. S. C. I. |
| Moniteur de la Photographie | Mon. de la P. |
| Photogram | Photogram |
| Photographic Art Journal | P. A. J. |
| Photo. Chronik. | P. C. |
| Photographic Club Epitome | P. C. E. |
| Photographische Correspondenz | P. Corr. |
| Photographic Era | P. E. |
| Photographic Journal | P. J. |
| Photo-Miniature | P. M. |
| Photographische Mitteilungen | P. Mitt. |
| Photographic News | P. N. |
| Photographic Quarterly | P. Q. |
| Photographic Record | P. R. |
| Photographic Review of Reviews | P. Rev. |
| Photographische Rundschau | P. Rund. |
| Photographic Societies' Reporter | P. Soc. Rep. |
| Photographic Scraps | P. S. |
| Photographic Work | P. W. |
| Photography | P. |
| Royal Photographic Society | R.P.S. |
| Society of Arts | S. A. |
| Yearbook of Photography | Y. P. |
| Zeitschrift für Instrumenten Kunde | Zeit. Inst. |
| Zeitschrift für physikalische Chem. | Zeit. Phys. Chem. |
| Zeitschrift für Wiss. P. | Zeit. Wiss. P. |



### 1881.

**1** HURTER, F. Actinometers, or Instruments for Measuring Light, British Patent, No. 1751 of 1881. [*See* p. 44].
Apr. 23.

### 1888.

**2** H. and D. Improvements in Instruments for Calculating Photographic Exposures. British Patent, No. 5545 of 1888. [*See* p. 50].
Apr. 14.

### 1889.

**3** ABNEY, W. de W. Photography and the Law of Error. P.N. **33**, 218.
Mar. 26.

**4** H. and D. The Actinograph. [*See* p. 51]. P. Soc. Rep. **1**, 165; P. Corr. **29**, 397.
Apr. 30.

**5** BOTHAMLEY, C. H. Amyl-Acetate Lamp. P.N., **33**, 521.
Aug. 9.

**6** ABNEY, W. de W. Testing Plates for Gradation. Y.P. **1890**, 52.
Dec.

### 1890.

**7** HURTER, F. An Instrument for the Measurement of Diffuse Daylight and the Actinograph. [*See* p. 70]. J.S.C.I. **9**, 370.
Apr. 2.

### 1890—*continued*.

**8** WATKINS, A. The Mathematical Calculation of Exposures. P.N. **34**, 319; P.Mitt. **27**, 64.
Apr. 25.

**9** H. and D. Photochemical Investigations and a New Method of Determination of the Sensitiveness of Photographic Plates. [*See* p. 76]. J.S.C.I. **9**, 455; P.N. **34**, 598, 674, 693, 738, 750, 772, 784, 809, 828, 842, 929; Dry Plates **1893**, 58, 65, 73, 81, 89, 97.
May 7.

**10** JONES, C. Negative Making. P. **2**, 429.
July 10.

**11** H. and D. The Action of Light upon the Sensitive Plate. Am. P. **12**, 25, 47.
July 11.

**12** WATTS, W. A. The Sensitiveness of Photographic Plates. Am. P. **12**, 67, 13.
July 25.

**13** ABNEY, W. de W. On the Accuracy of the Grease Spot Photometer for Measuring the Density of Photographic Plates, and a note on the Sector Photometer. [*See* p. 123]. J.S.C.I. **9**, 722.
July 31.

**14** H. and D. Reply to Captain Abney. [*See* p. 131]. J.S.C.I. **9**, 725.
July 31.

**1890**—*continued.*

**15** MICHALKE, Dr.  Actinometriche Unter-
Aug.  suchungen.  i. Abhängigkeit der Schwärzung von Belichtungszeit und Licht-Intersität.  ii. Bezichung Zurschen Indicirter Helligkeit und Belichtungs-dauer.  P.Mitt. **27**, 123–8, 261–4, 290–2, 305–6, 1 fig.

**16** H. and D.  Sensitiveness of Plates.
Aug.  Am. P. **12**, 99.
8.

**17** ABNEY, W. de W.  Measuring Density of
Aug.  Negatives.  P. **2**, 511.
14.

**18** H. and D.  Measuring the Density of
Aug.  Negatives.  [*See* p. 133].  P. **2**, 547.
28.

**19** ABNEY, W. de W.  On Measuring Densi-
Sept.  ties of Negatives.  P. **2**, 574.
11.

**20** ABNEY, W. de W.  The Grease-Spot and
Sept.  Sector Photometers.  [Reply to Hurter
25.  and Driffield, Aug. 28].  P. **2**, 611–612.

**21** H. and D.  The Grease-Spot and Sector
Oct.  Photometers.  [Reply to Abney, Sept.
2.  25].  P. **2**, 632.

**22** ABNEY, W. de W.  On the Density of
Oct.  Negatives.  C.C.J. **4**, 191 ; B.J.P. **37**,
9.  712.  Camera **5**, 136.

**23** JONES, C.  Density Ratios as affected by
Nov.  Development.  P.J. **15** (N.S.), 3.
11.

**24** ABNEY, W. de W.  Grease-Spot Photo-
Dec.  meter Measures.  J.S.C. I. **10**, 18.
10.

**25** H. and D.  The Sector and Grease-Spot
Dec.  Photometers and their results.  [*See*
10.  p. 139].  J.S.C.I. **10**, 20.

## 1891.

**26** H. and D.  The Sector and Grease-Spot
Jan.  Photometers and their Results.  [*See*
14.  p. 175].  J.S.C.I. **10**, 98–100.

**27** H. and D.  Relation between Photo-
Jan.  graphic Negatives and their Positives.
14.  [*See* p. 163].  J.S.C.I. **10**, 100–104. Translated in Eder's J. **1893**, p. 18.

**28** SCHUMANN, V. Determining the Sensitive-
Jan.  ness of Photographic Plates by the
16.  Spectrograph.  Chem. N. **63**, 33 ; P. **3**, 73.

**29** HURTER, F.  Action of Light on the
Jan.  Sensitive Film.  [Liverpool Physical
19.  Society, *see* p. 151].  P. **3**, 120, 135.

**30** B.J.P. (Editorial).  Sensitometer Indica-
Jan.  tions.  [On Schuman, Jan. 16].  B.J.P.
23.  **36**, 51.

**1891**—*continued.*

**31** ANXIOUS ENQUIRER.  H. and D.'s Paper
Feb.  and Dr. Emerson.  P.A.J. **4**, 135.
28.

**32** VOGEL, H. W.  Ueber Messung der
Mar.  Helligkeit des Lichtes resp. der Empfindlichkeit von Platten durch die sogenannte Anfangswirkung.  P. Mitt. **27**, 355.

**33** ROBINSON, H. P.  Messrs. Hurter and
Mar.  Driffield's Pronouncements.  P.A.J. **4**,
7.  151.

**34** JONES, C.  The Principles of Negative
Mar.  Making.  P. **3**, 161–162.
12.

**35** H. and D.  Reply to H. P. Robinson.
Mar.  [Mar. 7].  P.A.J. **4**, 166.
14.

**36** H. and D.  Reply to Chapman Jones.
Mar.  [Mar. 12].  P. **3**, 205.
26.

**37** KOHN, C. A.  The Teachings of a Chemical
Apr.  Actinometer.  P.Q. **2**, 237–245.

**38** ACWORTH, J. J.  The Relation between
Apr.  Absorption and Sensitiveness of Sensitised Plates.  P.Q. **2**, 197–226.  Wiedemann's Annalen N.F. **42**, 371.

**39** HURTER, F.  The Sector and Grease-Spot
Apr.  Photometers.  [*See* p. 180].  J.S.C.I.
1.  **10**, 318.

**40** JONES, C.  Hurter and Driffield's Investi-
Apr.  gations.  [Reply to H. and D., Mar. 26].
2.  P. **3**, 221.

**41** H. and D.  Exposure *v.* Development.
Apr.  [Reply to E.A.D. in previous issue].
3.  Am. P. **13**, 239.

**42** H. and D.  Photochemical Investigations.
Apr.  [Article following Anxious Enquirer,
4.  Feb. 28, and H. P. Robinson, Mar. 7]. P.A.J. **4**, 208, 222, 238.

**43** H. and D.  H. and D.'s Papers.  [Reply
May  on Gradation and Latitude].  P.A.J. **4**,
2.  275.

**44** PHILLIPS, R. C.  The Researches of H.
May  and D.  B.J.P. **38**, 326.
22.

**45** ADDENBROKE, G. L., MACKIE, A.,
May  JONES, C., HURTER, F., and others.
26.  Influence of Development on Gradation.  P.J. **15** (N.S.), 171 ; P. **3**, 359 ; Am. P. **13**, 404.

**46** VOGEL, H. W.  Kritik der gebräuchlichen
June  Photometer.  P. Mitt. **28**, 73–75.
1.

**47** HURTER, F.  The Influence of Develop-
June  ment on Gradation.  P.A.J. **4**, p. 339.
6.

**1891**—*continued.*

**48** BURTON, W. K. A Few Considerations
June concerning the Rendering of " Tones "
11. in Photographs. P. **3**, 371–372.

**49** H. and D. Reply to Burton. [June 11].
June P. **3**, 375.
18.

**50** DAVISON, G. Shall we Renounce ?
July [Criticism of H. and D. work]. P.Q. **2**,
1. 275–282.

**51** PHOTOGRAPHIC CLUB. Sensitometry. Dis-
July cussion. [By Spurge, Cowan, Bedford,
1. &c.]. P.C.E. **189–91**, 66.

**52** JONES, C. Discussion on Gradation.
July [C.J. contends can alter Density Ratios
10. by Development. Dr. Hurter present].
P.J. **15** (N.S.), 172.

**53** WILLIAMS, G. F. Spectroscopic Deter-
July mination of the Sensitiveness of Plates.
24. B.J.P. **38**, 469, 490.

**54** BURTON, W. K. Hurter and Driffield
Sept. Theories. [Reply to Hurter and
17. Driffield, June 18]. P. **3**, 601.

**1892.**

**55** HOPWOOD, J. R. Ratio of gradation.
Jan. B.J.P. **39**, 53.
22.

**56** H. and D. The Actinograph. Am. P. **15**,
Jan. 84, 100.
29.

**57** MICHAEL, M. J. Ratio of Gradation.
Feb. [Reply to Hopwood, Jan. 22]. B.J.P.
10. **39**, 93.

**58** H. and D. Ratio of gradation. [Reply
Feb. to Michael, Feb. 5]. B.J.P. **39**, 102.
12.

**59** NOVERRE, W. L. The Actinograph.
Feb. [Referring to H. and D., Jan. 29].
5. Am. P. **15**, 112.

**60** BOLTON, W. B. Ratios of Gradation.
Mar. B.J.P. **39**, 148, 196, 230 ; P. Rev.
4. **1892**, 175.

**61** FREE LANCE. On Things in General.
Mar. [Comment on Michael, Feb. 5, H. and D.
4. Feb. 12]. B.J.P. **39**, 150.

**62** H. and D. Editorial on Letter from
Mar. H. and D. Am. P. **15**, 200.
11.

**63** CHANNON, H. J. Ratio of Gradation.
Mar. B.J.P. **39**, 173.
11.

**64** NOVERRE, W. L. The Actinograph.
Mar. Am, P. **15**, 203.
11.

**65** H. and D. Ratio of Gradation. [Reply
Mar. to Channon, Mar. 11]. B.J.P. **39**, 181.
18.

**1892**—*continued.*

**66** NOVERRE, W. L. The Actinograph.
Mar. [Still claiming reply]. Am. P. **15**, 226.
18.

**67** PHILLIPS, R. C. Ratio of Gradation.
Mar. [Reply to Free Lance, Mar. 4]. B.J.P.
18. **39**, 190.

**68** SPURGE, J. B. Sensitometers. C.C.J. **6**,
Mar. 66 ; Eder's J. **1894**, 366.
23.

**69** FREE LANCE. Ratio of Gradation.
Mar. [Reply to Phillips, Mar. 18]. B.J.P.
25. **39**, 206.

**70** MARION and Co. The Actinoagraph.
Mar. [Reply to Noverre, Feb. 12]. Am. P.
25. **15**, 246.

**71** H. and D. The Actinoagraph. [Reply
Mar. to Noverre, Feb. 12]. Am. P. **15**, 245.
25.

**72** CHANNON, H. J. Ratio of Gradation.
Apr. [Reply to H. and D., Mar. 18]. B.J.P.
1. **39**, 223.

**73** NOVERRE, W. L. The Actinograph.
Apr. [Reply to H. and D, Mar. 25]. Am. P.
8. **15**, 284 ; correction, 302.

**74** PHILLIPS, R. C. Ratio of Gradation.
Apr. [Reply to Free Lance, Mar. 25]. B.J.P.
8. **39**, 239.

**75** WATKINS, A. Correct Exposure and the
Apr. Speed of Plates. P. **4**, 254.
21.

**76** CHANNON, H. J. Ratio of Gradation.
Apr. [" Since my last letter I have greatly
22. altered my opinions."] B.J.P. **39**,
261.

**77** PHILLIPS, R. C. Ratio of Gradation.
Apr. [Reply to a remark by Free Lance,
22. B.J.P. pp. 244–5]. B.J.P. **39**, 270.

**78** H. and D. Ratio of Gradation. [Reply
Apr. to Channon, Apr. 1]. B.J.P. **39**, 270.
22.

**79** PLUVINEL, A. de la B. La Mesure de
May l'opacité des Clichés Bull. Soc. Belg.
P. **1892**, 548.

**80** H. and D. Ratio of Gradation. [Reply
May to Channon, Apr. 22]. B.J.P. **39**, 297.
6.

**81** COWAN, A. The Actinograph. [At
May Camera Club]. P.N. **36**, 403 ; C.C.J.
23. **6**, p. 116.

**82** CHANNON, H. J. Ratio of Gradation.
May [Reply to H. and D., Apr. 22]. B.J.P.
27. **39**, 344.

**83** BOLAS, T. The Work of H. and D.
June P.W. **1**, 87, 98, 176, 206.
24.

**84** EDER, J. M. Ein neuer Aktinograph von
Aug. Hurter und Driffield. P. Corr. **29**, 396.

**1892**—*continued.*

**85** H. and D.   Relative Speed of Plates.
Aug.
25.
[Depends on batch].   P. **4,** 540 ; Dry
Plates, Sept. **1892,** 5.

**86** CADETT and NEALL.   Comment on Hurter
Sept.
and Driffield's letter.   [Aug. 25].   Dry
Plates, Sept. **1892,** 6.

**87** H. and D.   A Standard Developer.
Sept.
23.
B.J.P. **39,** 613–614.

**88** CADETT, J.   The Watkins Exposure
Nov.
Meter.   [As compared with H. and D.
Actinograph].   Dry Plates, Nov. **1892,**
1.

**89** CHANNON, H. J.   Ratio of Gradation.
Nov.
B.J.P. Almanac, **1893,** 661.

**90** STERRY, J.   Speed of Plates.   [Watkins
Nov.
17.
and H. and D.. methods compared].
P. **4,** 734.

**91** PHOTOGRAPHIC NEWS (Editorial).   Under
Nov.
18.
Exposure ? or Cold Developer ?   P.N.
**36,** 744 ; Dry Plates, Dec. **1892,** 12.

**92** H. and D.   La Mesure de l'opacité des
Dec.
Clichés.   [Reply to Pluvinel].   Bull.
Soc. Belg. **1892,** 974.

**93** WATKINS, A.   The Watkins Exposure
Dec.
Meter.   [Reply to Cadett, Nov.].   Dry
Plates, Dec. **1892,** 13.

**94** CADETT and NEALL.   Under Exposure ?
Dec.
or Cold Developer ?   [Comment on
Photographic News, Nov. 11].   Dry
Plates, Dec. **1892,** 11.

**95** H. and D.   The Speed of Plates.   [Corre-
Dec.
2.
spondence with Imperial Co. as to
assumed ratio between Watkins and
H. and D. numbers].   Am. P. **16,** 403 ;
P. **4,** 767.

**96** WATKINS, A.   The Speed of Dry Plates.
Dec.
8.
[Reply to Sterry, Nov. 17].   P. **4,** 782.

**97** IMPERIAL DRY PLATE CO., LTD.   The
Dec.
9.
Speed of Plates.   [Referring to corre-
spondence with H. and D., Dec. 2].
Am. P. **16,** 433 ; P. **4,** 781.

**98** STERRY, J.   Speed of Plates.   [Reply to
Dec.
22.
Watkins, Dec. 8].   P. **4,** 815.

### 1893.

**99** MARION and Co.   Neuer Aktinograph von
H. and D.   Eders J., **1893,** 391.

**100** COWAN, A.   Speed Testing by H. and
Jan.
5.
D.'s method.   P. Rev. **2,** 52 ; P.W. **2,**
23.

**1893**—*continued.*

**101** ARMSTRONG, H. E.   The Chemical changes
Jan.
25.
attending   Photographic   Operations.
J.C.C. **7,** 48, 71 ; P.N. **37,** 75.

**102** WILLIAMS, G. F.   Determination of Plate
Jan.
27.
Speeds.   B.J.P. **40,** 57, 69.

**103** CADETT, J.   The Comparative Readings
Feb.
of Sensitiveness and the Relation of
Density thereto.   Dry Plates, Feb.
**1893,** 25.

**104** WATKINS, A.   Determination of Plate
Feb.
3.
Speeds.   [Reply to Williams, Jan. 27].
B.J.P. **40,** 77.

**105** MARION and Co.   Determination of Plate
Feb.
10.
Speeds.   [Reply to Williams, Jan. 27].
B.J.P. **40,** 94.

**106** CADETT, J.   Determination of Plate
Feb.
10.
Speeds.   [Reply to Williams, Jan. 27].
B.J.P. **40,** 94.

**107** H. and D.   Determination of Plate Speeds.
Feb.
10.
[Reply to Williams, Jan. 27].   B.J.P.
**40,** 93.

**108** AMATEUR PHOTOGRAPHER (Editorial).   A
Feb.
17.
Standard Light.   Am. P. **17,** 107, 123,
143.

**109** WILLIAMS, G. F.   The Speed-Testing Con-
Feb.
17.
troversy.   [Reply to H. and D., Feb. 10].
B.J.P. **40,** 111.

**110** H. and D.   Determination of Plate Speeds.
Feb.
24.
[Reply to Williams, Feb. 17].   B.J.P.
**40,** 118.

**111** PRINGLE, A.   Is Exposure the Factor in
Mar.
2.
Practical Negative Making ?   [Refers
to Armstrong, Jan. 26].   P. **5,** 129.

**112** CADETT, J.   Speed Testing.   [Reply to
Mar.
3.
Williams, Feb. 17].   B.J.P. **40,** 143.

**113** BREBNER, H.   Normal and Solarising
Mar.
24.
Densities.   B.J.P. **40,** 185.

**114** CHANNON, H. J.   The Influence of Develop-
Mar.
24.
ment on Gradation.   B.J.P. **40,** 183,
197.

**115** COWAN, A. (jun.).   Nomenclature as to
Apr.
28.
Speed of Plates.   [Reply to Williams,
Apr. 14].   P.W. **2,** 200.

**116** ABNEY, W. de W.   Rapidity of Plates.
Apr.
13.
C.C.J. **7,** 126, 135, 161 ; Eders J.
**1894,** 36.

**117** ELDER, H. M.   On the Effect of Light
Apr.
13.
on Photographic Plates.   [Hurter
speaking].   C.C.J. **7,** 131, 161 ; Eders J.
**1894,** 22.

**1893—*continued*.**

**118** HURTER, F. " The Speed of Plates " and
Apr. " The Effect of Light on Plates."
13. [Camera Club discussion on Abney and
Elders Papers, *see* p. 199]. J.C.C.,
July **1893**, No. 86.

**119** WILLIAMS, G. F. Determination of Plate
Apr. Speeds. [Reply to criticism]. B.J.P.
14. **40**, 229, 265 ; Am. P. **18**, 248 ; P.W.
**2**, 171.

**120** H. and D. Influence of Development on
Apr. Gradation. [Reply to Channon, Mar.
21. 24]. B.J.P. **40**, 248.

**121** BREBNER, H. Photographic Metastasis.
Apr. [The Mathematics of Density]. B.J.P.
28. **40**, 261, 591.

**122** COWAN, A. Determination of Plate
Apr. Speeds. [Reply to Williams, Ap. 14].
28. B.J.P. **40**, 262 ; Am. P. 17, 284 ;
P.W. **2**, 195.

**123** CHANNON, H. J. Determination of the
Apr. Speed of Plates. [Reply to H. and D.,
28. Apr. 21]. B.J.P. **40**, 270.

**124** CADETT and NEALL. Speed Determination.
May [In reply to Williams' paper and letters].
Dry Plates, May **1893**, 49.

**125** H. and D. Preface. [To reprint of paper
May of May 7, 1890, noting progress since
that date]. Dry Plates, May **1893**,
57.

**126** WILLIAMS, G. F. Determination of Plate
May Speeds. [Following his paper, Jan. 27].
12. P.N. **37**, 293.

**127** COWAN, A. Determination of Plate Speeds.
May [A reply to Mr. Williams, May 12].
19. P.N. **37**, 308.

**128** BURTON, W. K. Density Ratios. P.
June Scraps **46**, 191 ; Am. P. **17**, 369.
1.

**129** COWAN, A. Compensation in Develop-
June ment for Variations in Exposure.
15. [Refers to Burton, June 1]. B.J.P. **40**,
389, 394 ; Am. P. **17**, 421 ; P.N. **37**,
695.

**130** FRY, H. H. Density Ratios and Exposure.
June [On Burton, June 1]. B.J.P. **40**, 375.
16.

**131** H. and D. Latitude in Exposure and
July Speed of Plates. [Plymouth Convention,
6. *see* p. 182]. P. **5**, Conven. Suppt.
22–28 ; Trs. Eders, J. **1894**, 157–78 ;
B.J.P. **40**, 456 ; P.N. **37**, 518, 538,
547 ; P.W. **1**, 325, 337.

**1893—*continued*.**

**132** BOTHAMLEY, C. H. Some points in con-
July nection with Development. B.J.P. **40**,
7. 444 ; P.N. **37**, 458 ; P. Conven. Suppt.,
July 13, 15 ; P.W. **2**, 344.

**133** BURTON, W. K. On the Power of Com-
July pensating in Development for Variation
7. in Exposure. B.J.P. **40**, 461 ; P.N.
**37**, 441, 452, 467 ; P. Suppt., July 13,
17.

**134** STERRY, J. Some Points in Connection
July with Development. [Reply to Both-
21. amley, July 14]. B.J.P. **40**, 456.

**135** CHANNON, H. J. The Influence of Develop-
Aug. ment on Gradation. B.J.P. **40**, 492.
4.

**136** BURTON, W. K. On the Range of Light
Nov. Impinging on a Plate during Exposure
14. in the Camera. [Criticising a paper by
Hurter and Driffield before the Photographic Convention at Plymouth, July
6]. P.J. **18**, 101 ; P.W. **2**, 581.

**137** DRIFFIELD, V. C. The Principles involved
Sept. in the Calculation of Exposures for
Contact Prints on Bromide Paper.
[Widnes P. Soc.]. B.J.P. **40**, 606.

**138** ELDER, H. M. The Speed of Plates :
Nov. a Criticism and a Reply. C.C.J. **7**,
23. 221 ; B.J.P. **40**, 785, 799 ; P.R. of R.
**1893**, 401 ; P.N. **37**, 775, 790, 812,
825.

**139** DIBDEN, W. J. Photometry in Relation
Dec. to Photography. [On the whitest
possible standard lamp]. Dry Plates
**1893**, 110.

**140** PHOTOGRAPHIC SOCIETY OF PHILADELPHIA.
Dec. Report of Special Committee appointed
to consider the Practicability of Recom-
mending a Uniform System of Marking
Plates. [Report in favour of H. and D.
system]. Am. P. **19**, 118, 148, 201 ;
P.W. **3**, 28 ; P.N. **38**, 53, 74.

**141** H. and D. Hurter and Driffield's Re-
Dec. search. [A reply to Elder, Nov. 23].
7. P. **5**, 175.

**142** BOLAS, T. H. and D. and their Critics.
Dec. P.W. **2**, 60.
22.

**143** H. and D. The Speed of Plates : a
Dec. Criticism and a Reply. [Reply to
22. Elder, Nov. 23]. B.J.P. **40**, 822 ; P. **6**,
14 ; P.W. **2**, 608.

**144** ELDER, H. M. The Speed of Plates : a
Criticism and a Reply. [Reply to
Hurter and Driffield, Dec. 22]. B.J.P.
**40**, 838.

### 1894.

**145** ABNEY, W. de W. Photometry. [At Soc. of Arts]. P.N. **38**, 499, 521, 542, 547.

**146** FARMER, E. H. The Work of H. and D.
Jan. 4. B.J.P. **41**, 21, 29, 38 ; P. **6**, 24 ; P.N. **38**, 57. 67, 83 ; P.W. **3**, 20, 31.

**147** H. and D. The Speed of Plates : a
Jan. 12. Criticism and a Reply. [Reply to Elder, Dec. 29]. B.J.P. **41**, 30 ; P. **6**, 47 ; P.W. **2**, 21.

**148** ELDER, H. M. The Speed of Plates : a
Jan. 19. Criticism and a Reply. [Reply to Hurter and Driffield, Jan. 12]. B.J.P. **41**, 46.

**149** H. and D. The Speed of Plates : a
Jan. 26. Criticism and a Reply. [Reply to Elder, Jan. 19]. B.J.P. **41**, 62.

**150** ELDER, H. M. The Speed of Plates : a
Feb. 2. Criticism and a Reply. [Reply to Hurter and Driffield, Jan. 26]. B.J.P. **41**, 79.

**151** WATKINS, A. A Method and Instrument
Feb. 14. for Timing Development. B.J.P. **41**, 120, 125 ; P.N. **38**, 115 ; P.W. **2**, 88, 101, 114.

**152** CADETT and NEALL (Editorial). [On
Mar. Modification of Dibden's Lamp as used by them]. D.P. **1894**, 123.

**153** PRINGLE, A. Negative Development.
Mar. 20. P.W. **3**, 184.

**154** MALLOCK, A. Photographic Action pro-
Mar. 24. duced by various Exposures and Intensities. [Elder Speaking in Discussion]. C.C.J. **8**, 120.

**155** STARNES, H. S. The Density of the
May 11. Photographic Image. B.J.P. **41**, 291.

**156** SCHEINER, Prof. Universal Sensitometer.
June. Zeitschrift f. Instrument K, **1894**, June ; Eders J., **1895**, 394 ; P. Mitt, **1895**, Feb. 1 ; B. Soc. Tran., **1895**, 215.

**157** COWAN, A. H. and D. System. P.C.E.
July 18. **1893–4**, 77 ; B.J.P. **41**, 476.

**158** WATKINS, A. Timing Development.
Oct. 24. P.C.E. **1893–4**, 88 ; B.J.P. **41**, 697, 700 ; A.P. **20**, 319.

**159** DRIFFIELD, V. C. The principles involved
Oct. 24. in Enlarging. [*See* p. 209]. B.J.P. **41**, 714, 724 ; P. **6**, 712 ; Dry Plates, Sept.–Nov. **1894**, 159.

### 1894—*continued*.

**160** EDWARDS, B. J. Timing Development.
Oct. 31. [Criticising Watkins, Oct. 24]. P.C.E. **1893–4**, 95 ; B.J.P. **41**, 718 ; P.N. **39**, 139.

**161** CADETT, J. Speed, Fog, Density and
Nov. Gradation. Dry Plates, Sept.–Nov. **1894**, 158.

**162** DIBDEN, W. J. Standards of Light.
Nov. 2. P. **6**, 712. Dry Plates, Sept.–Nov. **1894**, 168.

**163** WATKINS, A. Timing Development.
Nov. 14. [Reply to Edwards, Oct. 31]. P.C.E. **1894**, 30 ; B.J.P. **41**, 745 ; P.N. **39**, 154.

**164** WATKINS, A. Timing Development. P.
Nov. 14. **6**, 744.

**165** EDWARDS, B. J. Control in Development.
Dec. 5. [Reply to Watkins, Oct. 24]. P.C.E. **1894–5**, 32 ; B.J.P. **40**, 789 ; P. **6**, 792.

### 1895.

**166** VOGEL, H. W. Uber ein praktisches photographisches Sensitometer und eine Normallichtquelle. P. Mitt. **1895**, 335, 351, 382.

**167** WATKINS, A. Control over Results in
Jan. 22. Development. P.J. **19**, 161 ; P.R. of R. **1895**, 74.

**168** CADETT, J. Reliable Testing of Plate
Feb. 8. Sensitiveness. [On adoption of Double Standard, according to Developer]. B.J.P. **42**, 94 ; P.N. **39**, 108.

**169** BOTHAMLEY, C. H. Sensitometry. P.
Feb. 14. **7**, 97.

**170** MARION and Co. The Speed of Plates.
Feb. 15. [Reply to Cadett, Feb. 8]. B.J.P. **42**, 111.

**171** WATKINS, A. Control in Development.
Feb. 20. [Reply to Edwards, Oct. 24]. B.J.P. **42**, 132 ; P.C.E. **1894–5**, 41.

**172** EDWARDS, B. J. Final Reply to Mr.
Feb. 20. Watkins. P.C.E. **1894–5**, 43 ; B.J.P. **42**, 133 ; P.N. **35**, 139.

**173** CADETT, J. Development and Fixing.
Feb. 21. [Alteration in Speed due to different Developers]. P.R.R. **1895**, 86 ; B.J.P. **42**, 133, 139 ; P. **7**, 137 ; P.N. **39**, 137, 141.

**174** CADETT, J. The Speed of Plates. [Reply
Feb. 22. to Marion and Co., Feb. 15]. B.J.P. **42**, 126.

**1895**—*continued.*

**175** GALE, J. R. C. and CADETT, J. Method
Mar.   of Determining Speed of Plates. Dry
Plates, **1895**, 170.

**176** H. and D. The Speed of Plates. [Reply
Mar.   to Cadett Feb 8, 22]. B.J.P. **42**, 141.
1

**177** WATKINS, A. The Speed of Plates.
Mar.   [Reply to Cadett, Feb. 8, 22]. B.J.P.
1.   **42**, 141.

**178** BECKETT, R. Comparative Rapidity of
Mar.   Plates. [Cadett explains Double mark-
5.   ing]. P.N. **39**, 173.

**179** CADETT, J. The Speed of Plates. [De-
Mar.   veloper and Fog. Reply to Watkins,
8.   Mar. 1]. B.J.P. **42**, 157.

**180** STERRY, J. The Speed of Plates. [Reply
Mar.   to Watkins, Mar. 1]. B.J.P. **42**, 174.
15.

**181** ARMSTRONG, H. E. The Chemical Changes
Apr.   Attending Photographic Operations,
2.   III. C.C.J. **9**, 71 ; B.J.P. **42**, 221 ;
P. **7**, 232 ; P.N. **39**, 234.

**182** ACWORTH, J. J. and Mrs. Notes on the
Apr.   Hurter and Driffield System of Speed
9.   Testing. With Discussion. P.J. **19**,
208.

**183** STERRY, J. A Reply to " Notes on the
May   Hurter and Driffield System of Speed
30.   Testing " by Dr. and Mrs. Acworth.
Apr. 9. P.J. **19**, 288.

**184** BOARD OF TRADE. Report on Standards
June   of Light. London 1895 [C–7743].
B.J.P. **42**, 391.

**185** ARMSTRONG, T. N. On a Standard Speed
July   for Dry Plates and Films. [Convention
5.   Paper]. P. **10**, 462 ; B.J.P. **45**, 453.

**186** ACWORTH, J. J. and Mrs. Exposure and
July   Development. [Answer to Sterry,
25.   May 30]. P.J. **19**, 361.

**187** STERRY, J. Exposure and Development :
Aug.   a Further Reply to Dr. and Mrs.
31.   Acworth, July 25. P.J. **19**, 371.

**188** H. and D. Dr. and Mrs. Acworth's Notes
Aug.   on the Hurter and Driffield System of
31.   Speed Testing, Apr. 9. P.J. **19**, 372 ;
P.N. **39**, 586.

**189** ACWORTH, J. J. and Mrs. Exposure and
Oct.   Development relatively considered : a
25.   Final Reply to Messrs. Hurter and
Driffield and to Mr. Sterry. P.J. **20**,
48.

**1895**—*continued.*

**190** ACWORTH, J. J. The Speed of Plates,
Dec.   with Some Methods of Determining the
19.   same. [Warneke, H. and D., Abney,
&c. With discussion]. C.C.J. **10**, 25 ;
B.J.P. **43**, 12.

**191** BURTON, W. K. The Ultimate Power of
Dec.   Developers as a Factor of the Rapidity
19.   of Plates. P. **7**, 802.

**192** BURTON, W. K. [Letter criticising Hurter
Dec.   and Driffield's communication, Aug. 31].
21.   P.J. **20**, 97.

**193** JONES, C. A New Form of Apparatus
Dec.   for Measuring the Densities of Photo-
21.   graphic Plates. P.J. **20**, 86, 93.

**1896.**

**194** ACWORTH, J. J. Die Lichtempfindlichkeit
oder Rapiditat von Platten. Eders, J.
**1896**, 192.

**195** BAYLEY, R. Child. Gelatine. P.J. **20**,
224.

**196** H. and D. On the Range of Light in
Jan.   Photographic Subjects. [Reply to Bur-
9.   ton's letter, Dec. 21]. P.J. **20**, 134.

**197** DIBDEN, W. J. The Standards of Light.
Jan.   [With discussion, Cadett speaking].
29.   S.A. **44**, 233 ; Dry Plates **1896**, 204.

**198** ROYAL PHOTOGRAPHIC SOCIETY. Report
Jan.   of Plate Speeds Committee. P.J. **20**,
31.   124 ; B.J.P. **43**, 119.

**199** JONES, C. Density Measuring. [With dis-
Feb.   cussion]. C.C.J. **10**, 67 ; B.J.P. **43**,
20.   139.

**200** H. and D. Density in Negatives. [Reply
Mar.   to Chapman Jones, Feb. 20]. B.J.P.
6.   **43**, 159.

**201** JONES, C. Density in Negatives. [Reply to
Mar.   H. and D., Mar. 6]. B.J.P. **43**, 175.
12.

**202** JONES, C. On Judging Densities. P. **8**,
Mar.   185.
19.

**203** ACWORTH, CADETT, H. and D., WALL.
Apr.   The Speed of Plates. Photogram **3**,
91.

**204** PHOTOGRAPHIC CLUB. Influence of the
Apr.   Colour of a Negative upon its Printing
1.   Qualities. Discussion. P.C.E. **1894–96**,
100 ; B.J.P. **43**, 236.

**205** CADETT, J. Developers and the Speed of
May   Plates. [Refers to discussion at Photo
8.   Club, Apr. 1]. B.J.P. **43**, 303 ; P. **8**,
243.

**1896**—*continued.*

**206** Burton, W. K. Allowance for Fog in
June 4. Testing Plates and in other cases.
P. **8**, 365.

**207** H. and D. The H. and D. System.
June 25. [Controverting editorial]. P. **8**, 426.

**208** Cadett and Neall. The H. and D.
July 2. System. [Supporting H. and D.,
June 25]. P. **8**, 440.

**209** B.J.P. Marion and Co.'s Works. [De-
July 3. scription of plate testing]. B.J.P. **43**,
422.

**210** Jones, C. The Sensitiveness of Ordinary
July 28. Plates to the less refrangible light.
P.J. **20**, 314.

**211** Abney, W. de W. On Scaling Warnerke's
Aug. 6. New Sensitometer. P. **8**, 509.

**212** Jones, C. A New Form of Apparatus for
Nov. 10. Measuring the Light Reflected from
Prints. P.J. **21**, 70 ; Eders, J. **1897**,
370.

### 1897.

**213** Cadett, J. Density. Dry Plates **3**, 30,
July 36.

**214** B.J.P. The Speed of Plates : H. and
Aug. 6. D.'s Theory Practically Tested. B.J.P.
**44**, 498, 515, 530.

**215** Cadett, J. Latitude of the Plate. Dry
Sept. Plates **3**, 42.

**216** Banks, E. Some little-known Developers.
Sept. 30. [London and Provincial Phot. Assn.
discussion turns on character of " perfect negative " silver and stain]. B.J.P.
**44**, 653.

**217** Bolton, W. B. A Perfect Negative.
Oct. 22. [Reply to Banks, Sept. 30]. B.J.P.
**44**, 678.

### 1898.

**218** Eder, J. M. Bestimmung der Empfindlichkeit der Trockenplatten. [Scheiners
Sensitometer]. P. Corr. **1898**, 654.

**219** Eder, J. M. Welches Princip der Sensito-
meter wäre Zur Construction eines
Normalsensitometers auzunehmen ? P.
Corr. **1898**, 409.

**220** Eder, J. M. Ueber die Sensitometrie von
photographischen Trocken-platten nach
den Beschlüssen des III Internat.
Congres. fur. Aug. Chem. 1898. Eders,
J. **1898**, 37.

**1898**—*continued.*

**221** Janko, P. von. Betrachtungen über
Sensitometrie. Eders, J. **1898**, 91.

**222** Watkins, A. Ueber Entwicklung. [Abs-
tract from Anthony's Annual]. P. Mitt.
**1898**, 73.

**223** H. and D. The Latent Image and its
Jan. 11. Development. [*See* p. 221]. P.J. **22**,
145, 187, 277, 360 ; Eders, J. **1899**, 193.

**224** Jones, C. Density Measurements. [His
Jan. 25. Improved Apparatus]. P.J. **22**, 170 ;
B.J.P. **45**, 58.

**225** Cadett, J. The R.P.S. Progress Medal
Feb. conferred on the H. and D. [Notes on
their work]. Dry Plates **1898**, 85.

**226** Marion and Co. The Actinograph.
Feb. 17. [Improved or Illustrated]. P. **10**,
110 ; B.J.P. **45**, 107.

**227** Banks, E. The Theory of the Latent
Feb. 25. Image. [Refers to H. and D.]. B.J.P.
**44**, 117.

**228** Hurter, F., 1844–98. Short Biography.
Mar. 17. Nature **57**, 469 ; B.J.P. **45**, 155 ; J.S.C.I.
**17**, 228.

**229** Free Lance. On things in general.
Mar. 18. [Critical : on H. and D. papers at
R.P.S.]. B.J.P. **44**, 166.

**230** Sterry, J. The Two Latent Images
Apr. 19. (Organic and Inorganic), Development
Before and After Fixing. P.J. **22** (N.S.),
264 ; Eders, J. **1899**, 289 ; B.J.P. **45**,
254.

**231** Hurter, F., 1844–98. The Life and Work
Apr. 27. of Ferdinand Hurter, Ph.D., con-
tributed by Members of the Liverpool
Section. [Of the Society of Chemical
Industry]. [Biography : His Work in
Manufacturing Chemistry, expecially
Electrolytic Alkali, Photometric Re-
searches, Bibliography]. J.S.C.I. **17**,
406.

**232** B.J.P. (Editorial). Development under
May 20. New Lights. [Refers to H. and D.'s
papers at R.P.S.]. B.J.P. **45**, 322.

**233** Rae. The Practical Measurement of
June 3. Plate Speeds. P.N. **42**, 353, 386, 401 ;
Eder, J. **1899**, 48.

**234** Bothamley, C. H. Some fundamental
July 15. points concerning Development. [Glas-
gow Convention, criticises H. and D.].
B.J.P. **45**, 457.

**1898**—*continued.*

235   GALE, J. R. C., and CADETT, J.   Practice
Oct.    of Photography : the Latent Image and
its Development. [Digest of H. and
D.'s later work]. Dry Plates **1898**, 36,
43, 51, 60, 68.

236   BOTHAMLEY, C. H.   Photographic De-
Nov.    velopers and Development. B.J.P.
23.    **45**, 825.

237   JONES, C.   The Sensitiveness of the Plate.
Dec.    [Results depend upon the Developer].
8.    P. **10**, 794.

238   JONES, C.   An Opacity Balance. P.J.
Dec.    **23**, 99 ; B.J.P. **45**, 813 ; Eders J. **1899**,
23.    456.

239   JONES, C.   On the Principal Causes of
Dec.    Discrepancies in Opacity Measurements.
23.    P.J. **23**, 102.

### 1899.

240   HARTMANN, J.   Ein Apparat zur exacten
Vergleichung der Schwärzung photographischen Platten. Eders, J. **13**, 107.

241   ENGLISH, E.   Uber die Wirkung inter-
mittender Belichtungen auf Bromsilbergelatine. Arch. Wiss. P. **1**, 117.

242   BREDIG, G.   Die Fortpflanzung des
Bildes von einer belichtete Schicht auf
eine unbelichtete in Abney-Versuch.
Eders, J. **13**, 357 ; Arch. Wiss. P. **2**, 54.

243   EDER, J. M.   Nochmals die Silberkeim-
theorie ! Die Silberkeimtheorie und
Verwandtes. P. Corr. **36**, 463, 650 ;
Arch. Wiss. P. **2**, 52. (Ref.)

244   LUTHER, R.   Remarks on the Latent
Image. P. Corr. **36**, 584 ; P.J. **24**, 47.

245   ROOD, C. N.   The Flicker Photometer.
B.J.P. **46**, 660 ; Arch. Wiss. P. **2**, 120
(Ref.) ; American Journal of Science
Sept. **1899**,

246   HINTON, A. H.   Sur le développement du
négatif. [Account of Bothamley v.
Hurter and Driffield controversy]. Mon.
de la P. **6**, 317–319.

247   READMAN, J. B.   The Chemistry of
Photography in relation to Development. B.J.P. **46**, 807 ; Arch. Wiss. P.
**2**, 122 (Ref.).

248   SCHWARZSCHILD, K.   Ueber Abweichun-
gen von Reciprocitätsgesetz für Bromsilber Gelatine. [Schwarzschild's Law.]
P. Corr. **36**, 109.

**1899**—*continued.*

249   SCHWARZSCHILD, K.   Bemerkungen zur
Sensitometrie. P. Corr. **36**, 398.

250   WATKINS, A.   Richtige Entwicklungzeit.
P. Rund **1899**, 390 ; Eders, J. **13**, 588.

251   LUPPO-CRAMER.   Der Begriff der Re-
Jan.    duktionskraft Photographischer Ent-
wickler. P. Mitt. **36**, 245 ; Arch. Wiss.
P. **2**, 28.

252   BOTHAMLEY, C. H.   Remarks on some
Jan.    recent papers concerning the Latent
1.    Photographic Image and its Development. [At R.P.S. criticism of H. and
D.]. P.J. **23**, 123 ; B.J.P. **46**, 29.

253   SCHEINER, J.   Die Verwendung der photo-
Jan.    graphischen Methoden in den exakten
1.    Wissenschaften, insbesondere in der
Astronomie. Arch. Wiss. P. **1**, 1.

254   ABEGG, R.   Die Silberkeimtheorie des
Jan.    latenten Bildes. Arch. Wiss. P. **1**, 15.
1.

255   PRECHT, J.   Die chemische Wirkung des
Jan.    Roten Lichtes. Arch. Wiss. P. **1**, 25,
1.    187.

256   GAEDICKE, J.   Einfluss höherer Tempera-
Jan.    turen auf des latente Bild. Eders, J.
1.    **13**, 122 ; Arch. Wiss. P. **1**, 25.

257   FERY, C.   Uber eine Normallichtquelle.
Jan.    [Acetylene Standard]. C.R. **126**, 1192 ;
1.    Arch. Wiss. P. **1**, 28.

258   ONIMUS, M.   Nouvel appareil pour me-
Jan.    surer la luminosité. C.R. **127**, 663 ;
1.    Arch. Wiss. P. **1**, 29.

259   PRECHT, J.   Neuer Uhtersuchungen über
Jan.    die Gültigkeit des Bunsen-Roscoeschen
1.    Gesetzes bei Bromsilbergelatine. Arch.
Wiss. P. **1**, 11, 57, 149.

260   ABNEY, W. de W.   Struktur des Nega-
Jan.    tivs. Apollo **7**, 75 ; Arch. Wiss. P. **1**,
1.    55.

261   ANDRESEN, M.   Zur Aktinometrie des
Jan.    Sonnenlichts. P. Corr. **35**, 502, 504 ;
1.    Arch. Wiss. P. **1**, 56.

262   LIESEGANG, R. E.   Das latente photo-
Feb.    graphische Bild. Chem. Zeit. **1**, 5 ;
1.    Arch. Wiss. P. **1**, 55.

263   SCHWARZSCHILD, K.   Uber Abweichung
Mar.    vom Reciprocitätsgesetz für Bromsilber-
1.    gelatine. P. Corr. **36**, 109 ; Arch. Wiss.
P. **1**, 73.

264   SCHWARZSCHILD, K.   Uber die Wirkung
Mar.    intermittierender Belichtung auf Brom-
1.    silbergelatine. P. Corr. **36**, 171–78 ;
Arch. Wiss. P. **1**, 103 (Ref.).

**1899**—*continued.*

**265** ABEGG, R. Die silberkeimtheorie des
Mar. latenten Bildes. Arch. Wiss. P. **1**, 15 ;
31. B.J.P. **46**, 196–97.

**266** ABEGG, R. Eine Theorie der photo-
May graphischen Entwickelung. Arch. Wiss.
1. P. **1**, 108.

**267** SCHAUM, K. Uber die Silberkeimwirkung
June beim Entwicklungsvorgang. Arch.
1. Wiss. P. **1**, 139.

**268** SCHUMANN, V. Zur Theorie des latenten
June Bildes. Arch. Wiss. P. **1**, 153.
1.

**269** EDER, J. M. Silbersub-bromide in latenten
June Lichtbilde auf Bromsilber und die
1. Silberkeimtheorie. P. Corr. **36**, 276,
332 ; Arch. Wiss. P. **1**, 155.

**270** HERTMANN, J. Apparat und methode
June zur photographischen Messung von
1. Flächenhelligkeiten. Zeit. Inst. 97 ;
Arch. Wiss. P. **1**, 156 (Ref.).

**271** DOUSE, M. P. Actinometre Automoteur.
July Bull. Soc. Fr. P. **15**, 370 ; B.J.P. **47**,
2. 228.

**272** RANDALL, J. A. A Self-recording Acti-
July nometer. B.J.P. **46**, 426.
7.

**273** BOTHAMLEY, C. H. Some Fundamental
July Points Concerning Development. B.J.P.
10. **46**, 453 ; Bull. Soc. Belg. P. **26**, 482 ;
Bull. Soc. Fr. P. **15**, 520 ; Arch. Wiss.
P. **2**, 24.

**274** SCHAUM, K. Concerning the Action of
July Nascent Silver in the Process of
28. Development. [Trs. from Arch. Wiss.
P.]. B.J.P. **46**, 469.

**275** SCHUMANN, V. Zur Theorie des latenten
July Bildes. Arch. Wiss. P. **1**, 153 ; P.J.
31. **23**, 313.

**276** MERCATOR, G. Silberkeim oder subhaloid-
Aug. theorie. Arch. Wiss. P. **1**, 199.
1.

**277** PIPER, C. W. The Action of Nascent
Aug. Silver in Development. [*Re* Schaum,
4. p. 469]. B.J.P. **46**, 493.

**278** LUTHER, R. Edersche Versuch und das
Aug. latente Bild. P. Corr. **36**, 584 ; B.J.P.
25. **46**, 664.

**279** LIESEGANG, R. E. Das korn der Negative.
Sept. Arch. Wiss. P. **1**, 229.
1.

**280** SCHWARZCHILD, K. Bermerkungen zur
Sept. sensitometrie. P. Corr. **36**, 398 ; Arch.
1 Wiss. P. **1**, 238 (Ref.).

**281** RANDELL, J. A. Actinograms and Self-
Sept. Recording Actinometer. B.J.P. **46**,
1. 426–27 ; Arch. Wiss. P. **1**, 239 (Ref.).

**282** ABEGG, R. Silberkeim-oder Subhaloid-
Oct. theorie. Arch. Wiss. P. **1**, 268.
1.

**283** LUTHER, R. Vorläufige notiz über die
Oct. natur des latenten Bildes und den
1. sogenannten Ederschen versuch. Arch.
Wiss. P. **1**, 272.

**284** ENGLISCH, E. Uber die Einwirkung von
Oct. Brom auf das latente Bild. [Also a
1. reply to Eders article, " Nochmals die
Silberkeimtheorie "]. Arch. Wiss. P. **1**,
282.

**285** PRECHT, J. Gesetz der photographischen
Oct. Wirkung der Rôntgenstrahlen. Arch.
1. Wiss. P. **1**, 260.

**286** MERCATOR, G. The Nascent-silver and
Oct. Subhaloid Theories. B.J.P. **46**, 628.
6.

**287** ABNEY, W. de W. Thickness of film.
Oct. [Camera Club]. B.J.P. **46**, 664 ; Arch.
12. Wiss. P. **2**, 57

**288** PRECHT, J. Uber ziffermässige Bestim-
Nov. mung photographischer Schwarzungen
1. und Entwicklungschleier. Arch. Wiss.
P. **1**, 292.

**289** EDER, J. M. Uber Schleier beim Ent-
Nov. wickeln der Platten und dessen ziffer-
1. mässige Bestimmung. P. Corr. **36**, 529 ;
Arch. Wiss. P. **1**, 295 (Ref.).

**290** PRECHT, J. Photographisches Analogon
Nov. zum Phônomen von Purkinje. [Com-
1. parison of amyl-acetate and benzene
lamps for sensitometric purposes, &c.].
Arch. Wiss. P. **1**, 277, and (Nachtrag),
311.

**291** PRECHT, J. Neue versuche zur Theorie
Dec. der photographischen Prozesse. Arch.
2. Wiss. P. **2**, 1.

**292** ABEGG, R. Die Silberkeim-oder subhaloid
Dec. theorie. Arch. Wiss. P. **1**, 268 ; B.J.P.
8. **46**, 773.

**293** EDER, J. M. Die Silberkeim Theorie und
Dec. Verwaucttes. P. Corr. **36**, 1650 ;
15. B.J.P. **46**, 788.

**294** ABNEY, W. de W. A Sensitometer for
Dec. Three-Colour Work. B.J.P. **46**, 814 ;
19. P.J. **24**, 121 ; Arch. Wiss. P. **2**, 123
(Ref.).

### 1900.

**295** EDER, J. M.  Modern Intensifiers and their Effect.  [From P. Corr. **37**, 23].  B.J.P. **47**, 68.

**296** EDER, J. M.  Bestimmung der Empfindlichkeit der Trockenplatten.  P. Corr. **37**, 170, 240 ; Arch. Wiss. P. **1**, 30.

**297** EDER, J. M.  System der sensitometrie photographischen Platten.  P. Corr. **37**, 241, 304, 364, 441, 495, 567, 625.

**298** GAEDICKE, J. B.  Der Penetrations Coefficient von Trocknen Platten für Lichtstrahlen.  Eders, J. **14**, 5.

**299** JONES, C.  Dichtigkeits-Bestimmungen.  Eders, J. **14**, 48.

**300** SCHWARZSCHILD, K.  Ueber Sensitometrische Regeln und ihre astronomische auwendung.  Eders, J. **14**, 161.

**301** MERCATOR, G.  Silberkeim-oder Subhaloidtheorie.  Arch. Wiss. P. **1**, 268.
Jan.

**302** ABEGG, R.  Zu Herrn Eders Artikel uber die Silberkeimtheorie.  Arch. Wiss. P. **2**, 31.
Jan.

**303** VOGEL, O.  Beitrag zur Kenntnis des Silbersub-bromids.  P. Mitt. **36**, 334 ; Arch. Wiss. P. **2**, 23 (Ref.).
Jan.

**304** ABEGG, R.  Die chemischen Vorgänge in der Photographie. Sechs Vorträge von Dr. R. Luther.  I. Latentes Bild, nach Luther ; II. Theorie des Eisenentwicklers, nach Luther ; III. Theoretisches über andere Entwickler, nach Luther ; IV. Theorie der Solarisation, nach Luther ; V. Theorie des samen Fixier-bades, nach Luther.  Arch. Wiss. **2**, 20, 76, 100.
Jan.

**305** SCHAUM, K.  Zur Theorie des photographischen Processe.  [Latent Image ; Development].  Arch. Wiss. **2**, 9.
Jan.

**306** LUTHER, R.  Untersuchungen über umkehrbare photochemische Vorgänge.  Arch. Wiss. P. **2**, 35.
Feb.

**307** ENGLISCH, E.  Kritische Bemerkung zur Theorie des latenten Bildes.  Arch. Wiss. P. **2**, 50–52.
Feb.

**308** HARTMAN, J.  A new Photographic Photometer.  B.J.P. **47**, 67.
Feb. 2.

**309** PRECHT, J.  Zur Sensitometrie photographischer Platten.  [Polemical].  Arch. Wiss. P. **2**, 81, 163.
Mar.

**1900**—*continued.*

**310** PRECHT, J.  Uber Ziffermässige Bestimmung photographischer Schwarzungen.  Arch. Wiss. P. **2**, 99.
Mar.

**311** LIESEGANG, R. E.  Umkehrbare photochemische Vorgänge.  [*Re* Luther, Arch. Wiss. P. **2**, 35 and 59].  Arch. Wiss. P. **2**, 111.
Mar. 17.

**312** WATKINS, A.  Some developers compared.  P.J. **24**, 221.
Mar. 27.

**313** PRECHT, J.  A Contribution to the Theory of Photographic Development.  [Arch. Wiss. P.   ]  B.J.P. **47**, 650.
May.

**314** JONES, C.  Effect of Wave-length on Gradation.  P.J. **24**, 279.
May 8.

**315** WATKINS, A.  Hydroquinone and Colour Impressions.  P.J. **24**, 287.
May 22.

**316** ENGLISCH, E.  Studien über die Solarisation bei Bromsilbergelatine.  Arch. Wiss. P. **2**, 242.
July 5.

**317** EDER, J. M.  Moderne Verstärker für Bromsilbergelatineplatten und ihr Schwärzungseffekt.  P. Corr. **37**, 23 ; Arch. Wiss. P. **2**, 147 (Ref.).
June.

**318** ENGLISCH, E.  Uber die Zeitlichen Vierlauf der durch das Licht verursachten Veranderungen der Bromsilbergelatine.  Arch. Wiss. P. **2**, 131.
July 9.

**319** EDER, J. M.  The effect of Intensification and Reduction.  [Trs. P. Corr. **37**].  B.J.P. **47**, 469.
July 27.

**320** IVES, F. E.  Gradation in red with Hydroquinone.  [*Re* Watkins, P.J. p. 287].  P.J. **24**, 336.
July 30.

**321** PRECHT, J., and STRECKER, W.  Versuche über die Silberkeimtheorie beim Entwicklungsvorgang.  Arch. Wiss. P. **2**, 158.
Aug.

**322** PRECHT, J.  Beitrage zur Theorie der photographischen Entwicklung.  Arch. Wiss. P. **2**, 155.
Aug.

**323** MARTENS, F. F.  Einige neue photometrische Apperate.  II. Ein neuer Photometeraufsatz.  III. Neuer Flammanmesser für Hefner-Lampen.  Arch. Wiss. P. **2**, 164.
Aug.

**324** PRECHT, J.  Herr Eder und die Sensitometrie.  [Polemical].  Arch. Wiss. P. **2**, 169.
Aug.

**1900**—*continued.*

**325** JANKO, P. von.  Intensification, comparative effect of various methods.  [P.
Aug.  Corr.  ].  B.J.P. **47**, 518.

**326** B.J.P.  Ilford Wedge Screens.  B.J.P.
Sept.  **47**, 662.
2.

**327** MARTENS, F. F.  Einige neue photometrische Apparate.  IV Uber ein neues
Oct.  Polarisationsphotometer.  Arch. Wiss.
P. **2**, 184.

**328** PRECHT, J., and ENGLISCH, E.  Uber die
Oct.  Abhängigkeit der Grösse Punktförmiger
Bilder auf Bromsilbergelatine von der
Entwicklung.  Arch. Wiss. P. **2**, 179.

**329** ABNEY, W. de W.  On the estimation of
Oct.  the luminosity of coloured surfaces used
for colour discs.  P.J. **24**, 319 ; Arch.
Wiss. P. **2**, 201 (Ref.).

**330** PICKERING, E. C.  Measurement of photographic intensities.  B.J.P. **47**, 505 ;
Oct.  Arch. Wiss. P. **2**, 203 (Ref.).

**331** ABNEY, W. de W.  Effect of thickness of
Oct.  the film on the image and on the
12.  sensitiveness of the plate.  C.C.J. **13**,
173–80 (4 figs.) ; B.J.P. **46**, 380 ; Eders,
J. **14**, 302–12.

**332** EDER, J. M.  System der Sensitometrie
Nov.  Photographischen Platten.  P. Corr. **37**,
6.  495, 567, 625.

## 1901.

**333** HOFFMANN, A.  Ein neues Photometer
zur Sensitometrie.  P. Corr. **38**, 91, 651.

**334** LUPPO-CRAMER.  Studien über die Natur
des latenten Lichtbildes.  P. Corr. **39**,
145, 218, 559 (correction 643) ; Trs.
B.J.P. **48**, 520, 552, 569, 820.

**335** MARTENS, F. F.  Ueber einen Apparat
zur Bestimmung der Schwärzung photographischer Platten.  P. Corr. **39**, 528.

**336** CADETT, J.  Exposure meters.  B.J.P. **48**,
Jan.  27.

**337** SCHAUM, K.  Uber die Struktur der
Jan.  Negative.  Arch. Wiss. P. **2**, 267.

**338** LIESEGANG, R. E.  Uber eine scheinbre
Jan.  Wirkung von Silberkernen auf Silberhaloide.  Arch. Wiss. P. **2**, 263.

**339** ABEGG, R.  Uber den Einfluss des Bindemittels auf den photochemischen effekt
Mar.  in Bromsilberemulsionen und die photochemische Induktion.  Arch. Wiss. P. **2**,
271.

**1901**—*continued.*

**340** ENGLISCH, E.  Eine Amyl-lampe für
Mar.  sensitometrische Zwecke.  Arch. Wiss.
P. **2**, 279 ; P. Mitt. **28**, 157.

**341** EDER, J. M.  Systeme der Sensitometrie
Mar.  photographischen Platten.  P. Corr. **37**,
241, 304, 364, 441, 497, 577, 628, 668,
736 ; Arch. Wiss. P. **2**, 282.

**342** ENGLISCH, E.  Nachträge zu meinem
Mar.  Abhandlungen über die Wirkung intermittierender Belichtungen.  [Arch. Wiss.
P. **1**, 117].  Arch. Wiss. P. **2**, 280.

**343** KRUSS, H.  Die Flamme der Hefnerlampe
Mar.  und die Messung ihrer Länge.  Arch.
Wiss. P. **2**, 285.

**344** JONES, C.  A Simple and Inclusive Method
Apr.  of Testing Plates.  P.J. **26**, 246.
23.

**345** JONES, C.  Plate Tester.  P. Corr. **39**, 430.
Apr.  Eders, J. **15**, 491 ; Bull. Soc. Belg. P.
23.  **28**, 391.

**346** MARTENS, F. F.  Uber einen Apparat zur
May.  Bestimmung der Schwärzung photographischen Platten.  P. Corr. **39**, 529.

**347** RANDALL, J. A.  The Problem of Actinometry.  [*Re* Hurter's Actinometer].
Nov.  B.J.P. **48**, 748.
14.

## 1902.

**348** FRIEDLAENDER, J. H.  I. Zur Theorie der
Entwicklung.  P. Corr. **39**, 252.

**349** EDER, J. M.  Systeme de Sensitometrie
des Plaques Photographiques.  [Trs. by
E. Belin].  Laboratoire d'Essais de la
Soc. Fr. de P. Gauthier-Villars, Paris,
1902.

**350** EDER, J. M.  System der Sensitometrie
photographischen Platten.  II. Abhandlung.  P. Corr. **39**, 386, 449, 504.

**351** SEBERT.  Appareil à pendule pour la
mesure de la sensibilité des preparations
photographiques.  Bull. Soc. Belg. P.
**29**, 184.

**352** LUPPO-CRAMER.  The Latent Image.
Jan.  B.J.P. **49**, 9.
3.

**353** SOMERVILLE, C. W.  Theory of Development.  [Weak developers].  P.N. **46**,
May  312.
16.

**354** HAMBLING, R. A.  Exposure and Development.  P.N. **46**, 343.
May
30.

**1902**—*continued.*

**355** WILBERT, M. I. Reversal. P. **14,** 502.
July 17.

**356** JONES, C. Testing and Description of Photographic Plates. Am. P. **36,** 310.
Oct. 10.

**357** RANDALL, J. A. Measuring the Transparency and Opacity of Negatives. P.C. **2,** 580.
Sept. 11.

**358** WATKINS, A. Some Aspects of Photographic Development. [At S.A.]. B.J.P. **49,** 1025.
Dec.

### 1903.

**359** LUPPO-CRAMER. Neue Untersuchungen zur Theorie der photographischen Vorgänge. P. Corr. **40,** 25, 89, 174, 224, 272, 354, 495, 611, 670–710.

**360** EDER, J. M. Uber die Sensitometrische Prüfung Gewöhnlichen und Orthochromatischen Platten. P. Corr. **40,** 426, 439 ; Eders, J. **16,** 394, 399.

**361** STERRY, J. Photography by Rule. Stiff and Sons, Ltd., London, 1903, 129 pages. [Methods founded on Hurter and Driffield's work].

**362** WATKINS, A. Quelques aperçus sur le developpement photographique. [Trs. from B.J.P. 1902, p. 1025]. Mon. de la P. **10,** 18.

**363** DRIFFIELD, V. C. Control of the Development Factor and a Note on Speed Determination. [*See* p. 293.] P.J. **43,** 16 ; Eders J. **17,** 289 ; B.J.P. **50,** 93.
Jan. 27.

**364** SHEPPARD, S. E., and MEES, C. E. K. On the Development Factor. P.J. **43,** 48 ; Eders J. **17,** 395.
Feb. 25.

**365** HOUDAILLE. Influence de la Temperature du Temps de jour. Bull. Soc. Fr. P. **19,** 256 ; Eders J. **17,** 463.
Mar. 6.

**366** BENNETT, H. W. Control in Gradation of Negative. [Criticises H. and D. and claims power of control by development]. P.J. **43,** 74.
Mar. 10.

**367** WALL, E. J. What is Development ? P.N. **47,** 167, 199.
Mar. 13.

**368** WATKINS, A. Mr. Bennett on Time Development. B.J.P. **50,** 338, 497, 617.
Apr. 24.

**369** PIPER, C. W. On Development Controversy. B.J.P. **50,** 366.
May 8.

**1903**—*continued.*

**370** BENNETT, H. W. Is Time Development Desirable ? [Reply to Watkins, Apr. 24, and Piper, May 8]. B.J.P. **50,** 449, 576, 658, 697, 778.
June 5.

**371** EDER, J. M. Sensitometrische Prüfung gewöhnlichen und orthochromatischen Platten. [Congress App. Chem. Berlin]. Zeit. Wiss. P. **1,** 119.
June 6.

**372** SHEPPARD, S. E., and MEES, C. E. K. On the Highest Development Factor Obtainable on any Plate. P.J. **43,** 199.
June 9.

**373** HOUDAILLE. Effect of Temperature on Development. B.J.P. **50,** 464.
June 12.

**374** ENGLISCH, E. Das verhalten der Bromsilbergelatine im Grenzgebiet der Solarisation. Zeit. Wiss. P. **1,** 364.
June 18.

**375** EDER, J. M. Magnesium and Photometry. [Edit. Note, Acad. Sc. Vien.]. B.J.P. **50,** 523.
July 3.

**376** DRECKER, J. Uber Intensitätsverhältnisse in photographische Lichthöfen. Zeit. Wiss. P. **1,** 183.
June 20.

**377** PRECHT, J. Die Methode der verzogerten Entwicklung. Zeit. Wiss. P. **1,** 262 ; Phys. Z. **1902, 3,** 426 ; Chem. Z. **1903,** 596.
Aug. 27.

**378** PRECHT, J. Einige Anwendungen der Methode der verzögerten Entwicklung. Zeit. Wiss. P. **1,** 355–57.
Aug. 28.

**379** RANDALL, J. A. Measuring the Transparency and Opacity of Negatives. Photo. Chron. **2,** 580.
Sept. 11.

**380** BAKER, H. Time Development. [*Re* Watkins-Bennett]. B.J.P. **50,** 758, 798, 856.
Sept. 18.

**381** SANGER-SHEPHERD. Accurate Exposure and Systematic Development. [C. C. Lecture]. B.J.P. **50,** 915.
Nov. 4.

**382** DRIFFIELD, V. C. The Hurter and Driffield System. [*See* p. 300.] Photo-Miniature No. 56, Tennant and Ward, New York, Dawbarn and Ward, Ltd., London. P.J. **44,** 133 (Review).
Nov. 15.

### 1904.

**383** CALLIER, A. Adaption de sensitometre scheiner à l'etude des plaques orthochromatiques. Bull. Soc. Belg. P. **31,** 184, 426.

# Bibliography

355

**1904**—*continued.*

**384** STERRY, J. Umkehrung des photographischen Bildes durch Unterexposition. P.J. **43**, 290 ; Zeit. Wiss. P. **2**, 187.

**385** SIMMANCE-ABADY. Das Simmance-Abady flimmer photometer Zeit. Wiss P. **2**, 435

**386** EDER, J. M., and VALENTA, E. Beitrage zur Photochemie und Spectralanalyse. P.J. **44**, 185 ; Photogram **1904**, 232.

**387** STERRY, J. The separation of Development into Primary and Secondary action. Effect on correct rendering of Light Values and Theory of Latent Image. P.J. **44**, 50 ; B.J.P. **51**, 315 ; Zeit. Wiss. P. **2**, 188.
Jan. 26.

**388** BELIN, E. Nouvelle méthode de determination de la sensibilité des preparations photographiques. Spectrosensitometrie Sinusoidale. Bull. Soc. Fr. P. **18**, 324.
Apr. 1.

**389** REEB, H. Theory of Development. Bull. Soc. Fr. P. **20**, 324.
Apr. 18.

**390** LUMIÈRE, A. and L., and A. SEYEWETZ. Einfluss der Natur der Entwickler auf die Grösse der Korns des reduzierten Silbers. Zeit. Wiss. P. **2**, 256.
June 22.

**391** MEES, C. E. K., and SHEPPARD, S. E " On Instruments for Sensitometric Investigation, with an historical résumé." [With Bibliography up to date]. P.J. **44**, 200 ; Zeit. Wiss. P. **2**, 303 (translation).
June 28.

**392** BRAUN, W. Uber die Natur des latenten Bildes. [Effect of oxygen on the formation of the latent image.] Zeit. Wiss. P. **2**, 290.
July 4.

**393** WALL, E. J. The Testing of Orthochromatic Plates. B.J.P. **51**, 926 ; Eders J. **18**, 356.
Sept. 28.

**394** CHANNON, H. J. Exposure and Density. [Criticises H. and D.'s Theory]. B.J.P. **51**, 845.
Sept. 30.

**395** PIZZIGHELLI, G. L'esame di lastre fotografiche. [Full account of methods of Eder, Scheiner, Callier, H. and D.]. Bol. Soc. Fot. It. **7**, 357.
Nov.

**396** ENGLISH, E. Die Zweite Umkehrung des Photographischen Bildes. Zeit. Wiss. P. **2**, 375.
Nov. 1.

**1904**—*continued.*

**397** MEES, C. E. K., and SHEPPARD, S.E. On the Sensitometry of Photographic Plates. [Thesis for B.Sc., Bibliography]. P.J. **44**, 282 ; Eders J. **19**, 355 ; Zeit. Wiss. P. **3**, 97.
Nov. 10.

**398** PRECHT, J. Löslichkeit des latenten, primär fixierten Bildes in Salpetersäure. Zeit. Wiss. P. **2**, 413.
Nov. 28.

**399** HERTZSPRUNG, E. Notiz über die spektrale Veränderung der gradation von Bromsilbergelatineplatten. Zeit. Wiss. P. **2**, 419.
Dec. 3.

**400** SHEPPARD, S. E., and MEES, C. E. K. The Theory of Photographic Processes : On the Chemical Dynamics of Development. P.J. **45**, 281 ; Zeit. Wiss. P. **3**, 97.
Dec. 20.

## 1905.

**401** EDER, J. M. Uber die Natur des latenten Licht bilder. Zeit. Wiss. P. **3**, 329 ; B.J.P. **52**, 950, 968.

**402** SHEPPARD, S. E. The Reversibility of Photographic Development and the Retarding Action of Soluble Bromide. J.C.S. **87**, i, 1311 ; Zeit. Wiss. P. **3**, 443.

**403** HARTMANN, J. P. Uber die Messung der Schwarzung photographischen Platten. Eders J. **19**, 89.

**404** LUPPO-CRAMER. Neue Untersuchungen zur Theorie des photographischen Vorgänge. P. Corr. **42**, 12, 118, 159, 254, 319, 374, 432, 478, 573.

**405** HERTZSPRUNG, E. Eine spectralphotometrische Methode. Zeit. Wiss. P. **3**, 15.
Jan. 5.

**406** JONES, C. Wave Length and Gradation. B.J.P. **52**, 13.
Jan. 6.

**407** PRECHT, J., und STENGER, E. Uber die chemische Farbenhelligkeit des Tageslichts. Zeit. Wiss. P. **3**, 27.
Jan. 12.

**408** PRECHT, J., und STENGER, E. Photochemische Farbenhelligkeit des Bogenlichts. Zeit. Wiss. P. **3**, 36.
Jan. 18.

**409** SHEPPARD, S. E., and MEES, C. E. K. The Theory of Photographic Processes. I. On the Chemical Dynamics of Development. [Thesis for Degree of B.S.C.]. P.J. **45**, 281.
Feb. 2.

**1905**—*continued.*

**410** PRECHT, J., und STENGER, E. Uber
Feb. 18. Bromsilbergelatine mit Entwicklerge-
halt. Charakteristische Kurve und
Verhalten in Solarisationsgebiet. Zeit.
Wiss. P. **3**, 76.

**411** PRECHT, J., und STENGER, E. Die
Feb. 6. Farbenwerte auf panchromatischen
Platten in ihrer Abhängigkeit von der
Entwicklungsdauer. Zeit. Wiss. P. **3**, 67.

**412** PRECHT, J. Bemerkung zur Solarisation.
Feb. 21. Zeit. Wiss. P. **3**, 75.

**413** BAYLEY, R. C. Time Development. [At
Feb. 24. S.A.]. B.J.P. **52**, 149, 168.

**414** FERGUSON, W. B., and HOWARD, B. F.
Feb. 28. Control of the Development Factor at
Various Temperatures. P.J. **45**, 118–26;
B.J.P. **52**, 249; Eders, J. **19**, 408.

**415** FÉRY, C. An Acetylene Light Standard.
Mar. Journal de Physique **3**, 838; P.J. **45**,
132.

**416** WILDERMANN, M. Galvanic Cells Pro-
Mar. duced by Action of Light. [H. and D.'s
equation in terms of E.M.F.]. Proc.
Roy. Soc. **74**, 369; P.J. **45**, 131.

**417** GOODWIN, W. Capacity of Different
Mar. 10. Printing Processes for Rendering Gradation. B.J.P. **52**, 187, 207, 227.

**418** OTSUKI, C. Influence of Length of Time
June 23. of Development on Degree of Darkening
of the Photographic Plate. B.J.P. **52**,
490.

**419** SHEPPARD, S. E., and MEES, C. E. K.
June 13. On Some Points in Modern Chemical
Theory and their Bearing on Develop-
ment. P.J. **45**, 241–48.

**420** EDER, J. M. Ueber die Natur des latenten
July 6. Lichtbildes. P. Corr. **42**, 423–26;
B.J.P. **52**, 950, 968.

**421** JOLY, J. The Latent Image. [Photo.
July 10. Convention, Dublin]. B.J.P. **52**, 551.

**422** LUTHER, R. Die Aufgaben der Photo-
July 26. chemie. Zeit. Wiss. P. **3**, 257; P.J.
**45**, 406 (Rev.).

**423** BAEKELAND, L. Photoretrogression, oder
Aug. 21. ders Verschwinden des latenten photographischen Bildes. Zeit. Wiss. P. **3**,
58.

**424** KING, E. S. Photographic Photometry.
Oct. [Astronomical at Harvard College Ob-
servatory]. P.B. **17**, 267; P.J. **45**, 344
(Rev.).

**1905**—*continued.*

**425** MEES, C. E. K. Report on " Barnet
Oct. Roll Films." P.J. **45**, 345.

**426** SHEPPARD, S. E., and MEES, C. E. K.
Oct. The Theory of Photographic Processes.
Part II. On the Chemical Dynamics of
Development, including the Microscopy
of the Image. [Paper reprinted from
the Royal Society]. P.J. **45**, 319;
Eders, J. **20**, 387; P. Corr. **43**, 129.

**427** JONES, C. Photography the Servant of
Nov. Science. [Trail Taylor lecture, criticism
on H. and D.]. P.J. **45**, 362.

**428** BELIN, E. Methode Spectro-sensito-
Dec. 1. metrique. Bull. Soc. Fr. P. **22**, 26;
B.J.P. **53**, 630.

**429** CHANNON, H. J. How the Density
Dec. 1. Ratios are Altered. B.J.P. **52**, 949.

**430** EDER, J. M. The Nature of the Latent
Dec. 1. Image. [Viennese Acad. Sc.]. B.J.P.
**52**, 950, 968.

### 1906.

**431** HOMOLKA, B. Untersuchungen über die
Wirkung der Bromkalien in der Bromsilbergelatine. [Indoxyl.]. P. Corr. **43**,
216; B.J.P. **54**, 136, 216, 267; Bull.
Soc. Fot. It. **19**, 9.

**432** LUMIERE and SEYEWETZ. Action of
Alkalis in Organic Developers. Bull.
Soc. Fr. de P. **22**, 32; P.J. **46**, 169.

**433** PREOBRAJENSKY, P. The Solarisation
Curve. Bull. Soc. Fr. 1906, 124–281;
P.J. **46**, 371.

**434** KINGDON, J. C. Considerations on the
Jan. 9. Nature of the Latent Image, &c. P.J.
**46**, 57; B.J.P. **53**, 36.

**435** CHANNON, H. J. The Latent Image.
Jan. 19. B.J.P. **53**, 78.

**436** MEES, C. E. K. The Latent Image.
Jan. 26. B.J.P. **53**, 78, 97.

**437** COUSIN, M. H., and BELLIENI, M. H.
Feb. 2. Appareil de Photometrie Photographique. [Intermittent exposure and
Schwarzchild's law]. Bull. Soc. Fr. P.
**22**, 471–78 (1 fig.).

**438** BULL, A. J. The Latent Image. [Lond.
Feb. 8. and Prov. P. Ass.]. B.J.P. **53**, 169.

**1906**—*continued.*

**439** MEES, C. E. K. The Interpretation of
Feb. 9. Sensitometric Tests. B.J.P. **53**, 104,
126, 143 ; also 179, 617, 636, 797, 857,
899.

**440** MEES, C. E. K., and SHEPPARD, S. E.
Feb. 27. The Estimation of the Colour Sensitiveness of Plates. P.J. **46**, 110.

**441** BAKER, T. T. Theory and Practice of
Mar. 4. Intensification. [Measurements and
curves]. B.J.P. **53**, 264, 284, 309.

**442** FERGUSON, W. B. A New Method of
Mar. 10. Calculating the Times of Development
at Various Temperatures. P.J. **46**,
182–89 ; B.J.P. **53**, 296 ; Eders, J. **21**,
474.

**443** CHANNON, H. J. A New Formula for
May 8. Expressing Density in Terms of Ex-
posure. [On H. and D. mathematics].
P.J. **46**, 216.

**444** SHEPPARD, S. E., and MEES, C. E. K.
May 25. The Theory of Fixation and the Action
of Thiosulphate in Development. [Bib-
liography]. P.J. **46**, 235.

**445** LUPPO-CRAMER. Nature of the Developed
June 8. Image. [P. Corr. 1906, 242]. B.J.P.
**53**, 449.

**446** LOCKETT, A. The Personal Element in
June 15. Factorial Development. B.J.P. **53**,
464, 502.

**447** PAYNE, A. A Note on the Sensitometry
June 15. of Plates. [Criticism of Mees and
Sheppard]. B.J.P. **53**, 478, 499, 558.

**448** SHEPPARD, S. E. The Sensitometry of
July 6. Plates. [*Re* Payne, p. 478]. B.J.P.
**53**, 538.

**449** FERGUSON, W. B. A Note on the Sensito-
July 27. metry of Plates. [Reply to Payne].
B.J.P. **53**, 598 (correction 857).

**450** ABNEY, W. de W. To make a Sensito-
Aug. meter for Three-Colour Work. P.J.
**46**, 298.

**451** REEB, H. Theory of Development.
Aug. [Abst. from Bull. Soc. Loraine de P.
**13**, 8]. P.J. **46**, 302.

**452** MEES, C. E. K. (Wratten and Wain-
Sept. 9. wright). Explains the Gradation
Photometer. P.J. **46**, 341.

**453** GASCOIGNE, A. The Sensitometry of
Sept. 12. Plates. B.J.P. **53**, 778, 797 (Mees),
817.

**1906**—*continued.*

**454** MEES, C. E. K. How Development occurs.
Oct. 31. [Lecture at Croydon C.C.]. B.J.P. **53**,
890–91, 986.

**455** MEES, C. E. K. Screened Acetylene
Nov. 9. Light. B.J.P. **53**, 899.

**456** BENNETT, H. W. Is Time Development
Nov. 28. desirable ? [Croydon C.C. Mees in
discussion]. B.J.P. **53**, 985 ; 1018
(Watkins).

**1907.**

**457** HOMOLKA, B. Untersuchungen über die
Natur des latenten und des negativen
photographischen Bildes. P. Corr. **44**,
55, 115.

**458** SHEPPARD, S. E., and MEES, C. E. K.
Jan. 8. The action of substances on the Latent
Image. P.J. **47**, 65 ; B.J.P. **54**, 33.

**459** COUSIN, H. The Comparator : a new
Jan. 11. photographic Photometer. B.J.P. **54**,
24.

**460** LUMIERE, L., and SEYEWETZ, A. Sur la
Jan. 18. difference d'intensité des voiles produits
par l'action des révélateurs sur les
plaques du gelatinobromure d'Argent
exposées et non exposées. Bull. Soc.
Fr. P. **23**, 101–04.

**461** LUMIERE and SEYEWETZ. The limits of
Feb. useful work in the Fixing Bath. P.J.
**47**, 129.

**462** EMICH, F. Zur Geschichte des latenten
Feb. 11. photographischen Bildes. Zeit. Wiss.
P. **5**, 107.

**463** SCHLOEMANN, E. Zur Kenntnis des
Feb. 12. latenten Bildes. Zeit. Wiss. P. **5**, 183.

**464** SCHEFFER, W. Microscopic researches on
Feb. 15. plate grain. B.J.P. **54**, 116, 271, 540.

**465** STERRY, J. Action of Oxidisers on the
Feb. 19. development of the Latent Image.
P.J. **47**, 170 ; B.J.P. **54**, 166, 171, 206
Eders, J. **21**, 364.

**466** HOMOLKA, B. The nature of the Latent
Feb. 22. Image and of the Negative Image
Indoxyl Development]. B.J.P. **54**,
136, 216, 267.

**467** MEES, C. E. K., and WRATTEN, S H.
Mar. 8. Development with insufficient reducer.
B.J P. **54**, 173. [*See* Ferguson, 206].

**468** LUMIERE, A. and L., and SEYEWETZ, A.
Mar. 15. Fog on Exposed and Unexposed Plates.
B.J.P. **54**, 195 ; Zeit. Wiss. P. **5**, 392.

**1907**—*continued.*

**469** CRANSTON, P. M.   Time of Development
Apr.   and Temperature.   [*Re* Houdaille and
4.    Ferguson].   B.J.P. **54**, 300, 358.

**470** FERGUSON,   W. B.   Variation of Time
May   of Development with Temperature.
3.    [Reply to Cranston   ].   B.J.P.
**54**, 337

**471** COLLINGRIDGE, H.   Variation of Time
Apr.   of Development with Temperature.
12.   [Houdaille's Law   ].   B.J.P.
**54**, 300.

**472** WALLACE, R. J.   Studies in Sensitometry.
May   [Review by Dr. Mees of paper in
Astrophysical Journal].   P.J. **47**, 246 ;
Eders, J. **21**, 425.

**473** SHEPPARD, S. E.   Time and Temperature
May   in Development.   [*Re* Houdaille and
3.    Ferguson].   B.J.P. **54**, 337.

**474** DEMOLE, E.   Experiments on the Latent
May   Image.   [Action of Ferricyanide].
10.   B.J.P. **54**, 346, 600.

**475** WALLACE, R. J.   The Daylight Sensito-
May   metry of Photographic Plates, &c.
17.   B.J.P. **54**, 368, 388, 408, 427 ; P.J. **57**,
247.

**476** MEES, C. E. K., and WRATTEN, S. H.
May   The Wedge Spectrographs.   B.J.P. **54**,
24.   384.

**477** LUPPO-CRAMER.   The Action of Reducers.
May   Intensification and Toning with Ferri-
24.   cyanide.   B.J.P. **54**, 385, 392.

**478** SHEPPARD, S. E., and MEES, C. E. K.
June   Investigations on the theory of the
Photographic Process.   London : Long-
man and Co.   [Review].   P.J. **47**, 284.

**479** SHEPPARD, S. E.   Wallace's Sensitometry.
June   [Criticisms].   B.J.P. **54**, 425.
7.

**480** MEES, C. E. K., and WRATTEN, S. H.
July   Variations in the Watkins, factor.
18.   [Hereford Convention].   B.J.P. **54**, 560.

**481** BECKER, A., and WERNER, A.   " Das
July   photographische Reziprozitätsgesetz für
30.   Bromsilbergelatine bei Erregung mit
Licht verschiedener Wellenläuge."   Zeit.
Wiss. P. **5**, 382.

**482** PRÉOBAJENSKY, P.   The Curve of Solarisa-
Aug.   tion and its Critical Points.   The
Solarisation Photometer.   P.J. **47**, 335,
339.   Bull. Imp. Soc. des Natur.
Moscau **1** and **2** (1906).

**1907**—*continued.*

**483** WERNER, A.   Das photographische Rezi-
Aug.   prozitätsgesetz bei sensibilisierten Brom-
14.   silbergelatinen.   Zeit. Wiss. P. **6**, 25.

**484** LUMIERE and SEYEWETZ.   Action of
Aug.   Water and Developing Solutions on
23.   Sensitiveness of Gelatino-Bromide
plates.   B.J.P. **54**, 632.

**485** PFUND, L.   The Pfund Photometer.
Aug.   B.J.P. **54**, 660.
30.

**486** SWITKOWSKI, J.   Aus dem Gebiete der
Oct.   Phomotrie.   P. Mitt. **34**, 457.
23.

**487** MEES and WRATTEN.   Dieyanin, Photo-
Dec.   graphy of the intra red.   P.J. **58**, 25.
17.

**488** WEISZ, H.   Researches on the Latent
Dec.   Image by means of plates free from
20.   Colloid.   B.J.P. **54**, 960.

**1908.**

**489** KIESER, K.   Die Sensitometrie der Ent-
wicklungspapiere.   Eders, J. **22**, 21.

**490** CALLIER, A.   Ueber den gegenwärtigen
Zustand der Empfindlichkeits-messing
(Sensitometrie) der Orthochromatische
Platten.   Eders, J. **22**, 81.

**491** CAREY-LEA.   Kolloides Silber und die
Photohaloide.   [Trs. by Luppo-Cramer].
Dresden : T. Stein Kopff.

**492** WENTZEL, F.   Beiträge zur optischen
Mar.   Sensibilisation der Chlorsilbergelatine.
Zeit. Wiss. P. **7**, 113.

**493** PIPER, C. W.   The Nature of Photo-
Mar.   graphic Images.   B.J.P. **55**, 195.
13.

**494** TRIVELLI, A. P. H.   Beitrag zur Kenntnis
Mar.   des Solarisationsphänomens und weit-
22.   erer Eigenschaften des latenten Bildes.
Zeit. Wiss. P. **6**, 197, 237, 272.

**495** PIPER, C. W.   Bromide in Farmer's
Apr.   Reducer.   B.J.P. **55**, 319 [Renwick,
24.   349].

**496** RENWICK, F. F.   Ferricyanide-Bromide-
May   Hypo Reducer.   B.J.P. **55**, 349.
1.

**497** WATKINS, A.   Development Speed of
May   Plates.   [Review   ].   B.J.P. **55**, 382,
15.   401.

**498** B.J.P. (Editorial).   Time Development.
May   [Watkins, Temperature].   B.J.P. **55**,
29.   410, 413.

**499** SCHEFFER, W.   Researches in the Action
June   of Reducers.   B.J.P. **55**, 472.
19.

**1908**—*continued.*

**500** TRIVELLI, A. P. H.   Beitrag zur Kenntnis der Silberhaloide.   Zeit. Wiss. P. **6**, 358.
June 24.

**501** WATKINS, A.   Time Development Calculator.   B.J.P. **55**, 646.
Aug. 21.

**502** WALLACE, R. J.   Relation of Astronomical Secondary Negatives to their Originals.   B.J.P. **55**, 619.
Aug. 24.

**503** TRIVELLI, A. P. H.   Die Warnerkesche Modifikation des Herschel-Effectes und die Bereitung der Substanz des latenten Bildes.   Zeit. Wiss. P. **6**, 438.
Sept. 1.

**504** BRYAN, G. H.   Test Slips in Factorial Development.   B.J.P. **55**, 677.
Sept. 4.

**505** WATKINS, A.   Prof. Bryan's Method of Factorial Development.   B.J.P. **55**, 678.
Sept. 4.

**506** CHANNON, H. J.   Rayon's continuateurs and Negative Rays.   B.J.P. **55**, 637–38, 756–58.
Sept. 9.

**507** MEES and WRATTEN.   Silver Acetylide Emulsion.   P.J. **58**, 338.
Oct.

**508** LEIMBACH, G.   Die absolute Strahlungsempfindlichkeit von Bromsilbergelatineplatten gegen Licht verschiedener Wellenlänge.   Zeit. Wiss. P. **7**, 157, 181.
Nov.

**509** RUSSELL, W. J.   Action of Resin and Allied Bodies on a Photographic Plate in the Dark.   P.J. **58**, 345 ; Pro. R.S.B. **80**.
Nov.

### 1909.

**510** CALLIER, A.   La diffusion de la lumière par les cliches.   Bull. Soc. Belg. P. **36**, 397–99.

**511** EDER, J. M.   Uber Sensitometrie und deren Bedeutung für den Handel mit Trockenplatten.   Eders, J. **22**, 78.

**512** IDZERDA, W. H.   Bemerkungen zu dem Artikel von A. P. H. Trivelli Beitrag zur kenntnis des Solarisationsphänomens und weiterer Eigenschaften des latenten Bildes.   Zeit. Wiss. P. **7**, 392.

**513** SCHAUM, K.   Uber den Clayden-Effekt und Solarisation.   Zeit. Wiss. P. **7**, 71, 144.

**514** TRIVELLI, A. P. H.   Beitrag zur Photochemie der Silber (sub) haloide.   Zeit. Wiss. P. **8**, 113.
Jan.

**1909**—*continued.*

**515** CALLIER, A.   The Absorption and Scatter of Light by Photographic Negatives Measured by means of the Marten's Polarization Photometer.   P.J. **49**, 200 ; Bull. Soc. Fr. P. **23**, 177, 223, 259 ; Zeit. Wiss. P. **7**, 257.
Mar. 9.

**516** CARNEGIE, D.   A Modification of the H. and D. Photometer.   B.J.P. **56**, 197.
Mar. 12.

**517** TRIVELLI, A. P. H.   Tageslichthervorrufung latenter Eindrücke der Photographischen Platte.   Zeit. Wiss. P. **7**, 144.
Apr.

**518** WRATTEN, S. H., and MEES, C. E. K.   Absorption Spectra.   P.J. **49**, 234.
Apr. 6.

**519** WALLACE, R. J., and LEMON, H. B.   Evaluation of Reciprocity Law, Basic Fog, and Exposure.   [From Astrophysical Journal **29**, No. 2].   B.J.P **56**, 378.
May 11.

**520** CONGRESS OF APP. CHEM.   Abney, Krohn, Mees, Renwick [Abst.].   B.J.P. **66**, 440.
June 4.

**521** BIERMANN, E. A.   The Speed Number of Plates.   [Corr., Watkins and Harris, 506].   B.J.P. **56**, 486, 522.
June 18.

**522** WATKINS, A.   Time Thermometer.   [Review ].   P.J. **49**, 310 ; B.J.P. **56**, 538.
July

**523** SCHAUM, K.   Uber den Herschel-Effekt.   Zeit. Wiss. P. **7**, 399.
July

**524** FERGUSON, W. B.   The Speed Number of Plates.   [What is H. and D.   Number *re* Watkins-Biermann letters].   B.J.P. **56**, 522.
July 2.

**525** WATKINS, A.   The Speed Numbers of Plates.   [Reply to Biermann ].   B.J.P. **56**, 542.
July 3.

**526** SHEPPARD, S. E.   Colloid Chemistry in Relation to Photography.   With Bibliography.   P.J. **49**, 320.
July 13.

**527** FERGUSON, W. B.   Development Factor, Watkins, Factor, Development Speeds.   P.J. **49**, 335.
Aug.

**528** STERRY, J.   Control in Development of Bromide and Gaslight Papers.   [Action of Bromides].   P.J. **49**, 359.
Aug. 12.

**529** SCHAUM, K.   Uber den Mechanismus der photochemischen Reaktion an Halogensilberschichten.   Zeit. Wiss. P. **7**, 401.
Sept.

**1909**—*continued.*

**530** MEES, C. E. K.   A Report on the Present
Sept. Condition of Sensitometry.   B.J.P.
3. 56, 685.

**531** BRYAN, G. H.   The Comparison and
Sept. Measurement of Density and Contrast.
17. [*See* Mees and Renwick, 770].   B.J.P.
56, 723.

**532** CHANNON, H. J.   The Action of the less
Oct. refrangible Rays upon Printed-out
Images.   P.J. 49, 342, 345.

**533** MEES, C. E. K.   Comparison and Measure-
Oct. ment of Density and Contrasts.   [*Re*
1. Bryan, 723].   B.J.P. 56, 770.

**534** RENWICK, F. F.   Comparison and Meas-
Oct. urement of Density and Contrasts.
1. [*Re* Bryan, 723].   B.J.P. 56, 770–71.

**535** WATKINS, A.   Some Recent Aids to Time
Oct. Development.   [Practical adaptation
15. of W. B. Ferguson's method].   P.J. 49,
367 ; B.J.P. 56, 913.

**536** WINTHER, C.   Uber Solarisation in wäss-
Oct. enger Lösung.   Zeit. Wiss. P. 8, 135.
20.

**537** CHANNON, H. J.   Various Latent Images.
Nov. P.J. 49, 375.

**538** TRIVELLI, A. P. H.   Antwort an Herrn
Nov. Dr. Lüppo-Cramer.   [In Phot. Korr.
1909, 81].   Zeit. Wiss. P. 7, 397.

**539** SCHAUM, K.   Uber die Begriffe ,, Absorp-
Nov. tion '' und ,, Extinktion.''   Zeit. Wiss.
P. 7, 406.

**540** TRIVELLI, A. P. H.   Antwort an Herrn
Nov. Idzerda.   [Zeit. Wiss. P. 7, 392].   Zeit.
Wiss. P. 7, 394.

**541** PORTER, A. W.   The Growth of the
Nov. Photographic Image.   [Trail Taylor
23. Memorial Lecture].   P.J. 49, 407 ;
B.J.P. 56, 1010.

**542** MAYER, H.   Uber eine elektrische Methode
Dec. zur Messung der durch Belichtung in
Chromatgelatineschichten verursachten
Veränderungen.   Zeit. Wiss. P. 8, 1–17.

**543** TRIVELLI, A. P. H.   Beitrag zu einer
Dec. Theorie des Reifungsprozesses der Silberhaloide.   Zeit. Wiss. P. 8, 17.

## 1910.

**544** GOLDBERG, L. W.   Uber die Automatische Herstellung der Character-
istischen Kurve.   Zeit. Wiss. P. 9,
323 ; B.J.P. 57, 642, 664.

**1910**—*continued.*

**545** LUTHER, R.   Automatic Method of
Obtaining the Characteristic Curve.
[Wedges, International Congress].
B.J.P. 57, 642, 664 ; Zeit. Wiss. P. 9, 323.

**546** GOLDBERG, E.   Densograph.   Ein
Registrierapparat zur Messung der
Schwarzung von Photographischen Platten.   Eders, J. 24, 226 ; B.J.P. 57,
649 ; Bull. Soc. F.P. 1910, 336.

**547** SCHAUM, K.   Antwort an W. H. Idzerda.
[*Loc. cit.* p. 234].   Zeit. Wiss. P. 8, 235.

**548** WATKINS, A.   Uber einige Neuerungen
in des Zeitenlwicklungs Methode.   [Fer-
guson's Methods].   Eders, J. 24, 45 ;
Bull. Soc. Fr. P. 1910, 152.

**549** SCHEFFER, W.   Uber versuche mit einer
einfachen ausfuhrungsform des Rohren-
photometers.   Eders, J. 24, 97.

**550** BANCROFT, W. D.   The Photographic
Jan. Plate.   Parts 1, 2, 3, 4.   The Emulsions.
Jour. Phys. Chem. 14, 12, 97, 201, 620 ;
P.J. 50, 377 ; Bull. Soc. Fr. P. 1910,
278.

**551** IDZERDA, W. H.   Zur Theorie des latenten
Mar. Bildes.   Zeit. Wiss. P. 8, 234.

**552** RENWICK, F. F.   Difficulties in Accurate
Mar. Plate Speed Determination.   P.J. 50,
15. 157 ; B.J.P. 57, 234, 324 ; Bull. Soc.
Fr. P. 1910, 337.

**553** RENWICK, F. F.   On a New Form of
Mar. Density or Opacity Measuring Ap-
15. paratus.   P.J. 50, 177.

**554** TRIVELLI, A. P. H.   Einfluss der Korn-
Apr. grösse bei der latenten und der sicht-
baren photochemischen Zersetzung der
Silberhaloide.   Zeit. Wiss. P. 9, 168.

**555** IDZERDA, W. H.   Antwort an Herrn K.
May Schaum.   Zeit. Wiss. P. 9, 103.

**556** LUMIERE, A. T. L., and SEYEWELZ, A.
May The Use of Bromide in Development
13. for Increase of Contrast.   B.J.P. 57,
361 ; Bull. Soc. Fr. P. 1910, 148.

**557** WATKINS, A.   Time Development.   [Brand
May of plate : temperature].   A.P. 51, 481,
17. 509 ; B.J.P. 57, 387.

**558** MEES, C. E. K., and WRATHEN, S. H.
May Development by Time.   [*Re* Ferguson
20. and Howard].   B.J.P. 57, 376 ; P.J. 50,
403.

**1910**—*continued.*

**559** ALVES, G. M.   Time Development: its
May   Excellences and its Abuses.   [P.E. ]
20.   B.J.P. **57**, 378.

**560** JONES, C.   Intensification by Mercuric
May   Chloride and Ferrous Oxalate.   P.J. **50**,
21.   238.

**561** WEIGERT, F.   Einfache Methode zur
June   Konstruktion von Schwarzungs Kuruen
Photographischer Platten.   Deutsche
Phys. Gesell. **12**, 491 ; Eders, J. **25**,
474–475 ; Chem. Zentralblatt. **1**, 1180.

**562** HELLER and STENGER.   Uber die Ab-
July   schwächung mit Persulfal.   Ze t. Wiss.
P. **9**, 73, 389.

**563** MEES and SHEPPARD.   Investigations on
July   Standard Light Source.   B.J.P. **57**,
627 ; P.J. **50**, 287.

**564** LUTHER, R.   De l'état actuel de nos
Aug.   Connaisances sur la Nature de l'image
Latente.   Bull. Soc. Fr. P. **1910**, 293 ;
B.J.P. **57**, 651.

**565** RENWICK, F. F.   Sources of Error and
Aug.   Difficulties in Dry Plate Sensitometers.
19.   B.J.P. **57**, 626 ; Bull. Soc. Fr. P. **1910**,
337.

**566** DESALME, J.   Chemical Theory of
Aug.   Development.   B.J.P. **57**, 643, 653 ;
26.   Rev. de Chim. Indust. **21**, 13 ; Bull.
Soc. F.P. **1910**, 183.

**567** GOLDBERG, E.   Gelatine Wedges.   B.J.P.
Aug.   **57**, 642, 648 ; Bull. Soc. F.P. **1910**,
26.   326 ; Eders, J. **24**, 149.

**568** NUTTING, P. G.   The Helium Standard
Sept.   Lamp.   B.J.P. **50**, 305.

**569** BRUSH, C. F.   Photographic Photometry.
Oct.   B.J.P. **57**, 781, 794.
14.

**570** CHANNON, H. J.   Reversal in Develop-
Nov.   ment.   [*Re* Trivelli, Zeit. Wiss. P. 1908].
11.   B.J.P. **57**, 886.

**571** FERGUSON, W. B.   Investigations on the
Nov.   Temperature Coefficient of a Pyro-
29.   Soda Developer.   P.J. **50**, 412 ; Eders,
J. **25**, 506 ; Bull. Soc. Fr. P. **27**, 175.

**572** WATKINS, A.   Variation of Temperature
Nov.   Coefficient for Different Plates.   P.J.
29.   **50**, 411.

**573** MEES, C. E. K., WATKINS, A., and
Nov.   FERGUSON, W. B.   Time Development.
29.   P.J. **50**, 403 ; B.J.P. **57**, 919 ; Eders, J.
**25**, 161.

**1910**—*continued.*

**574** RENWICK, F. F.   The Physical Process
Dec.   of Development.   [Criticism of Mee's
9.   Paper at R.P.S.].   B.J.P. **57**, 942.

**575** SCHEFFER, W.   Scatter, a Demonstration
Dec.   of, in Turbid Liquid.   B.J.P. **57**, 941.
12.

**576** B.J.P. Editorial.   Discrepancies in Plate
Dec.   speed Numbers.   B.J.P. **57**, 946.
16.

**577** SCHEFFER, W.   The Present State of
Dec.   Microscopic Research with regard to
20.   Dry Plates.   P.J. **51**, 276.

**1911.**

**578** DESALME, J.   Sur ia Théorie du Dévelop-
ment.   [From Electro-Ionic point of
view].   Bull. Soc. Belge P. **41**, 148 ;
Bull. Soc. Fr. P. **1911**, 75.

**579** GOLDBERG, E.   Studien über die Detail-
wiedergabe in der Photographie.   Zeit.
Wiss. P. **9**, 313, 323.

**580** GOLDBERG, E., LUTHER, R., and WEIGERT,
F.   Uber die Automatische Herstellung
der Charakteristischen Kurve.   Zeit.
Wiss. P. **9**, 323 ; B.J.P. **57**, 642, 664.

**581** MIETHE, A.   Neuer Schwärtzung-Messer
für Negative.   Eders, J. **25**, 256.

**582** TRIVELLI, A.   Ostwalds Gesetz der
Umwandlungstufen der Silberhaloide.
[Theory of Latent Image].   Zeit. Wiss.
P. **9**, 185.

**583** RENWICK, F.   Physical Process of
Jan.   Development.   B.J.P. **58**, 75.
23.

**584** JONES, C.   On the Relationship between
Mar.   the Size of the Particle and the Colour
7.   of the Image.   P.J. **51**, 159 ; B.J.P.
**58**, 339, 381 ; Bull. Soc. Fr. P. **1911**,
357.

**585** DOW, J. S., and MACKINNEY.   Surface
Mar.   Brightness, its Measurement and its
28.   Application to Photography.   P.J. **51**,
188.

**586** RENWICK, F. F.   The Calculation of
Apr.   Gamma Infinity.   P.J. **51**, 213 ; Bull.
Soc. Fr. P. **1911**, 352.

**587** JONES, C.   The Ilford Wedge Screen.
Apr.   B.J.P. **58**, 265.

**588** TRIVELLI, A. P. H.   Uber die Natur der
Apr.   Schaumschen Substanz B.   [Theory of
Latent Image-subhaloid].   Zeit. Wiss.
P. **9**, 187.

## 1911—*continued.*

**589** MEES, C. E. K., and PIPER, C. W. On
Apr. 11.    the Fogging Power of Developers.
P.J. **51**, 226 ; B.J.P. **58**, 312, 491, 515 ;
Bull. Soc. Fr. P. **1912**, 44.

**590** SANGER-SHEPHERD, E. The Cause of
June 13.    Reversal and its Remedy, with some
Notes on the Photographic Process.
[Caldwell's Hydrazine]. P.J. **51**, 249 ;
B.J.P. **58**, 603 ; Bull. Soc. Fr. P. **1912**,
250.

**591** CALLIER, A. Powerful Intensification of
June 16.    Gelatine Plates. B.J.P. **58**, 452 ; Bull.
Soc. Belge P. **1911**, 165.

**592** TRIVELLI, A. Dark-room Safe Lights
July 14.    B.J.P. **58**, 474 ; Bull. Soc. Belge P.
**1911**.

**593** PERLEY, G. A. Experiments on Solariza-
June 23.    tion. B.J.P. **58**, 478, 496, 556, 572,
590 ; Jour. Phys. Chem. **13**, 630 ;
Bull. Soc. Fr. P. **1911**, 174.

**594** CLAYDEN, A. W. Experiments on
July 13.    Reversal and Clayden Effect. B.J.P.
**58**, 449.

**595** CHANNON, H. J. Experiments on
Aug. 4.    Solarization. [*Re* Perley, 478]. B.J.P.
**58**, 617.

**596** BOURGEOIS, L. Effect of Alkali in
Aug. 28.    Photographic Development. B.J.P.
**58**, 650, 669, 685, 725, 742, 760, 780.

**597** STERRY, J. Reversal and Re-Reversal.
Sept. 19.    P.J. **51**, 320 ; B.J.P. **58**, 820.

**598** STERRY, J. Light and Development.
Sept. 19.    P.J. **51**, 322 ; B.J.P. **58**, 820 ; Bull.
Soc. Fr. P. **27**, 251.

**599** SANGER-SHEPHERD, E. Density Meter.
Oct. 24.    Patent No. 23,429, Oct. 24, 1911 ;
B.J.P. **58** 926 ; Eders J. **26**, 383.

**600** RAYLEIGH. On the General Problem of
Nov.    Photographic Reproduction. Phil.
Mag. **1911**, 734 ; B.J.P. **58**, 994 ; Bull.
Soc. Fr. P. **1912**, 221.

**601** FERGUSON, W. B. A New Density Meter.
Nov. 21.    [The Use of Wedge Screens]. P.J. **51**,
405 ; B.J.P. **59**, 24 ; Eders, J. **26**, 469 ;
Bull. Soc. Fr. P. **1912**, 252.

**602** RENWICK, F. F. Wedge Screens and
Nov. 21.    some of their Uses. P.J. **51**, 414 ;
B.J.P. **59**, 45, 62 ; Eders, J. **28**, 469 ;
Bull. Soc. Fr. P. **1912**, 166.

RENWICK, F. F. What is Halation ?
Nov. 24    B.J.P. **58**, 894.

## 1912.

**604** LIESEGANG, R. E., und LUPPO-CRAMER.
Zur Kolloidchemie der Photographischer Bildentwicklung. Eders. J. **28**,
18.

**605** RENWICK, F. F. Natürgetreu Photographie. Eders, J. **28**, 106.

**606** NOVAK, F. Uber Papierskalenphoto-
meter. [Absorption by Diffusing
Media]. Eders J. **28**, 189.

**607** STARK, J. Sur le noircissement dans le
cas de l'éclairement normal : spectro-
photometrie photographique. [Schwarz-
schild's Law]. Ann. des Phys. **35**, 401 ;
Bull. Soc. Fr. P. **1912**, 250.

**608** GEIGER, L. Schwarzung und Photometrie Photographischen Platten.
[Schwarzschild's Law]. Eders J. **28**,
466 ; Ann. d. Phys. **37**, 68 ; Bull. Soc.
Fr. P. **1912**, 251 ; Jour. de Phys. **1912**,
144.

**609** VON KLENCK, G. Thermo-Entwicklung.
P. Mitt. **39**, 232.

**610** WATKINS, A. " Photography : its Prin-
Jan.    ciples and Applications." Constable
and Co., Ltd. 1911. P.J. **52**, 28.

**611** SANGER-SHEPHERD. The S.S. Density
Jan. 12.    Meter. B.J.P. **59**, 31 (Review) ; 925.

**612** B.J.P. Editorial. Density Measurements
Jan. 19.    of Fog. [Ferguson's method]. B.J.P.
**59**, 39.

**613** B.J.P. Editorial. Testing Plates with
Mar. 8.    Cheap Appliances. B.J.P. **59**, 171, 190.

**614** MEES, C. E. K. The Characteristic Curve.
Mar. 15.    B.J.P. **59**, 190.

**615** CLERC, L. P., and DESALME, J. Intensi-
Mar. 22.    fication with Copper and Tin. B.J.P.
**59**, 215, 266 ; Bull. Soc. Fr. P. **1912**,
96, 99.

**616** RENWICK, F. F. Under-exposure Period.
Apr. 12.    B.J.P. **59**, 289, 312 ; Eders, J. **26**, 106 ;
Bull. Soc. Fr. P. **1912**, 281.

**617** WATKINS, A. New Methods of Speed and
Apr. 16.    Gamma Testing. P.J. **52**, 206 ; B.J.P.
**59**, 316.

**618** MEES and WELBORNE-PIPER. On the
Apr. 23.    Fogging Power of Developers. II.
Sulphite Fog. P.J. **52**, 221 ; B.J.P.
**59**, 337, 342, 428, 441, 465 ; Bull. Soc.
Fr. P. **1912**, 44.

**1912**—*continued.*

**619** Bancroft, W. D., and Gordon, M. A.
May. The Silver Equivalent of Hydroquinone,
etc. B.J.P. **59**, 788.

**620** Renwick, F. F. Photographic Photo-
May metry and the Measurement of Densi-
14. ties. B.J.P. **59**, 394 ; Eders, J. **28**, 384 ;
P.J. **52**, 250, 260 ; Bull. Soc. Fr. P.
**1913**, 237.

**621** Nichols, E. L. Measurements of Day-
May light. B.J.P. **59**, 364, 403, 427.
16.

**622** Schuller, A. Das Schwarzungsgesetz
May fester lichtempfindlicher Schichten.
23. [Mathematical]. Zeit. Wiss. P. **11**, 277.

**623** Banerjee, S. N. Density Measurements
May with Sanger-Shepherd Meter. B.J.P.
27. **59**, 434, 435.

**624** B.J.P. Editorial. Errors in Photometry.
July [By Wedge methods]. B.J.P. **59**, 513,
7. 514, 668.

**625** Brigham, W. F. Dish Time Develop-
Aug. ment. B.J.P. **59**, 671.
30.

**626** Bancroft, W. D. The Effect of Bromide.
Sept. B.J.P. **59**, 878.

**627** Matthews, J. H., and Barmeir, F. E.
Sept. Electropotentials of Certain Photographic Developers and a Possible
Explanation of Photographic Development. B.J.P. **59**, 897.

**628** Renwick, F. F. Wedge Screens and
Sept. Scatter Error. B.J.P. **59**, 717.
13.

**629** Ferguson, W. B. Bar Photometer for
Oct. Measuring Densities by Non-Parallel
1. Rays. P.J. **52**, 283 ; B.J.P. **59**, 772.

**630** Luther, R. The Physical Chemistry of
Oct. Negative Processes. [Trail Taylor
8. Lecture]. P.J. **52**, 291 ; B.J.P. **59**,
915 ; Bull. Soc. Fr. P. **29**, 338.

**631** Jones, C. The Scattering of Light by
Nov. Small Particles. P.J. **52**, 349.
12.

**632** Bancroft, W. D. The Latent Image.
Nov. B.J.P. **59**, 881.
15.

## 1913.

**633** Allen, H. S. Photoelectricity, etc.
Longman, Green and Co. 1913. (Review.)
P.J. **54**, 108.

**634** Goldberg, E. G. Das Auflösungsver-
mögen von Photographischen Platten.
Zeit. Wiss. P. **12**, 77.

**1913**—*continued.*

**635** Kieser, K. Gradation und Schwartzung
von Entwicklungspapieres. Eders, J.
**27**, 135.

**636** Renwick, F. F. Die Tonabstufung in
den photographischen positiven Kopier-
prozessen. Eders J. **27**, 117 ; **28**, 122.

**637** Lehmann, E. Zur Theorie der Tiefen-
entwicklung. P. Mitt. **40**, 55.

**638** Piper, C. W. Some General Principles
Jan. of Physical Chemistry and Their Ap-
17. plication in Photography. [On Luther's
Lecture]. B.J.P. **60**, 45, 119.

**639** Stenger, E., and Heller, H. Uber die
Mar. Abschwächung mit Persulfat. [III.
Mitteilung]. Zeit. Wiss. P. **12**, 309.

**640** Renwick, F. F. The Under-exposure
Mar. Period in Theory and Practice. P.J.
11. **53**, 127 ; Bull. Soc. Fr. P. **1913**, 374.

**641** Renwick, F. F. The Effects of Inter-
May Reflexion on Density Values. P.J. **53**,
20. 203 ; B.J.P. **60**, 611.

**642** Schuller, A. The Sensitometry of
Sept. Print-out Paper. [P. Rund. **1913**,
26. 279]. B.J.P. **60**, 746.

**643** Callier, A. Experiments in Photo-
Oct. graphic Research Work, and in the
14. Construction of Photometric Instruments. B.J.P. **60**, 951, 972 ; P.J. **53**,
242.

**644** Ferguson, W. B. Testing Ordinary and
Nov. Orthochromatic Plates for Compara-
18. tive Speed by Daylight. P.J. **53**, 297 ;
B.J.P. **60**, 901, 919 ; B.J.P. **61**, 26.

**645** Mees, C. E. K. The Physical Chemistry
Dec. of Photographic Development. B.J.P.
5. **60**, 935.

## 1914.

Note.—It has not been possible to obtain continental
photographic literature for reference after this date.

**646** Hughes, A. L. Photo-Electricity. [Cam-
bridge University Press]. (Review.)
P.J. **54**, 191.

**647** Kron, E. Ueber das Schwarzungsgesetz Photographisches Platten. Eders,
J. **28**, 6.

**648** Renwick, F. F. Die Tonabstufungen in
Positiven Bildern auf Papier. Eders, J.
**28**, 122.

**1914**—*continued.*

**649** SHEPPARD, S. E. Photo-Chemistry. Longmans, Green and Co., 1914. (Review.) P. J. **54**, 301.

**650** STENGER, E. Die Messung der Lichtempfindlichkeit Photographischer Platten. Eders, J. **28**, 112.

**651**
Jan.
1.
EWEST, H. Beiträge zur quantitativen Spectral Photographie. [Condensed trans. by Renwick, " Quantitative Spectrophotography "]. P. J. **54**, 99.

**652**
Jan.
9.
MEES, C. E. K. The Calculation of Exposure. B. J. P. **61**, 21.

**653**
Feb.
NUTTING, P. G. The Brightness of Optical Images. P. J. **54**, 187.

**654**
Mar.
SEEMAN, H. Ungleichmässigkeiten der Photographischen Entwicklung. Zeit. Wiss. P. **13**, 333.

**655**
Mar.
STENGER, E. Die Messung der Lichtempfindlichkeit Photographischer Platten. Eders, J. **1914**, 113.

**656**
Mar.
10.
RENWICK, F. F. An Instrument for the Study of Gradation and Measurement of Gamma. [Wedge Screens]. P. J. **54**, 163.

**657**
Mar.
10.
RENWICK, F. F. Improved Form of Ferguson Bench Photometer. P. J. **54**, 167.

**658**
Mar.
17.
ALLEN, H. S. The Formation of the Latent Image on the Photographic Plate. [Electrons, etc.]. P. J. **54**, 175.

**659**
Mar.
27.
B. J. P. Editorial. The Latent Image. [*Re* H. S. Allen's paper]. B. J. P. **61**, 243.

**660**
Apr.
STENGER, E. Die Sabatiersche Bildumkehrung. Zeit. Wiss. P. **13**, 369 ; Eders, J. **1914**, 356.

**661**
Apr.
TUGMAN, O. Distribution of Silver Grains in the Developed Photographic Image. P. J. **54**, 270.

**662**
June
9.
CROWTHER, R. E. A New Method of Rendering Photographic Plates immune from Reversal by Over-exposure. P. J. **54**, 250 ; B. J. P. **61**, 533 ; Eders, J. **1914**, 307.

**663**
July
17.
VALENTA, E. The Chemical Analysis of Gelatine Dry Plates. B. J. P. **61**, 557 ; P. Corr.

**664**
Aug.
VOLMER, M., and SCHAUM, K. Uber Progressive und Regressive Vorgänge au Halogensilberschichten. Zeit. Wiss. P. **15**, 1.

**1914**—*continued.*

**665**
Aug.
7.
STEADMAN, F. M. A Simple Unit Method of Measuring the Actinic Effect of Illuminants, both Primary and Secondary, in the Practice of Photography. B. J. P. **61**, 612, 628, 645, 658, 666, 667.

**666**
Nov.
SHEPPARD, S. E. Photo-Chemistry. Longmans. 1914. P. J. **54**, 301.

**667**
Nov.
10.
JONES, L. A., NUTTING, P. G. and MEES, C. E. K. The Sensitometry of Photographic Papers. P. J. **54**, 342.

**668**
Dec.
STENGER, E., and HELLER, H. Uber die Abschwächung mit Persulfat. [4. Mitteilung]. Zeit. Wiss. P. **14**, 177.

**1915.**

**669** RENWICK, F. F. The Sensitometry of Photographic Papers. P. J. **55**, 29.

**670**
Jan.
1.
JONES, NUTTING and MEES. The Sensitometry of Photographic Papers. B. J. P. **62**, 9, 22, 38.

**671**
Feb.
SCHROTT, K. Empfindlichkeitsbestimmung nach Metrischen Massen. Zeit. Wiss. P. **14**, 223.

**672**
Mar.
9.
BULL, A. J., and JOLLEY, A. C. A Characteristic of Selective Absorption. P. J. **55**, 134.

**673**
Mar.
12.
MEES, C. E. K. The Physics of the Photographic Process. B. J. P. **62**, 165, 183, 221.

**674**
Apr.
13.
CROWTHER, R. E. Thio-indoxyl Development and its Bearing on the Theory of the Latent Image. P. J. **55**, 186.

**675**
May.
LIESEGANG, R. E. Polychromie des Silbers. Zeit. Wiss. P. **14**, 343.

**676**
May
11.
BLOCH, O. Some Plate Troubles, Common and Uncommon. P. J. **55**, 219.

**677**
June.
NORDENSON, H. Zur Frage von der ,, zerstäubenden " Wirkung des Lichtes, mit besonderer Rücksicht auf die Photographische Probleme. Zeit. Wiss. **15**, 1.

**678**
June
4.
RENWICK, F. F. Plate Speed Testing and the Characteristic Curve. [Letter *re* Editorial, 331]. B. J. P. **62**, 374, 405, 422.

**679**
Sept.
LUPPO-CRAMER. Uber die Zerstäubung der Silberhaloide durch das Licht. Zeit. Wiss. P. **15**, 125.

**1915**—*continued.*

**680** ANDERSON, A. H.   Developing Calculator.
Sept. 10.   [Review.] B.J.P. **62**, 595, 662.

**681** TUGMAN, O.   The Resolving Power of
Nov. 16.   Photographic Plates.   P.J. **55**, 292.


### 1916.

**682** LUPPO-CRAMER.   Speed and Size of
Grain.   Chem. Zeit. **40**, 304.

**683** NORDENSON, H.   Uber die vermutete
Jan.   ,, zerstäubande '' Wirkung des Lichtes.
[Polemical—*see* same vol. I and 125].
Zeit. Wiss. P. **15**, 288.

**684** RENWICK, F. F.   Some Deductions from
Jan.   Schwarzschild's rule].   P.J. **56**, 11.

**685** HENDERSON, A.   [Speed and Gradation
Jan. 7.   of Papers, Contact-printing, Opacity
Measurement.   [Exposure Wheel, photo-
meter].   B.J.P. **63**, 311.

**686** BLOCH, O., and RENWICK, F. F.   The
Jan. 11.   Opacity of Diffusing Media.   [Improved
Ferguson Photometer].   P.J. **56**, 49.

**687** CHANNON, H. J.   Resolving Power of
Feb. 16.   Photographic Plates.   [*Re* Tugman, **55**,
292].   P.J. **56**, 74.

**688** FERGUSON, W. B., and RENWICK, F. F.
May 9.   Description of the Hurter and Driffield
Apparatus.   P.J. **56**, 168 ; B.J.P. **63**,
285.

**689** RHEDEN, J.   Uber den Einfluss der
Aug.   Vorbelichtung auf die Wiedergabe
Schwacher Lichteindrücke auf der
Photographischen Platte.   Zeit. Wiss.
P. **16**, 33, 92.

**690** ODENCRANTS, A.   Sensitometrische Ap-
Sept.   parate und deren Fehlerquellen.   [With
very full bibliography].   Zeit. Wiss. P.
**16**, 69.

**691** RENWICK, F. F.   Tone Reproduction and
Nov. 10.   its Limitations.   [Range in landscape,
etc.].   P.J. **56**, 222 ; B.J.P. **63**, 675,
689.

### 1917.

**692** BLOCH, O.   Plate Speeds, Selective
Jan. 9.   Absorption of Neutral Wedge, Failure
of Reciprocity Law, Velocity Constant.
P.J. **57**, 51.

**693** COUSINS, G. P.   Illuminating Factors in
Jan. 12.   Enlarging.   [Absorption of Light by
diffusing media].   B.J.P. **64**, 16, 17.

**1917**—*continued.*

**694** CHANNON, H. J.   The Influence of Time
Jan. 23.   upon the Latent Image.   P.J. **57**, 72.

**695** EMERSON, P. H.   Tone Reproduction and
Feb.   its Limitations.   [Criticising Renwick's
Lecture].   P.J. **57**, 95.

**696** HOMOLKA.   The Latent Image and
Feb. 16.   Developers.   B.J.P. **64**, 81.

**697** EDER, J. M.   Der Einfluss der Vorbelich-
Mar.   tung auf die Wiedergabe Schwächer
Lichteindrücke auf der Photograph-
ischen Platte.   Zeit. Wiss. P. **16**, 219.

**698** JONES, C.   The Relationship between the
Apr.   Size of the Particle and the Colour of
the Image.   [Correction of former
Paper, P.J. **51**, 159].   P.J. **57**, 158.

**699** ODENCRANTS, A.   Was muss man von
Apr.   einer Theorie des latenten Bildes for-
dern ?   Ze't. Wiss. P. **16**, 261.

**700** HNATEK, A.   Die minimalen Photo-
June   graphisch noch Wiedergebbaren Helligkeitskontraste.   Zeit. Wiss. P. **16**, 323.

**701** STORR, B. V.   Photographic Processes,
July 13.   Theoretical and Practical.   [Review of
year's work, J.S.C.I.].   B.J.P. **64**, 364.

**702** BECHER, S., and WINTERSTEIN, M.   Iod
Aug.   und Iod-Thiocarbamide als Subtraktive
Abschwächer für Negativ und Positiv.
Zeit. Wiss. P. **17**, 1.

**703** RHEDEN, J.   Uber den Einfluss der
Aug.   Vorbelichtung auf die Wiedergabe
Schwacher Lichteindrücke auf die
Photographischen Platte.   Zeit. Wiss.
P. **17**, 33.

**704** HODGSON, M. B.   Physical Characteristics
Oct. 19.   of the Elementary Grains of a Photographic Plate.   B.J.P. **64**, 532, 542.

**705** LIESEGANG, R. E.   Die minimalen
Dec.   Photographisch noch Wiedergebbaren
Helligkeitskontraste.   Zeit. Wiss. P. **17**,
142.

**706** HODGSON, M. B.   The Sensitometry of
Dec. 28.   X-ray Materials.   B.J.P. **64**, 654.

**707** HOLST, G., and HAMBRUGER, L.   Uber
Dec. 20.   eine Methode zur Bestimmung Spek-
traler Intensitäten auf Photographischen Wege.   Zeit. Wiss. P. **17**, 264.

### 1918.

**708** Channon, H. J., Renwick, F. F. and Storr, B. The Behaviour of Scattering Media in Fully Diffused Light. Proc. Roy. Soc. **94**, 222 ; P.J. **58**, 121 ; B.J.P. **64**, 358.

**709** Jones, L. A., and Wilsey, R. B. The Spectral Selectivity of Photographic Deposits. P.J. **58**, 70.
Feb.

**710** Nietz, A. H., and Huse, K. The Sensitometry of Photographic Intensification. P.J. **58**, 81.
Feb.

**711** Renwick, F. F. The Relation between Optical Density and Quantity of Deposit in Prints. P.J. **58**, 102.
Feb. 5.

**712** Renwick, F. F. The Covering Power of Pigments with reference to Photographic Prints. [Extension of study of diffusing media]. P.J. **58**, 140.
Feb. 5.

### 1918—*continued*.

**713** Ferguson, Renwick and Benson, D. E. The F.R.B. Photometer. P.J. **58**, 155 ; B.J.P. **65**, 128, 213, 224.
Mar. 10.

**714** Krohn, F. W. T. The Mechanism of Development of the Image in a Dry Plate Negative. P.J. **58**, 179 ; B.J.P. **65**, 412, 425, 437.
Apr. 16.

**715** Ferguson, W. B. The Early Work of Hurter and Driffield. [1st H. and D. Memorial Lecture]. P.J. **58**, 205 ; B.J.P. **65**, 229, 327, 339, 347.
May 14.

**716** Slater, W. F. The Negative. P.J. **58**, 225.
June 11.

**717** Kingdon, J. C. Causes of Variation in the Watkins' Factor for Different Developers. P.J. **58**, 270.
Nov. 12.

# NAME INDEX.

NOTE.—Numbers after **B**. refer to paragraphs of Bibliography.